LAST TO LEAVE THE FIELD

LAST TO LEAVE THE FIELD

The Life and Letters of First Sergeant Ambrose Henry Hayward, 28th Pennsylvania Volunteer Infantry

Edited by Timothy J. Orr

Voices of the Civil War
Peter S. Carmichael, Series Editor

The University of Tennessee Press / Knoxville

The Voices of the Civil War series makes available a variety of primary source materials that illuminate issues on the battlefield, the home front, and the western front, as well as other aspects of this historic era. The series contextualizes the personal accounts within the framework of the latest scholarship and expands established knowledge by offering new perspectives, new materials, and new voices.

Copyright © 2010 by The University of Tennessee Press / Knoxville. All Rights Reserved. Manufactured in the United States of America. First Edition.

The paper in this book meets the requirements of American National Standards Institute / National Information Standards Organization specification Z39.48-1992 (Permanence of Paper). It contains 30 percent post-consumer waste and is certified by the Forest Stewardship Council.

Library of Congress Cataloging-in-Publication Data

Hayward, Ambrose Henry, 1840–1864.
Last to leave the field: the life and letters of First Sergeant Ambrose Henry Hayward, 28th Pennsylvania Volunteer Infantry / edited by Timothy J. Orr.
    p. cm. — (Voices of the Civil War)
Includes bibliographical references and index.
ISBN-13: 978-1-57233-729-9 (hardcover)
ISBN-10: 1-57233-729-X (hardcover)

1. Hayward, Ambrose Henry, 1840–1864—Correspondence.
2. United States. Army. Pennsylvania Infantry Regiment, 28th (1861–1865)
3. Soldiers—Massachusetts—Brockton—Correspondence.
4. Soldiers—Pennsylvania—Philadelphia—Correspondence.
5. Pennsylvania—History—Civil War, 1861–1865—Personal narratives.
6. United States—History—Civil War, 1861–1865—Personal narratives.
7. Pennsylvania—History—Civil War, 1861–1865—Regimental histories.
8. United States—History—Civil War, 1861–1865—Regimental histories.
9. Hayward family—Correspondence.
10. Brockton (Mass.)—Biography.
  I. Orr, Timothy J.
 II. Title.

E527.528th .H39 2010
973.7'448—dc22
2010030036

To Laura,
Who should have a thousand books dedicated to her

Contents

FIGURES

MAPS

FOREWORD

ON SEPTEMBER 23, 1863, AMBROSE HENRY HAYWARD AND HIS COMRADES IN the 28th Pennsylvania Infantry left their camps along the Rapidan River before dawn, filing onto trains for destination unknown. As the cars neared Washington D.C., they learned that they were departing Virginia for good. "Our hearts gladened with the hope that we were to leave the detested soil of Virginia," Hayward wrote, "the blighted land sickening to the sight of all Soldiers." The farther the train carried the Pennsylvanians away from the war front, the more reckless Hayward's fellow soldiers became. It was as if they felt invincible now that they were liberated from the killing fields of the Old Dominion. After passing by the picturesque countryside of western Maryland and before taking in the towering mountains of West Virginia, some of Hayward's comrades secured some whiskey. Within minutes stoic veterans lost themselves in a drunken spree, turning into frenzied soldiers who apparently could not survive the day without feeling the gut rush of standing on the precipice of death.

A number of drunken men clambered up the side of the train while it was moving at full speed. They swayed forwards and backwards, standing atop the cars until one soldier smashed his head against the overhang of a bridge. Another man fell between two cars, the wheels instantly crushing both of his thighs. Hayward thought it was horrible to see this helpless, drunken soldier sprawled across the tracks, with a canteen of whiskey hanging from his neck, as the train rumbled over him. In Ohio Hayward and his comrades jumped off the cars and viciously assaulted a party of Irish workers who were known to have Copperhead sympathies. The violent adventure of his regiment did not end upon entering Indiana, where scores of soldiers purchased rum at bargain prices, downing the bottles with a fierce joy until they were "crazy" drunk. One inebriated man took the butt of his rifle and cracked it against the skull of his comrade, killing the man instantly, for the simple reason that he was following him. Before the train finally halted at Duck River Bridge in Tennessee, after covering

1,120 miles in ten days, the soldiers grew so tired of their cramped quarters that they took their rifles and knocked holes in the wooden walls of the cars over the feeble protests of the conductor.

While Hayward was somewhat shocked by the wild behavior of his comrades, he reported these disturbing incidents in a very matter-of-fact way. He made no attempt to sanitize his experiences; nor was he convulsed in anxiety by a war whose violence was so pervasive and intense that it had consumed his comrades. Their heavy drinking, constant fighting, and general unruliness must have convinced Hayward that too many of his fellow soldiers had surrendered to the darker impulses of organized killing. It appears that he avoided a similar descent into darkness, largely saved by his devotion to the high ideals of the Union cause. Yet, he was no longer an idealistic recruit by 1863; he saw the world for what it was rather than what he wanted it to be. Unspeakable carnage on the battlefield and pervasive immorality in camp shattered his early illusion that the side which acted with the greatest courage and nobility would win a war of glory. The business of war was reprehensibly bloody, and Hayward made no attempt to hide it. While he was like many Victorians who were reluctant to showcase man's barbarity, Hayward's form of narration was exceptional, for his letters do not have the feel of a scripted performance as do so many other Civil War letters. He writes as he speaks, bringing to the modern reader a stream-of-consciousness flow that gives us access to a range of dark and painful feelings that the vast majority of Civil War soldiers almost always repressed. After Chancellorsville, for instance, Hayward made no attempt to turn the battlefield into a stage of high drama and heroism. His writings convey the jagged emotions that followed the immediate and overwhelming exhilaration of surviving battle: "[I] have again seen my comrades fall and heard their dying groans. yes I have been spared perhaps to witness the like again. . . . the mens faces still bare the mark of terror."

Last to Leave the Field is superbly edited by Timothy Orr, a veteran historian of Gettysburg National Park and more recently the recipient of a doctorate in history at Pennsylvania State University. Years before, while an undergraduate at Gettysburg College, Orr encountered Hayward's rich wartime correspondence in the library's special collections; and, as the volume's detailed notes reveal, he has devoted considerable time since then to contextualizing the life and times of this soldier. Throughout this book, Orr identifies portals for the reader to explore the inner world of Hayward, allowing us to see that, even among soldiers who were highly patriotic and exceedingly brave, powerful notions of duty and a sustaining love for country could not ease the agony of having to watch human beings slaughter each other with impunity. "I saw poor Fithian when he was struck," Hayward wrote after an 1863 battle. "He had just spoke to me about his gun. it would not go off. the ball struck him in his side. he droped his Rifle. I saw that I could not reach him. I turned away dreading to see him roll down the mountain. I could tell you more of such tales but it is as unpleasent for me to bring them back to my memories as it is for you to read them."

Peter S. Carmichael
Civil War Institute at Gettysburg College

ACKNOWLEDGMENTS

DURING THE PROCESS OF WRITING THIS BOOK, I HAD THE PLEASURE OF WORK-ing with many talented people whose contributions have aided my efforts.

First, I would like to thank Gettysburg College Special Collections Archive at Musselman Library for allowing me the opportunity to edit and publish the Hayward Collection. I bestow a hearty thanks to the staff: Karen Dupell Drickamer, Christine Amadure, Leia Kay Dunn-Marple, Jennifer Chesney, and Melodie Ann Foster.

Second, I would like to thank the faculty of the Department of History at Gettysburg College for all their generous time and energy teaching me the craft of history back when I began this project. Thanks go to J. Matthew Gallman, Gabor Boritt, Christina Ericson-Hanson, Timothy Shannon, Michael Birkner, William Bowman, and Magdalena Sanchez.

I would also like to thank the faculty and graduate students in the Department of History and Religious Studies at the Pennsylvania State University, to whom I owe my graduate training and assistance in editing this book. Thanks go to Carol Reardon, Mark E. Neely Jr., William A. Blair, Amy Greenberg, William Pencak, Robert Sandow, Michael T. Smith, Dave R. Siry, Matthew R. Isham, James Adam Rogers, Leah Vincent, Andrew J. Prymak, David Greenspoon, James Bailey, Alfred Wallace, Will Bryan, Jonathan Steplyk, and Chad Chalfont.

Also, I would like to thank the staff at Gettysburg National Military Park. I have had the honor of working alongside many talented historians and interpreters, all of whom offered tremendous aid in increasing my knowledge of the Civil War. Most notable, I would like to thank Eric A. Campbell. Eric's keen wisdom and helpful suggestions shaped this project from its infant stages. I am exceedingly grateful for his help. Other heartfelt thanks go out to D. Scott Hartwig, Barb Sanders, Karlton Smith, Troy D. Harman, Gregory A. Coco, Rick Bartol, Terry Latschar, Bert Barnett, Joe Wurzer, Wayne Motts, and others too numerous to mention. A special thank-you goes to John Heiser, my talented cartographer.

Other talented individuals who have helped me along the way include Michael Comeau and the staff at Massachusetts State Historical Archives, Keith S. Bohannon at West Georgia University, Max Moeller and the staff at Historical Society of Pennsylvania, and Jonathan Stayer and Rich Saylor at Pennsylvania State Archives in Harrisburg.

I would also like to thank Peter S. Carmichael for taking such an important interest in this project, advancing its publication, and suggesting revisions. Many thanks also go to Scot Danforth, Thomas Wells, and the folks at University of Tennessee Press who made this project a reality. My appreciation goes to Mike Lynch, Molly Bompane, and Rodney Foytik at the U.S. Army Military History Institute and to Lieutenant Colonel Fred Stevens of the Massachusetts Commandery of the Military Order of the Loyal Legion for helping to uncover a photograph of Sergeant Hayward. Thanks also go to Aaron Sheehan-Dean for his insightful recommendations in revising my narrative.

In addition, I would like to thank my friends and family for nurturing my Civil War fascination. Thanks go to my siblings, Katie and Andy; my grandmother Regina Schaub; and my friends L. Jason Rose, D. James Flook, Raffi E. Andonian, W. David Wiseman, Andrew R. W. N. Dangel, Philip W. Lyons, Aaron Cummings, Alicia Santoliquido, and Jackie K. Richardson-LaRue. Also, a most especial thank-you goes to my wonderful fiancée, Laura E. Lawfer, who, although she joined me long after this project was conceived, offered me so much help that I cannot fathom a time without her loving, invaluable assistance.

Last, I would like to thank my parents, Douglas and Cynthia Orr, for their everlasting support in helping me find my way in life. Without them, none of this would have been possible.

INTRODUCTION

I PRESENT TO THE READER THE COLLECTED, EDITED, AND ANNOTATED LETTERS of First Sergeant Ambrose Henry Hayward, 28th Pennsylvania Volunteer Infantry. This collection of original letters—kept at Gettysburg College's special collections archive—documents the military career of a twenty-one-year-old needle-maker-turned-soldier who served for three years in the Union army, only to fall mortally wounded during the Atlanta Campaign of 1864. This collection consists of 133 letters, beginning in April 1861 and ending in August 1864, shortly after Hayward's mortal wounding at the Battle of Pine Knob. Of these letters, 119 are written by Hayward to his family: his father, Ambrose Hayward, Sr.; his mother, Hannah Howland Hayward; his brothers, Augustus, Melville, Albert, and John Parker; and his sister, Cora. His letters begin on April 14, 1861, and end on May 28, 1864. Three letters are written by Hayward's brother, Melville, concerning his service with the 7th New York State Militia, and another is written by Melville's law partner, Paul J. Fish. Nine letters are written by soldiers from the 28th Pennsylvania to Hayward's family addressing such issues as Hayward's promotion, his brief hospitalization for fever in June 1862, and his untimely death at Chattanooga's General Hospital. Two of these are touching letters of condolence written by First Lieutenant Aaron Lazarus and Private William Roberts Jr., two of Hayward's close friends. Finally, this collection includes one letter written by Ambrose Hayward Sr. concerning his son's internment.[1] Altogether, this collection paints a vivid portrait of the wartime service of a skillful soldier and his family caught in the fires of sectional conflict.

In recent years there has been a dramatic increase in the publication of edited volumes of Civil War soldier letters. Consequently, I am hard-pressed to justify the publication of another. However, to my mind, the account of a single person—whether he or she be soldier or civilian, Northerner or Southerner, free or slave—who experienced our nation's costliest conflict is an instructional exercise in the personal nature of the forces of history. Henry Hayward's tale is both exceptional and representative. In many ways, this man's wartime experience progressed as it did for millions of other young recruits. Like his brothers-in-arms, he witnessed the exhilarating beginnings of the war in 1861 when hot-blooded rhetoric and lofty ideals propelled men into the ranks by hundreds of thousands. Like countless others, the unanticipated carnage and sorrow of the war's later months distressed Hayward in profound ways. But, although morose and sometimes critical of Union leadership, Hayward did not shirk his duty. Some of his comrades shrank from the challenge and yearned for the war's speedy conclusion; others simply deserted the ranks and ran for home. But like a majority of the Union army, Henry Hayward reaffirmed his commitment to the cause amid the Union's imperiled moments in 1863. Hayward vowed not to return home until he had seen the United States emerge intact from its "dark days." Finally, like millions of other Civil War infantrymen, Hayward experienced the grim hardships of war firsthand: long marches, inclement conditions, malnutrition, horrendous battles, and the mournful loss of comrades. In many ways, then, Hayward's voice offers a clear depiction of the army experience as seen by countless fighting men.

But in other important ways Hayward's tale reveals certain idiosyncrasies. As a Massachusetts native in a Pennsylvania regiment, Hayward brought a unique political and regional perspective to his service, and he offered a distinct assessment of his comrades and his opponents. In his letters Hayward described his commitment to his friends and family in North Bridgewater and Philadelphia. Hayward's letters reveal the strong connections between soldier life and the northern community, proving that home front and battlefront continually intersected. A strong-hearted Republican and a loving brother, son, and uncle, Hayward never let the primary recipients of his letters—his immediate family—forget where he came from and for what ideals he fought.

As an orderly sergeant, Hayward wrote letters that give readers a rare glimpse into the life of a Union noncommissioned officer on whose shoulders devolved the training and disciplining of raw recruits. Throughout the war Hayward had to assess the capabilities of soldiers below him (and at times officers above him) and impart his wisdom on the rank and file, ultimately conveying to them acceptable notions of gallantry, duty, and honor.

As a member of the 28th Pennsylvania, Hayward's letters offer readers an uncommon viewpoint. Simply put, the 28th Pennsylvania lacks a unit history, so his writings fashion an irreplaceable window into the lives of the enlisted men in this well-used veteran regiment. Also, as a soldier who served in Brigadier General John White Geary's "White Star Division," Hayward's letters are equally valuable. Few other soldiers in the Union army experienced the war as this division did. These soldiers from Pennsylvania, New York, and Ohio served in the Eastern Theater, fighting in horrendous engagements along the Potomac River and in the Shenandoah Valley, but they also served with the Army of the Potomac during many of its classic campaigns: Antietam, Chancellorsville, and Gettysburg. Then, in 1863, the division transferred to the Western Theater, engaging Confederate forces during the Chattanooga and Atlanta campaigns. Only a select few soldiers viewed these sections of the country or engaged in this assortment of battles.

Hayward's commentaries connected him with many of the war's larger themes. Frequently he commented upon slavery, emancipation, and race. Hayward, it seemed, supported abolition early in the war because he believed it would punish those he blamed for starting the conflict, the slaveholders of South Carolina. Quite tellingly, he wrote in April 1861 that "they at the South are Slaveholders. we at the North are their Slaves."[2] Clearly, Hayward saw slavery as a threat to white Northerners, and he acknowledged that war for the Union had to extinguish slavery to achieve complete victory. Like most Union soldiers, however, Hayward did not go out of his way to befriend black people. He treated runaways cordially, but his writings indulged in racial stereotypes and epithets, underscoring the complexity of northern soldiers' relationships to slavery and race. Rarely, it seems, did abolitionism and racial progressivism go hand in hand.

Hayward's letters also expostulated on the war's purpose. Frequently he reaffirmed his unwavering commitment to restoring the Union, which—as he often editorialized—had seen its best days. Although Hayward never compromised his fondness for battling for the cause, his initial idealism did not last the entire war. Because he witnessed deaths of comrades in battle—some of whom died in shockingly dehumanizing ways—the war gradually hardened him. When he retold stories from his major engagements, Hayward often stopped short, admitting to his family that he had to repress painful memories. The war's increasing brutality produced an inner war for Hayward, one that tested his ability to adjust to a world saturated with violence. Through it all, Hayward tried not to sacrifice his faith in the political goals of restoring the Union. In this capacity, Hayward's letters might reconcile two seemingly antagonistic trends in Civil War soldier historiography. Gerald Linderman's 1987 book, *Embattled Courage*, suggested that common soldiers became increasingly pitiless, less romantic, and further removed from the ideology that compelled them to enlist. Conversely, James McPherson, author of *What They Fought For* and *For Cause and Comrades*, claimed that soldiers demonstrated an inner resilience, adhering to their initial motivations despite the staggering butcher's bill. Hayward's letters reveal the mind-set of a soldier seared by the horrors of combat who still kept his faith in the cause. Perhaps some soldiers simultaneously exhibited the symptoms analyzed by Linderman and McPherson.[3]

Even more fascinating, Hayward's letters reveal a rare stream-of-consciousness approach to letter writing that diverged from most Victorian correspondents. Many Civil War–era letter writers—even those who wrote from army camps—followed a formulaic approach that stressed proper presentation, the "appropriateness" of certain subject matter, and limitations on secret disclosure. In Hayward's letters his conscious thoughts flowed unfettered. He endeavored to communicate his deepest emotions to his family as they came to him. Except for his restriction of the hurtful memories of battle, few of his letters suggest significant internal expurgation. A humorous moment from June 1863 revealed his intent to convey his uncensored feelings to his father. While writing in his tent, his company commander interrupted him. Rather than deleting the unfinished sentence, Hayward intentionally included it in the letter, commenting upon its incompleteness. He wrote, "I . . . have returned again to my writing but lost that Idea as you will notice I left of[f] at [']we have[']. who knows but what I was starting of at the time, with some great illustration or a poetic strain which would have been worthy of the pen of Byron or Saxe. but it is lost to the world for I scratched my head for 10 minutes and it would not come out." It is difficult to explain the origins of Hayward's garrulous style of correspondence, but in any case his letters offer scholars an opportunity to understand the deeper emotions of a complex individual. They also demonstrate the ways in which Civil War soldiers tried to communicate the images and feelings of the war to concerned family members back home.[4]

Hayward's letters reveal the complexities of camp life, conscription, the training of substitutes, Union military leadership, and the operation of military campaigns. They also prove that he had a tight circle of friends. He admired bravery and fortitude, and he singled out the bravest of his company by acquiring their pictures and sending them home to his family as wartime mementos. Politically, Hayward adhered to Republican Party planks, including its aversion to armistice talks and its support of conscription. However, as much as he applauded the first federal draft—and chuckled when Copperheads got drafted—he suggested ways for his brothers to dodge conscription. Hayward also had a complex relationship with substitutes, a consequence of federal drafting. He held a low opinion of men who substituted for draftees, often denouncing their ignorance or incompetence. Although he tried his best to maintain professionalism and drill the substitutes under a fair standard of discipline, Hayward did not stop cruel pranks that his veterans perpetrated upon green recruits. His indifference sometimes caused veterans to alienate unwelcome or naive substitutes. Hayward's opinion of leadership changed too. He spoke differently of several commanders as the war progressed, perhaps none so much as his first regimental commander, the illustrious politician Colonel (later Major General) John W. Geary. Early in the war Hayward described Geary with unshakeable reverence. But after participating in a few of Geary's poorly conceived battle plans, Hayward gradually acknowledged Geary's faults as a commander and even began to criticize him for his shameless glory hunting.

Hayward's letters additionally described his interactions with white Southerners. Although the 28th Pennsylvania rarely found itself in a position to regulate wartime occupation, Hayward repeatedly encountered southern civilians, Confederate deserters, and prisoners. Similar to his other worldly opinions, Hayward exhibited complex emotion when he dealt with them. Early in the war, he tried to differentiate between southern Unionists and Confederates, but as the war dragged on and no end appeared in sight, he became less concerned with respecting private property in the South, even if that property may have belonged to a citizen who harbored Unionist sentiments. Hayward allowed his men to forage for provisions under limited supervision, and he sometimes applauded the seizure of Confederate property. Yet, although Hayward made several bloodthirsty remarks about exacting vengeance against Turner Ashby's cavalry early in the war, Hayward never insulted his adversaries—at least his letters never indicated that he did—and he offered all surrendering soldiers the usual mercies. Hayward did not mind speaking with prisoners or with nearby Confederate pickets on the war question. It seems that he tried to understand the motivations of the enemy. Inevitably, he concluded that no matter which way he looked at it the Confederate cause appeared foolish. A striking incident occurred at Chattanooga, Tennessee, in 1863, elucidating Hayward's unflagging adherence to the preservation of the Union. After encountering a demoralized Alabama prisoner, he wrote, "they [the Confederate prisoners] expressed themselves freely on the War question, admitting the hopelessness of their cause. they were very bitter against their leaders, especially the Alabamaans. they told us that the war would soon close with us, but to them there would be no peace untill their leaders were exterminated." This interview lifted Hayward's optimism. Rejoicing at the Union's military success at Chattanooga, he wrote, "They could not hold Lookout [Mountain] which is proof enough that they cannot hold on to their Confederacy." In most instances, Hayward encountered Southerners with the intent of validating the morality of his cause.[5]

It should be recognized that Hayward marked his life with incomparable bravery. Although many other Union soldiers passed their testing of courage and stared down the grim face of battle, Hayward represented a breed of warrior who demanded more from himself during a time of crisis. As one of his officers recalled, Hayward was usually the "first to spring forward and the last to leave the field."[6] Hayward never paused when danger came, and out of a zealous passion for duty, he often participated in recklessly courageous acts, displays that impressed and perhaps even mystified his fellow soldiers. Hayward resolved to sacrifice his life for the Union cause if need be, and unfortunately he did so when on June 19, 1864, he died of wounds received in combat at the age of twenty-four.

I must admit I have always been impressed with the brilliant range of experiences, opinions, maturity, resilience, intelligence, bravery, and fortitude represented by those who fought—and died—in this most transformative of American eras. Many men who served in the Civil War revealed their deepest emotions, thoughts—even vices—in their uncensored letters home. Some displayed symptoms of cowardice; some exhibited outright criminal behavior. But a great many more expressed principles that stirred lofty passions of the human heart. In the end, though, Civil War soldiers represented ordinary Americans swept up by the fires of war, men who were forced to stick to or depart from their peacetime morals as best they knew how. These letters tell us a story—an engaging, inspiring, and ultimately tragic story—one that I think should be told.

EDITORIAL METHOD

THE PURPOSE OF THIS BOOK IS TO PRESENT THE AMBROSE HENRY HAYWARD letters in a comprehensible format with the least amount of editing. Spelling mistakes and grammatical errors have been purposefully included to preserve historical accuracy.

I have inserted edits when only three instances have arisen. First, as unobtrusively as possible, I have added words to sentences in cases where Hayward's vocabulary failed to promote readability. Second, whenever Hayward wrote the greeting "dear brother" at the beginning of his letters, I have added the brother's name if it can be determined. Third, if Hayward drew a picture or wrote in the margins of the letter, I have added bracketed text to explain the position of Hayward's image or postscript.

Generally, I have retained Hayward's punctuation mistakes; however, some explanation of Hayward's use of punctuation should be made. Hayward used commas and periods interchangeably. Also, he sometimes used the end of a line to symbolize the end of a sentence. To increase confusion, Hayward blotted his pen on the same paper on which he wrote. This caused him to insert random dots between words. Thus, Hayward's intended use of commas and periods cannot be fully known. To deal with this, I have simply left in the presumed commas and periods and silently removed the unnecessary ones. I have dealt with other punctuation differently. Hayward almost never used question marks or obscure punctuation, and consequently there is no way to know if he understood their correct service. Thus, question marks have been added as "[?]" to denote the end of questions and, on occasion, other infrequent punctuation marks have been added within brackets where I have deemed them appropriate. Overall, my editing is designed to present the letters as they physically appear, but with limited editing to allow casual readers a chance to examine the letters with unnecessary interruption.

The chapters are organized chronologically and are sorted by military campaign. Each chapter is preceded by a brief contextual introduction designed to explain the principle historical changes that shaped Hayward's life. The letters for each period follow that introduction.

THE LIFE AND LETTERS OF FIRST SERGEANT
AMBROSE HENRY HAYWARD

Chapter 1

"INDEPENDENCE STILL LIVES"

FROM NORTH BRIDGEWATER TO PHILADELPHIA, MAY 21, 1840–JULY 28, 1861

AMBROSE HENRY HAYWARD WAS BORN ON MAY 21, 1840, IN NORTH Bridgewater, Massachusetts. His father, Ambrose Hayward—a thirty-year-old dry goods merchant—had lived in North Bridgewater most of his life. The Hayward family descended from one of the first residents of Old Bridgewater town, Thomas Hayward, who settled in Plymouth Colony in 1638. Hayward's mother, Hannah Howland Hayward, came from a family of thirteen siblings in West Barnstable, Massachusetts, nine of whom were still living by the outbreak of the Civil War. On April 11, 1833, at age twenty-five, she married Ambrose Hayward and they took up residence in North Bridgewater at 48 Green Street. Hannah Hayward gave birth to her first child, Augustus, on September 1, 1834. Over the next fourteen years, she bore another six children: Melville, in 1836; Hannah Corinna, or "Cora," in 1838; Ambrose Henry, or simply "Henry," in 1840; Albert Francis, in 1842; Julius Freeman, in 1844; and John Parker, in 1848. Only one of the Hayward siblings did not live past childhood. Sadly, Julius Freeman Hayward died from the effects of dysentery on October 25, 1849, at age four years and eleven months. Almost nothing is known about how Julius's death affected Henry, who was then nine years old. In a time when child mortality was ever-present, such an event probably seemed commonplace, but almost certainly this tragic event had to have impressed upon Henry the frailty of human life.

Henry Hayward's hometown, North Bridgewater (present-day Brockton), sat in the northwest corner of Plymouth County, about twenty miles south of Boston. The town had expanded rapidly in the 1850s. In the five years leading up to the war, it grew by about 1,300 people. Throughout the decade, it steadily increased as a manufacturing center for clothing, dry goods, furniture, hardware, footwear, and musical instruments. By the Civil War, North Bridgewater encompassed about 13,000 acres and contained 6,584 inhabitants. It also had 1,377 families, 1,023 dwellings, 10 churches, 14 free schools, 1 private school, 2 academies, 1 bank, 5 fire companies, and a total property valuation of $2,173,965. It was, as one chronicler stated, "a live place."[1]

Hayward's hometown was important to him. Throughout his wartime correspondence, he ruminated nostalgically about his youth. Writing from Point of Rocks, Maryland, in 1861, he asked his youngest brother, John Parker, for particulars about the beauty of Katey Meadow and the fish biting in Porter's Upper Pond. Two years later, while in Tennessee, Hayward reflected on his elementary school days: "I look back to my School Boy days at times and wonder at the Changes time has made. I never dreamed that I would be a Soldier In those days of Compositions." His youth in North Bridgewater stood at the center of Hayward's life, and throughout his service in the Union army, he kept up-to-date on events in Plymouth County by receiving his town's newspaper, the *North Bridgewater Gazette*—his most cherished reading material.[2]

Religion also played a large role in Hayward's early life. At age seven he received a baptism from Reverend Warren Goddard, a leading member of the New Church, a religion founded on the works of Swedish mystic Emanuel Swedenborg. Although Hayward rarely mentioned his faith in his letters, a fellow soldier in Hayward's company substantiated his devotion to the New Church. As Private William Roberts Jr. wrote to his sister in January 1864, "I hope Harry Hayward called at the house. He is a noble fellow. . . . His folks as you are perhaps aware are ardent New Church people, & he is the same."[3]

However, Hayward's family—more than any other institution—stood at the core of his existence. During the war, he devotedly sent portions of his pay to support his parents and siblings. His letters recurrently expressed an eagerness to remain informed about their lives. When his sister, Cora, mistakenly addressed one of her letters to the wrong regiment, Hayward expressed himself heartbroken. Although this mistake cost Hayward a few photographs, he lamented that he could never read her missing letter. He wrote, "I would have rather received the letter than the Photo for I can get more of them, but you cannot again bring your mind to bare upon the same subjects which were contained in the letter that is lost. I know it has done some poor Soldiers heart good for I always read yours with great pleasure."[4]

Perhaps no incident better illustrated Hayward's deep attachment to his family than the birth on March 19, 1862, of his nephew, Arthur Augustus Hayward. Hayward took pleasure in calling himself "Uncle Corporal," and when he received a *carte-de-visite* of his nephew in October, he described the way it affected him. He wrote to his brother, Augustus, stating, "I received your last with the baby enclosed. I do not know when I have been so pleased as I was to get that little picture. when ever I feel cross, I go to my knapsack and take a look at the little chub and go away smileing. I have Coras and Johny Parker and Alberts, which I value highly." He wrote to his father that same week, explaining how he kept all his family photographs in his knapsack, regularly laying them out to gaze upon them.[5]

Before the outbreak of the Civil War, Hayward's two older brothers, Augustus and Melville, departed North Bridgewater to find profitable employment. Augustus, age twenty-seven, married in 1858 and settled in New York City, finding employment as a clerk. Meanwhile, Melville, age twenty-four, graduated from North Bridgewater's Adelphian Academy in 1850, and in 1857 he received admission to the New York bar. By the eve of the war, Melville practiced law alongside his uncle, Paul J. Fish, in Williamsburgh, New York. Sometime in mid-1860, Hayward followed his brothers' footsteps and left his parents' house. His letters offer only a few clues to explain why he decided it was time to make his way in the world. On March 1, 1863, Hayward wrote to his sister, stating, "it is nearly three years since I left my native place to go forth upon the world to find some peculiar place where my wild discontented Spirit could find repose, and since I have been in the army I think I have roamed untill I am satisfied." Although eagerness to appease a "wild discontented Spirit" undoubtedly played a large part in Hayward's decision to leave, the example from his older siblings probably contributed, inducing him to move to a larger city.[6]

Hayward settled in Philadelphia, where he moved into a boardinghouse at 402 North Front Street. Hayward found employment at Keith and Battles's Pin-Maker, a needle manufactory owned by Horace Grenville Keith and Joseph Battles, two former residents of North Bridgewater. At over 565,000 inhabitants, Philadelphia was the second largest city in the United States. Although it dwarfed North Bridgewater in terms of size, it mirrored Hayward's hometown in a few principal ways. Philadelphia had blossomed economically in recent decades, thanks to the proliferation of textile and shoe manufactories. For a needle-maker like Hayward, Philadelphia was an ideal place to work. It was a "live place," complete with social distractions and a strong religious atmosphere, and Hayward even found a New Church in which he could worship. In addition, Philadelphia deeply invested itself in the Union. Although a significant number of Philadelphians had southern connections, the Quaker City's history, its antislavery traditions, and its rising Republican Party allied it with the industrial North. It did not resemble a New England town, to be sure—in fact, Hayward could hardly fathom why it took so long for Philadelphians to become aroused by disunion—but when the war came, Philadelphia responded in a manner befitting any patriotic city of the North.

Life changed dramatically for all Philadelphia residents, including Hayward, on April 12, 1861. That day, Confederate military forces in South Carolina opened fire on the federal garrison at Fort Sumter. In response, President Abraham Lincoln called for 75,000 volunteer militiamen to mobilize, serve for three months, and subdue the rebellion. Philadelphia's quota stood at 8,000 men, the equivalent to eight regiments of infantry. In response, the Quaker City sprang to life. One resident claimed that the city was in "a state of dangerous excitement." Everywhere, citizens began establishing recruiting stations, armories, and barracks. One volunteer remembered, "In Philadelphia business was suspended, . . . [and] the armories of the volunteer companies were crowded to overflowing with men drilling night and day, the public parks of the city were given up for the same purpose, and the quietude of the Sabbath was forgotten amidst the preparation for war." In a mere seven days volunteers filled all eight regiments.[7]

Back in North Bridgewater, patriotic citizens formed two volunteer units, one company of infantry and one company of cavalry. When word of this reached Hayward in Philadelphia, he enthusiastically expressed a desire to enlist. He wrote to his brother, "they at the South are Slaveholders. we at the North are their Slaves. unless we Imediately dispute every step they have taken against the Federal Government it is not going to better this affair, neither will it be Sufficient to place the U.S. where it was before Lincoln's Election." Hayward's parents objected to his desire to fight. Fearing that army life would use him too roughly, his mother discouraged such thoughts. Not wanting to violate her wishes, he at first elected to remain, as he put it, a "Hayward reserve."[8]

On April 23, Hayward received a sudden shock when he learned that his brother Melville had already enlisted and was serving with the 7th New York State Militia, quartered in Washington. Since Philadelphia's three-month regiments had nearly filled, it annoyed Hayward to think that he had missed his only chance of fighting against the rebellion, but he received another opportunity on May 3, when Secretary of War Simon Cameron called for 42,000 volunteers to serve for three years. Cameron called upon Pennsylvania to provide 4,000 men, all to be sworn directly into federal service. He appointed three colonels and sent them to Philadelphia to commence recruiting.

President Lincoln personally appointed a fourth Pennsylvania colonel, selecting the illustrious John White Geary, an officer whom Hayward soon admired. Geary had served as the first mayor of San Francisco and had been governor of Kansas Territory during the strife that reigned there in 1856. Although he was first and foremost a politician, Geary possessed some military experience. During the Mexican-American War, he served as lieutenant colonel in the 2nd Pennsylvania Volunteer Infantry. Now Geary hoped to raise a regiment under President Lincoln's authority, this one in time becoming the 28th Pennsylvania Volunteer Infantry. Geary arrived at Philadelphia in mid-June and began selecting companies for his regiment.

By that time, Hayward had already joined a local militia company, the 2nd Company, Independent Grays, quartered at 602 Arch Street. On May 21—his twenty-first birthday—Hayward signed his name to this company's roster. When he enlisted, the examining surgeon noted that Hayward stood five foot six and one-half inches tall and had gray eyes and sandy hair. Three men, Captain George D. Hammar, First Lieutenant Gilbert L. Parker, and Second Lieutenant Joseph W. Hammar, officered the 2nd Company, Independent Grays. Unfortunately, Hayward and his new comrades had to wait six weeks to muster in. Because officials took no steps to regulate recruiting in Philadelphia, dozens of recruiters established enrolling stations and competed against each other. As a result, few companies filled their minimum requirements quickly. When Geary arrived in town, sixty-six companies applied for admission to his regiment and each hoped that acceptance might speed the pace of recruitment.

In July, Geary attached the 2nd Company, Independent Grays, to the 28th Pennsylvania. On July 6, after four hard weeks of recruiting, the Independent Grays mustered in as Company D and then established its first bivouac, Camp Coleman at Oxford Park, just north of the city. Once there, it joined nine other companies: three more from Philadelphia, one from Hazleton, one from Mount Pleasant, one from Mauch Chunk, one from Elizabeth and Allegheny Valley, one from Sewickley, and one from Pittsburgh. At Camp Coleman, the soldiers of the 28th Pennsylvania received uniforms—black-trimmed gray coats and trousers—and they also received arms, British-made Enfield rifled muskets equipped with sword bayonets. The regimental field and staff officers also procured accoutrements, tenting supplies, and rations, while benevolent visitors from Philadelphia brought socks, havelocks, and edible treats for the men. Throughout July the men of Geary's regiment commenced training for war. According to one reporter, "The drill to which the men have been subjected while encamped at Oxford Park, has brought them into a good state, and the Regiment is almost in condition to take the field for active work."[9] While at Camp Coleman, the soldiers elected their noncommissioned officers, and Hayward received a promotion to Company D's eighth corporal. Hayward admitted he did not actively seek the position, but he proudly delighted in his advancement. He wrote his brother, "It was rather unexpected to me as I made no particular exertion for a position in our fine company but allow me to inform you that it would not be only the truth for you and the rest of the family at large and to all whome it may Concern by addressing me in the future after this maner. ahem. Corporal Hayward."[10]

On July 22 news of the Union defeat at Bull Run reached Philadelphia, and Colonel Geary, anticipating mobilization orders, directed his men to prepare to march at a moment's notice. On July 27 the 28th Pennsylvania boarded ships at Tacony and landed at Walnut Street wharf. The regiment paraded through the streets of Philadelphia amid enthusiastic cheering. The soldiers boarded a train at the Baltimore depot "amid the parting cheers of the people gathered around the neighborhood," wrote a reporter. "Few regiments have left the city better equipped than this."[11] The next day, the regiment experienced a four-hour layover in Baltimore. Tension remained high since the Pennsylvanians expected trouble from Baltimore's secessionists. Geary ordered his men to distribute ammunition and load their weapons. Geary wrote afterwards, "My determination was, if there had been the slightest insult offered to my regiment, to have resented it instantly, and if necessary fired the city." Luckily, no incidents marred the 28th Pennsylvania's passage. The soldiers boarded cars at Camden Street Station and took the Baltimore and Ohio Railroad to the Shenandoah Valley. Commissary Sergeant David B. Hilt remembered the journey: "Various were the greetings we received along the route. At some places where there were Union men, we were joyfully greeted; at others, we met with nothing but sullen morose looks." The 28th Pennsylvania arrived at Sandy Hook, Maryland, at 3:00 P.M. on July 28. Once there, it joined a division commanded by Major General Nathaniel Prentiss Banks. Thousands of three-month troops, many of them from Pennsylvania, met the new volunteers at Sandy Hook, but they boarded trains to return home, their terms of service having expired. Tension mounted as the men of the 28th Pennsylvania realized that Confederate forces across the river might at any moment attack them in their vulnerable state. Still, a few itched for a fight. Sergeant Hilt wrote, "We . . . think we can give them a pretty tough reception."[12] Thus, sixty-eight days after signing his name as a soldier, Henry Hayward had finally reached the front.

1

Philadelphia Sunday Ap 14

Dear Brother [Augustus or Melville],

I recived yours last week and was glad to hear from you. my mind labours under a high state of excitement this morn (I confess it is to easily brought to that state). I have been reading the morning news and to see the Black hearted Traitors after commencing this Unnatural War exult and rejoice and make their boast they will unfurl the Palmeto Rag over the Capitol at Washington !! hear !! hear !! and over Fanuel Hall. they at the South are Slaveholders. we at the North are their Slaves. unless we Imediately dispute every step they have taken against the Federal Government it is not going to better this affair, neither will it be Sufficient to place the U.S. where it was before Lincoln's Election. an assault has been commited.[13] there are rongs to redress. there is a great lesson to be taught. South Carolina began this conflict and she should see it Closed. She has commenced the tragedy. let the Cast act and the Curtain Fall. Invade the State with pure American blood and never leave it untill it is left as waste and desolate as when the Sun rose on its free Soil 200 Years Ago. I have a feeling at times of late, a kind of burning in my bosom since these troubles have commenced.

it may brake out and prehaps Induce me to take a step that I should hereafter regret. (not on my own account.) for he who dares not come at his country's call is a coward (I never answered to that name). the South are boasting that they will yet unfurl the Confederate Flag and march north. it seems that this is the only thing that has aroused the Sleepy North. they are drove to it. now let them Show their mettel. I was down to the Navy Yard this morning when a dispatch came for the Water Witch to Steam up. they are fitting out the Sloop of War Princetown. the St. Lawrence is here dismantled.[14] this Week will tell some tales. write very soon. how is the post office, and I have not heard from Green St lately.[15] the old saying is that where there is a will, there is a way. It does not work well in this case. Jake brought a (will) but it dont make a Way. I am still makeing needles. Why dont the columbus 5 go and put out Fort Sumpter[?][16] I will tell you what will.

Independence
Still Lives

A Henry Hayward

2

Philadelphia Friday M-y 3

Dear Father,

After makeing two or three efforts to write, I have at last got seated to Inform you of what is transpireing in our City. the people here have begun to [grow] more quite and are not so easily excited as at first. the Soldiers are perfecting themselves more and more every day. they seem impacient for the field. every one has a smile upon his face. you would suppose they were going to a muster on a pleasure Excursion.[17] I recived a Paper & Letter yesterday, also Coras last.[18] I read over the names of Dr Hichborn's Company. I am acquainted with nearly all.[19] there will be enquirees about them where ever they move. I have enlisted In defence of the Stars & Stripes not yet.) but as you said if I had only been home you would not have objected. would that I had been for I feel proud of such a noble brave band under the Command of the Doctor, but are you not mistaken about the time they enlisted[?] can it be for 5 years[?] but before going farther I will propose 11 Cheers for the Squire. it made me mad to think that he should get the start of me on the Volunteer list. I think he has gone to see if he can get in with Old Abe and get an office). any how, he has taken the wind out of my sails. I shall act as a Hayward reserve if no more, but he made me mad again. I heard they was expected Friday night, so Saturday morning I arose at quarter to 5 and went up to the Baltimore Depot to see the Famous 7th and was around amongst them for 2 hours. [I] looked at each one closely, and thought I seen them all. [I] went to work the next morning, told my boss I had seen the big 7th. 2 or 3 days after they had gone I noticed in the Gazette[20] I had a Brother with them. you can only Imagin my surprise.

I took of my Apron told my boss I did not feel like work (a kind of head ache). I went up to both of the post Offices to see if there was a letter for me to Confirm the article. I would not belive it untill I got a letter from him yesterday.[21] I see there is another young Hayward in the Paper this week. he must not get Excited when the alarm Strikes but move moderate and Steady. tell Cora to Hurry up her letter. I want to hear what she has to say before I enlist. I cannot find anyone that favours it. If I were to think of going I should ask the advice of a Doctor.

HEN

3

Philadelphia Fri[22]

Dear Father,

I understood by your last that I should hear from Cora soon. that is why I delayed writeing. I recived a letter from Joe yesterday.[23] by him I learn that you have had a fire and that our sceanery was destroyed. the loss does not trouble me much [during] these days of Destruction. at any other time I might have Considerd it bad news. I got no gazette last week or this, so I am minus the particulars. continued on page 2 [*written in bottom margin*]

the Scott Legion went to camp this morning at Suffolk Park. this is one of our crack Regiments.[24] I have been out of work for 4 weeks. My Boss was oweing me $45 and the kind fool paid me off in needles, and I have been trying to dispose of them at any price with some success.[25] I was oweing Alice & Rebeca $20.[26] I have sold 12 dollars worth which makes 12/14 their Due. I dont like to do one thing to long. I have loafed long enough. I understand that Honest old Abe has taken the contract to remodel Old Union and build up another in the Republican style, and in order to make a sure thing of it he is employing men to remove all obstructions [*"look Page 3" and a finger pointing to page three is written in the bottom margin*] that come in their way. now if I thought he was mean enough to pay of his help in needles I would not have any thing to do with him. I have enlisted with the Independent Greys, a fine body of young men. I am acquainted with most all of them. we are attached to the Chippawa Regiment.[27] I guess Mell had a chance to do duty at Alex-da. the weather is lovely here. I hear you are haveing it cold. write if you have heard from Mell. I have had only one letter from him. I must go to the Armory and attend to drill. if you will answer this soon you will heare from me with further Particulars. Murry Hall has gone with Conl. Bakers N.Y. California Reg.[28] we shall be inspected next week. I am not obliged to serve untill after we have been Musterd in.

Henry

I enlisted the day I was 21

4

Philadelphia Sun Jun 2

Sister Cora,

I have felt much relived since I recived Mother's and your letter. Mothers letter affected me to the same extent as would a dose of Medicine. [It] Braced me up. Now all that I am waiting for is to get on the March—In order that you may be more settled on my case. I will state that it was no sudden move but an Idea for a long while thought and studyed upon when in the shop. I fully comprehend all of the dangers and hardships and will submit willingly to my fate. We expect to be musterd in Monday if nothing turns up. Pen-a has nothing to do with us with her rotten Clothing. We are Uncle Sams boys and he will Cloth us. our Company is composed mostly of Clerks, some rich mens sons. we shall be well cared for. our Capt (Hammer) and 2 Leut are brothers. 1 Leut Parker is a graduate from a Millitary School. we hold them in very high esteem.[29] they are men that will do all in their power for the Comfort of the men under them. I have plenty of help in fitting out for the Campaign. a Miss [*"Old Maid" written in margin*] Baker made me a very useful article which she calls a needle case. it is [a] foot long with three little bags in it. it now contains a doz needles, thread, Sticken plaster, a string, a variety of Buttons, lead pencil, linen, bandages, Lint, &c, &c. She and her good old mother have worked hard for 4 week gathering up old sheets of the neighbors and made them into bandages for the Volunteers. they also made 1000 needle cases like mine, put in all the articles, and presented them to the American Rangers Reg. she raised some of the money to by the needles and plasters. they made them all by their own fingers. now they offer to make as many Havelock if any one will furnish the Cloth. they are going to give me one. I was up to the Baltimore depot to see the N. Y. Seventh come in Friday night. I waited untill 12 ock and then went home to bed. got up early Saturday morn, went down their again to see if they had come, and while I was up their they was over in Camden. I was Cross all day long but I have come to the conclusion that it was not my fault I did not see him.[30] our papers generaly speak highly of the 7th. they have done all that they agreed to and have returned with honor. I have sold all of my Singer needles. it [is] quite a discount. I shall be able to leave square with all I think. I have 200 Wheeler & Wilson needles left. I think I shall send my trunk home. Our Armory is at the South west Corner of Sixth And Arch, Independent Greys Attached to the Chippawa Regiment, Colonel Seymour.[31] We have not got our number yet. I noticed the letter in the Gazzett from Mel. quite a contrast from the one from Fort Monroe. I noticed also the Freeman In arms. 21 years ago I was an Infant in arms, now I am to arms in Infantry, Just as I expected. I am going to put a fish line in my needle case. I will stump you to write again and I will answer soon.

Direct to Philadelphia next (not to Kensington) but same as you did the last.

A. Henry Hayward

[*in margin on page 3*] I wish I was a Zouave[32]

5

Philadelphia Jun 9

Dear Brother [Albert],[33]

I still maintain my position although we have not yet been musterd in to service, but we expect to be this week [on] Wednesday. the news this week has not been of much importance, which has the effect to make the people of the Quaker City loose their Patriotism. it needs a briliant Battle and a Glorious Victory to arouse them to [a] sense of duty. we expect two Regiments to leave this week. the Home Guards make a parade quite often. they have splendid Gray Uniforms and with their nice clean choakers and Kid Gloves they have the appearence of ladies Soldiers. they are not thought much of here with the exception of the ladies of Walnut St. there is where the money has gone to that the Volunteers aught to have had and the rest has been stolen.[34] the Ship John Truck's which has laid so long under water at the Arch street wharf was raised yesterday. they got her out into the stream and she went down again having broke a chain. she was being towed between two schooners. they was going to run her onto a bar. the Markets are well suplied with fruits and vegetables. we had Strawberrys two week ago. Peas are plenty. one of my Washington Friends that was larning his trade at Reany & Neafeys Kensington has gone home. he is for the Union. if I get to Wa-n he will hunt me up. the[y] will launch a big Iron Steamer at Reany & Nafeys this week. it has been Charterd by [the] U.S. which makes three new ones that are having their engins put in [as] soon as possible for [the] U.S.[35] I recived a letter from Joe dated F.W.[36] he is in good Spirits. Rebecca is going to give me a bottle of Campfire. she thinks it is so good to bathe the Head. the Old lady (Jersey) Burns came down stairs with a little white yarn twisted around a big peice of paper. I belive she said it would come [in] handy to tie up sore fingers. she also gave me a peice of Casteal Soap done up in a linen rag. she said she had it in the house 7 years. it was about the size of two new cents. her gifts wont take up much room so I shall except of them all. I can put them both in each ear. but I was greatly Oblige to her. if I get the present I have had promised me it will be worth having. I will tell you where I get it. Ed Mason is going to make me a little package of Medicine as a gift. My old Boss has gone to Springfield Mass to work in the Arsenal. the I. G. have got their Haverlocks.[37] the Regiments head quarters will be at the U.S. Building on Chestnut St. [on] Tuesday.

then Each Company will have a chance to see each other. the Colonel says ours is the Cracked one, and we know it. I notice you have a !!Green!! St. but how about the Post Office[?]

I dont hear from Mel, the Seventh

love to all,
A. Henry Hayward

[*in upper margin on first page*] a Fellow member of the I. G. died this morning.

[*written in pencil on first page*] I. G. Independent Grays

6

Philadelphia Sun J 23

Dear Sister,

I recived yours of the 18th and pursued its contents with much interest. I noticed by one of our city Papers that a severe Tempest had visited Plymouth County but said nothing about calling at Aunt Howards. Have you called on Mrs Bassett yet[?][38] I think I can see the Fair Twain In my minds Eye. I used to often speak of the fine Company of Dr Hich[born]s, was familiar with all of the names. I was in Keith & Battles when I opened my letters. we were much surprised. whoever is the cause of it should have more respect for N. B. say nothing about the shame and Disgrace that must fall upon their own heads. we have watched the papers closely to see when Websters Reg.[39] was coming, and we would have waited at the Depot all night to greet our N. B. friends. but if N. B. is not Represented they will go through Phil-d. without our particular notice. I met Mr. Ansilin[40] on Arch St the other day. he made a short stop. he has been stoping in N.Y. he is now in Washington. It has been quite hot here with frequent showers. the markets are full of fruit. I did leave my boarding House for two or three days and took my meales at eating houses and bunked with the boys at the Armory[41] (their was three of us in all). Rebecca thought that I was musterd in and was getting my Rations [*written in margin: "does not connect with when"*] when she knew I was not = she insisted upon my staying with them untill I was wich I was unwillingly submitted to. she said I was just as wellcome as though it was my Fathers own House. I will be hanged if I would not Marry them both if they was not so old. I shall never forget the many favors I have recived from their hands, and if at any time Father should come to Phil,d. he must call and see them. 402 North Front St. Miss Alice Shotwell. I have got $2.50 in cash, so I am not Broke, and about 200 needles (to sell if I can), but this is the way I am going to do[:] I shall wait untill I get my Uniform and then Folks will know that I am a (Volunteer), which I hope will have the effect to create a simpathy and induce them to bye. I have found out two New Church men In our Company. one is a Mr. Roberts.[42] he sings in the Choir at Rev Mr Berns Church. he says Rev Mr Goddard[43] has stoped at his Fathers house often. he has been east to attend Conventions often. he is well acquainted with James Pettie of Abington. the other gent is a Mr Swope of Frankford.[44] if you will tell me who you stoped with when you was here I would like [to hear] it. their is 3 Reg waiting here for Mustering orders. we expect our Colnel home Monday with the orders, and if he does not come soon we shall attach ourselves to another Reg. we circulated cards with the intention to be musterd in Thursday but it did not come off. our company march up to Dr Boardmans Church and was presented with a blue woolen Shirt, a pair of draws, and a red Flannel Stomach ache Belt.[45] when we got to the Armory and opened the shirts their was a needle case and 2 or 3 tracks fell out. We also got tin dipers & tin plates give to us and a promise of knives & Forks. Tell Father if he will consider his letter answerd I Will consider myself 3 cts in. I have given no one Authority to open your letters. this letter looks as if it was done. if I work on it much longer I shall spoil it. I shall let you know when I am mustered in. Write soon. What is John up to[?][46] (pay) my best wishes to all.

A Henry Hayward

I have recived no paper for 3 weeks. if you direct them to Kensington I will tell you when to stop.

7

Camp Coleman, Wednesday July 10

Dear Brother [Albert],

The reason I have not wrote before is because I wanted to be musterd in first and write from Camp. after anxiously waiting I can now proceed to give you the particulars in full as far as I have had Experiance. after waiting for weeks for Col Seymour, we gave him the slip and attached ourselves to Col. Geary Reg. we left our Armory, six & Arch, on Saturday last and took up our March for oxford bioling Park, situated 2½ miles from Frankford, It [is] pleasently situated on high ground with excellent water &c.[47] Col Geary as a man is a perfect Gentleman. he seldom speaks without a smile, and for his ability as a Soldier, he is to much known without any comments from me. his distinguished fame as Gov. of Kanssas and his experiance as Leiu Col in the War of Mexico has placed him in such a position that the war Department put such confidence in him that he has but little trouble in geting what he asks for.[48] Consequently, we are to be equiped (as he says) in the best maner possible. his companys are composed of western Pena. men from coal Mt. It will be the best Reg from the Keystone State. there is one company from Hestonville of the largest men I ever saw, and if a consumptive man was to look at them for 1 hour it would do him good. they came here fully equiped by the Capt. Father who is worth $8,000,000 [and he is a] coal Merchant.[49] we are the youngest Company on the Ground and i have heard the most active. we have the best officers. they are so kind to us that the wildest boys take advantage of it. our tents are on high and dry ground and with the others make a fine appearance. they come in large numbers from the city and county to see us. we mess six in a tent. Mr. Roberts is with me. his father came to camp yesterday and brought a basket of provisions. we lived high untill that had gone, then we came down a Coupple of pegs. some one in our mess has somethin brought to them quite often so we shall get used to Uncle Sams board gradualy. I am looking for the Quakers every day, as they said they should certainly come. I shall go to the city on furlogh to morrow to get, I hope, a letter or paper, an see the folks. we expect to stay here two or three weeks. we all march to the creek once a day to bath. I washed my clothes yesterday and Ironed them by laying in them at night. We are not with out our amusements. we have a fine Glee Club in our Company. Roberts and I are the Principles. some of the boys are going to get Instruments. our Leiu Col. Korpony is [a] distinguished Military Man. he has seen service in Europe. he was a Col in the Mexican war with our present Col Geary as his Leutenant Col. now it is right in reverse.[50] with such competent men we expect to see some fighting. It was rather unexpected to me as I made no particular exertion for a position in our fine company but allow me to inform you that it would not be only the truth for you and the rest of the family at large and to all whome it may Concern by addressing me in the future after this maner. ahem. Corporal Hayward.[51] how do you think that looks on paper[?] this is the first time I have seen it. I must get the Stripes sowed on my shirt to morrow. it is hard work to write with 200 men surrounding me with their yelp singing &c. and I have come very neer stoping 2 or 3 times. I must try to write to mell to morrow as I have not wrote to him for some time. direct as usal to Phil. I will tell you when to discontinue. I am enjoying good health, sleep well nights. we get as good grub as could be expected. [I] have no fault to find. I do not soak my crackers but two hours. so you see they are not as hard as stove covers[52] and the pork has 9 streaks of fat to one of lean. [I] had bean soup last night like mothers when she has them boiled for the bake house but with all this you may think we have hard times but we laugh the meals away by cracking jokes and Crackers, but I put mine in my Coffe as my teeth wont stand it. Well I will have a Smoke and then it will be time for the dress Parade.[53] write soon. love to all (how is Augustus and Wife[?])[54]

A. Henry Hayward.

8

Camp Coleman, Frankford July 23

Dear Sister,

With much haste I have to inform you that Col Geary has recived orders to be in rediness to march in one hours. the boys were wild with Patriotism on hearing the news which came soon after we heard of the repulse of Federal forces from Manassas.[55] Col Geary steped before his Reg and made a noble speech, Speaking of the defeat of our own forces and by Complimenting his own 28th. We are kept on our feet constantly, going throu the Regimental Drill and practicing charging at the Double quick. we were aroused Monday morning to one o clock with all haste. we formed in Company, and ran double quick to the parade ground where the Companys were formed in line of Battle. all formed, the oficer in command gave the word charge. we set up a yell (which we always do on a charge) and started. we got over the ground so fast and made such a noise we could not hear the commands. we stoped when we come to a high fence which surrounds [the camp] but not untill they commenced to climb the fence. the next morning we heard from Frankford. they were very much alarmed. they thought we were Mutining. Part of our Rifles came last night. we should have the rest today. they are the Enfield Sword Bayonet.[56] there is a rumor in camp that we leave to morrow but it is not authentic. I will give untill Saturday or Sunday. Some of the Companys are not full. we are all ready to start. some of the boys are packing their knapsack. their was 5 ladies to see me yesterday. they came loaded down with baskets and bundles of good things[:] pies, cakes, large loaf homemade bread, 2 large loafs of cake, peaches, some fancy cake, and many doughnuts. one of my mess mates comes to tell me that wagons are ordered to move us to morrow, that we shall march to night in the cool to the cars. I have heard by the morning paper that that we [are to] join the Division of Gen Banks at Harpers Ferry.[57] if all that i have wrote takes place before Thursday night I will write enough to let you know. I recived a paper at the camp yesterday. the conveniences I have to write is a tin plate on my knee. the boys are all alive with [the] Ecitement of moveing and i must join them. the Corporal H sends his best wishes to all. be composed. we will get them at their old tricks of runing again. the Stars and Stripes must sink or swim.

Corp A H Hayward

Comp D, Capt Hammer
28th Reg P. V.
Col Geary
Commandg

Chapter 2

"WE ARE NOT WITHOUT OUR SPORT"

GUARDING THE POTOMAC,
JULY 28, 1861–FEBRUARY 24, 1862

IMMEDIATELY AFTER THE 28TH PENNSYLVANIA ARRIVED AT SANDY Hook, the regiment's new division commander, General Banks, put the men to work. Banks expected them to guard the shores of the Potomac River between Maryland Heights and South Mountain. One soldier wrote, "A constant lookout is kept upon the commanding points in the vicinity, as an attack may be made at any time, although no Rebel forces are yet visible. We have companies detailed nightly for scouting and picket duty."[1] Within the first few days, many new regiments joined the division, including the 12th Massachusetts, the regiment that contained Hayward's North Bridgewater friends. Naturally, Hayward spent some of his free time visiting the Bay State regiment's encampment and catching up on the news from home.

Performing guard duty along the Potomac was no easy task; tensions ran high and rumors abounded that Confederate forces under General Joseph E. Johnston would soon attack. Still, the exigencies of war required the 28th Pennsylvania to remain on the front lines despite their incomplete state of readiness. Potomac guard duty tested Hayward's physical endurance. On the night of August 13, Banks ordered the regiment to march to Point of Rocks, Maryland, ten miles away. The night was dark and stormy, and Colonel Geary, unused to such adverse circumstances, lost his way in the thickets. After a confusing night march, backtracking and sloshing through creeks, the 28th Pennsylvania reached its destination after covering a distance of twenty-three miles. Sergeant David Hilt wrote, "The regiment moved o'er hill and dale, amid the pitchy darkness of the night, now wading streamlets, now climbing hills, until they at last reached Point of Rocks, about noon the next day, (Wednesday,) weary, tired, foot-sore, and hungry." Immediately upon arrival, Hayward had to stand guard duty. Without rest, in stifling summer heat, he patrolled his beat without complaint. This personal success proved to Hayward that he could endure the harsh, physical demands of army life.[2]

At Point of Rocks, Banks ordered the 28th Pennsylvania to patrol the area between Nolan's Ferry and Antietam Aqueduct. Accordingly, the regiment established picket posts at four-hundred-yard intervals for twenty-five miles along the towpath of the Chesapeake and Ohio Canal. Company D held a post below Berlin. For the next four weeks, Hayward and his comrades skirmished with Confederate guerrillas, searched Maryland citizens for contraband, and arrested suspected spies and secession sympathizers. The pickets always remained alert, as they constantly expected an attack from the Virginia shore. Also, the Pennsylvanians operated with no reserve because the rest of the division had pulled back to Frederick. One 28th Pennsylvania soldier wrote later, "If General Johnston, who has been at Leesburg, (thirteen miles from us) had *really* known of our small numbers, he would, no doubt, have tried to 'wipe us out' long ago. His force numbers about 15,000. Some kind fortune has protected us."[3] The pickets lived in small shanties behind the towpath. They constructed hovels from "borrowed" fence rails, lumber, straw, and leaves. After packing the materials together with clay and laying down stolen boards and straw for a floor, the shanties, in the words of one soldier, made "quite a comfortable residence." Every other day, one man from each post hiked to the company commissary to receive two days' rations, and the pickets cooked their meals behind the towpath.[4]

Union and Confederate skirmishers regularly skirmished across the river, and oftentimes the 28th Pennsylvania initiated these fights. Geary wrote to his wife in September, "It is almost constant skirmish here, even now the guns of my pickets are being discharged in the darkness of the night at some object either fancied or real."[5] Although Geary forbade soldiers from crossing the river, his men did it anyway. On September 1 Captain George Hammar selected fifteen men from Company D, including Hayward, to swim across the Potomac and liberate thirty-nine head of cattle from the Virginia shore. Hayward called it a "bold Expidition," and the event became the talk of the regiment for weeks.[6]

The men of the 28th Pennsylvania appear to have made unauthorized incursions quite frequently. When a reporter for the

Philadelphia Public Ledger visited the 28th Pennsylvania's picket line in late September, he remembered the rambunctious behavior of Hayward's Company D:

> We walked down the tow-path to see some "Philadelphia Boys" in Company D, Captain Hammer. . . . When it is known that the enemy are occasionally seen at almost every point along this river, it is an act of temerity to venture singly on the "sacred soil." . . . Continuing down the tow-path to Captain Hammer's quarters, we had barely reached them when we heard voices and shouting upon the other side of the Potomac. Our "boys" sang out, "Here they come," and rushed down toward the river. We were at a loss to comprehend the meaning of it all, but presently six men and seven horses emerged from the thicket and were speedily splashing through the water toward our picket. The shouting and laughter of the men, the fright and stumbling of the horses, whereby the riders were partially ducked, added to the sense of danger that they were in from the bullets of the enemy, made an exciting scene that will be long remembered by those who witnessed it. . . . The men belonged to Company D.[7]

The 28th Pennsylvania's occupation of the Potomac border forced Hayward to consider some of the broader aspects of the war, including the army's policy toward southern citizens and the confiscation of enslaved property. Hayward and his comrades faced little difficulty when it came to seizing private property for practical purposes. The Pennsylvanians stole fence rails for firewood or raided nearby farms for hogs and chickens with no regret. Neither did Hayward find it hard to intrude upon citizens' homes, such as when he and a comrade went begging for pies at an unnamed Maryland residence. During the war's early days, Hayward made a conscious effort to differentiate between southern Unionists and those who supported the Confederacy. He supposed that not all residents in the Maryland-Virginia borderland agreed with secession. However, as the war progressed and Hayward faced increasing contempt from occupied southern communities, his attitude changed to outright suspicion of all who lived on the "detested Sacred Soil."[8]

During the Potomac occupation, Hayward had plenty of opportunity to interact with "contrabands," slaves who escaped to freedom by running away to Union lines. By autumn 1861 the

Union army had yet to embark upon an official policy regarding black refugees. At every encounter Hayward and his companions had the option of returning runaways to their owners if they saw fit. It seems that Hayward and his comrades never resorted to this option. In all cases, Hayward sustained slaves' self-liberation. Hayward also dealt with African Americans cordially. Unlike other Union soldiers, he never exhibited outright racial hatred; however, his writings often stereotyped black people, portraying them as silly beings or social inferiors. In one instance, after Hayward had given up his gray uniform jacket in exchange for a blue one, he had no problem donating his old coat to a black camp follower as others in his regiment had done. However, Hayward joked with the ex-slaves by telling that the gray jacket made them look like Confederates. The purpose, it seemed, was solely to get a rise out of them. Thus, Hayward's letters unveil the complex relationship that some white Union soldiers had with slavery and race. Hayward was hardly a racial progressive, but he seemed to treat runaways affably and he supported emancipation before it became an official military policy.[9]

During this time, several new companies joined the 28th Pennsylvania. At the approval of the War Department, Geary increased his regiment to fifteen companies, or 1,500 men. Three new companies—L, N, and O—originating from Pittsburgh, Hazleton, and Huntingdon—joined the regiment on September 1. Two more companies from Philadelphia—M and P—joined in late September and mid-October. Also, about this time, Geary organized a four-gun battery—Battery E, 1st Pennsylvania Light Artillery—to be attached to the regiment.

Meanwhile, action along the Potomac began to increase, and on October 16 Henry Hayward fought his first major battle at Bolivar Heights, Virginia. On October 15, under orders from General Banks, Geary's regiment, now augmented with supporting companies from other regiments and some artillery, returned to Sandy Hook. Geary's hodgepodge force crossed the river on ferry boats and occupied the towns of Harpers Ferry and Bolivar. Banks directed Geary to seize a store of grain secreted in a nearby mill intended for the Confederates. The bluecoats removed most of the grain on the fifteenth, but Geary had to leave behind Companies D and F of the 28th Pennsylvania to secure the crossing for the next day's operation. These two companies took position on Bolivar Heights, a three-hundred-foot acclivity directly west of Bolivar.

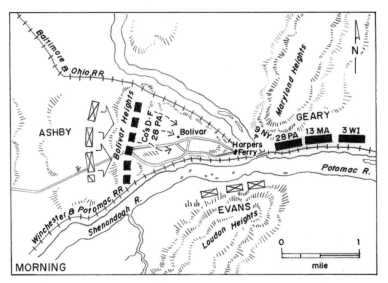

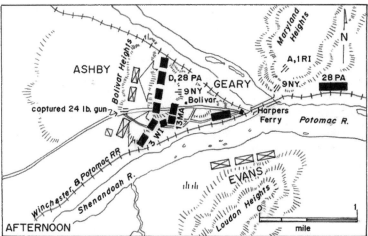

The Battle of Bolivar Heights, October 16, 1861. Map by John Heiser.

The next day, at 7:00 A.M., a mixed force of Confederate infantry, artillery, mounted infantry, and cavalry under the direction of Brigadier General Nathan G. Evans and Lieutenant Colonel Turner Ashby approached Bolivar Heights from the west. Hoping to drive the federals across the river, these Confederates attacked Geary's skirmishers. Ashby's cavalry charged the heights, forcing Hayward and his fellow soldiers from Companies D and F to retreat toward Bolivar in great haste. The Pennsylvanians fled so quickly they had to abandon their knapsacks to the Confederates. Once in Bolivar, the two companies reassembled and established a defensive barricade. Shortly before noon, Colonel Geary arrived with two more companies from the 28th Pennsylvania, three companies each from the 13th Massachusetts and 3rd Wisconsin, and two sections of artillery. The total Union force numbered about 600 men. The Confederate force, including a small detachment of Virginia infantry and artillery on Loudoun Heights, numbered about 550. Hayward, however, felt confident in victory; he had unbridled faith in the capabilities of Colonel Geary. In describing his commander in battle, Hayward wrote, "one thing now seemed to be wanting. it was some great Head to lead us. he soon made his appearence mounted on a horse galloping at full speed. we now breathed freer for we knew our cause was safe in the Hands of Col Geary."[10]

At 1:30 P.M. Geary launched a counterattack. The four companies of the 28th Pennsylvania stormed the northern section of Bolivar Heights while the three companies from the 3rd Wisconsin ascended the heights' southeastern face. One soldier from Company D wrote that "the order was then given to 'forward' with the artillery, which was moved steadily along until within 400 yards of their breastworks, when the troops were commanded to charge; they all pushed up the hill and the enemy retreated back to where they were in the morning."[11] At one point during the advance, Company D repulsed a mounted cavalry charge. The Philadelphians held their fire until the cavalry reached a distance of twenty yards. They unleashed a volley, dropping a few horsemen from their saddles, scattering the rest in disarray. Wrote one soldier, "The fire was so quick and disastrous as to throw the cavalry into confusion, and our men ran into them and after them, with their bayonets."[12]

The bloodiest part of the day came when the Wisconsin soldiers impetuously charged the Confederate artillery on the heights. The Wisconsin companies lost a few men in the scuffle, and a countercharge launched by Ashby's cavalry briefly drove them from the guns. Corporal John O. Foering of Company D wrote, "The Wisconsin boys were too rash; they went right up to the cannon's mouth, contrary to Colonel Geary's orders, and four of them were shot down. They would have captured a piece of rifled cannon, had not a squad of cavalry charged upon them from behind a house."[13] Still, the Confederate cavalrymen could not rescue the artillery. During the fight, the axel to a twenty-four-pound Columbiad broke and the retreating Confederates reluctantly abandoned it. By the end of the afternoon, Ashby's and Evans's men were in full retreat to Halltown, three miles away, and the Union soldiers triumphantly declared victory. At the end of the battle, Geary called the men of Companies D and F into line, and according to one soldier, he "thanked them for the service they had rendered and the bravery they had evinced upon that day, and said as they had a hard fight of eight hours, and fresh companies had arrived, he would relieve them, entrusting to their care the camp, which he said might be attacked at any moment. He again thanked them, in his name, and the name of the Government."[14]

The battle produced an unimpressive butcher's bill. Union forces counted thirteen losses (four killed, one captured, one mortally wounded and captured, and seven wounded), while Confederate forces tallied fourteen casualties (one killed, nine wounded, and four captured). Both sides proved equally raw, and the fight had been marred by confusion since both sides predominantly wore gray uniforms. However, Ashby's withdrawal and the seizure of the impressive twenty-four-pound artillery piece filled Hayward with assurance that the war might be won. "Hurrah three Cheers. the yankees are the Boys," he wrote his father exuberantly.[15]

Hayward did his best to describe an altogether new experience: combat. "I have not forgot the feeling which the first shot produced. we all looked curiously at each other as much as to say lookout for your head. father used to say when in a hard tempest you need not be afraid of the flash when it begins to thunder, but in this case you have to look out you dont get struck after it thunders. I never thought I should see the time when I should be dogeing cannon balls, but I did that day." He may have been raw, but Hayward, like many of his comrades, believed he had passed his first test of courage.[16]

The battle also filled Hayward and his comrades with bitter hatred for their enemies. Near the end of the fight, Ashby's cavalry stabbed and stripped the body of a Wisconsin soldier who had been killed during the attack on the artillery. One 28th Pennsylvania soldier wrote, "When these fiends in human shape again meet the Twenty-eighth, they shall feel their vengeance."[17] Hayward concurred; he wrote to his father, "It has not been beleived by many persons that the Rebels could be guilty of the many barberous acts that they have been accused of, but what I tell you is true. they bayonetted the wounded Wisconsin men and plunderd them of their clothing even to their shoes and stockings. they took an old man from his family only for his Union sentiments. they took a young man from his wife to make him join their ranks."[18]

Naturally, the soldiers of the 28th Pennsylvania reveled in their achievement. One soldier in Company D called the victory a "glorious one." Another soldier wrote, "We have had a brisk battle, and whipped the enemy. 'The Twenty-eighth!' What a magical effect the above syllables have upon all true and loyal hearts. Well may Pennsylvanians be proud of the gallant Twenty-eighth, with its brave Col. Geary. The action of the 16th instant, will long be remembered in the annals of history."[19] However, the celebration was short lived. On October 22 news of the Union disaster at Ball's Bluff reached the Pennsylvanians, and Banks immediately ordered Geary to send his regiment to Edwards Ferry to block any impending Confederate attacks originating from Leesburg. Within six hours Geary's twenty-mile picket line reassembled itself into a column, and Geary marched ten companies to the ferry. Geary told his wife that "some 30,000 or 35,000 men of the army got themselves into a scrape here, and the glorious '28th' had to come down to the rescue."[20] Five companies, including Company D, remained at Point of Rocks to protect the regimental encampment. After three days at the ferry, Geary's column returned to Point of Rocks. Five days later, on October 31, the regiment received its colors in a beautiful formal ceremony. A committee from Philadelphia subscribed funds to purchase "a beautiful suite of colors," a national color and a blue regimental color. Geary delivered a speech of gratitude, and afterward the regimental chaplain, Charles W. Heisley, blessed the colors. Recalled one soldier, "A fervent Amen, I know, welled up from every heart."[21]

The month of November passed quietly for Hayward and the rest of the 28th Pennsylvania. The War Department forbade them from trekking into enemy territory because the regiment still wore gray uniforms.[22] New blue uniforms did not arrive until late December. Thus, as cold weather moved in, the men acquiesced to the notion that they would close out the year without another major engagement. While at their new encampment, "Camp Goodman," the soldiers appraised their situation. In November, Hayward began losing patience with his company officers: "Capt [George D. Hammar] goes [to Philadelphia] Sunday and if he would act with the wish of the Co he would stay there. he is soft. we are disappointed in all our commisioned officers. we are the worst drill Co in the Regt, . . . they dont seem to look at the Interest of the men." Although his regiment had beaten the enemy at Bolivar Heights, Hayward believed that Company D required more time to prepare for the coming battles.[23]

Despite the hiatus in campaigning, the Pennsylvanians kept busy. On December 20–21 they finally received their new uniforms, dark blue frock coats, dark blue trousers, forage caps, and dress hats. One officer stated, "Our men were proud of their 'long-tailed blues' beneath their cross belts and waist belts." On Christmas Day, the regiment hosted a holiday pageant for the ladies of Maryland. Several hundred ladies arrived in the morning and sat on benches before a "gaily decorated stage," replete with flags, tri-colored lanterns, and evergreen wreaths. The program consisted of a symphony played by the regimental band, a comic song performed by the "Geary Glee Club," a choir performance sung by several soldiers, a speech delivered by Colonel Geary, two comic plays, and one grand drama performed by casts from the regiment. Hayward played the character of "Cowpens" in the one-hour comic play, "The Yankee Peddler, or, The Farce of the Virginian Outwitted." The festivities continued all day and ended at 11:00 P.M. The women expressed themselves pleased. "What fine-looking young men," one remarked. Another "silvery voice" exclaimed, "I wonder if anybody carries their pictures." Participants dubbed the pageant a complete success. One Pennsylvanian wrote, "The gala did not flag in interest, and at 11 P.M., when the curtain dropped for the last time, more than one wish was expressed that they could linger on." Lieutenant Thomas H. Elliot, the stage manager, added, "Camp Goodman was the star towards which the pleasure skiffs of the Marylanders were steering to welcome Christmas, and afterwards to treasure up in memory's storehouse as an epoch of gladness."[24]

Throughout December and January, the 28th Pennsylvania focused on its military discipline. One officer wrote, "We drilled morning, noon, and evening." Quickly the regiment's abilities began to improve. Continued the same officer, "Old soldiers rattled through the manual with twice the ease they did before, and recruits stepped into their places with a felicitous confidence and good success. Awkward squads toed the mark, whisked their eyes right and left, and dropped the butts of their rifles without crushing their corns. All seem to have entered deep into the mysteries of flank and file, and were full-fledged heroes before they knew it."[25]

In January and February 1862, the 28th Pennsylvania continued guard duty along the Potomac. Each week usually resulted in a small skirmish or a short artillery barrage. One soldier wrote, "Seldom a week passes that the rebels do not favor us with a little token of their regard at some point along our lines, where they think we may be a little unguarded."[26] The soldiers eagerly anticipated a grand advance, but the rough winter weather did not cooperate. On January 22 one member of the 28th Pennsylvania lamented that the "continuation of falling weather has, for the time, frustrated the plan of operation along the river. The roads are now, and will be, unless the weather should grow cold, entirely impassible to the heavy wheels of our artillery and army wagons, so that it seems very probable we shall lie inactive a little longer."[27]

Naturally, idleness bred frustration, which in turn bred alcoholism. Geary, however, would not let liquor infect his regiment. When signs of abuse surfaced, he commenced a crusade to make the 28th Pennsylvania a temperance regiment. One soldier wrote, "Liquor has been put out of reach wherever found, and kindly persuasion and strict moral example has released the inebriate from his fetters." Geary drafted orders requiring his men to arrest and punish any sutlers who attempted to sell alcohol to the regiment. The Pennsylvanians usually put arrested whiskey dealers to work chopping wood, cleaning latrines, or clearing brush, or they punished them by placing them under guard or by chaining an iron ball to their leg. One soldier commented, "Venders of the obnoxious fluid . . . swept the quarters of the men, cleared the ground of brush and stone, and otherwise manually labored. Huts have been burned to the ground where their owners have clandestinely contributed to lessen the esteem, worthiness and alacrity of the soldiers by dethroning his reason." Another Pennsylvanian related, "Yesterday the provost guard cleared out four more persons for selling liquor to the soldiers, and sent them to the guard house where they amuse themselves by chopping wood and policing the camp." Geary went so far as to order the provost guard to search private packages delivered to his soldiers and destroy, as one soldier wrote, any sign of "the liquid devil . . . found secreted in them." Nearby Union regiments noticed the forced sobriety of the 28th Pennsylvania, and they nicknamed it the "Goldstream Regiment."[28]

Finally, in late February orders reached the 28th Pennsylvania calling the men to action. Under a directive from President Lincoln, General Banks, now in command of the Army of the Shenandoah, planned to cross the Potomac on February 24 and engage Confederate forces in the Shenandoah Valley. Upon hearing the news, Geary went to Banks's headquarters in Frederick to receive his instructions. On Washington's Birthday, the 28th Pennsylvania's second in command, Lieutenant Colonel Gabriel

De Korponay, reviewed the regiment and declared it fit for campaign duty. The next day at tattoo, the company officers issued orders to the enlisted men, telling them to pack their gear and be ready for the march. Hayward excitedly wrote his brother Albert, "the canal Boats along the line have been accumulating at the Point and other Places for the last week. . . . a forward movement looks very probable. we are waiting orders."[29] At long last, Hayward and his regiment were going on the offensive.

9

Dear Sister,

I recived your last letter at camp Coleman. in my answer to it I stated the possibility of my leaving for the seat of war soon. such was the case. we moved sooner than I expected more on account of the defeat at Manassas. we packed knapsacks and strocke our tents Saturday morning at six oclock. it was a very hot day when we took up our line of march to Tacony (which is situated 4 miles from the park on the Delaware). after having marched a dusty road and tasted well the sweets of a Soldiers life, we embarked on a Steamer for Philadelphia. we then formed a line and marched up Chestnut amid the shouts and cheers of an excited multitude. having arrived at the Baltimore depot, we took cars for Baltimore from hence to New Sandy Hook where we arrived Sunday night at 5 oclock, being very glad to know that our journey had been accomplished. we will now go back to Phil-d. and speak of a few of the Incidents which occured on our Journey. the weather was so hot and our knapsacks and traping so heavey that 4 or 5 droped down on the road going from the park to Tacony. passing down the Delaware, salutes were fired and crowds who had gathered on the wharfs along the river cheered us on our way untill we arrived at the foot of Walnut St. we did not stop any length of time in Phil-d. for that reason I did not have [a] chance to see many of my friends. I did want to go to the Pinmaker once more, but I had been there but a day or two before. I saw Horace Keith on the march up Chestnut.[30] there was much cheering all along the way. the Star Spangled banner was displayed by the ladies who would come out the door with the flag in their hands and wave it untill we had passed. when we [were] within 5 miles of Harpers Ferry their was a little girl and what looked like her aged mother standing [in] front of the door waving the flag with the grey haired Father waving his hat. it looked as if they only dared to display it only when the occasion required. when we were near the Ferry we would pass some places where the people would look ugly at us. we would go a little farther and come to the slave cabins. the old nigs and the little darks would jump up and down as if they were in a Methodist Meeting. after we got out of the cars we started for Harpers Ferry which is 2 miles from Sandy Hook. but orders came for us to pitch our tents where we were as the Union troops were retreating from the Ferry to occupy what they consider a stronger hold. but know doubt it is [a] millitary move yet to be made known. we are well fortified upon all of the hills around. it is difficult to tell how strong our forces are but I think it doesnt exceed 15,000. it is said that Johnson is near with a large army, but we all sleep well nights. there are many rumors going through the camp at different times, but they begin from nothing and end the same way.[31] you better belive, I was tickled when I found out at Baltimore that the Mass 12th was here. the[y] came here only the night before us. I am over to their if [indecipherable word] when ever I get a moment to spare. it reminds me much of home. we talk of old times, of every thing we used to do in days gone by. we hardly realize that the Rebel foes are lurking about so neer us. I know most of them. I have seen all of the officers except the Captain who has happened to be away when I have been their. the music of their band is familiar. I can hear it from our quarters.[32] I must now close, for it is time for a dress parade. it [is] hard to write letters as you will see by this but take you time and study it out dont read to fast. stop at the commas. and if you see any periods count [to] 4. give my love to all. writ soon. I will write oftener when I feel lik it.

[unsigned]

10

Camp Banks Harpers Ferry, Thursday Aug 8

Dear Brother,

The first letter I recived after reaching here was from you. It did not take me long to read it. it must be you were short, like myself. I intend to use up all of mine in this letter. I have put of lying as long as I could as they ask 8 times its value here. when you write use light paper, and you can send me a sheet with your letter. I have sent 4 letters. 2 to Phil, one to Mell, one to Cora. there is quite a differance between camp life here and that at Camp Coleman. we have exciting times occasionaly. last Monday as Corp. Roberts and I was returning from the river where we had been washing our clothes, we noticed the men of the N. Y. 9th Reg runing in every direction halloing and shouting as if they were crazy. soon the drums began to beat from every quarter. we hastened on and soon came up to a squad of men. they told us to hurry to our camp as we were attacked and they were fighting over the Mountains. we pushed on at the double quick and reached our camp were we found the Reg drawed up in Battle line with the Drums still beating the Alarm.[33] I soon had on my equipments, and with my canteen full of fresh water right from the spring, was ready for the march. but it was no go for a courier came dashing up and informed our Colonel that it was a false alarm, thus relieving the minds of our gallant 28th from the thoughts of meeting the Rebels, and change the attack upon salt pork and Hard Crackers as it was past the time. during the excitement a member of company I was caping his rifel when it went of and the ball passed through the head of one of his owne Company killing him instantly.[34] Yesterday delegations from each company attended the funeral of a member Comp E who died in the Hospital of Fever. he was sick when he enlisted, and while here his captain offered to give him an honerable Discharge, but he refused saying, he had come with the Company, and he would die with them. they raised $76 to send him home.[35] Last Tuesday our forces stationed at a place called Point of Rocks, a few miles from here, had a skirmish with a company of Rebel Cavelary when they killed 3 men took 8 prisoners and 20 horses. a captain of the New York company that engaged with them brought them to our camp where they were put under Guard by the Regulars. the N. Y. captain was fired at 9 times with out affect, but the last ball went through his whiskers. when they were passing by the soldiers the men would cry out bring out the rope, here is a good limb, &c. which made these poor fellows look uneasy. all they wanted was to be let alone. I suppose they have taken the oath before this and left for home minus their horses.[36] I see they have got up something else for a change. our Colonel is a Temperance man and he does not allow whiskey within smelling distance of the camp. He got wind that a person was selling Union Whiskey to the boys. down went a Corp Guard and brought him to the Colonels tent. the Col passed Sentance and he is now serving it out by walking around a sentinel with a heavey canon Ball resting on his shoulder which he is to do for an hour. there is 4 more just been brought in for the same offence who are now in the Guard House waiting for the Colonel to come.[37] the roads leading to the camp are filled with farm wagons selling pies, cakes, butter, Eggs, &c. to the Soldiers. most of the produce they ask double price for, but the boys will bye with a little beating down. we were a little afraid of poison at first but that does not keep us from eating them. I bye [*indecipherable word*] the 3 for 2 cents worth so as to make the needfull hold out. there is a talk of our going to Fort MacHenry next week, but I shall not belive it untill we strike tents. I should like the change. not that I dislike this place, but you know I am always ready for a change. Monday night our company went out on picket duty. we went out about 5 miles. while we were on our way we came up with a party of Soldiers from the Mass 13th who were fixing up a wagon that had broke down. it was quite late and dark when we came to them. We thought for certain that we should have a brush. we sent three men ahead with a sargent who challenged them. they could not give the countersign. our men told them they were our prisoners but they stroke a light and with a little explanation we passed along. they were much alarmed. our company stood back ready to fire at the word go. had they been foolish enough to run we not knowing who they were would have fired at them, but they stood their ground. the 12th Mass have moved up the road one mile and I have not been up there. I was to their camp when they broke up and saw them in line for the first time. they looked well. Sergant Sampson had the Colors. I shall try to go up their with the Gayzette to morrow.[38] I recived a letter and paper to day. I see Mell is with you. tell him to take the gun and go out on picket duty. he asked if I recived a letter from Father with stamp. I did also notice my name in the Gayzette as being in the 27. it is the 28th. My trunk is at my old Boarding place, 402 North Front. their was about 400 of our Reg went out on target practice. when it came to our company about 16 fired before it came to me. not one of them hit the tree. I raised my Rifle, brought my poor right eye to bare on the mark, [and] fired. [I] hit the tree fare. Col Geary said good shot. wait and get back numbers of these leaves and get them bound. I Still Live. Neary Dead.

[*Missing page*][39]

hard but I knew it was my duty and I done it willingly. [I] was relived from duty at 12 oclock today [after] 3 hrs. I stood it like a Major. but the night was cold with a heavey dew, and in going the rounds to relieve the guard I had to go through bushes and tall grass which wet me through. but when of duty I would lay my gum Blanket on the grass, put my woolen Blanket over my overcoat, and lay down and rest untill 5. [I] was roused with the unwelcome cry of Corporal of the Guard post 11 or 14 as the case might be, when I would have to go see what was wanted. I made my first arrest yesterday. [I] took 3 men beside myself to arrest a man that escaped from our guard house when we broke up camp at Harpers Ferry. he had been seen at a tavern at Point of Rocks when a Corporals Guard was sent for him. after they had been gone a short time, word came to our guard house that he had just went into the woods opposite our camp. I was sent with haste with a guard of 3 men with orders to take him dead or alive. we caped our Peices, and enterd the woods. two of my men that were in advance had passed by him when I discoverd him in a stooping position and went up to him. [I] asked him if he was not attached to Gearys Regt. he said he was not. [I] asked him if he was not the man that was confined at the guard house at Camp Banks. he said he was not. I told him he was the man I wanted and orderd the guard to take him. he swore he could not be taken and would not go. I then said to him that as he would not go by fair means he must by fowl.

when he simmerd down and I walked him into camp, he was a desperate man, and they shaved his head and drumed him out of camp Imediately with the words on his brest Theif, Vagabond, & Drunkerd.[40] I have now toke yours and Hannah letter from my pocket to see what questions there are to answer. I recived the little Book guid to Soldier Health. I still retain use of all of my limbs but walking sticks are a little sore. I told some of you in one of my late letters that I did recive postage stamps from Cora. I did read to Alice & Rebecca part of the contents of one of your letters. I cannot keep it out of my head but what this letter is for Cora but it is not for Gus. I wrote in Alberts letter about my trunk which perhaps you did not recive when your last was wrote. tell Hannah the Rebel Picketts can not have me without a fight. has Wilson Orr come on here with an other Regt or [is he] to join the 12th[?] I shall not be likely to see him unless we go back to Harpers Ferry.[41] Friday Aug 16, I am up bright and early. feel well and hearty, and with my old Barell head for a writing desk. [I] will try to fill up smuty peice of paper which was attached to Rebbeca's letter. 200 men from Rhode Island have jest arrived to recruit up the R. I. Battery which came with us from Harpers Ferry. Col Geary is acting Brigadier General whil here. the number of our forces stationed here is 2200[:] 28th N.Y., 28th Pa, one comp of Regular Cavalry, and the R. I. Battery. Col. Geary formerly lived here and owned stock in the Bridge which was destroyed here by the Rebels.[42] they say this morn that we marched 30 miles. it is hard to tell just the distance. our men stood it well. we feel proud of it and [are] ready for an other. give my respects to your wife. tell mother I should like to have a Johny Cake. will answer Cora's soon. I was told this minute that we are under marching orders for Washington. you will see in the papers of our arrival their if it is so. love to all (Henry)

I forgot to say that we captured 2 slaves when we were on picket who had run away from their masters. we brought them in.[43]

11

Point of Rocks Maryland Thurs[44]

Dear Brother [Augustus],

With much haste I proceede to Answer your letter. We recived orders at 4 oclock Tuesday afternoon at camp Banks to Strike tents and pack knapsacks and get ready to march that night. [We] could not find out where we were going, but every one had a guess. a few hours found us drawed up in line ready to move. after waiting for a while, we started, the night was quite dark, it being a misty rain and the roads were in a dreadfull mudy condition. we headed down the river which gave us to understand that our destination was either Point of Rocks or Frederick. We had our knapsacks carried in the Waggons. we could never [have] carried them on our backs, as we found out before going far. in many places the mud was over shoe, but we found no fault about that. it was Climbing the high mountains known as the Blue Ridge [that we found fault with]. thus we traveled for hours, occasionaly halting, when the boys would whisper along the Plattoon, what is up now[?] we get under way again and come to a young river, which would explain all. when we came to these streams we new what came next. it was a mountain to climb. after reaching the sumit, we could easily hear the rumbling of our heavey baggage Waggons in the rear. the hills are so long and steep that they had to chain the wheels in descending. the most exciting and provoking part of my story remains to be told. Col Geary, with his guide and body guard, were in advance and when we were within 5 miles of our destination they mistook the way which caused, as you will soon see, some little excitement and a very fatiging March. we had been furnished before starting with 36 rounds of Ammunition which had a smell of blood and gave us much to think about in the way of seeing bloody fields and the Idea of driving the Rebels if we met them at the point of our Sword Bayonetts. after proceeding on our misguided way for a mile and a half, a rocket was seen to burst in the sky over our heads. this was strange indeed. the nervous trembled, wile the more brave walked calmly, all ready to obey at the word of Command. suddenly the Regt came to a halt, and soon the Leut Col came trotting along the line mounted on his horse with the Command, load at will, which I did with a steady hand. now we all thought we should have a fight and some could immagin bodys of men in the woods. we got under way again [but] could not find out where it came from. it might have been our own men, but most think it was from the Virginia side. we marched on, supposing Col Geary would soon take us on to the right road. we came to a halt again, and found out that we could go this way on to the right road but it was impossible for the baggage to get over. the Col then went to a house nearby and aroused the inmate to know if there was any way that we could make out with out going back. he soon returned with the planter [and] with a lantern. he gave us orders to file up the large cut side of the road with rails which was done. Whil this was going on, three men were detailed to search a cornfield where a man had been seen spying on us but he was not found. we got of once more [and] soon came to a house where we marched through the barn yard causing the cows to bellow, and the roosters to crow, and the farmer harnessing his horse was to act as [a] guide untill we were once more on the direct road. it was now nearly morning and we found ourselves in beautifull country with mountains on every sides as before and a distance of 10 miles to walk before we should get our coffee. we were all very tired but we pushed on and reached Point of rocks at 11 oclock Wednesday fore noon, after walking a distance of 23 miles, correct way being 13, but hark, hear, hear. I had to go on duty the night of our arrival as Corporal of the guard without chance to rest or get any sleep. (Henry)[45]

12

Dear Sister,

It is very uncertain about my geting another chance to write untill we can get once more settled. our camp has been in an uproar since our departure from Sandy Hook. the strictest watch has been kept by our Col upon all the hills on the Virginia side, and all the roads leading to our camp are well guarded. I suppose you have heard by the papers of the evacuation of Sandy Hook of Gen Banks army. our 28th acted as the advance guard and will now remain to cover their retreat.[47] we have been drilling lately as skirmishers. last night 3 of our companys left for Sandy Hook to relive a Regt, the last of Banks Div. Col Geary made a patriotic speech to his men before they left. they are under the command of Lt Col Korponey. they are orderd to keep the Rebels from crossing the Potomac if possible. if they are to strong for them, they will retreat untill they join us. if we cannot check them we are to fall back to a town 9 miles below where we shall meet with more Federal Troops. Col Geary in his speech said that no Regt. in the U. S. service held the same position of honor and such a dangerous position as the 28th. to day two of our men who have been in the hospital most of the time since we have been in camp are to be sent home. the officers are orderd to send all of their baggage below to some town so that nothing will trouble our movements. I think before this reaches you we shall have buckled on our Armor and to the Field or woods have gone to meet the treacherous Foe. I recived Fathers letter yesterday accompanied with a blank. it is not worth while to pay extra for sending paper. if we go to Frederick I can get some. you need not direct any more letters to this place unless I write. I shall be glad when we do vacate it for it is the most unhealthy place I have seen. yet for one week we have not seen the sun. yesterday it shown for a few minutes, but it soon discoverd its mistake and retreated. one of my messmates had a box come from Phild the other day and we have been liveing on fancy cakes, sawel, &c. our company hires two men to do the cooking, and we pay them $1 a month. they make us good soups, and we live much better than we should without them. I wrote to Augustus a few days ago. please tell me if he recived it. I took a guard Wednesday night to escort three reporters for Frank Leslies[48] and other papers to the Telegraph ofice. they are a jolly set of men. Mr. Elliot, the Editor of the Evening Journal Phild, is stopping with us. he has a son, a Lieutenant in Company C.[49] the boys are all to work [on] fixing their Guns to day and I must not be behind. we all take pride in keeping them looking well. I am in good health and ready for a brush (or my Mush). I expect to hear of great news From Washington soon, but it will be a week old before we get it if we stay here. I hope we shall have to make an honorable retreat from Point of Rocks, but not from Point of Bayonett. we con-fist-to-taked[50] some green Corn yesterday when we went to bathe. our Captain did not say no. they had to swim across the Canal to get it. some would stand and throw it a cross while others would swim with it in their arms. I thought I would not trespass, but one large ear hit near my close and I took possesion of it, and I am going to boil it for my dinner to day if it is possible. I will write again soon.

Love to all,
Corp. A. Henry
Hayward

13

Somewhere, Aug. 30th, 61

Dear Sister,

It is so long since I last wrote that I am uncertain wheather I answered your last or not but I am certain I answered Augustus and told you that I was then at a place called Point of Rocks, Md. but [I] did not expect to be [there] long. now I wish to know if he recived my letter, and when any of you write please say we recived yours of such a date, then I can tell you if I miss any. I recived the box which Father so kindly forwarded. it was Thursday night Ag 29 when I recived it. [I] could not rest easy untill it was opened, which was soon done by placeing my large sword bayonett under the cover. when I came to the cakes I stoped as I had already been intrudeing on the super hour. the seeds tasted like Home, but the cakes [smelled] stronger of the Box. but for all that it did not save them from be-ing devoured by a hungry mouth. the stockings I am much in need of one pair, and when I came to the paper, you could have heard me say that is just what I have been wanting and could not get, as there is no stores in 3 miles [in] any direction you can go. In Augustus letter I stated of the possibility of an attack from the Rebels across the river from Point of Rocks. the night I sent his letter which is the last thing I wrote, orders came from the Col to strike tents, pack knapsacks, and we all expected we were to march, but we afterwards found out that they was going to send our baggag ahead so that it would not be in the way and should have no trouble with it in case we should be obliged to retreat. we soon got the teams loaded and they left. no one doubted but what we should follow them the next day. we lay down on the ground with our Rifels by our side ready to answer the first call, but the night was quiet and the morning dawned upon the spot which but the day before showed a pleasant and well regulated camp but was now the picture of some hasty work, which showed itself by the boys going around to the spots where their tents stood to pick up what in the hurry they had left to spoil on the ground. It was now breakfast time and we began to study among ourselves what to do. all of our possesions had gone. but in such a country as this we laugh at the Idea of starving, especially when their was no less than 30 Hogs and young pigs feasting upon the leavings of Uncle Sams grub[—]which his boys are none to saveing[—]had left in the straw and around the tents. not many minutes had passed before we heard a squeling and soon the boys came along tuging a fine porker after them, and as we had two or three buchers in our company, he was dressed and many a fine pig was eaten that morn. breakfast over, we were carless for our diner, leting that take care of itself. our company has been out on picket duty for one week. we are streched a distance of 4 miles in squads of 3-5 7-11-15, &c. the whole Regt reaches a distance of 18, between the Potomac and the Ohio and Chespeak Cannal. we live in little huts made of rails coverd with branches, leaves, and hay. we all like it very much and the boys object to going back to camp. we do not know how long we shall stay. I am with a Pickett of 15 men [at] The Capt Hadquarters. this is a place where they tried to cross when Company A was stationed here. we have to keep strict watch at night and [we go] of of duty at daylight. I have not recived any letter from Ruf, But one from Fred,[51] untill I recived those in the Box which [I referred to]. tel Ruf I will answer soon. I have got a towel, 3 combs, and plenty of soap but they are with my knapsack with the baggage, 20 miles from here with Banks Div. I have not seen the mass 12 for three weeks. I will not try to get all I want to write on this paper.

the Mass 13th is at Sandy Hook, which is all with ours that is left of Banks div. I will try to get there letter I have to the owners. I gave Corp Roberts the correct address where to write (if I should get lost in the woods). the night we stroke tents I recived a letter from Mell date Aug 24th. [I] recived a Gazzette [on] Wednesday. did you not hear of the removal of Banks Div 3 weeks ago from Harpers Ferry[?] the nearest town from our pickett is Berlin which is 2 miles [away]. our Regt headquarters are at (Point of Rocks). we have a post man from our company who goes along the line of Picketts at 10 A.M. and takes the letters to P. of R. and comes back in the afternoon with the mail. their was a canon brought from Berlin the other night down to our Pickett to fire at a barn across the river wich was supposed to be a rendevous of the Rebels, but they could not batter it down. yester day two daring boys of our Company D swam and waded across with matches tied in their Hair and set it on fire, when it burned to the ground. the day we came here we had no duty to do untill night when we were to relive Company H. to pass the time away, four of us went around in the country to see what we could see and of course get something to eat. we came to a large house, went into the back way untill we came to the kitchen where we saw nigger servents. one of our party who said to go ahead and do the talking spoke politely to the lady of the house, who was for the Union and to tel her we had been on a long tramp. Would, if she could spare it, [offer some food, for we would] like a small byte. certainly. certainly. walk in, you are welcome to such as we have, which proved to be (O dear) nice home bread, Black current jelly milk, Tomattos, &c. the little nigs would look astonished to see the Soldiers. I guess I will tell no more for I fear I shall get reprimanded in your next, but we are not without our sport.

Henry

this is a fat letter it is only 4 sheets Direct to Point of Rocks

14

Headquarters Comp. D, Tues. Sep. 3d

Dear Father,

As I had some news which I thought would Interest you and others, I hasten to inform you of the affair, being one of the gallant band who accomplished it. we were informed a few days ago by a Union Man that there was a large herd of beef cattle on the Virginia side belonging to a man by the name of Grub who was also a Union man, that if we could go and get them we could have them for the Regt. all was kept quiet untill the arrangements were made. Sunday afternoon our own Capt. came from Headquarters P of R and told us he had an expidition for us and wanted 15 picked men. we all new what was up. the party was soon selected, your son being among the number. after relieving ourselves of part of our attire we commenced to ford the Potomac. as we were not acquainted with the direct way we made but slow progress. the current was much stronger than we expected. the water was up to our arms but we considered this but a small part of our undertaking. we soon made the Virginia Shore, and after buckling on our trappings which were brought over on a boat, we shoulderd our Rifels and marched carefully on. we had a Negro guide who was a slave to the man who owned the cattle, and we depended upon him to show us our game. after walking a distance of 1½ mile through a thick wood we came out on to a large tract of cleard ground where we found them. we now seperated and commenced to take possesion when a man made his appearence on horse back near where a Seargent and myself were standing.[52] we asked if he belonged here [and] he said he did. [We asked] if he owned the cattle. he did. we told him we had come for them which seemed to surprise him. he asked us if we were Federal troops. we told him we were, and our orders were to take them, and if he wanted to talk he must do it on the way back to the river. he said if we insisted he supposed they must go and soon set up familiar a call when they all came to him and he coaxed them to the banks of the Potomac. we did not see a Rebel even though we were within 3 miles of their camp, but it was done so quick that when they find it out, it will be in time to be to late to help themselves. the man told us that the Commissary of the Rebel Army had been there but a day ago and wanted them bad but could pay but a poor price with poor paper. we told him they were not safe there but would be on the other side. at least we thought so. but we have not got them across yet, and they disliked to leave the Sacred Soil, but with a good deal of hooting and flurishing of Rifels we got them in. when they got in the Channel they would not go farther but commenced to swim around in a ring. we now thought we had lost them for we had expected to see them drowned. we could not drive them and we thought we would look out for ourselves for they looked wildly at us. they were soon taken down with the strong current and came to where they could touch and made their way to firm land. we were yet in the Middle of the River. but soon we saw our Prizes appear on the banks. we gave 3 cheers for Comp D and waddled along, perfectly satisfied with the result of the bold Expidition of our little band in rescuing from the hands of the Rebels 39 as fine beef cattle as you would wish to see. they are now at our Headquarters at P. of R. and the man on Horse Back glad they are where they are, but if it was known he said so they would Hang him. he is afraid of it as it is.[53] I send enclosed a little Sprig taken from the Sacred soil which I thought would please the ladys. I wrote to Cora 2 or 3 days ago. Well and fataning (Henry)

15

Headquarters, Comp D, Wed. 4th
Dear Brother John,

I have not heard from you for a long time. I should like to know very much if there is a change in the looks of things around Katey Meadow, and do the fish bite well at the Upper Pond[?] are Barbereys thick[?] let Ephraim Bretts Grapes Alone, unless they are ripe.[54] Who did you go to [obscured word] to last and who is going to keep next[?] how old are you and are you growing fast[?] send your length by white strings in your next. have you made any improvements in your Penmanship[?] I should like to see a specimen. my letter to Father Embraces one subject. if I can think of anything I will try to give you the news. yesterday 3 Cannal boats loaded with the Mass 13th from Harpers Ferry passed by our post on their way to join Banks Div. I belive they are to be relived by the M-d first.[55] Col Geary got word that the Rebels would attempt an attack last night oweing I suppose to the departure of the 13th, but a smartt Shower came up late in the Evening, which perhaps prevented it. 2 companys of the 12 had a skirmish with the Rebels Monday. they say they killed 6 of the Rebels, [but] one of their number was wounded. I was at our old Encampment Monday at Point of Rocks. it looked familiar. 3 more companys of the 5 which are being raised in Phil-d arrived last week to join our Regt. the other 2 will be here soon which will make us nearly 1500 strong.[56] to see their Uniforms and look at ours looks as if we had seen some service. Col Geary says that our Confiscated Cattl are worth $2700. our 1st Leiut. Parker is going to take the names of those that Captured them and see if he cannot get for us what he thinks we are entitled to a bounty from the Government. I recived the N. Y. Times from Mel with his letter on the Seventh Regt. it was a good production. I was out hunting the other day but as I had nothing but my Rifel, I could not get small game, which was all I could see. but we found another good diner at a large Plantation, and what do you think John[?] I set to a nice table and had a little black Slave set near me with a corn husk broom to brush the flys away. what a change from a seat on the ground with a peice of Pork in one hand and a hard cracker in the other. we have once in a while some gay old sports. I was at Berlin yesterday which is a mile from here. I suppose Albert is Black enough to be Soldier after comeing from the Cape. give my love to all. tell (Sis) to write soon. Direct to Point of Rocks. my whiskers grow fast.

Henry.

16

Headquarters Sunday Sept 15

Dear Brother [Albert],

I recieved your letter written after your return from the cape. at the same time I recieved two from Father, one of which had been delayed which was wrote soon after the Box was sent directed to Washington. I notice in your last that the Dragoons had responded to the Call of the Gov. and were recruiting for the War.[57] North Bridgewater shall be rememberd and receive her Honors when the History of the Rebelion is being written. the victory of Gen. Butler on the N. C. coast brightend the boys up when they heard it.[58] we have been looking patiently for such an event to happen to cheer us on and to convince us that the arderous dutys which we have been so long performing on the wild shores of the Potomac were not all in vain. we have been on Pickett duty nearly 4 weeks and hardly a day has passed but what we have had rumors of attacks that were to be made from the Rebels on the other side. but they have not troubled us, but threatened in the way of an attempt to erect a Battery a short distance above us, and to show that we were not found wanting in a case of emergency, Col. Geary was right after them with 2 Rifeled Canon and the necessary articles accompanying them such as the surgon and assistant. yesterday an enginer passing by on a train made motions to us by bringing his arms up as if on the act of fireing a musket and pointed towards Harpers Ferry. we understood him and learned afterwards that they had been fighting near Harpers Ferry, wounding a boat man severly. they have commeced runing boats on the canal from the mountains for fall and winter markets. yesterday one of our Union men from the Virginia shore (who has taken quite a fancy to Comp D since we captured the cattle) was seen waveing the truce in the shape of a Virginia news paper. our Capt orderd the boat from the canal to the river which was quickly done and maned and made for the other shore. they soon made land when the Union man and our Capt went in to secret covers. what passed between is not for us to know. he handed the Capt a Leesburgh sheet. they pushed off and came back to quarters. we then formed around the Capt while he read to us the bigest lies that ever was put in print concerning our army and the late victory at Hatteras. it confirmed the reports of sickness in their army and of their Hospitals filled to overflowing, and it also had letters from farmers pleading to General Lee for protection of their produce which is taken with a promise to pay but no one can be found who will be responsible. while I write the booming of canon can be distinctly heard from down the river. we shall find out the cause when the boat men come up to night. I [was] very much surprised to see my letter published in the Gazette. if I had dreamed of such a thing I should not have wrote so careless. if it is your intention to make them public ocassionly use judgement in selecting the one which reads the best. six days rations have just come up to us in the cars, so we are good for another week. we have not yet been payed off, and if it does not come soon there will be a row. I must go and get diner. we go back into the country after our vegeatabls. we shall have to day green shell beans, Pumpkin Potatoes, onions, and Pork boiled together. by Gollys, that makes us fat. write soon. love to all

                                              Henry

[*in upper margin*] this is a slip of a Mexican Rose for Cora. I received the Journal.

17

Dear Father,

We have been liveing in unusal excitement for the past week which makes me behind in answering letters. we had a smart skirmish last week with the Rebels. it terminated after a short engagement without doing any injury to our boys who behaved manfully. our Comp went in on double quick during the Pickets as they passed by their posts. after returning the enemy were discoverd opposite of our quarters in considerable numbers. we took shelter in our Rifel Pitt and behind trees and opened fire but on account of the great distance it was without effect.[59] yesterday a dispatch was received from Headquarters that the Rebels were in large numbers near Point of Rocks and intended crossing, but they did not make their appearence. we are geting ready for cold weather as we see no signs of going to camp and last nights frost told in plain words that winter was not far away. we intend makeing a log Hut as their is plenty of material handy and we are the Boys that can make one. there is a fruit we gather which tastes and looks like the bannanes. Comp A went over into Virginia last week and took 3 Prisoners 8 horses 13 Head of Cattle.[60] since our adventure all the Companys have tried to come up to us, but they have not done it yet. I have got 7 letters to answr and when I have done it I am going to shut down for I get so many ahead I can not find Courage to begin. I am writeing now with all kinds of noises around me. [There is] one party makeing a House out of ruins of the Burnt Bridge which has drifted down opposite of our quarters from Berlin. there is 7 in our shanty, and when we get our Hut built I shall be at more liberty to write. I went to Knoxville Saturday to get my Brogs mended and now keep my feet dry. The Cobler works on the Zubion French style and is just as good as a Union man.[61] he said that if the Legislature of Maryland had passed the ordinance of secesion that the State House would have been blown and the traitors with it, as there was 7 kegs of Powder concealed under the building that he was knowing to.[62] he told me of the many trials that he passed throug at the commencement of trouble. he said that one night 6 men, himself, and wife, and the wife of another in [the] party defended their homes from Rebels who came over from Harpers Ferry. the Rebels were 3 times their number but he says the presence of the women shamed them away. we have not got payed off yet. have not heard from Mel for a long time. I received a letter from John Richardson & E. P. Couch.[63] [I] Received [the] Gazette. [I] weigh 133 lbs. [I] gained 9 lbs. since I left Phil-. one of my Mess Received a Box which is the second one [we received] since we have been on picket. [It came] from Phil. with a variety of Leauxuries. for two days we had Soda Crackers,

Home made Bread, Preserved Peaches, Pickeld Oysters, Sardens, Pickeld Tomatoes, and what more do you want[?] all [was] used up except two bundles of Black Tea which is a raeriti after [the] continual flow of Coffee for most 4 months. [I] will try to write again in 3 days. (love to all)

A. Henry Hayward

18

named after our Major
Camp Tyndale Wed Oct 2d 61-

Dear Father,

I have layed everything connected with camp life aside to enjoy the pleasure of writing home once more. so much has transpirede since I last wrote that I shall not be able to tell you half the news. we were releived unexpectedly Monday Afternoon from Picket duty by Comp N. we obeyed the order reluctantly as we had nearly finished our winter quarters and settled down for at least 2 weeks duty. soon the word fall in was given. we packed knapsacks and after a march of 3 hours arrived in Camp which is now located on a beautifull site 1 mile from Point of Rocks. here we found our new companions togeather with the band who had joined us from Phil-d while we were away. on the hill in the distance the 12th Indiana Regt. have encamped. they have releived 3 of our Comps on Picket duty and will soon releive them all. I think in less than 2 weeks our Regt will be on the move. yesterday 12 of our men and 12 from each Comp left for Washington to get a Battery of six guns which will be attached to our Regt. we shall have a cavalry Comp also in a few days which will make us the most efficeint Regt in the Service.[64] one of our comrades died yesterday after a short illness of 5 days. he was a fine man and a trusty soldier. I assisted in laying him out. we put on his uniform and one of the boys took of his own necktie and tied it around the neck of young Manley as a last token of Respect. our Comp turned out and escorted the remains to the depot where a Corp Guard took it in charge and will convey him to his distressed parents in Phil-d.[65] our Regt at present is rather sickly. our Comp has about 12 on the sick list. last Sunday we went to Berlin to hear a Sermon From our Chaplin.[66] he told them how they could be protectd in their rights, the reason why we the 28th were here and the effect we had made upon a certain portion of the people [in] this part of the state.

Thursday Morning 3

I was obliged to lay this aside last night for Battalion Parade and must cut this short if I want It to go this morn as it is time for Company drill. it is a lovely morning and I feel as happy as a Clam. I am very grateful that my health is so singularly spared after going through the same hardships the rest of my Comrards have endured, which Picket duty mite bring upon the most hardy. I must Close. the drums beat. I have learned to love the shrill sound, but then the band strikes up. I am amazed I am so fond of Music. in haste, good bye, love to all. I have not heard from Cora for a long time.

Corp A. Henry
Hayward

19

Camp Tyndale, Sunday Oct 13th -61

Dear Sister,

As I have nothing particular to attend to at present, I thought I would use the time in writing to you. Nothing has transpired in Camp since I last wrote worthy of note. there has been quite a change in the weather which is quite Coole and changable. I was on duty last night as Corporal of the Guard and [it] was a night I never experienced. the wind blowed and the rain pored down in torrents and in going the rounds to releive [the] Guard I was oblige to feel my way along with my Rifel in going through the woods. I got no sleep that night. the morning found me bright and Smart, good for another trip. it is all in getting use to it. we had preaching today under the trees by our good Chaplin who is working much good among the Soldiers. we have a Regimental Choir who perform their part of the service with great credit to themselves. it is general talk in camp that we have lost our Gallant Lieut Col De Korponay who has been appointed to the Command of another Regt. in Washington as Colonel.[67] he was much respected by all of the men. Gen Bakers Brigade[68] is 8 miles from us at a place called Poolsville. one of his men (who has a Brother in our Company) was at our camp to day. they have new uniforms of Blue since the late fatal mistake hapend to them.[69] I understand ours are at Frederic Md. which will be forwarded soon. wont I feel spruce when I shed this dirty gray for a true Blue[?][70] I must have boots, and stockings, thick woolen under Clothes to keep Comfortable very soon. I am in no great hurry at present. I shall try to get a pass to go to Frederick to do my shoping. I had my watch brought on from Phil-d when the Corp returned that went last week. I find it very handy in releiving the Guard. a young friend and myself took a cruise the other day. he being a watch maker of Course [he] understood the nature of Clocks.[71] we came up to a house and asked the time of day. the lady said the Clock was out of order. he said he could fix it for her. she told him it was useless as there had been a Clock Repairer there but a short time before. we walked in by her consent. I took a seat, took out my Meershaum [pipe], and smoked for the amusement of the Children while he (my friend) with a pair of Ear nippers Commenced to repair the Clock which he soon got to ticking. he said the job was worth a half dollar. but if she would bake him two or 3 pies it [would be] satisfactory. she seemed to be very much pleased with the bargain, hearing the ticking of the clock which had been silent so long. she said certainly and more. he said 3 would do. we made a Soldier bow and started for camp. a few days after we got the Pies, [we ate them] and they Died. I intend writing to Father, Enclosing a likeness of Old Abe and to of his Plasters.[72]

Much love to all,

Henry

20

Camp Tyndale Sun Oct 13

Dear Father,

I have wrote Cora what little news I could think of. I will only say (as I have not much time before supper) that I have been payed off for 2 months service the amount being $24.26. I send Enclosed $15, the rest of which I thought I would retain for needfull purposes to by boots, Clothing, &c. I did intend to send this in the morning, but it just occured to me that as there was no mail to day, there will be a great many Treasure Notes go in tomorrows mail and if any one has an eye on it with the intention of Robing it they would do it to morrow. so I will delay this untill Tuesday Morn.[73] 8 oclock Sunday Eve.

Since writing this afternoon orders have come to take one day rations and march after the drums beat the retreat. it is a very secret movement but I have found out by a confidential Friend that it is to Nolans Ferry. the Night is beautiful and cool and I am ready for the March. one of my Mess Mates will stay with a squad to guard our quarters. I shall let him mail my letter. the boys are singing God Bless our Native Land And I must join in the Chorus.

Comp D and F are the ones detailed for the expedition.

love to all, Henry

21

Point of Rocks Thur 17

Dear Father,

I have passed through my first Great Battle.[74] I only write this morning that you may know that I live.

We fought 8 hours against fearfull odds. we captured a big 32 pounder which we brought with us on the Maryland shore last night. our Brave Colonel saved us and gave us the victory he promised us if we would but obey his orders. we retook our position that we had to leave when they opened on us with their artillery. you will see all in the papers for the present. the Col made a complimentary speech to [Companies] D & F, then sent us to camp to rest. I am only a little exhausted and sore.

[I] will write to morrow. they captured many of our blankets and overcoats, mine included. a number of our men [from] the 28th were wounded.

in haste, Henry

I had this feather in my cap before the Battle and it went through it.

22

Camp Tyndale Point of Rocks, Fri Oct 18th -61

Dear Father,

Having recoverde from the labor and excitement which I experienced on Wed-d the 16th, I will try to give you some Idea of what we passed through on that day.

it was a fine morning and we had not drank our coffee which was ready and waiting when one of our men noticed a colum of men advancing at the edge of the woods towards our lines. the first intimation we had of their intention [was when] they opened on us with a peice of artillery.[75] we returned fire with our Rifels but with what effect we could not tell. we kept our position for a while, when it was discovered that the enemy were intending to out flank us with their cavalry.[76] at the commencement of the Battle a courier was dispatched to inform Col Geary and bring up the reserve. Capt Copeland[77] who was in command orderd us to retire back to Bolivar and wait reinforcements which we did in good order. we were afraid our pickets on the left would be cut of so we looked anxiously for them to make their appearence. they soon came up completely exhausted followed closely by the Rebel Cavalry. the reserve had now arrived and gave us much hope. they consisted of 2 companys of the Wisconsin Regt and 2 of the Mass 13th, together with D & F of the 28th Penn, which made up our little band that was to meet the Rebels when they made their appearence.[78] but one thing now seemed to be wanting. it was some great Head to lead us. he soon made his appearence mounted on a horse galloping at full speed. we now breathed freer for we knew our cause was safe in the Hands of Col Geary. the Rebels again opened fire with their 32 poundr, which they had now planted in the middle of the street and were pouring death and destruction all along the way taring down fences and throwing up the dirt. we all took shelter behind houses and trees and poured bullets into the men by the thousands. at one time their cavalry was preparing for a Charge but we turned their course and they went up the hill at full gallop but not untill we had emptyed many of their sadles. as soon as the Rebels had assembled in large numbers, the battery on Loudon Hights opened on our left.[79] at the same time our own cannon on Maryland Hights tryed to assist us but their balls fell short and came right among us.[80] we hardly knew where to put our backs as we wished to keep our faces towards the enemy. the Col sent a messenger for them to stop fireing and bring a peice across the river. the fireing had ceased on Loudon hights having been silenced by our guns from across the river. our Gallant Col told us to be patient and not expose ourselves for he had sent to Point of Rocks for 5 Companys of our Regt and one peice of the New York 9th battery. he told us to obey his orders and he would soon lead us to a Glorious Victory. Comp A & G had now arrived from Berlin. A was sent out on our right to deploye as skirmishers. our peice of artilery which had now crossed the river came up on a double quick. I expected to see the horses cut down every minute by the balls of the big Gun which had been keeping up a constant fire for six hours, but they escaped and soon got their peice to bear on the rebel gun. the Col. orderd the wisconsin boys to [move] forward on the left with the massachusetts boys, while D & F advanced supporting the artillery. the big gun was soon silenced. our Col gave orders to fix bayonett, then cried out, Charge my boys, which we did with a vengeance, scattering the terror stricken Rebels before us like sheep, leaving behind them their big Columbiad which was once the property of the United States and her true sons had now come to claim it.[81] there is a great many incidents connected with the Battle which I shall not be able to write about this time. It has not been beleived by many persons that the Rebels could be guilty of the many barberous acts that they have been accused of, but what I tell you is true. they bayonetted the wounded Wisconsin men and plunderd them of their clothing even to their shoes and stockings. they took an old man from his family only for his Union sentiments.[82] they took a young man from his wife to make him join their ranks. we took 4 prisoners. one was their Chaplin, a minister named North. he is the very picture of Secession and the Devil.[83] we took a man from his house that sent up signals to them the night before the attack and who shot a wisconsin boy from his window. we had 2 men taken prisoner, one a Corp from Comp A, the other from the Wisconsin Comp.[84] they wanted to exchange prisoners with us the very night of the Battle. Col Geary received a disturbed asking for parson North in exchange for the Corp of Comp A, but as he is the back bone of secesion in and around the country we shall keep him North. Col Geary was wounded in the early part of the engagement slightly.[85] he knows no fear. the Massachusetts boys are worthy of much praise and were often complimented highly by our boys. but I never saw such daring bravery as the Wisconsin boys showed. but let me not forget to speake of my owne comrads. I was [not] disappointed to see them behave so cool. I must close this now. I receive the Gazzette yesterday for the first time in 4 or 5 weeks. love to all, write soon.

Henry

23

Camp Tyndale, Point of Rocks, Md, Thursd Oct 24

Dear Father,

As I had nothing particular to do and pen and Ink handy I thought I would write a few lines for the fun of it. the weather is fine this morning but our once lively camp appears deserted. Tuesday night 10 Companys of the Gallant 28th under the Command of our Gallant Col Geary took their leave to join their Div under Gen Banks. I shall not soon forget the appearance of these men as they stood in line before they moved on their journey that night. [It] was one of the darkest with a fine misty rain. not a word or whisper could be heard, but all minds were in deep study of what might be their fate before the sun should set again. but soon the noble form of our Col was seen moving along in the darkness seated on his proud steed. he made a few remarks to them. in conclusion he said (Cross the bridge on tip toe). they now moved on but under the weight of the knapsacks and [with] such muddy walking they made slow progress. while they passed me 4 men fell down. I now went to my tent but laid some time thinking of the poor fellows marching along the tow path of the Canal.[86] Comp D, F, M remain behind to guard the camp and protect Point of Rocks. we have 2 Companys on the Banks of the Potomac which are now doing the duty of 5. we may join our Regt at any time. it is imposible to tell where we are unless we look sharp. we are moved so much, but the 28th shines in Phil-d. nothing else is talked of but the 28th. The Editor of the Phil-d Eve Journal is now in Camp. Capt McKabe of Comp O took 4 boxes of Sabers and a lot of Horse Pistols the other day at a place near Frederick.[87] I forgot to say in my other letter that I saw James Smith in Comp I of the Mass 13th.[88] we sent all of our prisoners, 7 in number to Fort McHenry before the Col left. so you see parson North has gone North. I see nothing yet very Promising for our Country. it yet swings in the balance. Oh that the Earth might swallow up those who would not be Americans. I recived the Boston Traveller, also the lead pencil letter. are you all well[?] I never was in better health. Hurrah three Cheers. the yankees are the Boys. I will close this now and it will go to day. love to all. [I] should like to hear from any of you.

Corporal Ambrose
Henry Hayward

[*two pictures drawn by Hayward*]
32 lbs taken at Bolivar
[*Union soldiers marching*]
for Charlestown

24

Dear Brother [Albert],
It has been quiet in and about Camp since I last wrote and I do not know as I shall be able to find items enough to fill this sheet. I received yours and Coras letter which I read with usual interest. you speak in your letter of the Gallant 13th as being the only one Conspicious in the Battle at Bolivar. it is perfectly natural for papers to speak in great praise of Regt hailing from their particular State. I look with as much interest and speak as boasting by the bravery of the Mass troops as any person. as it is, I am in a Regt from Penn., I feel the same spirit animates me and I can fight as willingly and brave in the 28th as I could in the 12th Mass. now for a few facts from one engaged from the time the first shot was fired untill the last. Comp D & F of the 28th the night before the engagement releived from picket duty Comp C of the 13th Mass and one Comp of Wisconsin men. they went back to the village and occupied houses and were to be used as a reserve in case D, F of the Pen 28th were attacked. you all have heard that an attack was made. the first shot was from a cannon which came whizing along and struck in the trees over our heads. I think there was about 13 men at the head quarters, which was the place they fired at first. I have not forgot the feeling which the first shot produced. we all looked curiously at each other as much as to say lookout for your head. father used to say when in a hard tempest you need not be afraid of the flash when it begins to thunder, but in this case you have to look out [so] you dont get struck after it thunders. I never thought I should see the time when I should be dogeing cannon balls, but I did that day. so you can see there was some one their besides Mass boys, and if you want to know who fought the bravest or was the most daring it was the Wisconsin boys. Col Geary says if they had obeyed his orders and not exposed themselves we should have accomplished the same and not one of them would have been killed. Col Geary put the Chaplin (who we took prisoner) in Charge of a Corporal from the Wisconsin Comp and myself. we brought him down to the Ferry. we afterwards went into a house and orderd dinners, which we eat with a relish after biteing cartridges of all day. it was here a fine young damsel gave us both a fancy feather saying you have won the day. I have got mine in my knapsack. shall wear it in the next engagement. we had [a] stand of Collors

presented to us Thursd. they were raised by private subscription in Phil-d. they are the most beautiful flags that ever floated to the breeze. Col Geary made one of his telling speeches.[89] then we give him three cheers. gracious. goodness. but it rained and blew some yesterday. I never went out of my tent once and you know what it was for[:] bean Soup. Monday Morning.

the drums are beating for morning drill and I have to drop my pen soon. last night we had an alarm. the word fall in were cried out by the Captains of the different Companys and soon we were in line ready for further orders. the long roll was sounded and all expected to soon meet the foe but it turned out to be a false alarm and we turned in and hugged the straw untill morning with out being disturbed. I was standing side of the Capt tent when the alarm was sounded. a Mr Elliot the Editor of the Eve Journal of Phil-d who has been a visitor at our camp for some time came runing up much excited and wanted his coat. he said we were attacked. I presume he will take the cars for Phil-d this morning. it is a fine morning this morning after the hard rain and I hope this week [will bring] about some event encorageing to the men. we are anxiously waiting to hear something favorable to our cause. I hope we dont winter this side of the Potomac. the Rebels have become uncomonly saucy since that affair at Edwards Ferry. we can see them in squads all along the river and yesterday they fired on our Picketts.

love to all. I must go drill.

Henry

25

Camp Tyndale Thurs Nov. 7th –61

Dear Sister,

I have once more placed myself in as comfortable a position as circumstances will allow in my tent to attempt in writing you a letter. it is evening and the dim light of the candle tells me it cannot be my companion for a sufficent length of time to see me through this sheet. we have lively times in Camp on these fine Moonlight nights. it is a novel sight to stand and cast your eyes around to see the many groups standing around the fires which are to be seen in every direction. where there was once long lines of fenceing, nothing remains to keep the cattle enclosed but briers and scrub bushes, the mischeivous soldiers having used them for bonfires. but, the land we occupy is owned by a seceshionist, which accounts for Col Geary leting the boys have as large a fire as they want by taking the bars.[90] we see the lights of two Signal stations which talk to each other nightly. one is from Gen Stones command.[91] the other is in the Mountains to our rear.

I was on duty last night. I have become so accustomed to be broken of my rest that I dont mind it. I intend rolling myself in a new Blankett (which I have procured from the Government) for the first time to night. you can not tell how much they are prized by us this time of year. I have been laying nights with a few feet of my mess mates Blankett overe me which he kindly loaned me, but he had such long elbows, that when he turned over he would take the Blankett with him, then I would be awakened with the shakes and would reach over and get it and tie a corner around my rist, after which I would lay in a dorment state untill morning. we expect our overcoats soon.

Friday Morning Nov 8th
soon the drums will beat for Company Drill. I must make my pen scratch faster or the cry fall in Co D I shall here with my letter unfinished. Soon after I was paid of I directed a letter to Rebecca the Quaker to know if she had a bill against me for board. I received an answer in which she stated there was a few weeks yet unsettled but she felt a delicacy in takeing anything as I had earned it at the risk of my life &c. I mailed a letter yesterday to her enclosing a $5 Treasury Note. I willingly paid it. they were so obliging to me while I was with them and boarded me so cheap. I shall have my trunk sent home soon. I have not been keeping it there because there was an unsettled account, but I want the expense of expressing it on takeing from my funds. We shall be paid of for 2 months service soon. the pay Rolls are already made out. I have lately drawed a new pair of shoes and 2 pair of thick woolen socks. I want Father to find out what would be the expense of sending a box the size of a Mason Soap Box to me. then I will let you know what you can buy for me. the express from Phil-d in such a box or larger is 50 cts. I received the Gazette. I will send a Ledger with a Letter from the 28th. I sent a Dispatch yesterday. if I were to send all the papers that have letters from the 28th I should have my hands full. Phil-d papers are full of items about the 28th. we are the boys that fear no noise and never cry to go Home. the Col is giving many furloughs lately. yesterday 2 officers and 2 men went to Phil-d. our Capt goes Sunday and if he would act with the wish of the Co he would stay there. he is soft. we are disappointed in all our commisioned officers. we are the worst drill Co in the Regt, but good at Skirmish. they dont seem to look at the Interest of the men. they are fine fellows on a dress parade. never mind, we make it up in Geary, but that picture dont look like him. the other one is a complete and perfect some one of Lieutenant Col De Korpony.[92] are you all well[?] I am in excellent Spirit and we all look anxiously for success of the sail boats. may they fix their compass for Charles town and go through it. we have got our big 32 in camp that we took at Bolivar.

fall in for drill.
I had live take a Pill.
love to all. write soon
Henry

26

Camp Goodman Nov 13th

Dear Father,

Yours of the 11th was received to day, which I hasten to answer. I have, after considering the case, thought it the cheapest way to send the articles which I mention to me. I shall be likely to get a better quality, and the price I shall be obliged to pay here will more than pay the expense of the Box. you will please buy one p-r of white nitt woolen under Shirts and two p-r nitt drs, these to be of the heveyest quality, one fine silk handkerchief, a p-r of gloves of your owne choice, one rubber Blankett if you can get it.[—] the best is the cheapest and have Clark Wentworth letter it A H H Co D 28th Regt P. V.[—]one pair of suspenders, and a box of Musterd, and if Hannah is willing, a paper of Smoking Tobacco. if you can find some kind of woolen Cap that will do to sleep in nights, such as Joe Robinson use to wear with no fore piece.[93] not on top. this is a bad pen. send a good one, a litle Yarn Arabic to do up News Papers for you, a few of Hunt & Wilders Crackers. ask Johney if he has not got a Jack knife to give me. I lost the one Father let me take. any kind of lead pencil will do. I shall have to lend it. I beleive there is a pair of Fountain 1 Shirts up stairs in a box. if so put them in. I can think of nothing more. send these as soon as possible to Point of Rocks, Md. the cost of these to come out of the Treasury Notes.

Thur-d Morn, 14th

A few more lines and I have done. I go on duty at 10 oclk and I must brush up my shoes, clean my Rifel, &c. the pay master will be here before thanksgiving. We have not got our New Uniform. the Likeness cost 50 cts. in my opinion it is not a good one. when I get a new uniform I will have another taken. our Pickets on the river talk with the Rebels. they say it is not them (the Virginians) that fire on our Picketts but it is the Missisipians, that they the Virginians are only fighting for their owne homes, [and] do not intend to go out of their owne State. I think you may here from me before you send the Box. we have moved in to the woods a short distance from our former encampment. Camp Goodman is named from one of the Staff, Doctor Goodman.[94] Melville sends me a New York Illustrated. I would sooner have a Gazette than any paper you can send. never mind any

Thanksgiving. if there is any room in the Box put in a Staff of Life. I got a Letter from Joe Freeman Tuesday. I continue to grow fat. I received a letter from Mell the other day offering me his Blankett. I have got no overcoat yet, but it is coming. when we got the news from the fleet we raised our Company flag on a tree near our quarters and there she floats. I think I get the news before you do as soon one of my messmates is in the Telegraph Office. I do not like the removal of Fremont.[95] Banks is very popular in his Div. we are liable to be moved any day. take your time in preparing the Box But let it be [as] Short as possible. remember me to all the Boys.

love to all,
Henry

27

Camp Goodman Nov 26th

Dear Father,

The Box arrived on Monday and glad I was to see it. if there had not been so much of (Herveys) sheet iron around it I would have been tempted to open it at the Depot and made a search for the Gloves as the morning was quite Cold, but my mess mate had a pair and between us we brought the Box safely to our tent. it is a pleasure that none can realize but a Soldier when he openes a box and eagerly catches at the different articles that have been placed in with so much Care by a Mother or Sister. the pie we had for dinner. it was so good we all laughed. the crackers are most all cracked and the Bread nearly devoured. the Mustard and Chocolate and tea will last for some time. to make it short, the contents of the Box pleased me very much and when the eatables have gone I shall have the clothing to wear and the best rubber Blanket in the Regt. I have not layed warm since Cold weather set in untill last night. I think much of the sleeping cap, especially the ear ties, which keeps it on my head. I am afraid Joe will miss it. I am thinking the rasins will be the cause of my not getting this of in time for the minute as they lay side of me, and I am continually picking. I am obliged to John Richardson of the fine apple. I just lit the big 6 ct Columbiad filled with Coras Tobbacco, but I guess it was Albert that chose it as he is the best judge, and when I wipe my nose with the Handkerchief dont I put on airs. we have not been paid of yet. I hope our new Clothes and monney will not come to geather. it will make us crazy. what I most wish is that we could go with the next expedition South, but they will not take us with our old uniform. Col Geary is on the Committy to examine Officers in Gen Banks Div. I pitty those that are not posted.[96] I have got a new overcoat and only one thing is wanting in it. that is (Rebels spare it). we had quite a snow

Storm Sunday. I was on duty Saturday night and the water froze quite hard in the canteens, but it is nothing when you get use to it. I can think of nothing more, but on the whole I think this is quite a Box letter.

love to all,
Henry

I received the Gazzette.

the bannar about the Pacific Railroad &c. hangs in our Tent. Col Geary made a remark when he passed by that is right anything but & 5 union.

28

Camp Goodman Dec 11

Dear Father,

In much haste I put myself in position to write a few lines to accompany the $20 note which, if it arrives safe, you will find enclosed. we were payed off last evening for 2 months amounting to $26. there was a general good time throughout the camp last night from the excitement of having once more seeing the Pay master. there was more excitement last week in this vicinity than usual. the long roll was beat off at night, and the boys orderd to take 2 days rations in their Haversacks. we waited for further orders from Gen Banks. they did not come so the men Slept on their arms. there was a constant cannonade distinctly heard from here yesterday. it lasted for many hours. we have not yet heard where it was. it was long and heaver than when we heard the cannonad of Balls Bluff. we were under Marching orders 2 days ago. our new Battery is with us. they have got 4 Parrott Guns that throw a 13 pound shell 4 miles.[97] if we had them at Bolivar we should never [have] captured the Big 32 for the Rebels would not [have] had a chance to brought it near enough. we are makeing arrangements for a joy time Christmas[:] Singing, Dramatics, &c. I was cast in the leading character in the Yankee Pedler but I give it up for I could not learn it in time as it was entirely out of my line.[98] I took another small character in the same peice. I must close soon as it is most mail time. Give my love to all of the family. I hope to hear you are all well. I never was in better health. oh, I like to forget I received a box from Phil-d (one of these Starch Boxes) full of goodys. it was from a lady in Kensington. there was in it a large loaf of Bread, a Big fruit cake, a large Bottle of Pepper sauce, writing paper, &c., and 4 pairs of Mittens to give to the Soldiers: I sent a Bulettin and the vision of McClellan.[99] I think he must of seen Stars. (We still live) at Point of Rocks.

Corp A Henry Hayward

29

Camp Goodman, Wed Dec 18

Dear Father,

I received your letter [on] Tues 17. I was very glad to hear that Augustus has been successfull in finding a situation. I have often thought of his case and wished he could find something to do to releive his mind, for I know he has seen his full share of trouble. I have not felt like enquiring into the matter when I have wrote home for fear he would hear of it, but wonderd often if he kept in good spirits.[100] Our new Uniforms have come at last.[101] we are to receive them today. I have not seen them yet so I cannot give a description of them, but I believe they are like the Mass 12th. we shall feel gay in them after sheding our Old Greys, which are the Color of Mustard [*indecipherable word*]. one of the many interesting events which occur in Camp came of Saturday night at Dress Parade. it was occasioned [to] be the presentation of a valuable sword by Col De Korponey to Leiut Edward Geary, Son of our Col. the Regt formed a hollow square, the Band taken the Centre when the presentation commenced. Col Geary stepped forward after Col De Korponey had finished his speach to make a few explanatory remarks concerning his Son. he said, fellow Soldiers I do not intend to make a speach for my Son, for the Gearys are well expected to speak for them selves. but said he, this young man did not come here expecting that such high honnors would be bestowed upon him. when he came here as a member of the Band, he was unsatisfied with his position as a Musician. he asked the consent of his father to take a Rifel and Join the Regt, which he was about doing when the Battery was talked of. he thaught he would have a fine chance to grattify his wishes, as he had made Artiller one of his close studys. I will here state that Col Geary, in the course of his remarks, said this young man now in his 16th year, when he was at Jefferson Colleuge, Stod 96 in his Class as an Arithmatician, and the highest that can be attained is 100. Young Geary goes to Washington to be examined before the board of Artillry Officers.[102] Col Geary told Gen Barry[103] to give him a stringent examination, and if he was not capable of the position of an officer to pass him by at once, for he was willing to go and serve his country in the ranks with the privates. he passed the examination, not a questine but what he answerd, Gen Barry remarking Leiut Geary is the right kind of a man for an Artillery Officer. Col Geary asked the Regt to excuse him if he should occasionally indulge in boyish ways. Young Geary came forward and made a fine speach in reply to Col De Korponey.

Young Geary is smart looking young man and has already attained the size of the average of men. Col Gearys Father was six years in the Revolutionary service under the imediate Command of Gen Washington.

he had a brother in the War of 1812, and if they would take Col John from point of Rocks he would stir up the Rebels or I am no judge. since we got our Parrotts, he does not allow them to come within 4 miles of the Potomac. the Companys in Camp have received orders to build log houses for winter quarters. one of our mess mates went to Frederick ysterday to purchase a Stove for $3. so you see we shall be nice and Comfortable and merry as a Swarm of Bees. Our Exhibition progresses finely. we meet at a farm house (where the Officers board) to rehearse and pass away the long Evenings very pleasant. Col Geary is doing all he can to make us proficient and give good entertainment. our Sutler is now absent to Baltimore, getting the curtain for the stage, Seceanery, &c. it will be a entertainment worthy of a Philadelphia Audience. when I shall have once more walked those boards do you not think it will call up many recollections of the days that have passed when I used to meet with my school mates to engage in similar pleasures[?] but I must not allow my mind to wander and dwell on subjects like this. there is an other Great National Play before the public and I have engaged to do my part and will do it as long as I am permitted to raise an arm. let England come. she is a fit Animal to pounce upon Strugling Liberty. if they can find reason to go to war with us for 2 Traitors what are ours when we fight to save our Country[?][104] I notice I have been going on at an awfull rate, but it is owing to the condition of my mind. I read 3 newsprs yesterday so I am a little excited. to wind up I will give you a riddle. perhaps you have heard it. why was Gen Baker virtualy dead and buried before the Battle of Balls Bluff[?] because he was under the (Gen) Banks of the Potomac with a (Gen) Stone at his head. I sent a Dis patch this morning. [I] received the Gazzett of Dec 11. tell Hannah and the Boys I should like to hear from them. Col Geary has annother son in the Band as a drummer, 8 or 9 years Old.[105] the weather has been quite moderate for 2 or 3 weeks, but it looks like snow now. it is quite a sight to see 2 or 3 men in the wood falling trees. it makes busy times for us. one young man like & cut his leg of the other day. he was taken to the hospital. I think I now have been writing at great length, but I cannot help it. I have not sufferd much from the cold since I put on my under Clothing. does Johney go to school now[?] if he does, when it is Composition day he can write me a letter. I am well. our dinner to day is been Soup. We like him. remember me to all the boys. tell Albert to tell Ruf Brett I should like hear from him or any of the Boys.

from your Red headed
Soldier
Henry

30

Dear Brother [Augustus],

You have doubtless seen in the papers the latest news from Point of Rocks which gives you to understand that them poor miserable crazy things called Rebels made another dash against the gallant 28th on the morning of the 18th. the Mountains from which their cannon played upon us is directly opposite to the one from which the Point of Rocks take its name and on which our observatory is situated. we have often wonderd why they sufferd us to remain here so long if it was possible to get cannon on the Heights and Col Geary often saying it was a thing impossible to get them there. but we have been located here so long and never allowing them to enjoy a bit of peace when they would show their faces that they have probably determined to shell us out if it took 1000 men and as many horses to get their cannon in position. well they have done this and aught to be praised for it for it was no small undertaking (you may praise them but it dont look well for mts) and then early in the morning they open their battery upon us, [we] never thinking it was from the mountain untill the shell come flying among us. we quickly got on our equipments and waited for orders, which were to fall back over the brow of the hill to the Parade Ground. we were next orderd in a secret way to the point of Rocks, and there they were divided 2 companys going to Knoxville and at different places, as we supposed it was a move on their part to cross, but I shall not beleive that untill I see them [on] this side. but I have not told you what stoped their sport. it was our Parrotts. they got into position at the second Shot and fired from the camp. the first shot took effect and knocked them clear to Leesburgh for that is the last [that] has been seen or heard from them. but our battery long kept up the firing and shelled the mountain for a while and then aimed for the houses where they had been seen to congregate.[106] they must not fool with Capt Knapp for his Father made the big Union Gun now at Fort Monroe,[107] and this young man Capt Knapp use to aim all his guns cast in his Father Foundry when they were proved by target practice. there was one solid shot struck within ten feet of Col De Korponeys tent. it was the second shot. he and his wife were in there. another struck the spring house where there were 4 men on guard to watch the spring. they dug up the shell and sold it for $100 to a man going to Pittsburgh. there was another solid to go to Phild for 50 cts. 3 guess it would make the Rebels mad if they knew the Yankees were speculating in their shells. one reason why none of us were harmed [was because] $2/3$ of their shells would not burst when they struck. but I guess I would not say any more about the Rebels. you hear enough about them. our new Uniforms have come, and we look gay in them. I have got a good fit. they are Regular Style Dark Blue Pants and Coat with a fatigue cap. the hats have not come yet. I received a letter from Mell Saturday. enclosed was one from Aunt Henrietta.[108] with this I shall send 3 papers which I thought would be Interesting to read in the store [on] the dull times. give my respect to all the Boys and the rest of the folks.

Henry

31

Camp Goodman P of R, Jan 6

Dear Sister,

Now is the winter of our discontent, made glorious by a Sibley Tent,[109] one of which we have. 13 of the best men in Co D makes up our mess. we are a lively set of time killers and enjoy ourselves very much hardly giving a thought to the gay world. we have been living under intense excitement for 3 or 4 days past. a dispatch came from the Signal post stateing that the Rebels were makeing preperation to shell us out again, they having a battery of six peices pointing towards our Camp. we had orders to sleep on our Arms with knapsacks packed. they have not yet attempted it. it may be that they expected we were about to cross and sent for the cannon to prevent us, as we were drawn up in line the night before to receive Gen Banks, [and] Vice Pres Hamlin.[110] Gen Banks is a very smart looking man but that is no news. Vice Prest Hamlin looks like a man that use to bring eggs to the Store to trade for candles. we had a Merry Christmas. I sent a Programme home. we have got 2 Union Guns that were presinted to the 28th. they are fired by turning a crank. the faster you turn it the more Rebels it will kill. it will throw a ball 4 miles. I cannot describe it but when the men saw it first they thought it was a sausage machine.[111] we have now 2 more Plays under way to be played when the Pay Master comes. I have the Character of George Acorns in the Toodles.[112] it is my style and I take much interest in studying it. we have a reading rehearsal for the first time to night. I am surprised Joe Battles did not forward my trunk 5 weeks ago when I requested him to. there was a hard snow storm Saturday. the sleighs are out and all nature is Clothed with its winter garb. but for all this we the Soldiers of the 28th are Cheerful as ever, but would not be prephaps if they thought that they were the object of to much grief and sorrow by the dear ones at home. I am in excellent health, stand my regular guard duty always in all kinds of weather, never have been on the sick list since I have been in the army. there is seldom a day passes with out a smile upon my features. I never have the blues, but on the whole, I am perfectly satisfied with my condition and want to be a Soldier as long as it is necessary to keep them to fight for the Union. 2 peices of our battery that were at Sandy Hook have gone to Hancock, also our big 32, which we Captured at Bolivar. it is rumored that we have got Marching orders which would please us all as we are all sick of Point of Rocks. we deserted our log Cabin and took a Sibly tent which Leut Parker procured for us. it is heated by a stove which comes with tents. I gave my washing out yesterday for the first time. it is so pesky Cold. I thought I would decline. we get Phild papers here the same morning they are printed in Phild. I received [a] Gazzette. I [can] think of nothing more. the Lion roared and the Eagle droped his wings. remember me to all enquiring Friends. yours of the 4 was answered on the 6th. the 28th Regt send their respects to mother.

Tuesd Morn 7

Col Geary returned from Frederick last night in a special Train. he is unwell. also his little son has been sick for a few days past.[113]

[unsigned]

32

Camp Goodman Jan 11

Dear Brother [Augustus, Melville, or John],

I received your long and interesting letter in good season. Our Camp has been full of various rumors and reports since I last wrote. everybody said as soon as the weather permitted we should be of and at them. this will suit the boys of the 28th. I know all at home will watch the movements of the 28 with great interest, and it will be our aim to prevent anything that shall happen to bring a Stain upon our good name which the whole Country acknowledg we bare.[114] Col Geary was presented a beautifull Sword last week from Co E. in his remarks he told us that much was expected from our Regt.[115] if the weather keeps as favorable for 2 weeks as it has been for 2 days something will be done and somebody will get hurt. now a little camp news and I must close. our lines have been close by watching the movements of the Rebels. they have become quite saucy. they killed a man at Harpers Ferry who was crossing to answer a flag of truce. this made our Col get up his Geary[116] and he orderd the torch to be applied to the houses which destroyed many of them.[117] they will learn soon not to trifel with our Geary. the Col learns from good authority that we are to be Shelled again and to be even with them. Sunday morning. 2 Parrot Guns from Frederick arrived here this morning. 2 of our guns [from] Knapps Battery came into camp. they are mow makeing a Brest work on the mountain to mask 2 peices. it is most time for Company Drill. write soon. I am in the best of health and if it must come, as sure it must, am eager for the affray. write soon.

Henry

33

Camp Goodman Jan 16th

Dear Brother [Albert],

I received you in a letter to day. it looks very natural and is a fine picture. you have grown very tall since I last saw you. I had mine taken this forenoon before I received yours. the boys say we look alike. we are having a touch of winter now. [We have] some snow and [it is] quite Cold. we are waiting anxiously for news from the Burnside expedition and the Mississipi fleet.[118] we may cross in 2 weeks or may not. It is impossible to tell. our Col is very busy at present. all of our officers are going through an examination at Frederick. we have 5 prisoners in Camp waiting to be exchanged for 5 of our men (the 28) now in the hands of the Traitors. the Pay master will be here soon. John Richardsons last letter did not reach me. I have been wondering why he did not write. I send you a programe of our next performance which will come if at the date mentioned it dont rain. one of our Sargents will go to Phild soon. I shall ask him to go to H. G. Keiths and have my trunk sent home. I had 3 or 4 good Shirts, 1 new one I never wore, my Over coat, and [a] Beaver Hat. the last is not worth much. all of the little nigger boys that sell cakes in camp wear our Old grey uniform which makes them look like Rebel Soldiers, but it makes them mad to tell them so. there was one big nigger selling milk in camp. we got him into our Sibly and asked him if he knew where there was a secession Flag. Yes Massa, he said. he told us and some of the boys say they are going to get it.

I must close now. give my respects to all of the Boys. tel John Parker to write. do you hear from Augustus and wife, and how is the winter with you[?] from your Brother,

Corp A. H. Hayward

34

Camp Goodman Feb 20

Dear Brother [Albert],

I received yours of the 17th in due season and hasten to answer it for I beleive it is some time since I have wrote home, but I know the news which you are daily receiving from the seat of our war is far more interesting than I can possibly send you from the Point of Rocks, but we Still maintain our position on the Point. our lines have been more quiet of late Since the destruction of a portion of Harpers Ferry.[119] our men are building a Fort on the Mountain near the Signal Station under the Direction of Col De Korponay. it is to be made for 4 Parrot Guns. Knapps 28 Battery are waiting for 2 more peices. we shall then have a full Battery of Six guns.[120] our

Guns were out for practice the other morning. Col Geary asked them to fire at a mark over in Dixie near [some] woods. they did so, when to our surprise a number of Cavalrymen went dashing away in all directions. we saw it. once we had disturbed a Hornets nest, the Artillry ceased fooling and went at [it] in earnest and did not Stop untill they had shelled out the woods thoroughly.[121] the canal Boats along the line have been accumulating at the Point and other Places for the last week. it is beleived they will be sent to Edwards Ferry. a forward movement looks very probable. we are waiting orders. our performance which was to come of on the 22 has been postponed as the weather looks very unfavorable. I lost the papere that gave the account of our last, but Sergt Devine has sent to Phild to See if he can get another one. if he does, I will send it soon. we are having a change now from the regular duties of camp. it is in the shape of Sham Battles with Blank Cartriges. the Artillery joins us. they play the Bass part. ask Johnny if I answered his last. I receive the Gazzette. I can think of nothing more. I have closed a letter to Mell to day. Col Geary went up to Sandy Hook this noon. he seldom goes up there with out ordering a Salute to the Rebels if there are any to be seen at the Ferry.

> love to all,
> Corp A. Henry
> Hayward

Chapter 3

"WE ALL SUPPOSED THE TIME FOR CHEWING CARTRIDGES HAD COME"

THE SHENANDOAH VALLEY CAMPAIGN, FEBRUARY 24–SEPTEMBER 1, 1862

ON FEBRUARY 24, AS PART OF GENERAL BANKS'S 37,000-MAN ARMY of the Shenandoah, the 28th Pennsylvania led the advance into enemy territory. Amid cold, blustery weather, the regiment used small boats to cross the Potomac River at Harpers Ferry. Unfortunately, two accidents marred this operation. Six men from Company P drowned suddenly when their boat—the fourth to cross—overturned in the strong current. Remembered one witness, "The water was very cold, and the men having all their accoutrements with knapsack[s] upon them, were unable to swim, and soon . . . all went down." After this accident, Geary ordered the men to use larger ferry boats. However, after seven companies made it across, a cable snapped, setting adrift one boat laden with over one hundred men. Providentially, this vessel did not overturn. The soldiers kept their cool, drew in the guy ropes, fastened them, and then swung the boat onto the Virginia shore. Banks ordered the crossing suspended for one day, and U.S. Engineers commenced building a pontoon bridge. The remaining companies of the 28th Pennsylvania crossed the next day, followed by the rest of Banks's troops. Despite these accidents, so wrote one Pennsylvanian, "Never was there an army more determined and confident of success, and although there must necessarily be many hardships incident to so grand a move, and many things to try the patience of the men, yet we hear no murmur of discontent."[1]

Banks intended to drive Confederate forces commanded by General Joseph E. Johnston from their defensive positions along the Potomac River. On March 2 Banks sent an expedition consisting of the 28th Pennsylvania, three companies of the 1st Michigan Cavalry, and two pieces of artillery to strike the Confederate flank at Lovettsville, Virginia. After marching through icy winter weather, this column reached its destination on March 4. Once at Lovettsville, it discovered that the enemy had evacuated the town. After a three-day rest, Geary pushed the expedition another seventeen miles to Waterford and then to Leesburg, where it arrived on March 7. Once in Leesburg, the bluecoats discovered that Johnston had abandoned the four forts that protected the town.[2] The bloodless victory roused hearty cheers from the men. The soldiers of the 28th Pennsylvania occupied Leesburg for three more days and, while in residence, they administered loyalty oaths to the populace and seized contraband slaves. The Pennsylvanians approached the population with peaceable intentions, and they proffered friendship to the town's Unionists. Declared one officer, "With affiliating protestations we lifted the cloud from the eyes of many of the deluded, and administered panegyrics to those afflicted with mental paralysis, which has begotten so many hasheesh visions of sectional independence." Generally, the occupation of Leesburg proceeded affably. When a fire erupted in the city, the men of the 28th Pennsylvania helped to put it out. One officer remembered, "The people implored them to remain with them as protectors."[3]

The 28th Pennsylvania left Leesburg on March 12 and headed southwest to Snickersville. After two days at this village, the regiment continued to Upperville, where it encamped for another nine days. Now deep in enemy territory, the men of the 28th Pennsylvania no longer met friendly faces. One soldier vividly remembered the women encountered at Upperville. "The young ladies are exotics," he wrote, "who, in their first conversation, will inform you at least three times where they finished their education. . . . These exquisite and luxurious creatures—some of whom, by-the-by, feed like little canaries, on delicate morsels at the table—at all events express much sympathy for the Rebel cause, not that they really think it a just one, but they have lovers in the field. This induces them to sing and play 'The Bonnie Blue Flag' and other Secession ballads, and warble 'Ever of Thee' to their absent gents in uniform." Undaunted, the Pennsylvanians replied with their own musical rejoinders. Lieutenant Thomas Elliot wrote, "A favorite song in the South is 'The Bonnie Blue Flag.' The first time we heard it sung here, by a fair-faced Secesh, it was thrown into the shade of silence by 'The Star Spangled Banner,' in all its dignity and martiality, performed by our band at Retreat. It is an item of news to these people to learn that 'Dixie' is a Philadelphia production. It is sung throughout the South and claimed as indigenous to the clime." The frosty reception from the Upperville women soured Hayward and his comrades on the possibility of a speedy sectional reconciliation. These early encounters suggest that the developing Union policy of a war against southern society emerged from these antagonistic relations between southern civilians and their occupiers.[4]

Since the commencement of the campaign, Geary's expedition had yet to engage Confederate troops. Colonel Turner Ashby's cavalry often skirmished with Geary's soldiers before they entered a particular town, but each time the Confederates gave way before a major battle could be joined. In late March the 28th Pennsylvania missed chances to engage Confederates at Aldie, Snickersville, and Philomont. But then on March 27, on the fields north of Middleburg, three hundred Confederate cavalrymen made a stand. Geary called the 28th Pennsylvania into line of battle, ordering his men to fix bayonets and charge. Excitement prevailed among the rank and file. "[W]e all supposed the time for chewing Cartridges had come," Hayward recalled. "[W]e thought of Bolivar and felt that all would be well."[5] However, the battle did not come to pass; the overwhelming numbers of the 28th Pennsylvania forced the Confederate cavalry to retreat, and the Pennsylvanians met only feeble resistance. A sergeant remembered, "Advancing upon them with fixed bayonets and a wild hurrah, we soon forced the 'chivalry' to give place before us."[6] Lieutenant Elliot remembered the eager rush of excitement that accompanied the charge into town: "The charge through Middleburg partook of all the excitement of a fierce battle. . . . Knapsacks, overcoats and blankets were thrown off, without halting, until the sides of the streets were barricaded with them. Rallying cries filled the air, and like a great machine, bearing destruction in its course, the body pushed on. . . . Horses dashed over the pavements, stores and dwellings were closed up, and the inhabitants, in the guilty conviction of their participation, terror-stricken, concealed themselves."[7]

The Pennsylvanians did not remain long at Middleburg. Banks recently brigaded the 28th Pennsylvania with four other regiments—the 28th New York, the 46th Pennsylvania, the 5th Connecticut, and the 1st Maryland—all commanded by Brigadier General Alpheus S. Williams. Banks wanted the regiment to press on and join the brigade at Warrenton. Over the next several days, the Pennsylvanians marched through White Plains, Thorough-fare Gap, Greenwich, Catlett's Station, and Warrenton. Then on April 7 Banks suddenly ordered the 28th Pennsylvania to return to White Plains to repel Confederate guerrillas. Since the commence-ment of the campaign, the regiment had marched 180 miles. Many of the marches took place over rough roads or through inclement weather. One sergeant described the march to Thoroughfare Gap as "one of the most difficult marches that we have encountered since the war opened. In some places the mud was about the con-sistency of soft mush, and from one to three feet in depth, and in other places the roads were obstructed by rocks of huge size." Another soldier remembered the three-day march back to White Plains, commenting, "The wind blew keenly, with heavy damp-ened breath, and a frozen rain beat sharply in our faces, succeeded by a darkened sky and a brisk snow-storm, which threatened to continue for all time to come. . . . Seven miles of severity had been gone through with . . . by an almost impenetrable fall of snow."[8]

On April 14 the 28th Pennsylvania reached Rectortown. There Geary erected his headquarters. Under orders from Banks, he was to disperse his regiment along the lines of the Manassas Gap Rail-road and make repairs to the rails, telegraph lines, and bridges destroyed by Confederate raiders. The following week, Geary commenced sending detachments to their assigned positions, and thus he scattered his men over thirty miles between Salem and Linden. Companies D and G held a position at Markham, a rail-road station near Manassas Gap. Hayward commanded "Picket Post Number 2," a post of six men, located at Wolf's Crag, the home of Colonel Turner Ashby, the one-time wealthy Farquier County planter and now a commander of cavalry in Lieutenant General Thomas J. "Stonewall" Jackson's Army of the Valley. The men of Companies D and G spent much of their time consorting with Ashby's slaves and plundering his house. Hayward raided the library and stole several books.[9]

Company D remained at Markham for four weeks. Once the workmen completed their repairs, Geary recalled the 28th Penn-sylvania's scattered companies to Rectortown. When Company D arrived, the men welcomed a new commander. On April 25, during Company D's absence, Geary received a promotion to brigadier general, and he took command of the brigade to which the 28th Pennsylvania belonged. Lieutenant Colonel Gabriel De Korponay, a veteran of the Hungarian Army, ascended to command the regiment. Although the men generally liked De Korponay, Geary considered him a drunkard and unfit to lead. Secretly, he did his best to force him to resign. However, in the meantime, Geary had to accept De Korponay as his replacement.[10] Most soldiers in the 28th Pennsylvania expressed sadness to see Geary leave, although as brigade commander he would never really be far away. Before Geary took his departure, the men purchased him a new dress sword, epaulettes, and a sash, wishing him the best of luck at his new command. Afterward, De Korponay addressed the despondent troops, promising to "do ample justice to the position which is entrusted to my hands."[11]

For most of the campaign thus far, the 28th Pennsylvania remained east of the Blue Ridge Mountains, fighting raiders and guerrillas. On the west side of the mountains, Banks directed the bulk of his army, squaring them off against Stonewall Jackson's Army of the Valley. The first months of campaigning went exceptionally well; Jackson retreated south in the face of Banks's advance, allowing the Unionists to occupy Winchester and Strasburg without a fight. Then, on May 23 Jackson suddenly struck Banks's flank at Front Royal, routing the Union defenders and severing his connection with the Manassas Gap Railroad. Banks withdrew his men to Winchester to prevent Jackson from cutting off his line of retreat. News of the defeat at Front Royal threw Geary's camp at Rectortown into anxious excitement. Fearing that his command would be unable to rejoin the main body of the Army of the Shenandoah, Geary hastened the remaining companies of the 28th Pennsylvania to Rectortown so he could abandon the Manassas Gap Railroad line and withdraw to safer latitudes. While Geary considered this a prudent course of action—he believed Confederates outnumbered him twenty to one—many subordinates considered his conduct disgraceful. Major Ariovistus Pardee of the 28th Pennsylvania wrote, "From all accounts the Gen. [Geary] has been badly frightened since the Front Royal affair. . . . Tents were struck, the part of the reg. there were in line fully expecting to be marched to the scene of action. Such was not the case however. . . . [N]ext to Jackson, Geary has contributed more to disturb the country than any other man."[12]

At any rate, Hayward did not participate in the withdrawal. On May 24, two days before Geary evacuated Rectortown, Hayward, then ill with fever, reported to sick call. The regimental surgeon, H. Earnest Goodman, declared him unfit for duty. Sometime thereafter Hayward received a transfer to a general hospital. Hayward's movements during this period are unclear. It seems likely that he remained with the 28th Pennsylvania's ambulance trains during the regiment's retreat from Rectortown. Probably, when the regiment reached Manassas Junction on May 27, Hayward went into a field hospital, and he remained there for an undetermined amount of time. Sometime prior to June 7, medical staff put Hayward on a railroad car and sent him to a general hospital in Alexandria. Hayward stayed at this hospital for only a few days. Medical personnel again transferred him to make way for wounded, who were arriving by boat from the Yorktown Peninsula. On June 8 Hayward arrived at Fort DeKalb, a fortification on Union-held Arlington Heights, and he stayed there over a month. However, on June 14, only six days after his arrival, his fever broke and he declared himself well enough to rejoin his regiment. Hayward wrote his father, "I wanted to go to my Regt but the Doctor did not see fit to send me. those he thought were able he sent but since I have got out here I have got as strong as I ever was and in good health."[13] Apparently, Hayward experienced difficulty locating the 28th Pennsylvania after Banks's disaster at Front Royal. Reports concerning Geary's movements oscillated between suspected unreliability and outright falsehood. Eventually, when accurate communication returned, Hayward located his regiment at Warrenton. There he rejoined it on July 14.

Hayward's absence caused him to miss very little. His regiment had spent most of the period maneuvering, never engaging Confederates in a pitched battle. However, the 28th Pennsylvania did have a new commander. In early July Colonel De Korponay took charge of a parole and exchange camp in Alexandria, so command of the regiment consequently fell to Lieutenant Colonel Hector Tyndale, a Philadelphia glass and porcelain importer and a noted abolitionist. Almost to a man, the soldiers of the 28th Pennsylvania despised Tyndale for his overly stern nature and his uncompromising attention to discipline. One private lamented, "Lieut. Colonel Tyndale is in command & I will not say what is generally thought of him but we have had some hard times since he has been in command."[14]

However, since Hayward's illness the general path of the war had changed immeasurably. The dual failures on the Peninsula and in the Shenandoah Valley induced radical Republicans in Congress to widen the conflict, adding confiscation of property as means of subduing the rebellion. Also, recent legislation now required Union soldiers to liberate contraband slaves who fled into their lines. This act did not noticeably alter procedure for the men of the 28th Pennsylvania, who, among other Union soldiers, had been liberating slaves on their own volition for months. Lincoln also called up 300,000 additional three-year volunteers to augment the 542,000 three-year troops called up in 1861. Finally, Lincoln looked for a new general to deliver a crushing blow to the rebellion. In June Lincoln selected Major General John Pope, a bombastic westerner noted for his hard-line approach toward southern civilians.

Pope took command of the newly created Army of Virginia, about 70,000 strong. The formation of the Army of Virginia consolidated three small armies into three corps, and it borrowed three additional corps from the Army of the Potomac. Under this new command structure, Banks's Army of the Shenandoah became the 2nd Corps, Army of Virginia. On July 16, under Pope's directive, the 28th Pennsylvania proceeded to Little Washington, where it finally linked up with Banks. The 28th Pennsylvania remained at this camp for eighteen days and while there spent ample time drilling and preparing for Pope's advance to Richmond. Banks reviewed the regiment on July 28 and Pope reviewed it on August 3. Two days later, Banks assigned the 28th Pennsylvania to a new brigade. Geary received command of the 1st Brigade, 2nd Division, 2nd Corps, Army of Virginia, and he wished the 28th Pennsylvania could accompany him to this new assignment. Banks graciously allowed the transfer; consequently, the 28th Pennsylvania joined four veteran Ohio units: the 5th, 7th, 29th, and 66th Ohio Volunteer Infantry Regiments.

Not long after being brigaded, the 28th Pennsylvania, along with the rest of Banks's corps, participated in an arduous march toward Gordonsville in an effort to cut the Virginia Central Railroad and destroy Stonewall Jackson's command, now merged with the Army of the Northern Virginia. For four days the regiment marched south over dusty roads in miserably hot weather, reaching Culpeper on August 8. The next day, Banks put his column on the road at 9:00 A.M., and then, ten miles south of Culpeper, it confronted Jackson's forces on the fields north of Cedar Mountain. The resultant battle went poorly for the federals. Although a portion of Jackson's line routed at the outset, timely Confederate reinforcements drove Banks's troops from the field, costing both sides a heavy toll: 3,700 casualties.

Although eager for the fray, the 28th Pennsylvania did not participate in this battle. Just a few miles north of the battlefield,

Banks directed Geary to send one regiment westward to occupy Thoroughfare Mountain and reestablish the signal station there. Geary selected the 28th Pennsylvania—1,043 men strong—for this assignment. Tyndale led the regiment on a long march beyond the right flank of Banks's corps. Along the route, it drove off a few Confederate cavalry scouts and suffered a few casualties from gunfire and heatstroke, but the regiment reached the mountain after much delay. Tyndale remembered, "It was one of the hottest days of that very hot summer, many men were sunstruck, and there was great difficulty in keeping the close order so necessary in the presence of the enemy." When the battle opened, Tyndale debated the possibility of rejoining the corps, but when no couriers arrived, he elected to remain in position and thus missed the battle.[15]

The day after the engagement at Cedar Mountain, August 10, a courier reached the 28th Pennsylvania and directed it to rejoin the shattered corps at Culpeper. After arriving at the town, the bulk of the regiment remained there for fourteen days. Then, on August 24, under Pope's orders, the regiment struck tents and withdrew twenty-one miles over the next three days to Warrenton Junction. On August 28, acting as Banks's rear guard, the 28th Pennsylvania fell back to Bristoe Station. The regiment encamped at this place for two days, missing Pope's bloody defeat at the Battle of Second Bull Run, August 28–30, a fight which cost Pope's army 14,462 casualties. On August 31 the regiment fell back again, this time to Bull Run Bridge—where the Orange and Alexandria Railroad crossed Bull Run—destroying any government property in its wake. This was done to prevent General Robert E. Lee's victorious Army of Northern Virginia from seizing any valuable war materiel.

On September 2 the 28th Pennsylvania continued moving east to Alexandria, where it joined the Army of the Potomac, recently removed from its campaign on the Yorktown Peninsula. At Washington, Lincoln relieved Pope from command and consolidated all Union forces around Washington under the authority of Major General George B. McClellan. Lincoln relieved Banks too, and McClellan summarily redesignated his corps the 12th Corps, Army of the Potomac. Thus, nearly eleven months since the skirmish at Bolivar Heights, Henry Hayward had yet to experience a major engagement. However, at that moment, Hayward's war was about to take a strange turn.

35

Dear Father,

I suppose you must know my whereabouts. we broke camp Sunday night at 1 oclock. [We] took cars for Sandy Hook. 3 comps of the 28 took posession at Harpers Ferry and held it for 1½ days before we could get the rest of the Reg across. our Pickets eat Dinner yesterday in sight of each other. to day at 1 oclock the Pontoon Bridg was put across. we then crossed in good order. to night 9000 men with 15 peices of Artillery occupy the place. Gen Banks and Staff [and] Gen McCellen and Staff are here. the troops are in the best of Spirits. they cheerd heartily as soon as the[y] trod the Soils of Old Virginia. the 28 lead the Advance. I understand McClellen has Telegraphed for more Troops. the Men are all Determined and we shall meet them like Men. you will hear from us soon I hope. the troops are quarterd in the deserted houses of Harpers Ferry and Bolivar. the Boys are all writing. I am in good health. [I] will write when ever fortune favors me with a chance. we quarterd for the last 2 nights in canal boats. we are not with out our sport for we are born to be merry when it dont rain. I received Coras letter. take your time and Study this out. I have taken my knapsack of but it seems as if it was there yet. I must now close. good bye,

Corp A Henry Hayward

Direct Harpers Ferry, Gen Banks Div.

36

Camp of the 28th, Lovettsville Va[17]

Dear Father,

I wrote last from Sandy Hook. I beleive all communication has been stoped untill we get in such a position as no harm can arise from it. 8 Co of the 28th crossed the Shenandoah River with 4 of Mich Cavalry and our Battery of 4 peices. we took posesion of Lovettsville on the first day of Spring. the Rebels fled on our approach. Six privates and an Officer were overtaken by our Scouts, togeather with a mailbag. we were most enthusiastically received by all the citizens. the women wept for joy. I felt that the hardships I had sufferd were all repaid when we saw we were the means of makeing so many hearts glad. the large number of refugees that followed us were met by their familys with tears in their eyes. you cannot form an Idea of the Suffering this war is causing to the People of Virginia. Hundreds have flocked into our lines since we have been here to save themselves from being pressed into service. Confederate Scrip will not pass here or in Leesburgh. Tea is worth $4 lb. Coffee cannot be had. the Women beg us for Salt and we give [it] to them. we have been reinforced with the rest of our Regt. we are now 1500 Strong of Infantry 400 Cl with 4 Peices of Artillry. we will fight like Tigers before they shall return to Destroy Little Massachusetts as the Rebels call it. we have packed up twice for a fight but they do not come. If we are overpowerd we have chosen our position to fall back, but never with out a fight while Geary has Command. It will be time enough to worry about me when you hear of a Battle. we live in houses on secesh Beef and hogs, Poultry, flour &c. Forageing Parties go out every day. we have sent 400 barells to Harpers Ferry besides corn. Col Geary was the Lion at Harpers Ferry. he was with Banks & McCllen. I saw many N. B. boys at the Ferry. I am for the Union and in good Health.

Henry

[*Upside down in top margin of first page*] Direct Harpers Ferry, Va, Gen Banks Div, Col Geary.

37

Leesburgh Va March 9

Dear Brother,

I was informed that a mail would leave here in 2 hours. we left Lovettsville at 5 ock PM Friday. we first took Posession of Fort Johnson, a most formable [fortress] it is. we Planted the Colors of the 28 on the Ramperts and Geary made a Speech. 4 Reg left on our approach and why they did we can not tell, unless it was that the Geary Boys were coming. we went into Waterford at 11oc. the people were all up hearing of our approach and greeted us with waving of handkerchiefs &c. one old man came out with his waggon and took the boys Knapsacks. I packed mine all the way. the mud was awfull, and as soon as the Regt would halt a moment the boys would drop down to get a little rest. the Cavalry that were in advance made a dash through the City capturing 2 or 3 Rebels. you will think it very Strange how we could occupie such a Strong fortified City with out a hard fight. It is as strange to us. there are 4 forts[:] 1 Johnson, Since named Geary, 2d Beauregard, 3 Evans, 4 Fort Hill. they pressed men last Sumer to build them, and they are not finished yet except Johnson. I am so full of items I do not know which to write first. I can not think that I am in Leesburgh and that Col Geary took it with his Little band.[18] this is a Hot Secession place but we dont mind them much. many have expressed themselves surprised to see that the detested Yankees look so well. they even admitt that we look much better than their own. Gen Stone is the shurist Traitor living. Gen Evans [was the] Rebel formerly in command here. [Stone] said he was a better Soldier than he (Evans) was.[19] they use to go to school togeather. 2 of the Mississipi 21 deserted to our Post when we were at Lovettsville. they both belong North. he said he was at the Battle of Bolivar with 3 peices that fired at us from Louden Heights. the Mississipi 17th got our blankets.[20] direct as before. good bye. love to all.

I am on guard to day. I would give $5 for a quart of baked Beans.

[*no signature*]

38

Upperville Va. Mar 15

Dear Father,

I have got only 2 minutes to write as the mail is of. we left Leesburgh 2 days ago for Winchester. finding Banks had possession, we changed our course towards Manassas. we captured 5 of Asbys Cavalry Last night when we came to town. I am well and in good Spirits.

Henry

39

White Plains, Va. Mar 30

Dear Father,

A mail goes tomorrow. that is news to me. we have been on a move for a week. the last time I wrote was from Upperville. we went from there to Alldie. as we came into the Town, Abercrombies Brigade was leaving it as they had received orders to return to Winchester.[21] we encamped there for the night when we followed them again. [We] took up our quarters at Snickersville. here we learned that the Battle of Winchester had been fought with Victory for the Union Troops.[22] the next morning Abercrombie Brigade passed our Camp going towards Alldie. here I had an Opportunity of seeing all of my Old Friends. the 12th Mass lead the Advance, and with the (+Band+) [*in lower margin it reads "No. Bridgewater Band"*] Playing Stiring Airs, It made me feel good all over. how eager I watched for a familiar Countenance. Soon Joe F noticed his Old Friend and came out of the ranks followed by many others. we had a hearty shake of the hand all around, Exchanged news, and talked of our late victories &c. I walked along with them for 2 miles, and as I expected to soon be on the march again, I went back to camp. here I heard we were to strike tents at 1 ock. I hastily put away a cup of been soup, put a peice of pork in my haversack, throwed myself upon the Straw and waited orders. the drums soon beat to prepare to strike Tents. the last tap strikes the drum and in an instant our little city of canvass is level to the ground. the teams drive up to their respective Co. the Baggage is put aboard. we sling Knapsacks and in a short time the 28th is in motion following the Brigade. we halt for the night at a place called Fillimont after a short march of 8 miles. we take up quarters on an Old Camp ground once occupied by a Rebel Regt. after refreshing ourselves with a nights rest, we brake Camp again. after marching 2 miles we came to an Encampment composed of the New York 9, 13th Mass, [and] 16 Ind.[23] we passed by them, turned of to the right on a road leading to Midellburgh. we had heard that a body of Rebels 1400 Strong were at this place, and Geary was the man to Dislodge them. we marched on with 2 companys of Cavalry in advance. scouting around, we noticed nothing that looked like Rebels untill we had reached within 2 miles of the town. order came down the line for quick time and as we gained the top of a hill, we noticed our Cavalry at a distance scouting around in a field, and some distance in their rear the first Battalion deployed as skirmishers. now the order comes for double quick, and as we went joggin along, we passed one of our peices of Artillery in position looking towards the town. we all supposed the time for chewing Cartridges had come, and we expected to soon meet the Rebels. we threw away our knapsacks, fixed bayonetts and with Geary at our head, enterd the town. soon the Cavalry came dashing in and told us we should see a fight soon for they were close upon them coming in force. all eyes we turned toward Geary as he shouted "forward Men." we thought of Bolivar and felt that all would be well. we soon came in sight of the Rebels Cavalry. they were at a halt, seeming to be on a study. which to do[?] Advance or retreat[?] as it was but one way and that was Advance, and as we were yet on double quick, we gave a yell. they turned quickly and Co H and one section of D that were in Advance sent a volley of bullets after them. one peice of Artillry got into position and sent them 3 shells. thus we have met the Enemy again but they are not ours. we left Midellburgh Saturdays morning for White Plains where we now are on the line of Manassass Gap Railroad that carried Reinforcements that Decided the day at Bulls Run.[24]

PS. as there is nothing personal in the big Sheet, I will say that I am in perfect health and enjoying myself as much as any Soldier in the Great Union Army. we have nothing to Complain about except Short Rations which cannot be helped as we are far from any Supplies, but we dont think of Starving as there [is] plenty of Secesh Beef and flour in this part of the country. we expect to move on to Warrington soon. get out the Map of Virginia and watch our progress. we have our Regt of 1500 men, 4 Co of Cavalry, [and] 4 peices of Artillery. Col Geary with his usal Shrewdness Devides us into 3 Regt when we encamp. we get no news, and to see a papere puts the whole Camp in an uproar. the 22d is the latest date I have seen. we had a Thunder Storm to day, which looks as if winter had broken. when we were on the march yesterday we were caught in a snow strom. but it look fair for better weather to morrow. the grass is gren and I heard the figs peek 2 weeks ago for the Union) Direct to Washington. did you get the paper called the Advance Guard[?][25]

> love to all,
> Henry

40

White Plains, Va. April 12

Dear Father,

As I have an opportunity of writeing a few lines I will give you a faint Idea of what I have been doing since I last wrote. I think my last was dated from this place. since then we moved to Thoroughfare Gap, from there to Grenich, from there to Calverts Station, from there to Warrenton, from there to Mt. Halom, from there to White Plains. at Calverts Station we again met Abercrombies Brigade also Blenkers Div. of Germans.[26] I had a chance to see all the Bridgewater Boys. they were all well, and in good Spirits. I witnessed a Dress Parad of the 12th Mass Regt. they Drill Splendid, much better than we can. we made a forced march to Warenton. this is the finest Place that we have yet seen in Virginia. we enterd the City with Colors flying and the Band Playing Dixie. we Marched through the Principle Street, Countermarched and went in to quarters on a fine field outside of the City. Major Tyndale in command of our Battalion told us to brush up and wash ourselves Clean that the Southern ladies might see that we were not made up of the Rough & scrapeings of the North but men far the superior of the Southern men. the next morning we broke up camp and started another march. after marching an hour, it commenced to rain, and from rain it turned into snow, which made the roads impassible. we made 4 miles only when we were obliged to camp in the wilderness with out provisions. we remained here 3 days. [We] called our camp Camp Starvation. we lived on sheep and beef which we had to forage for. we expected to meet supply here at White Plains. [We] expect them here to night. if they come we shall leave for Middelburgh tomorrow on our way to join the Div. we go by the way of Snickersville and Winchester. if we make the above place it will be three times we have camped there. the weather is fine to day overhead but awfull muddy water under foot. Collis Zouaves or what was Banks body Guard are with us. they joined us at Warrenton on their way to join the Div. they are a fine body of men 100 Strong with a splendid Uniform.[27] Gen Blenkers Div. passed our camp at Warrenton on their way to join Fremont. they are all Duch. they have no tents and what they did when the Storm came on I have not heard. we had hard work to keep comfortable in our Siblys with fire in the Stove. I have not heard from home for 4 or 5 weeks. I get no papers any more. the[y] do not let them come. when we get with the Div I hope we shall have a change in camp affairs. I am in good health. we are all waiting to hear the news. love to all. I will write again soon.

Henry

Direct Gen Banks Div.

[*In different handwriting*]
This is a pattern of my sack, just what I wanted
Mary Good[28] and is better
I expect to hear from Henry again soon. Harmon is at home—Says he saw H ten days ago—"We miss you at home mother"

Father[29]

41

Rectortown Va. April 15th

Dear Sister,

I received yours, Parkers, &c. of the sixth at a time when it was most welcome. I had not heard from N. B. for so long a time. the same mail brought late papers to some of the boys in our mess containing the Glorious News of the Battle at Pitsburgh Landing.[30] the camp was wild with excitement. the band played. at the same time we could hear the booming of cannon firing Salutes at Washington. last Sunday, the train came in from Manasses with Provisions for us poor hungrey half Starved Subjects of Uncle Sam. When the Engine made its appearence (as it was the first train that it has run under the Stars and Stripes) the boys set up a yell, Crackers, Crackers, and started for the Depot. the Zouaves who were on Guard tried to stop us from leaving the Camp but we run the blockade and we found on arriving at the cars the boys had burst open a Box and were filling their pockets with crackers. some of the our men had a barrell of Whiskey and 2 or 3 Larger Beer aboard. as soon as the Colonel was made known of the fact he orderd the head stove in. so the proprietor of the Licquor did not get his money back. we Stroke Tents at White Plains early yesterday morning [and] arrived at this forsaken Place last night[, a] distance [of] 10 miles. the sceanery of this Place is most beautifull. last night a body of troops were seen at a distance towards Manases Gap, but they were beleived to be our men. Col [Geary] sent a squad of Cavalry to look after them. you may think we make some strange moves and so we do. but we know wiser heads than ours are at the helm. our hasty leave from White Plains at the first will be easily explained by the little paragraph I cut from the N.Y. Times. it was an awfull night when we got notice to Pack Knapsacks and such a road, well, Jordans is no Comparison. you asked in your last what became of our

Knapsacks at the foot race we had at Midelburgh. the rear guard that came up with the waggons saved them for us and we got them all safe. at least I am quite sure of it when I am on the march. the last time we were Paid of was at Point of Rocks. we dont want any money. no chance to spend it here. Thursday. but the Orderly just came in and says there is a prospect of our makeing a longer stay. for want of something else to write I will say that I am still enjoying good health and have got a Haversack full of crackers with two nice peices of Pork. I have just drawn my ration of flour, and the boys are mixen it up and if we dont have some nice Slap Jacks for diner it will be Strange. tell Parker I will write soon and answer the rest. write soon. I must look after my Dinner.

from your Uncle
Corporal[31]
Hayward

42

Camp Beautifull
Markham, Va.
28th Reg't, Co. D, U.S.A.,
1862[32]

Dear Brother,

I am seated under the shade of a cherry tree in front of the House owned and formally occupied by Col Turner Ashby of the Confederate Cavalry Service. there are a family of his faithfull slaves who still remain here to take care of his place. he was once quite wealthy. [He] owned at one time 60 slaves, but being a great Gambler lost them all. he had a large Library but the boys have taken up the largest shares and they are scatterd around in the different tents.[33] some of the boys have parts of old uniforms found in his house which they wear around camp. there are 2 comp stationed here, D & G, 2 more 6 miles up the railroad at Linden, and 2 more at the bridge on the Shenandoah. the head quarters of xGen Gearyx are still at Rectortown. we were paid off at Rectortown just before we marched for Markham. I sent $25 By our Chaplin who went to Philadelphia where he was to mail it for N. B. write if you received it. I received 2 Gazettes and 2 New York papers and a letter from Mell and one from Aunt Beldens to day.[34] we were mustered for pay last monday and will be payed off again soon. trains run to and fro by our camp, and as soon as the large bridge is finished across the Shenandoah I think the whole Regt will move up. Contrabands arive daily at our camp. they tell us strang storys. we send all up to the General with a few hard crackers for lunch. we see the rebel cavalry on the hills at different times but I dont think they will venture very near our lines. we live like Lords since we have left the Regt. I help to eat a fine chicken that belonged to Col Ashby. there was as many as 30 Chicks [that] lost their lives the night we arrived here. we killed an ox that belonged to him the other day, but it was strong tainted with Garlic. we could not eat it.[35] the Peach trees have been in full blossom for 10 days. the mountains are all robed with green and nature in all its loveliness trys to make happy the troubled spirits of this distracted country. I received a letter from John A. Richardson the other day. [I] will answer soon. I did not think the Gallant 28 would halt along side of a rail road, but it seems we are. I think we shall eventually join Banks now that our Geary is a General[36] where he can find a field to display his masterly Millitary Genus,[37] but it is quite evident that it needs a smart man to open this road and troops that have a good name so as to economize numbers, as there are numerous Gurilla bands in this section of the country. since the cars have began to run we get late papers with all the important news such as the fall of New Orleans, [the] Gallant Conduct of the Mass Boys before Yorktown &c., &c.[38] I am Glad I am a Mass Boy although fighting under the flag of the Keystone State. I watch with much interest the movements of the Mass Regiments. if you have a map you will notice we are in Manassus Gap. send me an Envelope in every letter you send as I am most out and [I have] no chance to buy. I have plenty of paper. by order of Corporal Hayward, love to all. write soon / Commanding No 2 Pickett Post Markham Va

43

Fort DeKalb
Dis. of Columbia June 14th

Dear Father,

I arrived here last Sunday. they cleared the Hospitals & Alexandria to make way for the Wounded from Richmond.[39] I wanted to go to my Regt but the Doctor did not see fit to send me. those he thought were able he sent but since I have got out here I have got as strong as I ever was and in good health. I have been trying to find out where my Regt is. I want you to send me a gold Dollar as I am broke. I was at Washington Thursday to find my Paymaster. the Pay Mast. General said he had gone to Pay of the Regt. so I shall miss this Regiment untill the next time unless I should see him again in Washington. there are about 200 Sick here. we live in Sibly Tents [with] boarded floors to sleep on. I go Strawberrying and fishing. there are 7 of the 28th here. send the dollar as soon as Possible for I want to answer Mells letter and I have got no Paper. I do not no what he will think because I have not wrote. I [*indecipherable word*] way I have seen the boys recive money. that way is to split open a card and then put it in and paste it up. I do not feel right staying away from my Regt so long. as soon as the money comes I shall go to the War Department at Washington and enquire for the 28 Regt P. V. Fort DeKalb is about 6 miles from Washington on Arlington Heights. there are nothing but forts as far as the eye can reach. love to all.

Henry

44

Fort De Kalb, July 4th

Dear Father,

I have been waiting to get an answer from the letter which I dated from this place, but I have come to the conclusion that you did not get it. there are about 200 Invalids here from the different Hospitals recruiting up their health. most of us are ready and waiting to be sent to their Regts. we have to wait [for] orders from Washington. it is impossible to write. there is so much powder being wasted about camp. there is 7 of us here from the 28th PV. we know not where our Regt is but Pope does.[40] I think all will yet be well at Richmond. the Evening Star of last night has an Official Dispatch from Mac. he still Lives and his boys are good for another Charge. I see in the paper to that the Stonewall is down. may it be so. if I were to write the Inscription on his grave, Stone it would be, here lies one of the Bravest of Generals who Died fighting for the Wickedest of all causes.[41] I was over to Washington to get payed the other day. you will find enclosed a $20. if you write direct to Fort De Kalb near Washington. I may be here 2 days longer or 2 weeks. my health is good. I want nothing but Encouraging news. love to all.

Henry

such a pen and such ink.

45

Camp in the Field[42]
Sixteen miles til Front Royal
July 9—1862

To Ambrose Hayward Esq.
Dear Sir,

This letter having been in my possesion for some time and being unable to have it forwarded to your son and my Friend and Companion in arms, "Harry," I took the liberty of opening it so as to take the money out and remail it to you in a more safe way. I succeeded in getting a new England note which will be more safe to mail. It is very probable if Harry gets very bad they will send him home. I have had no communication from him since he has been away. I dont think any of the letters you directed to this company since his sickness has reached him. with my Kindest Regards to him, should he succeed in getting home, And my best wishes for the welfare of yourself & family.

I remain your most
Obediant servant
Edwin F. Paul[43]
1st sergt. Co. D 28th P.V.
Gearys Brigade
Banks Division

an answer is solicited
Direct
Via Washington D.C.

46

Camp Warrenton Jul 15th

Dear Father,

I arrived here (from Washington) yesterday. the boys were all glad to see me although they did not expect to see [me] as they had heard I was about to be discharged. I asked the Orderly Sargent if he had any letters for me. he said he had just mailed 2 for me at fort De Kalb (of July 7, 9th) I have not heard from home since I was in the Hospital at Alexandria. I saw Corp. Joe Freeman at Alexandria. he does not look well. they have taken our Tents from us. I met them going to the cars as I was coming into Camp. I found the Regt. spread all over the field. we have made a shelter by driving 4 stakes into the ground and placeing a blanket over us, so you may judge of the apperance of our camp. I found the boys much disheartened and they enquired eagerly of me for the latest news. I told them as bright and encourageing a story as I could. there are many camps arround us. all present the same appearence as ours. we are to have the Shelter tent soon. they will be better than none. we may move at any hour or we may stay for weeks. there is no use in hideing it, our troops are discouraged. they have lost their confidence in some one. they feel as if they have been duped. now what will right this condition of affairs is a decisive Victory. they want news, but of the right kind.

Wednesday morn, 16th. it is reported we move in one hour towards Cullpepper Court house. my health is good and I am determined as long as I am able to shoulder a muskett to remain true to the Cause. I must Close now and take my Coffee. this Photograph is a Quaker Boy. he is one of my mess mates. his name is Powell Thorne.[44]

love to all,

Corp. A. Henry Hayward

if we dont march to day I shall write to Mell. there are 4 Regts of infantry and Bests Regular Battery in Gearys Brigade.

47

July 22d

Camp at Little Washington

Dear Father,

I write once again that you may know that I have received all of the back letters which you sent to me while I was at Fort De Kalb. Seargent Paul received your letter and read it in my presence. he sends his regards to you. the Pay master was here yesterday and payed us off. he might as well [have] given it to the Suttlers at once for they get most of it in the End. our Regt has been furnished with Shelter tents. one of my mess mates bought an extra one and we have cut it up and made a marque of the other. the Shelter tents are made to accomedate 2. we have 3 in our tent. Gen Banks was in our camp [on] Sunday. his headquarters are 2 miles below this place. he is much liked by his command. Pope is concentrating his army around here. they are gaining confidence and are in the best of spirits since the Troops have begun to pour in by our camp. I am expecting to see the 12th Mass. come in every day. I think we shall be on the move soon, and when we do start we expect to move right over !!Stonewalls!! or any obstructions that we may meet on the Road to Richmond. my dear little rifel has been Shamefully abused while I was away. I found all the rest of my things in good order. it is not true as was reported in the papers that Geary burnt all of his tents and camp Equipage while on the retreat from Thourafare Gap. it was the 104 N.Y.V.[45] many of our boys got new jackets which they left. they also burnt many Navy Pistols. the 2 days march which I have passed through since I have joined the Regt I shall not soon forget. it rained in Torrents all the time we were on the march and for one day after we arrived here. I put on dry clothes after the first days march only to get wet again when we started in the morning. the mountain streems were swollen in to rivers and it was a sight to behold to see the boys plunge into them and hold onto each other while they crossed. Officers and men both shared alike and both Slept in the wet and mud that night. the fields are full of blackberrys. our Potatoes, and beans, and peaches will soon be ready to confiscate. I suppose you have read General Popes Orders.[46] Send me 50 cts worth of Postage stamps and a Gazzette. give my respects to all the boys. Enclosed you will find $20. tell mother I expect to do more writing when the Stamps come. one of my mess mates just gave me a cake with apple sauce on it, so I dont feel like writeing any more. I am in the best of health and ready for the Advance.

love to all
(Henry)

48

Aug 2d
Camp at Little Washington

Dear Brother [Albert],

I have this minute finished reading your letter. I received one from father yesterday, neither one of which say anything about the Letter which I sent from here 10 days ago containing $20 which I had just received from the Pay master. it may turn up during the war. I have been in good health since I joined my Regt. we are Encamped in a healthy locality and it looks as if we might stay here a while if the Rebels will permit us. we have had two Div. Parades here. the one we had yesterday was in respect for the Memmory of Prest. Martin Van Buren.[47] our Divs [and] Gen Williams [Division][48] of Banks army Corps made a fine appeerence. the 28th moved as a brigade. Gen Geary has not his brigade made up yet. it is expected that the Zouaves de Afrique, formerly Banks body Guard, will make up one of the Regts. you should see Geary once with his (fix ups) on if you want to see the finest looking Soldier in the army. from what we can learn Banks expects great things from the 28 when the time comes. at Div Drill the other day, our Regt was orderd to form hollow square. we did so. Gen Banks soon dashed by and took position near us on a hill. soon one of his aids went up to the Cavalry which was formed for a Charge. the bugle sounded the Charge. on they come with sabers drawn, yelling like mad men. Geary quickly gave the order to receive cavalry. we did so and they made no impression on our lines. they tried it a second time with a like result. we had five bush whackers in the guard house. they were taken by our scouts. we get papers daily here, 24 hours old. the weather is so very hot here the water most boils in our canteens. tell father it was me that met the National Guard in Washington and enquird for Mell.[49] I should like the Gazzette while I stop here. I have wrote to Mell to find out the Directions to write to Augustus. I should like to know the Directions to write to Aunt Belden, as she wrote to me a long while ago and I forgot the directions. what is Parker doing now and is Cora keeping schooll[?] write soon. I should like to hear from Grand Mother.

Corp A. Henry
Hayward

49

Camp near Culpepper, Aug 17
Head Quarters, Co "D" 28th Regt, 186[2]

Dear Sister,

Yours of the 8th inst. came to hand in good time. I received it when we were resting, waiting orders to March. I am much obliged to you for that pepper. I find use for it every day. I will tell you what part the 28th took in the late battle as the few lines I sent to Father gave no particulars.[50] Gearys Brigade left Culpepper in the Hotest part of the day, and, as we supposed, [it was] only to take a more advanced position. when we were about 5 miles out of town we could hear the report of the Artillery distinctly. soon Gen Banks and Staff dashed by us and rode towards the front. we moved at quick time. the dust was most suffocating, and when we would come to a stream the boys would rush out of the ranks and soon change the collor of the water to a dirty Yellow. Gen Geary who had not shown himself since Banks passed us came rideing up and when opposite of the collors orderd a halt. he made a few hasty remarks to the 28th. (I wish I could remember them) he told us that the enemy had driven our men from the hill, which was used by the Signal Corps the day before, and that the 28th had been orderd by Gen Banks to take the hill and hold it at all hazards untill further orders. Gen Geary said he should move with the remainder of the Brigade in another direction where he would be able to give us assistance if necessary. you will see by this that all that was expected to be done that day was given us to do and they watched our advance with great interest. we moved on through the dense wood with guns loaded ready for action at a moments notice. we had been from the Brigade 3 hours when a brisk canonade opened on our left. we felt certain that Geary had been attacked. when we came to the open country we could see the Shells bursting in every direction. we kept on untill nearly sunsett with the battle raging furiously all the while. we were on the march and we had made up our minds for a desperate fight when we should reach Telegraph hill. but fortune favored the 28th once more and when we reached the hill we found the Rebels had fled and were then fighting Geary. one of our advance was shot by a bush whacker. we pulled down some wheat Stacks nearby, made our beds, and soon forgot the dangers we had past. the next morning the Signal Corps informed Gen Pope of the movements of the enemy who could be seen by the naked eye from this hill. Gen Banks sent an orderly after us to bring us in but he never reached us. our Col sent 2 cavalry men back to have our waggons sent to us, but they were both taken prisoners. but soon a lar[g]e body of Cavalry reached us with orders to report back to Headquarters by another road. when we reached Culpepper we heard of the fate of Geary and his Brigade and the many Stories that were in circulation about us. Captain Elliot of Gen Gearys Staff reported to Gen. Banks that we were all cut to peices. we were kept in line of battle for 2 days after we came back. all is quiet now along the lines of the Army of Virginia. Gen Banks Div. is placed Hors De Combat,[51] having Sustained the whole attack of the Rebel force. Banks is one of the Ablest Generals in the Union Army and Geary is a Tiger.[52] the Division has retired from the front to rest and recruit. the Place we marched to on the day of the Battle is James City. do send those pictures you spoke of in your letter. I have a portfolio I can keep them in. the weather has been a little cooler for a few days back. I am in the best of health. troops are coming in every day. I was over to see the Mass 12th the other day. I must prepare for Dress parade.

love to all. write soon,

Henry

I was on a march [on] the 8th. [I] received [the] Gazette of Aug 13th.

50

Camp Culpepper,
Head Quarters, Co. "D" 28th Regt 1862[53]

Dear Brother [Augustus],

We have come to a halt once more where I am in hopes to remain long enough to write a few letters. you have heard of Gen Geary being wounded in the late battle and I suppose you are anxious to no what part the 28th took in the affair. we were orderd by Gen Banks to proceed to James City and take possesion of Telegraph Hill which was ocupied by our men as a Signal Station but had been driven from it the day before. we were in formed by Geary that several thousand of the enemys Cavalry were there but we must take it and hold it at all hazzards. we gave 3 cheers for Geary and 3 for the 28 and marched on turning to the right, Geary with the rest of the brigade takeing a road to the left. we had not gone far when a furious cannonade opened and we all knew Geary was at work. we kept on expecting our turn would come soon, but we found them not and we took the hill with out opposition. we beleive that they discoverd Geary first and left the hill as our march was through a dense wood. we all thought from the tone of Gearys remarks that he had got the work to do and would be ready to assist us if we were overpowerd. no one supposed that the Rebels had crossed the Rapidan in such large numbers, but it was their intention to make a sudden move and take Culpepper before Pope could get his troops up, but Stonewall could not get through Banks. Gen Geary fought like a tiger and did not leave the field untill he got his second wound. the 4 Regt that went into battle with him the 5, 7, 29, 66, were cut up teribley.[54] Banks Div. is placed Hors de Combat. it only numberd about 7000 men before it went in. now it is about 4500. they have been orderd to lay by for a while and rest and recruit up. I was over to 12 Mass Camp the other day. I saw Capt Hammond who inquired after you.[55] my health is first rate and I am in good Spirits for I think when Pope gets ready he will go through. I wrote home some time ago to get your directions. I received a letter from Cora yesterday who gave them to me. it is very hot here. [It is] awfull on a march, breathing dust and drinking muddy water. I must Close. write soon. I should like to hear if your family are all well. I hear Grandmother is no more.[56]

> Direct Corp A. Henry
> Hayward, Co. D 28
> Regt. P. V. Gen Gearys
> Brigade
> Banks Div.
> Culpepper Va

[on bottom and margin in different handwriting][57]

I have just received this from Henry and forward the same to you. I am well. they commence enrolling the names this week.[58] Col Corcoran is to have great reception here on Thursday. the old 69th escort him from Washington.[59]

Chapter 4

"Baltimore Is a Slumbering Volcano"

MELVILLE HAYWARD IN BALTIMORE, MAY 25–SEPTEMBER 5, 1862

On May 21, in reaction to a fear that Confederate forces in the Shenandoah Valley might seize Washington, New York Governor Edwin D. Morgan called up twelve regiments of New York National Guard. Among the units called up was the 7th New York State Militia. Hayward's older brother, Melville, once again returned to the front.

Melville Hayward's regiment left New York City on May 25 and arrived in Baltimore one week later. Melville saw no combat during his second tour of duty, although he had ample opportunity to interact with Baltimore's civilian population. About half of Baltimore's 212,000 residents possessed southern loyalties, and Melville experienced the city's fractious nature in a very personal way. Interestingly, he attended service at Baltimore's New Jerusalem Church—the oldest New Church in the country—despite the pastor's avowed secessionism. Melville wrote to Cora telling her that he "formed the acquaintance of a Mr. Hinkley, a Lawyer here who is a New Churchman and a Secessionist. He treated me very courteously and we talked very freely on the War question— He is personally a very amiable and pleasant gentleman. I have had several invitations out to Supper." Undoubtedly, it unnerved Melville to dine with the enemy. Generally, he feared that Baltimore seethed with unrest. "Baltimore is a slumbering volcano," he wrote, "the secession fires might burst forth at any time."[1]

The 7th New York quartered in Baltimore for three months. In early September it returned to New York City and mustered out of service. The following chapter includes three letters written by Melville Hayward and one written by his law partner, Paul J. Fish.

51

Brother & Sister Hayward [Albert and Cora],

I do not know whether you have heard by Augustus, in the News papers that 7th Regt and consequently Mel—will have gone again to Washington. M. had been rather indisposed for some wks—and I induced him to spend a little time at Tarrytown in our new place (farm of 5 acres) upon the hills—He went Thursday & staid till Monday—was considerably [*indecipherable word*]—on the way down yesterday—he had a call for his 7th,[2]—Miss Howland (Mary) was aboard coming down on her way to Barnstable—she took the F R boat last Evening.[3] Mel got ready—& left last Evening by Steamboat & Amboy R R to W last Evening & is before now probably in Washington. They Expect to protect the City at that time & return—The most I fear is that marching with the heavy Knapsack will be too much for M—but he has the will to Ease his hardships when others cannot—He really gained health and thoughts in his former campaign and he somehow feels as well if not better than when he started before—besides I think the way is clear and [there are] no hardships to encounter. His cousin and the ladies helped him off & filled his knapsack with comforts.

E. was quite unwell last week but [is] better now.[4]

Hope mother has had no serious drawbacks.

Let us hear from you soon—. We have heard nothing from Henry in a good while—He is now safe I suppose in McDowells division[5]

Affly Yours
P. J. Fish[6]

Love to Cora & the other children—Fanny[7] and Mary are going to [the] Female Seminary in Tarrytown.[8]

52

Dear Sister,

Your letters have both arrived and I will proceed to answer them (the first one I have discovered before). I have been absent from camp the past week on guard duty. Twelve of us were stationed at the U.S. Medical Purveyors Office. We had six hours leave of absence to go to the city every day—I visited the Washington Monument and most of the objects of interest in the city. I formed the acquaintance of a Mr. Hinkley, a Lawyer here who is a New Churchman and a Secessionist.[9] He treated me very courteously and we talked very freely on the War question—He is personally a very amiable and pleasant gentleman. I have had several invitations out to Supper—I had a pleasant ride out to Druid Hill Park the other day—The Superintendent drove me about the grounds in his carriage. I met a gentleman there who said he would introduce me some time to his friend Hayward who is a great Union man here. Hayward is a common name in Baltimore—We were quartered at the Union Relief Association[10] and I saw soldiers there from every part of the country who had been in the different battles with Banks, Fremont, [and] McClellan. The Association has a lunch room for soldiers, ham, cheese, bread & coffee. I found a good grocery near by Kept by an old Williamsburgher. "Aunty" the old black woman brought me corn cake, and from the Grocery I got eggs, strawberries, milk, &c. The Eutaw House[11] is near by where I could wash and bathe and I met there several Williamsburghers on their travels—Clinton Berry who lived opposite Mr Corwins died there last week. We were sworn into the service of the United States for 3 months. All but one in our company swore in—I went to the Col. and got a promise of a furlough for 30 days to go home and attend to my business whenever I wish (Ewell, Fish, Jackson, & Alderman Fish attend to it now)—The Col. says if McClellan is successful we shall all go home immediately. We got into camp yesterday from our guard duty and it was pleasant to get back again to our old quarters. I am excused from company and battalion drills to day being a little sick from drinking too much tea last night which had some Kind of herbs in it not raised in China—We had an immense crowd at our Dress Parade. a great many secessionists were present to hear our splendid band— Also several Officers of the 47th.[12] Lewis & Mr. Johnson have gone home and many other officers—Those military celebrities I will attend to. I have not had my photo taken—I am afraid it would not suit you—I look rather rough.

In reading your first letter a second time I am quite amused at your allusion to my feats and adventures. I am quite famous that way. It is one of the sunny features of a campaign and I make it pleasant while I can. There is a rumor today that we are going to Winchester—I have no particular ambition to go to battle but as a member of the Seventh I go with it wherever it goes. I have not heard from Henry. I will write him where he now is—It is possible that the Reg. may go to Washington. If possible I will go on there. I shall want first to hear from him—Remember me to all—All of you write often if only a few lines. Tell mother to write a short letter as to the plan of yours and Fannies. I will speak about it to the Colonel and tell him to hurry home the Regiment. Tell Father, Albert, & Johnny to write. I must write to Uncle F. today.[13]

Yours, Mellville

53

Camp Federal Hill
Baltimore, Md July 10 1862

Dear Aunt Howland,[14]

After a period of very hot weather, a North East storm has commenced and our Drills and parades are suspended. I shall to day answer some of my neglected correspondents and you among them—I have heard from you through several sources and also from Grandmother—You have heard of our change of camp to Federal Hill. I suppose It is a pleasant location over-looking the city of Baltimore and Chesapeake Bay and we generally have a sea breeze on the hottest days. Yesterday I went down to Fort McHenry in a Boat—It was a pleasant sail and quite a relief to get out of camp and enjoy the sea breeze. We had fishing tackle and I caught an Eel—at Fort McHenry the Williamsburgh 47th Regt are encamped. Col Joe Meserole Lieut Col. Sangster—Major Young &c., (formerly Elire Johnson was Major who returned and married Mrs Culbert)[15]—I visited them and dined with the officers—I Know most of them—[In] This weather our Barracks are more comfortable than tents—We sleep in Bunks arranged like the Berths of a steamboat—During the hot weather I have taken my Blanket and slept in the open air.

Before McClellans repulse [I] had expected that we should return by this time, but now we shall be detained the whole 3 months. Whether we shall go further South is uncertain—Baltimore is a slumbering volcano and the secession fires might burst forth at any time—We occupy an important position and I believe the government wish us to remain here—On the Fourth of July we fired [a] salute from our heavy guns and reverberations through the city must have made the secesh tremble—our duties here are not very arduous—We have our daily drills and parades and our turn at standing guard and various other matters to take up our time—I was on guard yesterday—In the afternoon I saw Dr. Cox in camp, the Rector of grace Church—He married a sister of the Hydes—[I] had a pleasant conversation with him.[16] He is a strong Union man and his congregations are rebels—

I have been to his Church since I have been here—I get a pass to go to town once a week and have seen the Cathedral, Monument Park, Mercantile Library and most places of public interest.[17]

12th   I have received a letter from Father to day & He says you are going to Neponsete and grandmother to No. Bridgewater. He says that Henry has recovered and will soon join his regiment—For some reason my letters fail to reach him. My health is very good and I hope I shall be quite hardy before the campaign is over. I was promised a furlough of 30 days by the Col. when I swore in but events since then may prevent my getting that time to go home and I think I should not ask it since the change in affairs. I had a letter from Jonnie at Amherst [and] also [one] from Augustus yesterday. I think I had better direct this to Neponset. I hope you will enjoy the summer—Please write me—letters are acceptable every day in camp. Remember me to all at Uncle Jabez and all my cousins.[18] Excuse my pencil lead. I hope you will be able to decipher it.

Yours,
Melville

54

Fort Federal Hill
Baltimore
July 23d 1862

Dear Father,

I enclose a pencil communication for the Gazette—If you have mind to ask Hannah or Albert to copy it or if they will take it as [it] is very well.

One of our company was in Washington the other day and just as he was getting into the cars came one stepped up and asked him if he knew me—He had just time to say yes and tell him I was well when the cars moved off—It was Henry. I wrote him enclosing a sheet of paper and stamp but [I] have received no answer. I am very well and getting fat—The weather has been very hot but now we have a North East storm.—

Your last letter said that Grand mother is with you or [is] expected to be—I hear so also from Aunt Belden at Amherst. if so remember me to her. I hope to see her if I can come home.

I shall try and get a furlough for 10 days on the 1st of August and more if possible—I went to church on Sunday where Mr. Hinkley preached. It is an old building, I think the oldest New Church structure in the country.[19] I have had a number of calls here and seen several Williamsburghers at the Hotels. We have had a number of distinguished visitors including Gen. Burnside.[20]

How do you get along for change[?] We are bothered here a great deal. I will write you more at length by and by—I hear from Williamsburgh often. All are well at Tarrytown. Remember me to all.

Are not you & Mother coming on to N. Y. to visit this year or Hannah[?] I will arrange about Johnny by and by.

Yours,
Melville

Chapter 5

"I HAVE SEEN DEATH IN EVERY SHAPE"

THE MARYLAND CAMPAIGN,
SEPTEMBER 1–DECEMBER 29, 1862

THE MARYLAND CAMPAIGN BEGAN STRANGELY FOR HENRY HAYWARD. On September 1 he received a special assignment. One day before being relieved of command, Major General Banks ordered a reconnaissance to ascertain the movements of Robert E. Lee's Army of Northern Virginia. Banks directed a member of his staff, Colonel John S. Clark, to select thirteen men from the 28th Pennsylvania to scout behind enemy lines. Officers from thirteen of the 28th Pennsylvania's fifteen companies each selected one man for this assignment. Lieutenant Joseph W. Hammar chose Hayward to represent Company D. Once assembled, the 28th Pennsylvania's scouts received orders to infiltrate Confederate lines near Centreville, move north toward the Potomac River, and send one man back through the lines each day to report the enemy's movements. When the party reached five members, the remainder could return.

This expedition ran into problems from the outset. The Battle of Chantilly unexpectedly delayed the scouts' incursion. They persisted with their endeavor, and on September 2 they gained access to Confederate lines near Vienna. On the fifth day, Confederate cavalry discovered their whereabouts and captured one member of the squad. Their mission now compromised, Sergeant Frank B. M. Bonsall of Company H, the detachment's senior member, decided to return to camp immediately. They learned what the army's senior leaders needed to know—Lee's army was on the move, heading north toward the Potomac River into Maryland. In a countryside now filled with stragglers, the 28th Pennsylvania's scouts encountered numerous Confederate soldiers and their African American servants searching for food. Each time, the

Pennsylvanians took them prisoner until their number of captives rose to nineteen. On the evening of September 6 the scouts intrepidly marched their prisoners across the Leesburg Pike in sight of countless enemy camps, and, astonishingly, the entire party reached the Potomac River undetected. Once there, Hayward and his comrades built a raft, crossed the river, and took their hostages to the Old Capitol Prison in Washington, D.C. They had spent seven days behind enemy lines eating only dried corn. Hayward referred to this scouting mission as "the boldest of the War."[1]

The scouts rejoined the regiment on September 8 to discover that their corps, the 2nd Corps, Army of Virginia, had been merged with the Army of the Potomac. Their corps now became the 12th Corps, Army of the Potomac, and its new commander was Major General Joseph K. F. Mansfield. Brigadier General George S. Greene commanded their division, the 2nd Division, and Lieutenant Colonel Hector Tyndale now commanded their brigade. Major Ariovistus J. Pardee Jr., son of a Hazleton coal baron, commanded the 28th Pennsylvania. While these command changes generally suited the Pennsylvanians, the appointment of Tyndale to brigade command greatly disturbed them. Major Pardee claimed that Tyndale was guilty of "overbearing conduct towards them," but "circumstances attending the campaign rendered it impossible then to wholly resent his tyranny and insolence." Pardee warned his father that Tyndale "has been most fortunate that we were not in a regular engagement as I fear he would, if the balls of the enemy spared him, been injured by his whole command."[2]

On September 9, the day after the scouts' return, the 12th Corps led the advance of the Army of the Potomac into Frederick, Maryland, where it arrived on September 13 at 11:00 A.M. In a nearby clover field, soldiers from the 27th Indiana fortuitously discovered an abandoned Confederate headquarters document that detailed the movements of the Army of Northern Virginia. This discovery prompted General McClellan to move his troops across Catoctin Mountain and South Mountain in an effort to engage the Confederate army before it captured the federal garrison at Harpers Ferry. Hayward and his comrades from the 28th Pennsylvania participated in several long marches, including a sixteen-mile night trek on September 14–15. The 12th Corps arrived at the village of Smoketown on September 16, northeast of the town of Sharpsburg. A few miles away, General Lee positioned his 39,000 soldiers along the banks of Antietam Creek, east of Sharpsburg, to defend against an inevitable attack delivered by the Army of the

Potomac. By most accounts, the Union march had been exhausting. As one chronicler later wrote, the men of the 28th Pennsylvania "were so overcome with fatigue and loss of sleep that they stacked arms and threw themselves down upon the plowed fields to seek the repose they so greatly needed."[3]

At first light on September 17, McClellan issued orders to the 1st and 12th Corps to drive the Confederate left flank toward Sharpsburg. After a hasty meal, Hayward and his comrades fell into line at 7:00 A.M. and marched to the sound of booming Confederate cannon posted on a rise called Hauser's Ridge. The 760 men of the 28th Pennsylvania led the brigade with the 5th, 7th, and 66th Ohio regiments—another 290 men altogether—following closely. Tyndale's brigade arrived at an open field northeast of what is today known as the East Woods. When it reached this field, it received rifle fire from Confederate skirmishers, wounding a few men. Beyond the woods the men of the 28th Pennsylvania could see a Confederate counterattack moving north, driving the panicked Pennsylvania Reserve Division through a large cornfield. The 28th Pennsylvania fixed bayonets and then leaped a stake and rider fence at the north edge of the East Woods.[4] The regiment punched in the right flank of Colonel Duncan K. McRae's North Carolina brigade and then paused along a fence separating the east edge of the cornfield from the west edge of the East Woods. Here the 28th Pennsylvania volleyed into the flank of another Confederate unit, Colonel Alfred Colquitt's Georgia and Alabama brigade. According to one Huntingdon County man from Company O, "At a word from Col. Tyndale . . . , one splendid burst of musketry came from the 28th directed in the corn. The Rebels, appalled by this unexpected and severe fire, fell back pell-mell in a perfect rout." A Hazleton man in Company A wrote home that, "We gave the war cry and in the corn field we rushed. Every corn stalk had a rebel. Here we mowed them down." Corporal John O. Foering of Hayward's Company D remembered, "The regiment poured such a murderous fire into their terror stricken ranks as to scatter them in every direction."[5]

The 28th Pennsylvania advanced southwest and into the cornfield with the Ohio regiments on its right. The 28th Pennsylvania's well-directed volley had filled the eastern portion of the field with the grim detritus of war.[6] Tyndale's brigade emerged from the south end of the cornfield and ascended a small crest northwest of the Samuel Mumma farm. Here Joseph M. Knap's battery and Captain John A. Tompkins's Battery A, 1st Rhode Island

Light Artillery, joined it. These two batteries protected the flanks as the brigade advanced west toward Dunker Church along the Hagerstown Road. At that moment, a Confederate counterattack, launched by Brigadier General Joseph B. Kershaw's South Carolina brigade, emerged from what is today called the West Woods, just behind the church. Tyndale's men dropped to the ground and waited until Kershaw's soldiers reached within fifty yards of their line, when, according to one participant, "our line sprang up and fired low and hurt their column most terribly." The 28th Pennsylvania advanced at a charge, routing the South Carolina brigade and capturing two artillery pieces abandoned by the Sumter Artillery. Here Hayward's tent mate, Corporal Jacob George Orth, captured the battle flag of the 7th South Carolina, after killing its bearer in a fierce hand-to-hand fight.[7]

Even though his men were no longer supported by other units, Tyndale pushed his brigade deep into the West Woods. There he ordered his men to use rocks, hollows, and crags to form a defensive position. Although three more regiments from other Union brigades came to reinforce Tyndale's errant battle line, both flanks were now unprotected. Tyndale admitted, "My position at this time was far in advance of our lines, and was, I believe, directly opposite the last position of the enemy and near the [Potomac] river bank, which commanded, I think, all positions in its front and rear." Tyndale correctly affirmed he had broken the Confederate line, and if he held this position long enough for reinforcements to arrive, the Confederate army would have had to retreat, if not surrender. However, Confederate officers vowed not to let Tyndale's soldiers remain in that position. Two more Confederate brigades —Brigadier General Robert Ransom Jr.'s brigade and Colonel Vannoy Manning's brigade—attacked Tyndale's position in the afternoon. According to Corporal John Foering, when Manning's brigade attacked from the left, "a panic seized the men and all the troops about the school house [Dunker Church] were compelled to fall back." By the time the 28th Pennsylvania commenced its withdrawal at 3:00 P.M., it had fought for nearly eight hours.

Throughout the battle, Henry Hayward displayed incredible bravery and pluck. He remained with his unit, even at its last stand. As the regiment retreated, Colonel Tyndale, who had just been shot off his third horse of the day, called for his troops to mount a final defense on the crest near the Mumma farm. Hayward paused with a small cluster of men from the 28th Pennsylvania and delivered a few parting shots as the remnant of his brigade retreated back to Antietam Creek. Meanwhile, Tyndale descended the small

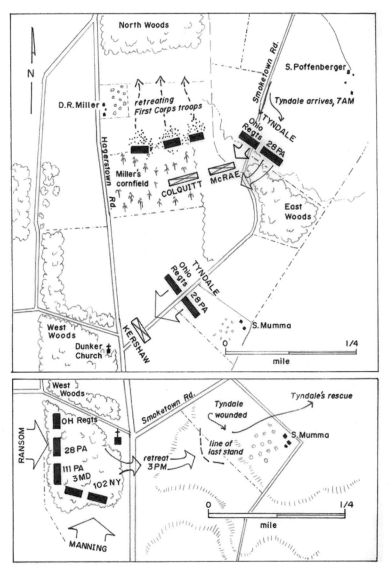

The Battle of Antietam, September 17, 1862. Map by John Heiser.

knoll and entered a field of hay mounds. He paused at a haystack, turning to the rear to entreat his men to retire in good order. Just then the Confederate line reached the crest and fired. A musket ball struck Tyndale in the back of his head and glanced downward into his neck, knocking him unconscious.

Hayward was among the last to leave the 28th Pennsylvania's final line of battle. As he retired, he passed Tyndale. Valiantly, Hayward began dragging his insensible commander from the field. Moments later, First Lieutenant Charles W. Borbridge of Company

I joined him and together they carried Tyndale to the rear. In what must have been a harrowing couple of minutes, Hayward, Borbridge, and Tyndale were exposed to a hail of enemy fire. At one point, a bullet passed through Hayward's cap, knocking it off his head. Hayward admitted to his brother, "there was no one who had a more narrow escape than myself. a ball knocked of[f] my cap and nearly took me from my feet. I put my hand up and saw there was no blood and Smiled." Eventually, Hayward and Borbridge transported Tyndale to safety, and through their courage, they saved his life. As they passed the Mumma farm, a brigade from the 6th Corps entered the fray and drove the Confederates back to the West Woods.[8]

The fight at Antietam cost the 28th Pennsylvania severely. The regiment took 760 men into the fight and lost 44 killed, 217 wounded, and 2 missing. The sight of the battlefield was traumatic in the extreme. The day after the battle, Hayward wrote to his father telling him how he thanked God for being allowed to pass through the "Blood[i]est Battle on record." Perhaps disturbed by the carnage, he continued, "I will not say much about the Bloody field for I saw sights to[o] horrible to relate. I have seen death in every shape." Nevertheless, the slaughter did not discourage his devotion to the cause. In the same letter, he reaffirmed, "I am well and in the best of Spirits. we must win."[9] In all, the Battle of Antietam—the single bloodiest day of the war—cost both sides 22,000 casualties.

The rescue of Lieutenant Colonel Tyndale earned Hayward great accolades from his comrades. Sergeant James C. Devine of Company D later remembered that Hayward's "conduct at this Battle cannot be surpassed." Another member of the 28th Pennsylvania marveled, "although greatly fatigued and exhausted from exposure, and scarcity of food, Sergeant Hayward was one of the most active in the battle of September 17th."[10] Although Tyndale was unconscious during the whole affair, he considered his rescue "a disinterested, noble, and courageous action." Strangely, Tyndale never learned the name of his benefactor. However, in 1871, during a speech before a group of veterans, Tyndale praised the valor of Borbridge and the corporal, "whose name is unknown," affirming that they "acted like true soldiers."[11]

The Army of Northern Virginia commenced its retreat on September 19, and the Army of the Potomac began its pursuit the next day. On September 21 the 28th Pennsylvania crossed the Potomac and entered Harpers Ferry, and on September 23 the Pennsylvanians established camp on Loudoun Heights. Four days later, amid much enthusiasm, General Geary returned from convalescence, taking command of the division to which the 28th Pennsylvania belonged. On October 2 President Lincoln reviewed Geary's division, and the men gave their commander in chief a twenty-one-gun salute. In mid-October Hayward received a temporary transfer to the pioneer corps, and for twenty days he commenced cutting timber for winter quarters. For a time it looked like the Army of the Potomac's active campaigning had ceased for 1862.

However, the army did not go into hibernation. On October 30 the 28th Pennsylvania removed to Bolivar Heights, and the next day, the War Department ordered the regiment's 3rd Battalion, consisting of Companies L, M, N, O, and P, to detach itself from the regiment and form Companies A, B, C, D, and E, 147th Pennsylvania Infantry. Major Pardee assumed command of the 147th Pennsylvania, now augmented by three fresh companies from Luzerne, Snyder, and Lehigh counties. At first the men of the 28th Pennsylvania vehemently protested the removal of the 3rd Battalion, but since these orders came from the War Department, they could do nothing but complain. Upon Pardee's promotion, command of the 28th Pennsylvania fell to Major William Raphael.

The 28th Pennsylvania continued campaigning into the winter. They regularly skirmished with Confederate forces during the next six weeks. On November 7 President Lincoln dismissed General McClellan, and two days later the Army of the Potomac's new commander, Major General Ambrose E. Burnside, commenced a campaign intended to put his army across the Rappahannock River by the end of the month. The advance elements of the 12th Corps began moving southeast to Leesburg and Fairfax to participate in this operation, but the 28th Pennsylvania remained behind at Bolivar Heights to decoy Confederate forces in the Shenandoah Valley. Meanwhile, Hayward's officers began filling the vacancies in Company D's noncommissioned staff. Hayward's valor at Antietam guaranteed his rapid advancement. On December 1 he received a promotion to fourth sergeant, surpassing six corporals ahead of him. Hayward told his sister, "I will only say that I have been a Marked man since the Battle of Antietam."[12]

The 28th Pennsylvania broke camp on December 10 and marched eight days to Dumfries, Virginia. Perhaps providentially, it did not arrive in time to participate in the bloody Union defeat at Fredericksburg on December 11–13. When the 28th Pennsylvania arrived at Dumfries, it rejoined its old brigade, now commanded by Colonel Charles Candy and containing the 147th Pennsylvania. On December 27–29, a portion of Geary's division halted a

Confederate cavalry raid launched by Major General James E. B. Stuart. After this, the Army of the Potomac received orders to construct winter quarters. Thus, after nineteen months of weary service, Hayward had yet to see an assured victory. Despite the accolades and honors he received for his participation in the daring scouting mission and his rescue of Hector Tyndale at Antietam, Hayward agonized to his father shortly before Christmas, "I do not think the Country is Safe."[13]

55

In Line of Battle near Frederick
Sept 11th

Dear Father,

We received notice that a mail would go to night. I am all right. [I am] in good health. [I have] no time to write. [The] mail has most gone. Gen Pope orderd 12 men from the 28th to go a Scouting. I was chosen from Co D. we left Bull Run Bridge [and] was gone 7 days. [We] joined the Regt at Rockville. we were 6 days in the Enemys lines. we were fired on by the Enemys the first time we tryed to go inside of their lines. the 5th day we were chased by the Rebel Cavalry near Aldie. [We] lost one man from Co B. we captured 16 Prisoners from Longstreetts and Jacksons Div. [—] Straglers. [We] built a raft at night and crossed the Potomac 5 miles below Leesburgh. [We] took the Prisoners to Washington. [We] met Col Clark of Banks Staff (the man that gave us instructions when we left). he reported it to Gen McClellen. he thanked us and orderd them to be turned over to the Provost Marshall. we took them to the Capitol Prison. I received your last letter with [a] Dollar enclosed [and] also papers. we expect a battle soon. I wish the Potomac would rise.

love to all,
Henry

when I get time I will write and give you more of the particulars about the Scouting party which was the boldest of the War.[14]

56

Sept 18th
Camp on the Field of Battle

Dear Father,

I thanked God last night that I was allowed to pass through the Bloodest Battle on record. our Brigade went in under the most discourageing circumstances. our men were being driven from their position and the shot and Shell had laid many low before we had got far to the front. we made a charge and drove the Rebels from the woods and continued on the advance untill we drove them from 3 fields. we took two peices of Artillery. our Regt has 5 Stand of collors. we counted 169 South Carolinians on one field this morning that we killed when they tryed to take a Battery that we were supporting.[15] it is hard to tell how many that are killed in the 28th, but they are many for we were under fire for 9¾ hours. our noble Col. Tyndale is dangerously wounded. Lt Borbridge and myself took him from the field. it happened when we were forced to retire towards night. he was one of the last to leave, beging the men to retire in order.[16] we were out flanked and the New York Regt broke through our ranks.[17] reinforcements came up and the rebels were driven back. we made for ourselves a name yesterday. we were highly complimented by Gen Williams[18] on the field. Gen W. Said the big Regt is doing the work and we were cheerd by the Ohio boys when we made the advance early in the day driving the Rebels before us. I will not say much about the Bloody field for I saw sights to horrible to relate. I have seen death in every shape. I must now close. a citizen will take this to Hagerstown. he is waiting. I am well and in the best of Spirits. we must win.

Corp A. Henry Hay

57

Sandy Hook, Sept. 21

Dear Brother [Augustus],

I received your last letter, also one from Mell. I went through the Bloody Battle of Sharpsburgh but how God only knows. our Brigade was brought up at a most discourageing time of the Battle. the Rebels were driving our men from the woods. we Advanced with a charge, driving the Rebels before us. Gen Williams made the remark that the Big Regt was doing the work this time. we still kept on the Advance untill we had drove them from 3 fields. at this time they had got 2 batterys to work on us. we held our ground and soon had a battery brought up to our support. the Rebels made a charge to take it but were repulsed with great Slaughter. the 28th took 4 stand of Collors and many prisoners. we killed Gen White. our Major has his horse.[19] the 28th won great praise from all the officers who wittnessed our advance. we were under fire for 9 hours. our foe was of the most desperate kind being South Carolinians and Texans. we lost many officers. Col. Tyndale acting Brigadier was mortally wounded and fell to the Ground. Lt. Borbridge and myself took him from the field. there was no one who had a more narrow escape than myself. a ball knocked of my cap and nearly took me from my feet. I put my hand up and saw there was no blood and Smilled. the loss in our Regt is about 45 killed and 210 wounded.[20] the Rebel loss is very heavey. we layed them out in 2 ranks. the Sights I have seen are to terrible to describe. I wish I could forget them. I will let you hear the rest from the papers. let Melville know that I am safe as soon as you get this. love to all. I am in good health.

Henry

58

Camp on Louden Heights Sept 28th

Dear Brother [Albert],

We have come to another halt and are now resting on the Mountains. Geary's Brigade was the first to cross the Potomac after the Great Battle of Antietam. the Bridges were all destroyed and so we had to ford it. we marched up through the town of Harpers Ferry, which looked as natural as when we left it nearly a year ago. when we arrived at Bolivar Heights we discoverd the Enemys Cavalry Pickets stationed on the Charlestown Pike. one Company was sent out to feel them and they disappeard. we occupied the place untill 3 ock P. M. the next day when Sumners Corps crossed.[21] the next day we were orderd to cross the Sheneandoah and climb the Mountains High. we done so, and for [it] we have been allowed to remain here in our Glory to rest nearly a week. I have often wished that some one of you at home could be here one evening to wittness a sun sett and look down on Harpers Ferry and see the camp fires of Sumner Corps. it was awfull cold sleeping up here for a few nights before we got our Knapsacks. we have great trouble in getting water, which we have to go at the foot of the Mt. to find, and such geting up Stairs you never did see. I think we earn our coffee when we get it. there was an unusual noisey time on Louden Heights Yesterday. (What for[?]) why[?] Gen. Geary made his appeerence and such a crazy set of boys could not be found in the Union army. the Capt of each Comp tried to form their men [in] front of their respective quarters and cheer him as he passed, but as soon as he showed himself they began to cheer all over the camp and the boys all made a rush towards him. he looks very well. his arm is yet tied up in a sling. he made a good speach to us, but as usual I can not think much of it. he said he was able to be with us once more and would take command in a few days. he said let the rebels attack Harpers Ferry now and we would see who would Hang out the White Flag. (9 cheers were given for that).[22] some of the Officers said last night that Geary said that he was going to take us of of this place [as] soon as possible. I wrote some time ago about a Scouting Party that left this Regt. I will now give you some Idea of what we went through and what a complete success it was. one non commissioned officer from 13 companies of the 28th were detailed to make up the party.[23] we received our instructions from Col.

Clark, Chief of Banks Staff.[24] he showed us with a map where the Rebels were supposed to lay and of their intentions to attack Washington. we were orderd to go light, takeing nothing but canteens and haversacks and Rifels. we had our choice going mounted or foot. we thought as we were to go where the Rebels we[re] so numerous we could get along better a foot. we were to send a man in every day untill the number should be reduced to 5, then we were all to come in. we had a pass that would take us any where in our lines (on to Richmond in the Rebels Lines). we could draw rations from any quarter master. we procured a Compass, Glass, and map and left Bull Run at 11 ock A.M. we expected to get through the Rebel lines at Centerville but when we reached our Picketts they told us it would [be] Impossible to get through there as they were skirmishing continuously with the Enemy. we moved on 9 miles further to the North. we did not find any of our Picketts here so we thought we could make another attempt. we moved cautiously through the woods untill we came to a cleared place. here we saw a farm House. we went up to it to enquire which way the Leesburg Pike was from there. we all layed down in a corn field waiting for the Seargent to come back who had gone to the House to get information. sudenly a volley of balls came hissing by, which caused us to retrace our steps at a double quick. fortunately no one was injured. when the Sergent came to us he said they told him at the house that we had better get away from there as our cavalry Picketts that were stationed there had been driven away 2 hours ago. we had not gone far before we met Karneys Div. in Battle Line and Skirmishers coming forward. we told the officer in command where we had been fired upon and where he would find the Rebels. they moved on and soon the Great Battle commenced in which Kearney and Steavens lost their lives.[25] we moved on for Fairfax, thinking it best not to attempt to enter their lines untill we had made many miles North. we Slept that night in Fairfax. we moved on again, in the morning feeling certain that we would have nothing to detain us on our night march except Gurillas, but those we could easily avoid. we passed through the villige of Vienna when we came suddenly upon 5 horsemen. 3 were Federal officers and 2 were Rebel Cavalry men who were escorting them to our lines to be released on their Parole. we watched them untill they had passed, then we moved on takeing a still more northerly direction. we sent our first dispatch in after we had met the Rebels with the officers. we now had 12 men.[26] we marched all that night to make up for the lost time as we had been marching away from the section of country that we were orderd to Scout, but we told Col. Clark in our dispatch that it was impossible to get into their lines at the place he thought we would be most likely to. we went around Drainsville at night. we could easily see the Rebels Cavalrys Pickets stationed near the town. we marched on for 3 days keeping [in] the woods most of the time. when we would gain a high bluff the Seargent in command[27] would go up a tree and take a survey with his glass. he could see Leesburg and the fortifications in Possesion of the rebels. the 4th night was one that we feared we would have trouble to make much advance. the Coctoctain Mt. were near at hand, and there was where we were orderd. for if we could reach the top, we could look down upon Aldie and the Valleys around. here we expected to find the Rebels encamped in mass, but we knew we should have some trouble in reaching it. we could see the rebels at the houses when we would come in sight of them. we came to the conclusion that we had arrived at the place where if we did not wish to be captured we must be very cautious. we saw the Rebel camp fires the day before and we knew by the direction that we had been travelling that we were among them. it was night but we were very tired and having a little coffee left in our haversacks we ventured to light a little fire in a deep gully where we then were resting. here we took out the map and with the aid of light of the burning embers tryed to study out where or near what place we had halted. we came to the conclusion that morning would find us near the base of the Mountain. our coffee being ready, we drank it, and like Soldiers we were soon at sleep with the night Owl for our guard. we saw by the morning light that we had not far to go to reach the base of our opperations and as we had not sent but one dispatch we were anxious to wait untill we could reach the Mt. we had one road to cross which gave us some uneasiness, for we had heard that night the enemys waggons moveing and the rumbling of Artillery over the Stoney road. each one being ready, we started and as we neared the road, one man was sent ahead to reconoiter while the rest of us laid low in the grass. suddenly 6 horsemen came out of the woods not far ahead and with revolvers drawn commanded us to halt.★[28] We Imediately beat a hasty retreat towards a thick wood with the Cavalry men in pursuit. but instead of going a great distance, we took the first place we came to that we thought would aford a suitable hideing place. soon the Rebels came dashing by and we breathed a little easier. yet we dare not move or speak above a whisper but must content ourselves with our situation untill darkness could assist us in our escape. we lay there all day, and a long one it was, for we had carried empty haversacks for 2 days past. once in the day we heard 2 men make the remark as they past us that they had searched the woods and could find no trace of them. when night came we took a vote as to what course would be best to pursue, to return or try to make the Mt. we were all of the opinion that as we had been discovered, search would be made in every quarter for us and we had learned from good authority that the Rebel army were moveing towards Leesburgh. so we came to the conclusion that if we could reach our lines safe, Col. Clark would be sattisfied. we got our party togeather and found that one man was missing.[29] we supposed that he had got behind when the Cavalry pursued us and we thought he might be the cause of having us all captured if he should let out anything when they questioned him. and for that reason we made quick time that night and reached goose creek early in the morning. (now the laugh comes in) as we came to a road and were about to cross we noticed 3 men dressed in grey armed and equiped dogeing behind trees. at first we attempted to avoid them for we felt certain they were on our track with more men behind them to assist, but we soon noticed they were the frightened men as well as ourselves. but we being the stronger party, we walked up to them and took them prisoners. they were much astonished to meet Yankees so far within their lines. we took their arms and equipment and threw them into the stream, [and] asked them some questions, which they readily answered. they said they belonged to Jackson Div, which had been moveing that night toward Leesburgh, and that they were stragilers in search of food. they said that the country around for miles were full of them and they thought we would find some trouble in makeing our way, especialy across Leesburgh Pike. we stood talking for some minutes meditateing on what course to pursue. some were in favor of leting them go, while most of us thought that our owne safety depended on keeping them. while we were talking we heard more voices coming the same way. one of the prisoners said there comes more of them, and sure enough another squad of 4 came in sight. we boldly walked up to them, for we had made up our minds to make a business of it as we could not help it. we took their arms from them, and all moved on thinking more might come and turn the tables on us. we could hear reports of musketts in every direction. the prisoners told us that it was the straglers shooting their breakfast. as we walked on we began to get quite familiar with the strangers, who by the way were quite respectable for Rebels, as they belonged to Georgia and Louisianna Regt. they told us they beleived they had fell in with pretty good boys and were very well satisfied. we were carefull to be very polite to them for we knew not at what minute we might come up with a large party of grey backs and be obliged to change arms. we thought we could get along very well if we met with no more, as there was 11 of us and 7 Rebels. but what they told us about finding the woods full of men proved true for we soon came up with another party of 3 and 2 Blacks cooking their breakfast. we served them like the first. [We] disarmed them, and through their equipments in to the drink. we told them to fall in and we moved on. we now had arrived near to Leesburgh Pike, but to cross it was another thing. we halted. the Sergeant in Command went ahead to see if it would do to attempt it. he came back with the word that the road was full of Straglers and army waggons going towards Leesburgh. we retraced our steps untill we came to a thick bushy place which was to be our hideing place for the day and where we must wait and watch our Prisoners untill darkness would once more assist us in our bold adventure. it was a riskey thought, but the only alternative left us. the Rebels were hungry for we had disturbed their meal. but we suffered with them for we had tasted nothing but roasted corn and green apples for 3 days. we thought we would venture to build a fire and go for corn and as one of the party had yet enough coffee left for another meal. we set about to get a little grub. we were not long in getting breakfast and when we invited the poor Reb to take hold and share it with us they seemed to be much pleased. they thought the salt was much better than they got, of a finer quality, and the coffee was something they had not tasted since secesh broke loose. as we sat talking, the guard which we had put out to the right and left had discoverd more Rebels coming lazily towards where we were. 3 or 4 of our men went out and hailed them and brought them in. they were much surprised to see more of their companions in the same fix. we wished they had not come. we did not want them, but to let them pass after we had been discovered would certainly result in our capture. soon another squad came along. we came to the conclusion that the smoke from the fire drew them towards us. we put out the fire and gave orders to the prisoners to talk very low. we had yet 5 hours before we could move, and if we could live that long without being discovered we should be very thankfull. but before night the number of our strangers black and white were 19. our number was 11. we looked at each other and wonderd if we should ever be fortunate enough to hand them over to Gen Banks and say these are our Prisoners. no, I could not think it. it seemed so impossible for as night approached fires were being lit up all around us and 2 Rebel soldiers had passed us on the opposite side of the creek, but seeing more grey backs than blue (most of us hideing) they only remarked see the straglers. when it was dark enough to crawl out of our hideing place, we got the prisoners in line and their names were called (which had been taken during the day) and formed into a line. one man was missing. he was one that was taken last and belonged to the 34 Va Regt of Longstreetts Div.[30] he seemed to have a dread of us and supposed one would kill him if he did not make his escape. we started but you can not Imagin my feelings for the boldest and most dareing part was to come. we had to pass Leesburgh Pike and in every direction your eyes would turn you could see nothing but the fires of the Straglers. we thought to go around would excite suspicion, but to walk boldly through them we might be taken for Strglers. so on we went, carrying our arms at a secure. we passed within 10 feet of a fire where 3 men were cooking. one says there is yankees. no says another, they are only Straglers. the reason they did not suspicion us was because there was so many more Grey backs than blue, and many of their men wear our uniforms. the prisoners could have gone their way if they had been so disposed. a little yell from them to their comrades at the fires would have brought hundreds to their assistence, but for some reason unknown to us, they held their place, and when we had got out of sight of the fires, we took a look not expecting to see them at all, but they were all true prisoners of war, except one of the cufferys who had given us the slip. but at one time I did not know wheather I was a prisoner or had prisoners in charge. this was one of the most dareing acts of the war, but even now we did not feel certain of our Safety for we might be pursued by their cavalry who might be put on our track by the man that got away from us. but no they did not come. we reached the banks of the Potomac and thanked God that we were safe. but we are not yet on Union Soil, but in a dangerous place between Leesburgh and Drainsville. we now lay down to rest while the Seargent goes to make a survey of the Country and see if he can find a boat or a ford to cross. he comes back and says the River is deep. we shall have to build a raft. well, there was no time to lose for we had 6 hours untill Sunrise. we marched up to a shed near the bank of the river [and] put the prisoners into it. they layed down and soon fell asleep. we put two guards over them while the rest of us worked to build a raft. after a considerable hard labor and wet feet to bost, we were ready to commence to cross. it would only hold 2 Rebels and with one of our men to push it we worked this way untill nearly 7 ock in the morning and then there was 3 Rebels to cross an 4 of us. one of our party discoverd a boat in a Sluice way which was soon halled out. it was a large one and would have put us all over in 3 trips. we that were left jumped aboard and were soon out in the stream where we could safely say good bye old Virginia. little did we think that while we were stealing away from the banks of the virginia Side with our precious load of Rebels that the army of Jackson & Longstrett were crossing into Maryland. where we had landed was an Island,[31] but we knew we were safe, with a good boat tied near by so we took our time and Yankee and Rebel set to work roasting corn and washing and cleaning perparetory to our triumphant march into Maryland. we were awfull hungry, in fact nearly starved, and we were not long in getting ready to push for the Union side of the river. when we landed we put them in 2 ranks and marched them down the tow Path. we now began to feel our authority and if we wanted to give an order we would do it and see that it was obeyed. the first stopping place we came to was a Cannal Lock. here we found a Federal Pickett Post. we halted here. 3 of our men went in search of food. they soon came back with a Ham and Plenty of bread. we Sliced it up and the Rebels walked in without being asked. we had to scrabble to get our share. a Union man that we got the Provisions from told us that we had better move down as soon as possible as the Rebel Cavalry were not far of. this astonished us. but we did not know anything to the contrary as we had been in the woods for 6 days. so we pushed on as fast as possible. we soon came to a canal boat which had stoped I suppose to hear the latest news from up the river. we told them it would not do to go on with that boat. he had better turn around Imediately. he did so, and we jumped aboard with our Prisoners and blessed the man that first invented the canal boat). It was now one week since we left our Regt. and this was the first time that we felt at ease, knowing that we were out of range of the Enemys Rifels. so you can judge for yourselves whether or no we were not a jolly crew. the Rebels attracted much attention as we passed by the different Villeages along the canal. after a long ride of 8 hours, we made the city of George-town, and it being quite late in the evening, we concluded to take up with the convienecs of the boat for a nights rest. by this time, the Seargent in Command who had been to report to the Provost Marshall returned with 12 men for Guard, which releived us from that duty, and we all were soon rocked in the cradle of the deep. we were awakened in the morning by the bugle call at Fort De Kalb which was not far distant, and once more (and we hoped for the last time) we called the roll of the traitors, for we had been in their company for so long that we were tired of seeing them and longed to meet once more the Union boys of the 28th. the Roll being called and all present, we started for the Soldiers Retreat. here we found Breakfast wait-ing and we walked in. poor Secesh smiled as he walked up to the table and grasped a peice of roast beef in one hand and a slice of warm bread in the other and a cup of Hot coffee near his plate. one of them said I reckon this is good living. very good said I. eat plenty of it. we have a great abundece of it, and I reckon they did for we had our segars half smoked up before they thought of leaving. and when they did get through they took a Sly glance at the table and fragments and as much as to say good bye. I shall never look back upon the like again. the Foreman of the Saloon filled up their Haver-sacks and we left for the Office of the Provost Marshalls. after a few ques-tions, we were orderd to take them to the Old Capitol Prison. we baught them some tobaco. they thanked us for the kind treatment which they had received from us while in our hands. we bade them adieu and hand them over to the Turnkey. after remaining in Washington a day we started to join our Regt which we found near Rockville Md. the Col was much surprised to see us as they had us returned on the Rolls as Prisoners. there was a gen-eral order issued from Gen Banks Headquarters complimenting us very highly for carrying out what they called the most daring feat of the War.[32] it was read [in] front of our Regt and 3 Cheers given with a will for the dare-ing Scouts of the 28th.

I receive all of the Gazzetts your father sends and all letters from home. I have been looking anxiously for those Photographs and hope to see them soon. if we had not gained the late Victory of the Battle of Antietam you would not have received this long letter. tell father I only want those small notes so I can Celebrate more extensively for we are now in the land of

Peaches, Tomattoes, Eggs, butter, and onions, &c., &c. enclosed you will find a peice of the Battle Flag of the 7th South Carolina Regt. George Orth, my mess mate, shot the traitor that waved it and took it from him. yesterday an order came to hand it over to headquarters as there had been an order issued to that effect from Gen Mcllelan.[33] he was so provoked by it that he tore of a Star and I tore of this peice. with much love to all I will now Close.

if I get another spell like this one I will tell you more about the battle of Sharpsburgh, that is what it should be called.

I remain in good health,
Corp. A. Henry
Hayward

P.S. give my best respects to Rufus Brett and Fred and all the boys. I should be happy to hear from them.

[*on back of the letter*] An account of our Scouting and position. Please preserve.

59

Camp on Louden Heights

Dear Father,

Yours of the 7th was received last night. Coras Came the night before, and I must say was the most wellcome. those faces looked so natural. I went to my Knapsack and brought Alberts out and arranged them according to age and then took a good long gaze at them. Augustus sent me his baby a few days ago. so you see I have quite a family. most of the boys have their Papas & Mamas with them. I should like to have mine. I should like to know in your next if you received all the letters I have wrote since the battle of Antietam. I sent the first one by a Citizen to Hagerstown. I wrote another from Sandy hook. did you get the Peice of Rebel flag[?] we have changed our camp about a mile from where the old camp was but no nearer a Spring. Abe Lincoln made us a ball last week. we fired a Salute and used him well as we could considering our situation.[34] they send up a balloon from Sumners Corps every day. we have a fine view from our camp. the mail carrier is one of my mess. he took the Position yesterday. he is arranging the mail now and is nearly ready to go, so I must make haste. I send in this mornings edition a few notes about the 28th which I suppose you are Interested in. the one headed Honor to the Brave I cut out of the Philadelphia Press which came to one of my mess mates.[35] I will write soon, perhaps Sunday to Cora.

in haste
Henry

60

Oct. 19th

Camp on Louden Heights

Head Quarters, Co. "D" 28th Regt 186[2]

Dear Brother [Augustus],

I received your last with the baby enclosed. I do not know when I have been so pleased as I was to get that little picture. when ever I feel cross, I go to my knapsack and take a look at the little chub and go away smileing. I have Coras and Johny Parker and Alberts, which I value highly. we have been laying in Camp here for a long time. from our camp you can look down to Harpers Ferry where Sumners Corps lays. it is quite a sight to look down upon their camps at night when the fires are all burning and the tents lighted up. we saw the engagement between our reconoitreing Party and the Rebels. we see them disperse the Rebels and advance to Charlestown. I think there will be a forward move soon. they send up a balloon often during the day. they seldom go as high as we are. every thing looks as if we might make a long stay here, but it will not do to put much faith in it for you can never be certain of anything connected with Millitary affairs. I am on detached duty for 20 days. the Party consists of a Lieut, 2 Seargents, 4 Corp, and 100 men. they are all armed with axes and are to work claring off the Mt. they will soon begin the Forts which are to be built here to command the Ferry. Geary is in Command, so they will not be built to be Surenderd. we have lately received a new supply of Clothing which we are very much in need of. I throwed away my overcoat and gum Blankett and Shelter tent just before we went into the fight at Antietam. we wore them straped around us, and they were much in the way to load and fire. I have got every thing but a rubber Blankett. I shall get one of them when I am paid off. we expect Sibleys Tents this week. we might as well have more of the Shelter tents. I beleive I have a letter from Melville which remains unanswerd. I shall try and do so soon but I have no time to myself, only Sundays. I get 25 cts. a day extra. I have nothing to do, only to watch to see that trees dont fall on me. I never was in better health. hopeing that the Country will yet be safe.

I remain Your Brother

Corp. A. Henry

Hayward

61

Dear Father,

The last time I wrote I was on Picket, but I noticed from reading your last that you had not then received it. last Sunday morning we were orderd out from under our blanketts at 2 oclk to procede on an other reconoisance. we passed the fires of the enemys out post before daylight, reached Charlestown before the breake of day. we halted there about one hour, and while our Artillery were shelling the woods where the rebels had fled, we were busy searching houses for the Rebels and we were quite successfull. having gatherd in about 20 Grey Backs, we were soon orderd (the 28) down the Berryville Pike with 2 peices of Artillery. When we [were] seeking the Rebels, we would open on them with shell. we marched in line of Battle for 3 miles through woods and over fields which was very tiresome. Gen Geary, thinking that he had punished the Rebs enough for captureing 3 of our boys, orderd us back. we reaching Bolivar, 9 ock Sunday Eve, having marched the distance of 22 m, with only [an] hours rest in Charlestown. while we were in that place, a fugitive [slave] was seen coming over the hill swinging his hat and takeing up the whole road to himself. he bowed to everyone he met as they all do, but this one more than usal polite, and he kept the boys in a roar of laughter as he passed by us. he said he had been trying to get with us a long time. one of my Company pointed to his feet size 21½ and asked him what he called them things. dem dems my boots. days going to take me de oder side of de ribber, right straight. and off he went through Charlestown without waiting for Gearys command to insure his protection. another little incident occured which may be of interest to the ladys of the house. one of our boys was in one of the fine houses in Charlestown when the lady of the house asked him if he had any tobacco. when he produced a plug which the high born Southern lady offerd him 50 cts for it, and when she had finished her purchase begged of him if he should chance to come this way again to bring her some and she would pay him any price for it. (how have the mighty fallen). can you beleive it[?] that high born Southern Madam would stoop so very low as to ask a yankee mudsill for a chew of tobacco. but it is even so (Cora I am glad you dont Chew tobacco).

Gen. Geary is acting Major General. we consider ourselves in winter Quarters. we expect to be payed off soon. I received $1.05 in U.S. Scrip. Little Mac is down as fast as he came up. he should have gone up by degrees to have been successfull. I do not beleive he ever was a corporal [*Hayward has drawn in corporal stripes here*].[36] the change suits every one as far as I can hear. I never have seen him, the Napoleon of France in the Washington of America. everyone who survived the Battle of Antietam layed down that night with the expectation of a renewal of the Battle with the rising of the sun, and why was it not done little Mac only knows. Yet he is a good General, so is Geary, and Banks. these are fearfull times and I feel sometimes as if the country would never survive the shock. it seems to me that there are men in the North who would give to Jeff Davis the Stars and Stripes to trample under his feet for the sake of the Office. if you look back to one of my letters I wrote from Phil-d you will notice that I then said that I thought America had seen its best days. I still hold to that Opinion. my Rifel is in good condition.

I remain in good health,
Corporal A. Henry
Hayward

Brother John, you wrote an excellent letter. I shall have something to say to you. I am looking for a letter from Cora every day to know about her visit to Boston. Send a few letter Stamps.

[*upside down on last page*] (Better late than never. Friday Nov. 14th)

62

Nov. 24th
Camp on Boliver Heights
Head Quarters, Co. "D" 28th Regt. 186[2]

Dear Brother [John Parker],

I was much pleased with your letter, and I hope you will make me glad again by writing me another soon. my Brigade has been out for six days past protecting the workman. 1000 Axeman have laid the trees low from the Shenandoah to the Potomac. we have left the Charlestown Pike open for Jackson to come and see us. we can bring three batterys to bear upon this road, and with the Rifel pitts and Breast works that are built and are yet to be built, we can hold this place as long as we can get amunition and Supplys. as we were coming in the other night, we met one of the F.F.V.[37] who had been stoped by our Pickets. he was makeing for Charlestown. he had two fine carriges with him, one with his Servants and Baggage while he and his family occupied the other. his horses had already been turned towards the Ferry and he sat weeping as we passed. I wondered as I passed him if he was weeping tears of pity for (U.S.) poor yankees as we trudged along through the rain and mud or because he had a dispatch hid in his boots that he was afraid would not reach secesh Headquarters in time. while we have been out we have found a number of new tents at the different houses which were carried off by the farmers. they use them to make bays and wagon Covers. we brought in 4 the last day. the Citizens of Boliver tell us that the Morning of the Surrender the farmers had their teams all back in the woods ready to drive in here and load up. they even came as far as Winchester. so certain were they that Miles would Surrender.[38] where we found tents and horses at the same house, we would borrow the horse to bring it to camp. we done this the other day at a farmers when the old hen came flying out at us. says she, ye didint come here arter the Rebels but to steal horses, and you orter be ashamed of yourselves. the Secesh call Geary the Kansas Ruffian. prehaps he is. I know he is Ruff on Secesh. 3 more of the 7th Ohio were captured while we were out the other day. the way they do it they leave the command to go out forageing (which is against orders) with out their arms. Geary gave orders the next day to our Pickets to shoot any one they saw out again. we open the Dramatic Season with a performance on Christmas. tell Father when he writes to tell me how to direct to J. W. Freeman. if ther can be another Gazzette with my letter in [it] procured at the Office send it. tell Father we do not expect to be payed off untill the first of Jan. I want Boots and Gloves, &c., &c.. Consequently Send me $10.

I remain in good health,
Corp. A. Henry
Hayward

I forgot to mention that we were called out the other day to repell the Advance of the Rebels who were seen coming this way. a few shots from our Battery turned them. we are always on the alert, awaiting orders to up and at them.

P.S. Thanksgiving Morn 27th

we returned from a reconoitering expedition last night. we were gone all day. [We] took some prisoners and any quanity of poultry. I have just got up from a Chicken stew and I must go and dress the other for dinner. you know I am an old hand at it.

love to all,
Henry

63

Dec 9th
Camp on Boliver Heights
Head Quarters, Co. "D" 28th Regt. 186[2]

Dear Sister,

I hasten to inform you that we are again on the move. we brake camp tomorrow at 5 ock A.M. I can form no Idea of where we are going. there are all kinds of rumors going about camp. I think we shall go to Fredericks-burg. tell Father that the $10 came in good time. I found it waiting for me after I got back from Winchester. You should not have expected me to be promoted untill there was a vacancy. that has occured. I am now fourth Sergeant.[39] I have no time to dwell upon the subject. I will only say that I have been a Marked man since the Battle of Antietam. my Boots are well greased for the March. the taps will soon sound, and the candle must go out. if I get a chance I will write again soon.

love to all,
Sergeant A. Henry
Hayward

Sergeant Edwin F. Paul is now a Prisoner at Winchester. he was taken on our return near Charlestown. I was promoted the night before we went to Winchester.[40] I went over the heads of six Corporals.

64

Camp on Occoquan River
Dec 20th

Dear Father,

the Postmaster just came in and says that a mail will go in 1 hour. it is now 8 ock P.M. and I have no time to write much.

I do not think the Country is Safe. love to all.

Sergeant A. Henry H.

65

Camp on Occoquan Creek, Dec 23d
Head Quarters, Co. "D" 28th Regt 186[2]

Dear Father,

It has been very cold here the past week. to day it is more mild, and I dare attempt to write a few lines. you must not expect any more long letters for the present but short ones and oftener. we were 8 days on the march from Boliver. we came to a final halt near Dumfries. the last day we made but 2 miles. we had to make roads through swamps by cutting down trees. it was intended that we should reach Fredericksburg in time to lure our part in the final assault but we stuck fast in the mud—both Seigel[41] and Geary. if you would like to form a faint Idea of the kind of road we had to travel, go find the muddyest place in Vinegar Swamp[42] then Imagin the soil yellow instead of Black. we heard all kinds of rumors while on the march. some times they were favorable and other times unfavorable. we were soon orderd backward and have been resting here since. we soon learned the facts that Burnside had been repulsed.[43] every one felt down hearted, for we had thought that the days of serious reverses had past and we had a night to think that with the great numbers that we had in the field under an experienced General would gladen our hearts with Victory. I have not yet wrote a complaining letter, and I do not intend to now, but I will say with a heart yet determined that I would like to see this great Slaughter of human beings brought to a close only with the Union as it was. we will take heart and look and wait for Banks or the Mississipi Expedition.[44] we have rumors in camp of a march to morrow. as usal we are going everywhere but nobody knows for certain where. my dutys now are much lighter than when I was a Corporal. I stand the winter weather thus far very well. we have not had much snow. we have not seen the Pay master yet. I was very fortunate in receiving that $10 before I left Boliver. if you can form any Idea what is going to become of Uncle Abe and his Government let me know in your next. I must stop here to write to Mell. love to all.

I remain in good health,
Sergeant A. Henry
Hayward

(a few more letter Stamps if you please)

First Sergeant Ambrose Henry Hayward. This photograph, mentioned in one of his letters to his father, was taken in Philadelphia on Hayward's veteran furlough in February 1864. Note Hayward's recently acquired first sergeant's stripes on his upper sleeve and his "veteran's service stripe" on his cuff, a symbol of his recent reenlistment as a "veteran volunteer." Courtesy of the Military Order of the Loyal Legion of the United States, Military History Institute (elsewhere abbreviated as MOLLUS-MHI).

Colonel John White Geary, shown here as commander of the 28th Pennsylvania. A stern disciplinarian, Geary impressed and inspired his men. During the war, he rose gradually, reaching the rank of brevet major general by the war's end. He also commanded the White Star Division, to which the 28th Pennsylvania belonged. Courtesy of MOLLUS-MHI.

Lieutenant Colonel Hector Tyndale. This gruff Philadelphia abolitionist eventually rose to brigade command. At Antietam Hayward saved his life by dragging him off the field after a gunshot wound to the back of the head had rendered Tyndale unconscious. Courtesy of the Military History Institute (elsewhere abbreviated as MHI).

Second Lieutenant Joseph W. Hammar eventually rose to the rank of captain and commanded Company D throughout many of its toughest engagements. In mid-1863 General Geary forced him to resign because of his poor performance at Chancellorsville. Courtesy of MHI.

First Sergeant Edwin F. Paul wrote a letter to Hayward's father on July 9, 1862. Paul feared that Hayward's illness might prevent him from returning to the army. In December, Confederates captured Paul and paroled him, an event that caused his reduction to private. Courtesy of MHI.

Sergeant Edward Pepper received a surgeon's discharge in November 1862, but he continued corresponding with his friends in Company D, even letting Hayward stay at his house while he was on furlough. Courtesy of MHI.

Color Sergeant Jacob George Orth was one of Hayward's tent mates. At Antietam Orth captured the battle flag of the 7th South Carolina, an act that earned him the Medal of Honor. Orth was the only soldier from the 28th Pennsylvania to earn such a distinction. At Chancellorsville he received a wound to the leg that put him out of service. Courtesy of MOLLUS-MHI.

Sergeant William H. Hiles was one of Hayward's close friends in Company D. On May 7, 1863, he died of a gunshot wound that he received to his leg during the Battle of Chancellorsville. Courtesy of MHI.

Major Lansford Foster Chapman commanded the 28th Pennsylvania at Chancellorsville. Chapman complimented Hayward for leading the regiment in its heroic charge. Moments later a Confederate ball claimed Chapman's life. Courtesy of MHI.

Captain John Hornbuckle Flynn commanded the 28th Pennsylvania during the Gettysburg and Atlanta campaigns. Although widely despised by his men, Flynn built up an impressive army career, and he ended the war as a brevet brigadier general. Courtesy of MHI.

Corporal Henry C. Fithian was one of Hayward's closest companions. Present in every major battle with the 28th Pennsylvania from the beginning of the war, Fithian was killed by Hayward's side at the Battle of Taylor's Ridge, November 27, 1863. He is now buried in Chattanooga National Cemetery. Courtesy of MOLLUS-MHI.

Sergeant John Oppell Foering had strong political connections in Philadelphia, and during Company D's veteran furlough he unsuccessfully schemed to steal the second lieutenancy from Hayward. Although his actions bore no fruit, Pennsylvania's adjutant general declined Hayward's advancement also. Following Hayward's death at Chattanooga, Foering rose rapidly through the ranks, ending the war as a captain. Courtesy of MHI.

Sergeant Henry Shadel, one of Hayward's tent mates later in the war, survived a wound at Gettysburg and served during the Atlanta Campaign. Courtesy of MHI.

The Battle of Pine Knob. On June 15, 1864, at Pine Knob, Georgia, the three brigades of Geary's White Star Division charged a series of log redoubts defended by Confederates commanded by Major General Patrick Cleburne and Major General William H. T. Walker. Although the Confederates retreated the next day, Geary's division lost eighty-two men killed and mortally wounded, among them First Sergeant Ambrose Henry Hayward, who died of his wounds four days after the battle.

Veterans of the 28th Pennsylvania at a reunion and dedication ceremony on Lookout Mountain, November 15, 1897. From *Pennsylvania at Chickamauga and Chattanooga*.

Hayward's grave marker in Chattanooga National Cemetery. Editor's photo.

Chapter 6

"THESE ARE AMERICA'S DARK DAYS"

WINTER QUARTERS,
DECEMBER 29, 1862–APRIL 27, 1863

ON DECEMBER 30 THE 28TH PENNSYLVANIA ESTABLISHED WINTER quarters at Dumfries, Virginia, and it remained there for sixteen weeks. During that period, a number of major military and political changes occurred. On January 1 President Lincoln's Emancipation Proclamation—announced on September 22—went into effect, freeing all slaves held in rebellious territory. Unlike many Union soldiers, Hayward did not express a strong opinion about this sweeping decision. However, he wrote one brief passage to his father: "to day the niggers are free. I wish Father Abraham would hurry up and free us." In all probability, Hayward's apathy did not reflect a shallow commitment to Lincoln's declaration. Although he never considered Lincoln a good president, Hayward staunchly supported the Republican administration throughout the war. His hope that Lincoln would "hurry up and free" the soldiers most likely expressed his fervent desire to do battle with the Confederate army again and bring an end to the war sooner rather than later.[1]

Hayward expressed his political opinion more openly when he discussed the Copperheads, the antiwar bloc of the Democratic Party. In response to the Union defeats at Fredericksburg and elsewhere, and also to the Democratic resurgence in the autumn congressional elections, antiwar Copperheads denounced the Lincoln administration, arguing that it had tyrannically mismanaged the war. An Ohio congressman, Clement Laird Vallandigham, led this charge. On January 14, 1863, during the third session of the Thirty-seventh Congress, Vallandigham, then "a lame duck," delivered the first in a series of antiwar, anti-administration speeches on the floor of the House of Representatives. Vallandigham told his Republican opponents:

> [Y]ou have not conquered the South. You never will. . . . The war for the Union is, in your hands, a most bloody and costly failure. The President confessed it on the 22d of September, solemnly, officially, under the broad seal of the United States. And he has now repeated the confession. The priests and rabbis of abolition have taught him that God will not prosper such a cause. War for the Union was abandoned; war for the negro openly begun, and with stronger battalions than before. With what success? Let the dead at Fredericksburg and Vicksburg answer. And, now, sir can this war continue? . . . I answer, no —not a day, not an hour.[2]

When news of Vallandigham's dissent reached the 28th Pennsylvania's camp, Hayward seethed over the notion that a northern congressman would dare consider armistice with the South. To Hayward, Vallandigham was a traitor of the worst kind, a northern rebel who stabbed Union soldiers in the back. On March 1 Hayward wrote his sister: "it seems that the good time has not yet come. they say the War must go on. I say let the war go on untill every traitor Copperheads and all are made to kneel to the Godess of Liberty. . . . I beleive that if such men as Vallandingham should come here and talk the way he does in Congress the Soldiers would kill him. we must have victory . . . to give our troops confidence and silence traitors in the North."[3]

Hayward was not alone in his anger. Many other soldiers in his regiment, regardless of their political affiliation, believed as he did. One member of the 28th Pennsylvania wrote, "We know we have a viler enemy in our rear than in our front. . . . The Rebels at home, it seems to us here, do not comprehend the full scope of their treason. They seem to think they are in the midst of a political campaign instead of the existence of the nation being at stake."[4] The days Hayward spent at the 28th Pennsylvania's winter quarters gave him time to reflect upon his personal conviction to the cause, and he ended up explaining to his sister why he chose to serve in the Union army in the first place: "these are the old original times that tried mens souls. these are Americas Dark days and if I live to see her pass through them and come out whole then my fondest hopes are realized." More than anything, Hayward hoped to live once more in a restored Union.[5]

It did not take long for Hayward and his comrades to put their feelings into words. On March 28 a committee from the 28th Pennsylvania drew up a series of eleven resolutions condemning the actions of the Copperheads. These resolutions encouraged the people of the North to "waive party prejudices, and unite heart and soul in the suppression of treason and the maintenance of consolidated authority." They also supported Lincoln's suspension of *habeas corpus,* approved the formation of Union League clubs, encouraged vigilante efforts to curtail Democratic dissent, spurned all proposals for armistice, and condemned Copperheads as "traitors of the worst class." The 28th Pennsylvania's officers forwarded these resolutions to several Pennsylvania newspapers, and Hayward happily clipped out a printed copy and sent it home to his parents to show what he and his comrades had done.[6]

A number of major organizational changes took place during this time. On January 26 Major General Joseph Hooker took command of the Army of the Potomac. In preparation for a spring campaign, Hooker held frequent reviews and inspections. He also initiated an army-wide system of identification. Hooker required all his troops to wear a badge, the shape and color of which identified each soldier's divisional affiliation. By regulations, soldiers in the 1st Division of each corps received a red badge, soldiers in the 2nd Division of each corps received a white badge, and soldiers in the 3rd Division of each corps received a blue badge. Hooker selected a star-shaped badge to represent the 12th Corps. Thus, since the 28th Pennsylvania belonged to the 2nd Division, 12th Corps, it received a white star badge. The soldiers in the 28th Pennsylvania—and the rest of the 2nd Division, for that matter—enjoyed this insignia immensely. It became a symbol of pride for them, and they proudly referred to themselves as the "White Star Division." In all, Hooker's changes breathed life into a despondent army. One Pennsylvanian wrote, "Our troops are in fine spirits and condition. Everything has combined, it seems, to enliven and inspirit us. General Hooker's efforts to remodel and improve the discipline of the whole command are felt in a very great degree here."[7]

Command changes occurred at other levels, too. Major General Henry W. Slocum, a New York Democrat, assumed command of the 12th Corps. Geary still retained command of the 12th Corps' 2nd Division, but Colonel Charles Candy permanently took command of the 1st Brigade, replacing the incapacitated Hector Tyndale. The 28th Pennsylvania also underwent a command change. Since November 1862, after Major Pardee resigned to accept command of the 147th Pennsylvania, Major William Raphael had commanded the regiment. However, General Geary disliked Raphael, and he used his authority as head of the 12th Corps' officer examination board to remove him. Colonel Pardee wrote his father, "For a long time there has been considerable plotting in the 28th Regt. One result has been effected. Maj. Raphael has been forced to resign. . . . Maj. Raphael was sent before the 'Examining Board.' The officers on it were his friends and after a slight examination they kindly told him that he could not pass the examination. . . . An officer has no earthly hope, if summoned before the Board, of passing simply that it is expressly understood that he is sent there to be broken if he does not resign."[8] On January 22 command of the 28th Pennsylvania fell to newly promoted Major Lansford Foster Chapman, a civil engineer from Mauch Chunk, Pennsylvania. Generally, the soldiers of the 28th Pennsylvania respected Chapman. One soldier wrote, "He has proven himself to be a good officer, and in the discharge of his duty is indefatigable. We all like him."[9]

Changes also occurred within the ranks of Company D. Not having any confidence in Company D's senior leadership, Geary pressured Captain George Hammar to resign, and he did so on March 22. Company D's first lieutenancy also went vacant when Gilbert L. Parker formally accepted a position as divisional assistant quartermaster on April 7. To fill the officer vacancies in Company D, the Adjutant General's Office at Harrisburg promoted Second Lieutenant Joseph Hammar to captain, First Sergeant James Devine to first lieutenant, and Second Sergeant Aaron Lazarus to second lieutenant. In late March Major Chapman advanced several sergeants as well. George T. Barnes became Company D's new first (or orderly) sergeant, Henry Hayward became its new second sergeant, William H. Hiles became its new third sergeant, Charles Longworth became its new fourth sergeant, and John O. Foering became its new fifth sergeant. Thus, Hayward's promotion to second sergeant made him the second highest noncommissioned officer in his company.

After another month of drilling, the Army of the Potomac went on the move. On April 27 the 28th Pennsylvania struck its tents and began marching to Stafford Court House. There it joined the rest of Geary's White Star Division. The division then marched to Hartwood Church, where it paused to rest. On the evening of April 28, it reached Kelly's Ford on the Rappahannock River, after covering a distance of thirty miles in two days. The weather was exceedingly warm, and one soldier in the 147th Pennsylvania called it "a very hard march. A great many men gave out. and some died on the road."[10]

At 10:00 A.M. the next day, Geary's division crossed a pontoon bridge near the ford. It covered another sixteen miles that day, reaching another river, the Rapidan, in the evening. A dense scrub forest known as "the Wilderness" stood beyond the Rapidan, and beyond that stood Lee's army, facing the opposite direction. This three-day forced march had put the 12th Corps, along with the bulk of the Union army—70,000 soldiers—on the flank and rear of the Army of Northern Virginia, and General Robert E. Lee still did not know it. Hayward and his comrades knew that another grand battle loomed ahead.

66

Dumfries Va. Jan 3d

Dear Father,

I hope we have got settled once more so that we can write and get a mail occasionaly. I have not received a letter from home since I left Boliver. the mail we got to day was an old one. we had quite an exciteing time in camp. on the 28th of Dec. word came that our Brigade at Dumfries had been attacked and scatterd through the country and that the Rebels were marching upon us with 5000 men and a six gun Battery. we were under arms the night before and at early morn on the 28 Gen Geary with the rest of the Div. and Gen Slocum[11] with the first Div. had arrived to reinforce us. Gen Green Brigade[12] was sent out on a by road where they met the Rebels and drove them before the rest of the troops could get up. we were sent a few days after to our Brigade at this place. we found that they had a smart fight but held their owne for a while and afterwards drove the rebels from the woods.[13] this is called by the Inhabitents the oldest Place in America. their are only a few houses here but they are very ancient. some of them were built of Brick that were sent from Scotland. the old Brick Court House is where Patrick Henry made one of his great speeches. it is draped in mourning that was placed there when Washington Died. we are encamped near an ancient burying ground.[14] the stones are crumbling down with age. there is also a great many graves of rebel Soldiers that were buryied here last winter. from this place the Rebels shelled our transports last winter. the landing where we get our provisions is 4 miles. I hear there is a large mail at the landing for us. the last paper we have seen was dated the 22. we fasted on New Years day. we were out of Provisions and none could be procured from any place but we have plenty now. to day the niggers are free. I wish Father

Abraham would hurry up and free us.[15] I am in good health and fine spirits. we expect the pay master on the 15th.

love to all,
Sergeant A. H.
Hayward

67

Camp at Dumfries, Jan 18th —63

Dear Father,

I received yours of the 12th inst. yesterday. I was highly pleased upon opening it to find your Photo—I have now quite a Collection of the family, all of which I highly prize. we are under marching orders. we hear the Pay master is coming. have you heard anything about it[?] I would not care if he never came if the Sutler would ever come with his Tobacco. we have been useing oak leaves as a substitute. there is a great many of our boys [who] have it sent to them weekly in papers. I see there has been a move in congress about mail matter to soldiers. if there is anything done you can have the Gazzette left at the Store, and if it is not Contraband put it in a Plug. I received a letter from J. W. Freeman. tell him I will answer [at] the first oppitunity. the weather has been quite cold here for a few days. I will answer all the following questions. I received most of all the Gazetts. I missed the one that spoke of my promotion. I am in the 12th Army Corps Commander Gen Slocum. 2d Div Commander Gen Geary (Kansas Ruffian). there are 2 Div. in our Corps. the first is commanded by Gen Williams. Col De Korponey was sick in Hospital at Washington. he has since been assigned to duty as commander of the Convelesent Camp.[16] Chaplin Heisley is host Chaplin at Harpers Ferry. Col Tyndale has nearly recoverd from his wound and is now in Washington. he is trying to have his five Companys brought back to the regt which were taken away in his absence. he will probably be a Brigadier General if he takes the field again.[17] Lieut Joseph Hammar is in command of Co D.[18] his brother George will resign.[19] Joe is a good man. he was in the Battle of Antietam. George was not. he lacks good sense, and there are many more like him in the army. I have seen late papers. I know the state of affairs. I am thankfull that I still retain my usual good health. with much love to all. I must now close.

Sergt. A. Henry
Hayward

(Monday morn. 19th)
clear & cold and the Sutler has not arrived.)

68

Camp at Dumfries Va Feb 23

Dear Brother [Albert],

I received yours of the 15th inst. [I] was glad to hear that all were well. we have had a great snow storm lasting for 3 days, the Snow having fell to the depth of 8 inches. there is no prospect of our moveing for sometime (more snow, more rest the boys say) I received the Tobacco in good time and the boys all thought it was first rate. I have just finished my supper. I have been feasting on the contents of a box which one of my messmates had sent to him. I must lay this aside untill morning, and as the mail leaves at 9 ock AM, I do not know as this sheet will get filled up. I just spoke to the boys to have them put on more Pork on the fire as it is quite Cold.

Tuesd Morn, 24th

I am [detailed] for Picket this morning. the Guard will mount in a few minutes and I must close. I would not send this but it is sometime since I wrote and mother will say something must be the matter with him. but I am in the best of health. It would not be best to risk a Box. tell Cora I received her letters. I beleive If I get a furlough it will be by the first of April, but do not expect me untill I write for you to kill the fatted Calf. I have been payed off nearly 3 weeks. send me some postage stamps. I must Close. love to all.

(Henry)

69

Camp at Dumfries Va. March 1st 63

Dear Sister,

The last time I heard from you was through Alberts letter when you justly complained of not receveing answers for 2 long letters that you had wrote to me. you will see by this that I have made an effort to repay you for your good deeds, even at a time when the Tariff on paper is so great as to command the attention of our Statesmen in Congress. but I do love to get letters when the mail comes and I do not expect to unless I do my part of the writing. I must confess it is quite an undertakeing for me to make up my mind to do so, but when once accomplished how eager I watch the arrival of the mail to receive an answer. One Year ago yesterday we crossed the Shenandoah. the night following that day is one long to be rememberd by the followers of Geary. we lay on the Banks of the Potomac while a little cold snow storm threatend our lives and made fires useless as you could not get near them, the wind was so violent. the next day we marched to

Lovettsville. after remaining there a few days, we moved on to Leesburgh. we soon took possesion of that strong hold, and with glad hearts and high hopes for the future we still moved on from place to place, driveing the Rebels before us, raising the Stars & Stripes upon the very poles, where but a few hours before our comming, floated the foul flag of treason. we thought we were doing much for the Great Cause, and it seemed that everywhere the work went Bravely on and that before another winter should come upon us Treason would have done its worst and this dreadfull Curse would disappear from our once Happy Country and restore us once more to our Homes and friends. but it seems that the good time has not yet come. they say the War must go on. I say let the war go on untill every traitor Copperheads and all are made to kneel to the Godess of Liberty. the army is yet true and Loyal but they feel as if there was not much chance for their lives with enemys on every side. I beleive that if such men as Vallandingham should come here and talk the way he does in Congress the Soldiers would kill him.[20] we must have victory at Vicksburgh & Charlestown to give our troops confidence and silence traitors in the North.[21] but I cannot dwell longer upon this subject with any pleasure to myself or anybody else. these are the old original times that tried mens souls. these are Americas Dark days and if I live to see her pass through them and come out whole then my fondest hopes are realized. I find this sheet is not half scribbled over yet. what shall I say to fill it out[?] I am afriad I shall get more than I bargined for before I have finished. Camp life is as dull as usuall, especially when it rains for then we can go into our shantys and sit and look at each other or go to bed. many choose the latter to save their rations. [On] evenings we congregate to gather in Shanty No 1 better known as the (Meremac) to the number of 20 and sing old worn out songs (for we have no chance of learning new ones) untill we get choaked with Tobacco smoke. then some one must dance untill he is very much exhausted, when he is allowed to rest and make room for some person that can quote a few passages from Shakespear. this is the way most of our evenings are passed at Dumfries. what else could we do to while away the hours[?] you might say read the papers, write letters, &c. but that must [be] done by day light for Uncle Sam only gives enough candle to us to see to make the bed. we consider it besides one of our few privalages to make as much noise in our own shantys as we like and this we can do with out the aid of a candle. Sergt. George Orth has returned from Philadelphia. his 10 days Furlough have expired. To day Orderly Sergt. James C. Devine leaves for Phil-d. we can easily tell who is on the Docket next for he wares a smile from morn untill night and I suppose carries it with him untill his return when you notice a sober thinking, long faced body which tells you at once that man has taken his furlough and wishes the war was over more than ever now.

I take much pleasure in anticipating my good time a comeing and have commenced laying out my plans for a triumphant entree into old N.B.[22] it is nearly three years since I left my native place to go forth upon the world to find some peculiar place where my wild discontented Spirit could find repose, and since I have been in the army I think I have roamed untill I am satisfied. but I suppose I shall see more of Virginia before my journy will be ended. we are having some beautifull weather now and it will not be many days if it continues before the army can move. I took a ramble yesterday over the hills and it was very pleasant after having been shut up in our rude huts for many days to breath in pure air and hear the birds sing. the climate here at present is like your owne May.

Tuesday Mar. 3d

As I expected, this was laid aside for want of items or to answer one of the many calls conected with the life of a Soldier. which of the two I will leave you to guess. I walked over to the camp of the 29th Ohio yesterday afternoon to witness their dress Parade. after that was over, they formed into a hollow Square when their Colonel read them a letter upon the state of affairs in their State. it spoke of a set of Traitors that were Plotting against the Government and poisening the minds of the people. after he had finished reading it, he requested them to express their minds upon the subject freely, with out any hesetation either for or against. he then said all those who entertained the views as expressed in that letter to signify it by saying aye when the whole Regt. burst out with one tumultuous aye. he then tryed the nays, but with no effect. then one of the Officers proposed three Cheers for the Constitution and three more for the President which were given with a will. then one of the Privates proposed three groans for the Copperheads which were given. I suppose this letter will go from one Ohio Regt. to the other and will then be sent home as a warning for all traitors at home.[23] I receive the Gazette quite regular. I shall wait untill the mail comes before I close this which will be to night. the mail goes every morning.

Wed-d. Mar. 4th

The maill came last night. I received the Gazette. all [is] quiet along the lines this morning. it is blowing up cold. I think the end of this is not far off. love to all. write soon.

Sergt. A. Henry
Hayward
Co. D, 28 Regt. P.V.

70

Camp of the 28th Regt. Dumfries Va. Mar 27th

Dear Brother J. P. H. [John Parker],

I have been waiting to hear from home for a long time but get no sattisfaction. so I will try you and I think it will not be long before I get a reply for you cannot certainly be as busy as the rest even if you are attending school. I received a letter from Joe Freeman last night. he says that he saw Albert and the latter told him that I might expect a letter Soon. I came of Picket this morning and I do not feel wide awake so you can expect nothing but a sleepy letter. we have had much stormy weather since I last wrote, but it broke away yesterday and to day it has the appearance of settled weather. the trees are begining to bud, the grass is looking green, birds are singing merrily and every thing looks like an early spring. If we can judge rightly by the papers I think the Union cause looks favorable and we all look for great News soon. we have been expecting fighting Joe Hooker to review us every day.[24] our Regt is very healthy this Spring, even with all the bad weather. the 147 Regt P.V. which is camped near us has lost 5 men since the first of January from sickness.[25] they buried a Soldier to day. the 28th has not as yet lost one since we left Boliver. Sergt. Aaron Lazarus is expected to return from his Furlough on Wednesday. the 2d Sergt. Barnes will be ready by the 5th. [He] will be expected back by the 17th and if nothing happens I shall get off by the 21st. unseen accidents often occur to delay the furloughs but when I am certain that I can name the date I will write. Capt. Hammer has resigned. Lieut Hammer has been promoted to Capt. 1st Lieut Gilbert L. Parker has been appointed Division Quartermast with the rank of Major. this leaves 2 vacencys in our company which will be filled by Orderly Sergt. James C. Devine and second Sergt. Aaron Lazarus. it thus makes 3d Sergent George T. Barnes Orderly[26] and A. Henry Hayward 2d Sergt. the drums are beating for Battalion Drill but the Picketts that came off this morning are excused. I have buisiness of importence to attend to now so with much love to all, I will close. I shall send this with my warrent which I hope will get through safe as I regard it as one of my relics of the war for the Union. Oh, I saw by the paper that Father fell and Injured himself but not dangerously, but [I] have not heard so by letter.[27] (dont forget to send a few stamps.)

(Henry)

Sat-d. Mar 28th

I hear from good authority that the Furloughs have been stoped but only for a few days. I think we shall move soon. Gen Hooker should never issued the order for Furloughs if he did not intend to keep them up. it will depress the spirits of the men very much. for my part I am not so much troubled by it, but I suppose it will be a disappointence for you at home. if it had been an order for 15 or 20 days it would be worth while to growl. who knows but what the men that would have been away on Furlough will at the next Battle turn the tide in our favor. it is raining this morning. (more rain, more rest)

(Cora, write)

(Henry)

Chapter 7

"LAST TO LEAVE THE FIELD"

THE CHANCELLORSVILLE CAMPAIGN, APRIL 27–MAY 23, 1863

THE 28TH PENNSYLVANIA, ALONG WITH THE REST OF GEARY'S DIVI-
sion, reached Germanna Ford on the Rapidan River at 4:00 P.M.,
April 29. When the White Stars arrived, they saw the 1st Division,
12th Corps, crossing one hundred yards below the ford. Fearful
of the deep water and swift current, Geary ordered his men to
fall out and construct a foot bridge using nearby logs and planks.
The division completed this task by 9:00 P.M. and bivouacked on
the south bank for the night. Early the next day, the division commenced its march east along the Plank Road, moving in the direction of Fredericksburg, where General Hooker hoped to smash the
rear of the Army of Northern Virginia. Near Wilderness Run, the
28th Pennsylvania skirmished with Confederate cavalry scouts,
losing two men, but this altercation did not impede the regiment's
march. At 2:00 P.M. the 28th Pennsylvania reached a small clearing
called Chancellorsville, a crossroads four miles south of the confluence of the Rapidan and Rappahannock rivers. One of Geary's
staff officers wrote, "we found the 'ville' to consist of *one* house; a
very fine one indeed for the country, being built very substantially
of brick and having an air of dignity and comfort about it indicating wealth, good breeding, and that genial hospitality for which
the F. F. V.'s [first families of Virginia] of olden time were wont to
be distinguished." This same officer noticed several ladies from
Chancellorsville who "eyed us with the curiosity natural to the
sex, heightened, no doubt, by the circumstances of our approach;
but they little dreamed of the fearful drama which was so soon to
be opened in their immediate presence."[1]

Geary placed his division about 150 yards south of the cross-roads with his 3rd Brigade on the right, his 2nd Brigade in the center, and his 1st Brigade on the left. The entire division faced south. The 28th Pennsylvania, part of the 1st Brigade, formed a line of battle with its right flank resting against the Plank Road and its left flank connecting with the right flank of the 7th Ohio. The 147th Pennsylvania stood on the other side of the road, and the rest of the 1st Brigade extended this line west, where it connected with the remainder of the division. Eight pieces of artillery—six from Knap's battery and a section under Lieutenant Edward Muhlenburg—guarded the road itself. In relation to the rest of the Army of the Potomac, Geary's division held a position near the center. The 2nd and 5th Corps took position on the 2nd Division's left, extending the line northeast across the Old Orange Turnpike and terminating at the banks of the Rappahannock. The 1st Division, 12th Corps, took a position on the 2nd Division's right near a plantation called Fairview. The 3rd and 11th Corps extended this flank further down the Plank Road, ending in the deep undergrowth two miles away.

Shortly after Geary placed his men, he ordered them to fortify their position with a barricade of timber and abatis—that is, a row of felled brush and tree trunks to serve as obstructions. Unfortunately, the division carried no entrenching tools, only worn-out pickaxes and spades that badly needed replacement. Nevertheless, the men improvised. Wrote one officer, "in the half clouded subdued moonlight were the men on their knees, busily engaged in bringing into this service any implement with which earth could be dug and cast up; sabre bayonets, swords, tin plates, tin cups, pieces of boards, and every imaginable contrivance was brought into requisition, and the morning dawn saw a long line of excellent earthwork covering and protecting the whole front of the Division from right to left."[2]

The battle commenced the next day, May 1. On the Union left, troops from the 2nd and 5th Corps opened the engagement by pressing against a Confederate position on Mount Zoan Church Ridge. However, General Hooker did not press home this attack with any supporting units. Instead, after incurring a few casualties, he ordered his men to retire to Chancellorsville. This fight provoked a response from the Confederate army. Within hours Confederate forces probed the Union line, looking for weak points. In the afternoon Geary advanced a small reconnaissance force, including the 28th Pennsylvania, south of the division's line of entrenchments. Geary's men encountered Confederate skirmishers and they commenced a one-hour fight, but after suffering only a few casualties, Geary's troops withdrew back into the breastworks.

The next evening the 28th Pennsylvania, with several other regiments from the 2nd Division, made another reconnaissance with the same results. According to instructions sent by General Hooker, Geary expected to find the Confederate army in retreat toward Gordonsville. Theoretically, a reconnaissance should have disrupted or captured the Confederate wagon trains. Instead, Geary found the enemy defending the area in force. He determined that Confederate infantry one mile south of Chancellorsville had thrown up heavy breastworks, and he declared that "overwhelming numbers of the enemy" stood in his front. Unable to make an attack with his "insufficient force," Geary again retired the 28th Pennsylvania and the other reconnaissance units to their entrenchments.[3]

Before the Union generals could do anything with this new information, disaster struck. At 5:00 P.M. 28,000 Confederates under Stonewall Jackson outflanked the right of the Union army and drove thousands of frightened soldiers from the Union 11th Corps pell-mell toward Chancellorsville. Luckily, a few steady soldiers kept their cool. Sergeant Hayward leaped from the ranks and halted the routed men as they sprinted through the 28th Pennsylvania's position. In conspicuous fashion, Hayward helped to organize these terrified soldiers into temporary units. First Lieutenant James C. Devine remembered, "when all was confusion Sergt. H. left his company and with fixed bayonet checked the progress of a number, and brought them to the Regt. where he furnished them with weapons. . . . by his voice and example he sought to stay the flying fugitives, and when all else failed the bayonet was applied."[4] As darkness fell, the Confederate attack stalled, giving the 28th Pennsylvania a chance to brace for a coming assault the next day.

By dawn on May 3 the Union line had reformed into a curved bow, and the 28th Pennsylvania still occupied a position near the center. Only now the Union right flank bent back toward Ely's Ford Road, near the confluence of the two rivers. Any federal units occupying the center would be attacked from three sides: east, west, and south. Just after sunrise, the Confederates renewed their attack, striking the 28th Pennsylvania's position with a series of assaults. Geary, who rode behind the 28th Pennsylvania, wrote, "At this stage of the action the enemy suffered severely at our hands. Candy's [1st] brigade seemed animated by a desire to contest single-handed the possession of the field, and before the deadly aim of our rifles rank after rank of rebel infantry went down, never to rise again."[5]

Shortly after 9:00 A.M. the 12th Corps commander, Major General Henry W. Slocum, believing that retreat was inevitable, ordered Geary to withdraw his division from the entrenchments and reform it near the Chancellor House. The bulk of the division withdrew about one hundred yards to the rear, and in response two Confederate brigades rushed into the abandoned breastworks. Two New York regiments in Geary's 3rd Brigade, unable to retire in time, commenced a hand-to-hand struggle with these Confederates. When this happened, General Hooker rode to Geary and ordered him to advance his men and reoccupy the entrenchments they had just deserted. Turning to the 28th and 147th Pennsylvania, Geary shouted, "Come on, boys, we will take them!" At this point, Hayward and another man from Company D, Orderly Sergeant George T. Barnes, surged forward, shouting words of encouragement to their fellow Pennsylvanians. The two regiments, followed by the rest of the 1st Brigade, leaped forward and retook the entrenchments after a brief hand-to-hand struggle. Lieutenant Devine recorded Hayward's prominence in the advance: "he being the first to spring forward and the last to leave the field; by his example the men renewed their efforts and we drove the enemy from our position with a heavy loss." He believed that Hayward's "coolness is proverbial."[6]

The 28th Pennsylvania held its position for another hour, at which time orders arrived instructing them to vacate their position. In the afternoon most of the Army of the Potomac, now thoroughly defeated, withdrew to a new position near United States Ford, where its soldiers constructed new entrenchments. On the morning of May 6, the army commenced recrossing the Rappahannock River on a pontoon bridge. By May 7, after covering a distance of twenty-five miles, the 28th Pennsylvania returned to its old campground near Aquia Creek.

In all, Chancellorsville produced a horrifying casualty toll for the 28th Pennsylvania. The regiment began the campaign with 315 men, but on May 4 it counted 101 casualties, including its commander, Major Lansford Chapman. Near the end of the fight on May 3, Chapman received a mortal gunshot wound to the chest. His frightened horse bolted into Confederate lines, and his body was not recovered until two years after the battle. Most of the casualties resulted from the regiment's desperate charge on the morning of May 3. Hayward's Company D suffered proportionately, losing twelve men killed, wounded, captured, or missing. Company D lost three noncommissioned officers. Orderly Sergeant George Barnes received a wound to the knee that kept him out of action for the rest of the war. Hayward's messmate, Color Sergeant Jacob George Orth, received a wound to the right thigh, ending his army service. Sergeant William H. Hiles, one of Hayward's close friends, received a leg wound from which he died four days later. Once again, Hayward discovered that he could barely describe the horrors of battle. In a terse letter to his father written on May 9, Hayward stated, "[I] have once more trod the bloody field of battle. have again seen my comrades fall and heard their dying groans. yes I have been spared perhaps to witness the like again. who ever read of such a terrible battle as we have endured . . .[?] the mens faces still bare the mark of terror."[7]

Not everyone in the 28th Pennsylvania behaved well during the battle. After the return to Aquia Creek, the regiment's new commander, Captain Conrad U. Meyer, the senior officer who took command upon Chapman's death, was found guilty of cowardice by a general court-martial. According to Adjutant Samuel Goodman, Meyer "should have taken command of this regiment upon the death of Major Chapman, instead of so doing, he willfully Deserted us, and fled for safety to the rear, notwithstanding the protestations of myself and others of the reg't, entreating him for 'God's sake to stand by us.'" In an uncharacteristically generous move, General Geary overruled the opinion of the court, allowing Meyer to resign his commission with honor. However, Geary also purged three other officers charged with cowardice at Chancellorsville, including Captain Joseph W. Hammar, commander of Company D. Instead of allowing these officers to stand trial by court-martial, Geary let them resign with the word "honorably" struck from their discharge papers.[8]

The Battle of Chancellorsville sifted the fainthearted from the courageous. While some officers faced charges of cowardice and misbehavior, other members of the 28th Pennsylvania received praise for their valor. On May 8, one day after the 28th Pennsylvania reached Aquia Creek, Hayward's new company commander, Lieutenant Devine, issued him a ten-day furlough, an award for his recent bravery. In accordance with General Orders Number 3 of the Army of the Potomac, companies without unauthorized absences could sanction limited furloughs to men with honorable service. As several soldiers from Company D had gone on furlough before the campaign began, Devine determined that Hayward should have his turn. Hayward departed on May 12, and he visited his family in North Bridgewater. On his return trip, he stopped one day in Philadelphia and then rejoined his regiment on May 23. Fully rested, he felt "Happy to go on duty" again.[9]

On May 22 Lieutenant Devine received a copy of General Orders Number 53, asking officers to submit names of any soldiers worthy of gallant or meritorious conduct at Chancellorsville. Devine immediately recommended Sergeant Barnes and Sergeant Hayward. He recommended Barnes for "honorable mention" in written orders for gallant service at Chancellorsville, but he recommended a higher honor for Hayward. In addition to his valiant conduct at Chancellorsville, Hayward had distinguished himself on numerous other occasions, including the scouting mission in September 1862 and the rescue of Hector Tyndale at Antietam. For these three citations, Devine recommended that Hayward receive the Medal of Honor.[10]

It is unknown if the officers at the Army of the Potomac's headquarters took Devine's commendation seriously. Quite possibly, no one ever saw it. Under regulations, Devine forwarded the recommendation to Captain Meyer, who never pursued any action because of his court-martial and subsequent resignation. Hayward discovered that he had been recommended for the Medal of Honor after he returned from furlough, but he modestly refused to pursue any action to attain it. Two months later, he explained his decision in a letter to his father: "[This was] the last I have heard from it. I received an extract of the order from the Lieutenant to day which will do as well for there are other[s] in the company which [have] done their duty as well that would not have got one."[11]

In any event, Hayward had little time to dwell upon his past laurels. Active operations soon recommenced as the Confederate Army of Northern Virginia attempted to invade the North for a second time.

71

Encampment 28th Pa. Vols.
Acquia Creek Va. May 8th 63

To H. C. Rodgers[12]
Asst. Adjt. Genl. 12th A.C.

Sir

I have the honor to transmit herewith a Furlough for Ambrose H. Hayward, a Sergeant of my Company. He has faithfully and honestly served as a soldier for 22 months, has never been absent or without leave. there being none absent from my company on Furlough agreeable to Genl. Orders No. 3 Head Quarters Army of the Potomac, I do most respectfully request that one be granted him for 10 days.

Very Respectfully,
Your Obed't Serv't
James C. Devine
2nd Lieut Comd'g Co.
"D", 28th P.V.

72

Camp on Acquia Creek, May 9th

Dear Father,

I have been [as] anxious to write as you have been to hear, but this is the first time the mail has been allowed to go since I left Dumfries. this must be short and to the point. (I still live) but have once more trod the bloody field of battle. have again seen my comrades fall and heard their dying groans. yes I have been spared perhaps to witness the like again. who ever read of such a terrible battle as we have endured on that Saturday night[?] the mens faces still bare the mark of terror. the 28th was the first to bleed. we have lost our gallant Major. I am the only Sergeant left for duty. our Orderly was shot dead, Hiles & Orth were wounded.[13] total Co D, 3 killed 4 wounded 4 missing.[14] total Regt. 97 killed wounded and missing.[15] the mail Closes in a few minutes. I have just taken my furlough into the Adjutants Office, but you know enough about war not to expect me home untill you see me.

love to all,
Henry

73

Encampment 28th, Pa. Vols.
Aquia Creek Va. May 22nd, 63

Capt. C. U. Meyer[16]
Commdg. 28th Pa. Vols.

Sir:
Extract[17]

x   x   x   x   x   x   x   x   x
II . . . . . In mentioning the actions of Sergt. Ambrose H. Hayward, Co. "D", 28th Pa. Vols, I would respectfully state that during the action of the

1st, 2nd, & 3rd inst, he behaved nobly, displaying qualities seldom found in a man occupying his position. his coolness is proverbial. in the heat of Battle of the 2nd when a portion of the right wing of the Army gave way, they came rushing en masse past our lines (we occupying the centre) and were passing through to the enemy's: when all was confusion Sergt. H. left his company and with fixed bayonet checked the progress of a number, and brought them to the Regt. where he furnished them with weapons. this was under a severe fire from right, left and centre. by his voice and example he sought to stay the flying fugitives, and when all else failed the bayonet was applied. On the morning of the 3rd his courage was again put to the test, it was a time requiring the energy and example of every good soldier; we had been driven from our position and formed to charge the enemy. conspicious among those in the advance was Sergt. Hayward, he being the first to spring forward and the last to leave the field; by his example the men renewed their efforts and we drove the enemy from our position with a heavy loss. On the field he was complimented by the Commdg. officer for his gallant behavior.[18]

Sergt. Hayward also bore a conspicious part in the Battle of Antietam being under a severe fire for 7 hours. his conduct at this Battle cannot be surpassed. at the latter part of the action when being driven from the field, the Col. Comdg Brigade (now Brig Genl. Hector Tyndale) was seriously wounded and left upon the field given up for dead. Sergt. Hayward in passing saw him, and with the assistance of Capt. B., and under a galling fire conveyed him from the field to a place of safety, which noble action saved his life.[19]

During the summer of '62 we formed part of the 2nd A. Corps (Banks) Army of Virginia under Genl. Pope. during the retreat from the Rappahannock, it became necessary to find out the exact position of the enemy and their movements. for this hazardous duty Sergts. Hayward & B. were selected with 12 men from the regt. they penetrated the enemys lines, where they remained 5 days living mostly on corn etc., after gaining the desired information they set out to return, which was safely accomplished with the loss of 1 man taken prisoner, bringing in 16 confederate prisoners; for this daring act the party was complimented by Genls McClellan and Banks in Special Orders — it was one of the daring feats of the war, and required much coolness and sagacity.[20]

I would respectfully request that a medal of honor be conferred [to] Sergeant Ambrose H. Hayward Co. "D", 28th Pa. Vols.

I am Sir,
Your Obedt. Servt.,
James C. Devine
1st Lieut, Commdg. Co.
"D", 28th Pa. Vols.

74

Camp on Aquia Creek, May 23d

Dear Father,

Here I am seated Turk fashion in my tent with the boys around me questioning me about my visit home. I had 9 hours in Phila and such a gay time I never had before. every where I stoped I was pervailed upon to seat myself to the table and I would excuse myself by takeing a cup of tea. I told them that considering the very short time I had to stay and the many places I had to call that it would be more satisfaction to myself and them also to talk instead of eat. well, the consequence was that I took about 11 suppers that night more or less. I made my headquarters at Quaker Hotel. A. & R. were very much surprised to see me.[21] [I] met all the boys at the Depot at 11ck P.M. [I] arrived at camp at 12 ock A.M. to day. [I] took dinner with the Lieutenants. I am now rested and feel gay and Happy to go on duty to-morrow. [The] boys like my Photos, first rate, sell well, all gone, order ½ doz more immediately, send them by mail 2 or 3 at a time. [I] met A. M. & A.[22] at the boat. [I] took breakfast aboard the boat. they had not been to breakfast. I had to eat again. I have done nothing but eat since I left N.B. [I] do not want another Furlough. [I] could not stand it to eat so much. I met Mr. Glover on the boat.[23] at Washington I ordered the Inquirer for 3 months for $1.50. tell me if you get them. Capt Joe Hammar has resigned. he has received an honorable discharge.[24] our Orderly is here in [the] Corps Hospital not seriously wounded. [I] shall call on him tomorrow. the weather is very warm. we have trees planted around the tents for a shade. tell Cora I have forgot the tune of Kingdom Coming.[25] I have so much upon my mind that it is impossible for me to steady myself to write as I would like to. you will notice the way it reads that 20 Ideas flirt across my mind at once but I think that I have the most important items condensed on this sheet, and I will releive my poor brain by bringing this epistle to a Close. love to all.

Henry

Monday morning, 25th

I should have sent this yesterday morning but forgot it. Lieut Murlenburgh is the man that I was talking with you about.[26]

Lieut Lazarus and I went down to see Sergt. Barnes yesterday. he is not so badly wounded but quite ill from exposure.

Henry

Chapter 8

"I HAVE DONE MY DUTY IN THE LAST GREAT CONTEST"

THE PENNSYLVANIA CAMPAIGN, MAY 23–SEPTEMBER 24, 1863

THE 28TH PENNSYLVANIA ENCAMPED AT AQUIA CREEK, VIRGINIA, until mid-June, when news of the Army of Northern Virginia's invasion spurred the Army of the Potomac to action. During the intervening time, the regiment encountered a number of changes. First, certain soldiers had to be promoted to fill vacancies produced by the Battle of Chancellorsville. Command of the 28th Pennsylvania now fell to Arkansas resident Thomas J. Ahl, promoted to colonel on June 3. For an unstated reason, Ahl declined to return to the regiment, instead choosing to remain on detached duty as commandant of the 12th Corps' ambulance train. In the meantime, Captain John Hornbuckle Flynn, an Irish-born Mexican-American War veteran, assumed command of the 28th Pennsylvania. Strangely, no promotions occurred in Company D. Although many of the remaining officers and noncommissioned officers had been cited for gallantry at Chancellorsville, Pennsylvania's military administration at Harrisburg declined to advance them. In the end, First Lieutenant Devine had to accept command of Company D without advancement, while Second Lieutenant Lazarus remained his executive officer. Hayward remained the company's second sergeant. However, because all infantry companies required an orderly sergeant to function properly, Hayward had to assume superior duties in place of the wounded Orderly Sergeant Barnes, who had been transferred to a general hospital in Philadelphia. So, although he did not officially hold the rank, Hayward now became Company D's acting orderly sergeant. Finally, on June 5 a shipment of U.S.-made Springfield rifled muskets arrived to replace the regiment's worn-out Enfields. Hayward welcomed this change. He wrote his father, "we shall like them very well when we get used to them. the sabre bayonet is so heavy to wear." However, this change tested his administrative skill. As acting orderly sergeant, Hayward had to exchange his company's firearms one by one, noting the serial numbers for each weapon issued and turned in.[1]

The 28th Pennsylvania broke camp on June 13, commencing its pursuit of Lee's army. Over the next five days, the regiment marched sixty miles, reaching Leesburg on June 18. This campaign took the regiment over dusty roads in dangerously muggy weather. Hayward told his father, "there was 18 dropped dead in our Corps yesterday. 13 in the first Div, 5 in the 2d. we all suffered with a terrible headache. it was the hardest march we have had yet."[2] All the while, tensions ran high. On June 19 Hayward witnessed his first military execution. Three 12th Corps soldiers convicted of desertion were executed by firing squad. Hayward wrote to his sister, "it is very hard but right. if it had been done in the first place I think it would have saved Conscription." On June 26 the 12th Corps crossed the Potomac River on a pontoon bridge at Edwards Ferry. Two days later, it arrived at Frederick, where the new army commander, Major General George Meade, received it. Few soldiers immediately knew about this sudden change in command. Initially, rumors circulated that George McClellan had replaced Hooker. Hayward earnestly hoped these rumors were true. Although he never held McClellan in high regard, he told his father, "I will cheer him the first time he passes our lines. anything to keep the people united."[3]

On June 30 the 12th Corps crossed the Mason-Dixon Line. As the bluecoats marched into Pennsylvania, scores of citizens greeted them with enthusiastic applause. Hayward wrote, "such lusty cheering I never heard before. . . . the smiles of the ladies, the many flags which we see on our advance, the cool spring water handed to us by the lovely ladies send us a peculiar healthy feeling through the whole system well calculated to lighten the Knapsack." Despite this excitement, Hayward recognized that the fate of the nation hung in the balance. "[W]e will whip them this time or fall by thousands," he declared. On July 1, with sixty rounds of ammunition distributed to each man, the 28th Pennsylvania rushed to join a battle in progress at Gettysburg, Pennsylvania.[4]

Hayward's regiment saw no fighting on the battle's first day. While a portion of the Union army engaged the Confederates, the

28th Pennsylvania marched eleven miles, arriving at the scene of action at 5:00 P.M., July 1. On July 2, at 8:00 A.M., it moved to the Union army's right flank on Culp's Hill. After standing in line of battle for over an hour, the 28th Pennsylvania received orders to advance down the wooded slope and skirmish along the banks of Rock Creek. As it turned out, this skirmish action proved vital to the Union defense of Culp's Hill because it allowed the rest of the 12th Corps to fortify the hill with heavy breastworks in relative safety. Sergeant John Foering remembered, "We were exchanging shots with the enemys skirmishers during the entire day, the Corps constructed temporary Breastworks with Rocks &c."[5] At 7:00 P.M., under orders from General Meade, the bulk of the 12th Corps, including the 28th Pennsylvania, attempted to redeploy near the Army of the Potomac's left flank, but in so doing became lost. While absent from the front, Confederate forces under Major General Edward Johnson occupied a portion of the 12th Corps' abandoned works. When the 12th Corps soldiers began making their way back in the dark, shortly after midnight on July 3, they bumped into these Confederates, who refused to give up the recently seized breastworks. Throughout the evening, random skirmishes erupted, with both sides chaotically stumbling into each other's positions.

Luckily, Colonel Charles Candy's 1st Brigade, to which the 28th Pennsylvania belonged, discovered that the entrenchments near the summit of the hill had not been taken. Geary's 3rd Brigade, under Brigadier General George S. Greene—the only portion of the 12th Corps that had been left behind to defend Culp's Hill—had resolutely protected them throughout the night. During the early morning hours of July 3, Candy's men began relieving Greene's men at the summit, on the so-called upper hill. At 6:00 A.M., Candy's 29th Ohio relieved Greene's 137th New York near the right flank of Greene's line. At 7:00 A.M., the 28th Pennsylvania relieved the 29th Ohio. This constant shuffling of fresh troops into and out of the entrenchments on the upper hill stirred the Confederates, causing them to attack. At 4:30 A.M., the acting commander of the 12th Corps, Major General Alpheus Williams, also ordered a cannonade to drive out Johnson's Confederates—now reinforced with three extra brigades—from their precarious position. Unable to endure the constant shelling and small arms fire, Johnson's men charged. In the rising daylight, the Confederates discovered that they held a small summit, today known as the lower hill, southeast of that section defended by Geary's division. Using the slope

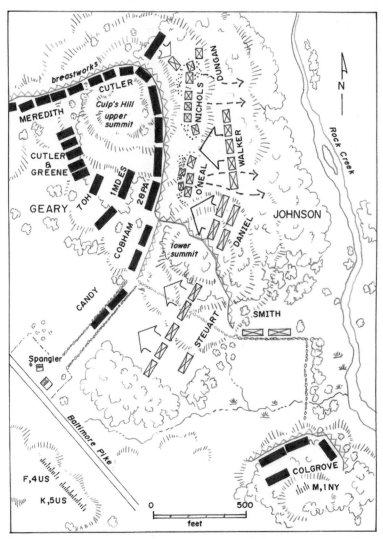

The Battle of Gettysburg, July 3, 1863. Map by John Heiser.

of the lower hill to gain momentum, elements from the Stonewall Division and Brigadier General Junius Daniel's North Carolina brigade charged into the ravine separating the two summits and then they surged up the opposite slope. They hoped to breach the Union works and drive the 12th Corps from the field. Waiting for them on the upper hill stood the 28th Pennsylvania and about one thousand of its comrades from Geary's 1st and 2nd Brigades.

The 28th Pennsylvania fought for almost two hours in the entrenchments, repulsing repeated Confederate assaults. During

The Life and Letters of First Sergeant Ambrose Henry Hayward that time, Hayward fired sixty-five rounds of ammunition. His rifle became so fouled that he had to ram his last charges with a stone. Private Henry Brown of Company A remembered:

> Down the opposite slope they came in beautiful alignment, their officers gallantly leading, —now up the hillside in our front, as if by sheer force of weight to bear us down. There was no retreat for the poor fellows in the front ranks who, with blanched faces, came up to be mowed down by companies. At twenty paces, ten, five, and even less intervening space, our minnie balls were planked into their unprotected bodies as we called out, "Remember Chancellorsville." The faces of the men in the front ranks exhibited that fear and dread that is akin to insanity, and yet, without any hope of success, they were driven to the slaughter. Their dead and wounded must have numbered by the thousands in front of our brigade.[6]

Sometime after 9:00 A.M. a battalion from an untested regiment, the 1st Maryland Eastern Shore Infantry, relieved the 28th Pennsylvania. It was a harrowing moment as the inexperienced Marylanders opened fire on the Confederates, shooting over the heads of the Pennsylvanians. Hayward complained, "they came up with a yell and fired a volly over our heads into the trees. we did not know what to make of it at first and like Chanc[el]lorsville hugged close to the ground untill they were stoped by the 7th Ohio who were in their rear."[7] After the initial confusion, the Marylanders ceased fire and exchanged places with the Pennsylvanians. The 28th Pennsylvania reentered the works sometime after midday, when they faced a second attack. Private Henry Brown wrote that this second attack—probably delivered by a portion of Brigadier General George H. Steuart's brigade—came within "a pace or two of the works when a thousand fingers press a thousand triggers, and all humanity is forgotten in the haste to load and kill. A thousand reel and fall. Then a perfect roar of musketry greets the ear. . . . The roar increases until it becomes deafening, as the poor misguided rebels run for their lives."[8] After this last attack, the Confederates kept up constant skirmish fire lasting well after dark. That evening, sometime after 8:00 P.M., the surviving men from Johnson's division withdrew, commencing the Confederate retreat to Virginia.

During this incredible twenty-four-hour firefight, the 28th Pennsylvania suffered lightly, losing only twenty-five men, including six killed or mortally wounded. Of these, Company D lost three men killed or mortally wounded: Private Lewis K. Boyce, Corporal James D. Butcher, and Third Sergeant Charles Longworth. Hayward helped bury Boyce and Butcher, and he helped to carry Longworth from the field to get treated for a gunshot wound to the knee. On July 14, Longworth died in a field hospital about two miles away. Hayward remarked ominously, "this make[s] 4 Sergts we have had wounded in the leg."[9]

Like many Union soldiers, Hayward rejoiced at the victory at Gettysburg. Although his legs involuntarily trembled after three days of marching and fighting, he informed his father that he was all right. The Army of the Potomac pursued the retreating Army of Northern Virginia for eight more days. At Williamsport, Maryland, along the banks of the Potomac, Hayward anticipated another engagement—"a terrible battle," he forecast—yet none came. The next day, the Army of Northern Virginia recrossed the river and escaped.[10]

The late summer months of 1863 took Hayward back to Virginia, but the fighting slowly sputtered to another standstill. He remarked in a letter to his father that "the boys say I have been getting fat since the battle of Gettysburgh. we do not know where the Rebels are but I suppose Meade does."[11] On July 18 the 28th Pennsylvania crossed the Potomac and it commenced a series of hard marches, including one trek that covered thirty-five miles in a single day. The regiment moved south along the Blue Ridge Mountains, heading through Snickersville and Manassas Gap, and eventually, it veered southeast toward the Rappahannock River. By early August, the regiment reached the banks of the Rappahannock, where it performed guard duty between Kelly's Ford and Ellis's Ford.

The biggest change of the late summer came with the arrival of substitutes to replenish the 28th Pennsylvania's depleted ranks. In March, Congress had established an enrollment act, allowing the president to administer a federal draft. This legislation also allowed drafted men to purchase substitutes to serve in their place. This concerned Hayward because, as acting orderly sergeant, his duties required him to teach any incoming substitutes proper infantry maneuvers. Hayward guessed he would have his work cut out for him. He supposed most substitutes had been drawn into the service by lucrative bounties, not patriotism. He told his father how he would train these incorrigibles during the hot weather: "we expect our Conscripts before long, and we Non Coms have got them to drill. I shall get my squad under a Shady tree and talk it into them instead of runing around with them."[12]

The substitutes arrived on September 18, after the regiment had already moved to Raccoon Ford on the Rapidan River, and Company D received thirty-seven. Hayward informed his father, "they are mostly old Soldiers, those that are not are as dumb as sticks." Two of the substitutes had been born in Germany, and they had not been in the United States more than eight days. They spoke no English, so Hayward had to deliver commands through an interpreter. Six days later, he complained to his sister, "the Substitutes are among us in all their ignorance. you have no Idea what a wretched creature a dumb man is. we have 2 out of our squad of 37 that Bobby Williams would call Block heads. I think sometimes that they will never learn. they are both Irishman of the Pick & Spade school."[13]

Hayward had precious little time to drill his new squad. On September 24 orders reached the 28th Pennsylvania directing the men to strike tents and march to Culpeper, where cars waited to take them to eastern Tennessee. The 28th Pennsylvania was heading to a new theater of operations. This movement filled Hayward with a renewed sense of optimism. Clearly, the year 1863 had tested his physical and emotion endurance. The rise of the Copperheads, the defeat at Chancellorsville, the exhausting forced marches in June, the shocking execution of deserters, the incompetence of the substitutes, and the heartrending deaths of close friends at Chancellorsville and Gettysburg had almost broken Hayward's will to fight. As his train sped away from Virginia, he spitefully vented his contempt toward the Old Dominion State: "our hearts gladened with the hope that we were to leave the detested soil of Virginia, the blighted land sickening to the sight of all Soldiers where 2 years of dreadfull marches and numerous struggles we have endured and the object not yet accomplished. thus we bid a long and hope last farewell to old Virginia." Although still dedicated to the cause, Hayward was no longer the naive recruit from 1861.[14]

75

No 2
Camp at Aquia Creek, Tue. June 2d

Dear Sister,

The wind blows a perfect gale. imagin me seated under my shelter, holding on to my sheet with one hand and rubing the dust out of my eyes with the other. this is the way we have lived for 3 days, inhaling dust and eating dirt. the boys all leave for the woods as soon as they have eaten their meals, but the poor Orderly must stay about quarters to be ready to answer to any calls. yesterday I wrapped my head up in a Phila Inquirer and laid down in my tent all afternoon and let it blow. when I arose I was as grey as a rebel with dirt. well !! there is one consolation. it does not spare the Officers, and they found that it was unbearable so Col. Candy Comd Brigd[15] took a ride out last night to find a new camp, and I suppose we shall be more comfortable in the future. at least it will not be so bad for the eyes. When you send those Photos keep the best for those that I promised around home. Soldiers are not at tall particular about the quallity of anything they get but more for the quantity. I hope that Mr. Frank Nash will get drafted and then will not be able to raise $300, and that (Webster) also.[16] do such things as those get mad when they are called cowards[?] it is a wonder they did not exempt themselves by going as cooks for the Nigger Regt. I did feel some what Demoralized when I was home to hear some people talk, but since I have rejoined the army and mingeled again with my comrades a good healthy hopefull feeling has come over me again. here there is but one feeling, one hope, one purpose. we are waiting anxiously to hear from Vickburgh.[17] I hope we shall be successfull. it is so long since we have had the pleasure of Cheering for a great Victory. I gave Augustus one of my Photos. you can give those out first to those I have promised. dont forget any one, and then order an other half doz. that will make 2 doz. Father will let you into my bank any time if you will ask him. was not I lucky in getting my furlough as I did for they have stoped again[?] perhaps Joe expects uncle Lee across the river to pay him a visit and he wants all of his boys to stay at home to give him a warm reception. should he come, he will find that the same spirit animates the Old Army of the Potomac that it has ever shown. Cora, my whiskers are growing very fast and I intend to let them. do remember me to all at home and abroad. my ink is getting so full of dirt that I am compelled to stop. (love to all)

Henry

76

No 3
Camp at Aquia Creek, June 5

Dear Father,

We have been payed of to day and I take the earlyest opportunity of releiving my pocket book of an over stock of greenbacks. tell Cora she need not expend it all for Photos without further orders from me. we have had many rumors through Camp about marching but I doubt them all. we are now beautifully located on a level plain near a grove of oaks. we have (Sergt. Hayward, Call the Company into line to exchange guns.[18] I done so and have returned again to my writing but lost that Idea as you will notice I left of at (we have). who knows but what I was starting of at the time, with some great illustration or a poetic strain which would have been worthy of the pen of Byron or Saxe.[19] but it is lost to the world for I scratched my head for 10 minutes and it would not come out. but we have (Sergt Hayward will you please hand me that book) now the old Springfield rifel. we shall like them very well when we get used to them. the sabre bayonet is so heavy to wear. (Sergt Hayward, has George Zeller got a gun[?])[20] I find that I shall have to leave the Marque untill the Lieut has the Company equiped or this will not go in the morning mail. in my own rude shelter I may enjoy peace. [*Here Hayward drew a hut with "here" inscribed on it.*] I do not find things so convenient for writing. instead of a chair & desk I have a log and board. we have our bunk raised from the ground 2 feet. our tent is well ventilated and well stocked with provisions, and considering the quallity of feathers (oak rails) we sleep well nights. as soon as we can get the chance we intend to cut a lot of pine boughs untill our nights will be passed dreamless. I received the Gazette a few days ago. we got no mail to day. I hope to recive a letter from home before you get this. Capt. Meyers has resigned. he stood his Court Martial but I think it turned against him for Gen Geary advised him to resign.[21] Capt. John Flyn is in Command.[22] I wrote to Cora a few days ago. enclosed you will find $32. the 2 dollar will not pass here. we dont like your Yankee money here in Virginia. (love to all)

Henry

Sat morn, June 6th
There was heavy canonading towards the Rappahannock last evening. we were orderd to be ready at a moments notice. all [is] quiet this morning. send reinforcements of stamps. (a few peny stamps also) I just took a fancy wash with fancy soap and mothers towell)

77

No. 4
Camp at Fairfax C. H. June 16

Dear Father,

We arrived here last night after a terrible suffocating march from Aquia Creek. we were only 2 doz makeing the distance of 40 miles. we came in (Co D) with only 9 Rifels, being only 2 more than we had on the march to South Mt. I was completely faged out, almost sick. I could not have made it without the assistance of the boys. Lieut Devine carried my Knapsack quite a distance while Tom Ashton carried my Rifel.[23] (Cora hemmed his hankerchief) I feel better now than I have at any time since I left N.B. I just came up from the creek where I enjoyed a good bath and feel like myself again. but I must get to work and get supper. I look into the Haversack, I notice Eggs, Cheese, condensed milk, Yankee Soap, &c. I guess we shall make out to night. the sutlers say they will have a fresh supply up in the morning. we are living gay at present. (so are the Rebels) I wish they would let the 28th go to Penna. the boys are burning to go as tired as they are. I think they should send a Corps of old troops up there to encourage the poor Conscrips. I have a sheet of Music that I am going to send to Cora. it was sent to Sergt. Hiles by Sergt Pepper[24] from Phila. the Lieut gave it to me and I thought Cora could lern to play it if it is a good one. you will notice that I am in a hurry. I do not know how long we shall remain here. you did not tell me in your last if you got the Inquirer. I notice my $32 is safe. there was 18 dropped dead in our Corps yesterday. 13 in the first Div, 5 in the 2d. we all suffered with a terrible headache. it was the hardest march we have had yet. $2/3$ of the Corps straggled. they are coming in all day. I notice the 7 N.Y. Regt is of for the war again. good boys) so are the gallant 6th Mass.[25]

yes I must Close. (on to Richmond Via Pena.) love to all. write when you feel like it, and sooner if possible. it must be known that the Kingdom Coming, &c. there, I have filled the sheet in 10 minutes. it will take you 20 to read. I hope it gets through the Rebel lines.

Henry

78

No 5
Camp of the 28th Regt. Leesburgh, Va June 21

Dear Sister,

I wrote this afternoon to one of my Comrades in the Gen Hospital at Germantown Pa, enclosing 2 Photos which I recived from you to day. they are for Sergt. Orth and P. F. Worsely.[26] they are both getting along very well. I have sent word to Frank Worsely to get me one of the late Sergt. Hiles Photos if he can possibly. I have not heard from Sergt Barnes since he was removed from the Hospital at Aquia Creek, but I am afraid it has made him worse as he was to sick to be moved much. we left Fairfax the same day which I wrote to Father. we arrived here friday night in the rain, and it has been raining ever since untill this noon when it broke away, and it is now very pleasant. we have heard heavy canonadeing all day in the direction of Snickers Gap. we are anxious to know what it is all about. for the last ½ hour it has ceased. we have not seen any late papers but have heard that the Rebs have left Pa. prehaps they heard the 12th Corps was moveing northward and that Geary belonged up there in that part of the country which they were makeing desolate. if they have been burning and plundering they will suffer the most in the end for the boys have made up their minds that they will be even with them by carrying matches in their pockets hereafter. Yesterday 3 men sufferd death for dessertion. it was the first time that it has been punished to the full extent of the law in our Corps. the whole Corps was drawn up in the large field where we are encamped. the sentence was read to them and the Chaplin prayed for them. then they were executed. it is very hard but right. if it had been done in the first place I think it would have saved Conscription.)[27] you must give Mr. Goddard one of my Photos, also Uncle Sumners little girl, and I think I promised Uncle Otis folks one.[28] I sent you a sheet of music when I was at Fairfax. the rations have just come and I must close. love to all.

> from,
> Uncle Henry

Monday noon. 22d

we moved camp this morning to a better location and better water near at hand. we have laid out a regular camp. the waggons have come up and we may remain here for 2 weeks or move in 2 minutes. I get the Gazette regularly. received [the] N.Y. Ledger from Mell yesterday.

79

Camp of the 28th near Hanover Pa June 30th

Dear Father,

we have just arrived and it is nearly dark, but I will write a few lines that you may know my whereabouts. we crossed the Pa line at ½ past 12 AM to day, and such lusty cheering I never heard before. all of our marches, which we have made since we crossed the Potomac, although quite lengthy, have been pleasure excursions to us compared to our travels in Old Virginia. the smiles of the ladies, the many flags which we see on our advance, the cool spring water handed to us by the lovely ladies send us a peculiar healthy feeling through the whole system well calculated to lighten the Knapsack. I wish I could describe the Country which we are now in. it is the best farming Country in the world. I only wonder that the Rebels have not tryed to get here before. I think they will be slow to leave for they never knew before what good liveing was. most of the farmers will not take anything for what we get, but work hard to supply us with everything that is in their power to do. our Cavalry had a skirmish where we now are.[29] we shall push on in the morning. I cannot describe the feeling of the army but they are very patriotic, never were more so. we will whip them this time or fall by thousands. we here that Hooker has been removed and that McClellan takes command.[30] I am sattisfied. I will cheer him the first time he passes our lines. anything to keep the people united. I hope it will sattisfie the Copperheads, and that the north will submit cheerfully to Conscription.[31] I shall hand this to some fair lady when we pass through Hanover tomorrow to mail for me. I hear we shall get a mail to night. excuse this for it is night while I am writing.

love to all,
Henry

Wed. Morn, July 1st

it is a lovely morning. we take 20 extra rounds of Cartridges and move at 8 ock AM. I had pork & crackers and onions for breakfast.[32]

Henry

80

July 6

6 ock AM

Camp of the 28 near Littletown Pa

Dear Father,

I will write untill the bugle sounds the call to fall in. you must not expect particulars this time. it will be enough for you to know this time that I have done my duty in the last great Contest and have not received a scratch. it has been a great victory thus far. our Division met the famous Stonewall Division and repulsed them in all their onsets. Co D went into the fight of the 3d inst with 26 enlisted men. we lost 2 killed and 6 wounded being nearly [cut in] ½. we left the battle field yesterday morning to follow up the enemy. [*Hayward wrote "cut them off" above the preceding sentence.*] we have just received orders to go no farther untill further orders as the enemy has made another stand or else they cannot get away. we were under fire for 3 days. I am all right with the exception of my legs which tremble under me. last night was the first night we have passed with out being disturbed since June 30. it rained hard but disturbed us not. love to all.

I shall write again soon.

Henry

this paper was taken from a dead rebel Sergt. by one of my Co [in] front of our entrenchments. he must have been a deserter and promoted while in the rebel service.[33]

81

28 P.V. in Line of Battle near Williamsport July 12

Dear Father,

Fearing that you did not get my last letter that I sent from Littletown after the Battle of Gettysburgh I will write a very few lines this morning. the mail will go in a few minutes. we have been following up the Enemy untill we are now face to face with them. firing with artillery has commenced on the right Wing. we may become engaged at any moment. we are ready. they have the choice in position and it will be a terrible battle. fall in is the order.

This is Corp Butcher killed in the Battle of Getysburgh.[34]

love to all,
Henry

82

Camp of the 28th Regt. P.V. Sandy Hook July 17th

Dear Father,

I have mailed one letter to you to day but I was so much hurried that it did not contain much of interest. my mind is not in that state of composure which it should be to write even now. the events of the past 2 weeks have been of such an exciteing Character that I have no controll over myself. we are begining to find out what has been transpireing while we were on the march. I now hear the cars a comeing and you must excuse me if I lay this aside to rush for a paper when they come. we are now camped on the same ground which we occupied nearly 2 years ago. what do the people of the North think now of the Old Army of the Potomac[?] have they not proved to the world that it has not been their fault that they have not won fields before[?] worn out and exausted as they were before they reached Gettysburgh, they have fought the flower of the Southern Army and compelled them to recross the Potomac. it is now a mere Skelleton but will make a splendid frame work for another army, that is if the roughs of New York will consent to reinforce us. I have no pacience with Abe Lincoln that he should [have] allowed such a riot to breake out there when the presence of a few troops could have quelled it before it became so monstrous.[35] he is certainly an excellant rail splitter but a very poor President. there is not one of the old Regts but what would have liked to have taken a rest (or would now) to New York or any other place where bayonetts are needed to carry out the laws. I am better pleased with the news from Port Hudson than any other place because Banks has been successfull with his niggers and nine months men. I have been afraid that he would fail, but now he has exceled them all.[36]

After I had returned from my furlough last spring I was much surprised after reading a copy of an order which the Lieutenant handed me which he told me he had sent to headquarters during my absence. he said there had been an order issued to send in names of those who had by their actions at Chancellorsville entitled themselves to medals of honor. soon after this, active operations commenced by the Army and that is the last I have heard from it. I received an extract of the order from the Lieutenant to day which will do as well for there are other in the company which [have] done their duty as well that would not have got one.[37] I will write about the battle of Gettysburgh [at] the first oppurtunity. I have not received a letter from home since the battle. send stamps.

love to all,
Henry

83

Camp of the 28th Regt. Sandy Hook Md. July 17 (Third Edition)
Dear Father,

I have this moment received yours of the 11 inst. you wished me to write on this page when I had the chance. I will take it now for the post master says we shall not have a chance to send again after the one that goes at 6 ock PM to day for some time. that looks like crossing the Potomac again soon. now is the time to move while we have them frightned. I was going to give you a full account of the doings of our Division in the late battle, but I shall now get the chance. on the morning of the 2d, the 28 was thrown forward as skirmishers or picketts while Geary and his men throwed up the works that afterwards proved so valuable.[38] on the night of the 2d, our Brigade was orderd to the right wing. [We] returned to our former position the same night. [On the] morning of the 3d the day of the great battle [we] laid in reserve supporting Kanes Brigade of our Div for 2 hours.[39] Lewis K. Boyce of our Company was killed at this time.[40] [We were] soon orderd to releive the 29th Ohio of our brigade who were in action in the entrenchments. we were in action 3 hours, during which time I fired 65 rounds of Amuntion. this is more than I have used in any battle. I often had to wait for my rifel to cool, raming the ball home with a stone. we were releived by the 1st Md Regt. (Home Brigade) the first time they were ever under fire. they came up with a yell and fired a volly over our heads into the trees. we did not know what to make of it at first and like Chanclorsville hugged close to the ground untill they were stoped by the 7th Ohio who were in their rear. they then advance and we retired.[41] our brigade then moved to the rear where we made coffee and eat a tremendious diner such as soldiers carry in their haversacks. we had not tasted of coffee for 20 hours (which is the main stay). it was at this time that the furious canonading commenced which the papers all speak of.[42] the shel burst and flew all around us. Capt. Flyn moved us again to where the rest of the Brigade laid. soon the Brigade move off by Regts. to find a place of safety for a short time untill we should be wanted again to the front. but there was no choice. we halted and each hunted a tree or stone to hide his head. I lay with six others behind a large stone with my face close to the ground watching the course of the Rebel shells. they would burst over us, [in] front of us, strike trees, and at one time threw dirt all over us. we would pass a joke upon it and think no more of it. there was bugeler hid behind a tree holding his horse. a shel came, struck the horse, and over he went. soon we heard the order fall in. we done so quickly and moved to our old position near the brest works waiting orders. we were orderd into the entrenchments at 8 ock P.M. [We] remained there untill 1 ock AM on the morning of the fourth. while we were in this last time a wounded rebel that had been laying near our works all day was brought in. he was most gone but he could tell us that he belonged to Jones Brigade of the Old Stone wall Div.[43] on July 4th I went with two others to bury Corporal Butcher and Lewis Boyce. we buried them as they have often marched side by side. we made them good head boards. I helped carry Sergt Longsworth of the field after we had been releived the first time.[44] this make 4 Sergts we have had wounded in the leg.

love to all,
Henry

wounded in Co D)	Sergt Chas Longsworth	Killed)	Corp Butcher
	Corporal Shadle[45]		Private Boyce
	Private Shenckle[46]		
	Private Williams[47]		
	Private Murphy[48]		
	Corp Ashton		

I received stamps in your last. this is a fat letter. you will have to send two for it.

84

Camp of the 28th Snickersville Va July 22

Dear Father,

we received orders that a mail would leave here this afternoon. I have not much time to write as there is to be a general Inspection at 2½ ock. my Rifel is in good condition so I can write untill the drums beat. the 2d,

3d, & 12th Corps crossed the Potomac at Harpers Ferry. we have been encamped here for 2 days in the same field where we pitched our tents before. The people here are sick of the war and long for peace on any terms. some of the boys told me yesterday that they offerd $20 in Confederate money for a dozen of biscuit and the women refused to take it saying they had rather have our little 25 cts notes for them. that must be a joke. the boys say I have been getting fat since the battle of Gettysburgh. we do not know where the Rebels are but I suppose Meade does. I hope we cannot find them while the weather is as hot as it is now. we expect our Conscripts before long, and we Non Coms have got them to drill. I shall get my squad under a Shady tree and talk it into them instead of runing around with them. we have received no mail for 5 days. when it does come I know I shall get letters and papers. this will be a costly Advance for the Virginians this time. some of the Soldiers burnt a barn the first day we crossed. they found Arms concealed in the hay. they catch all the chickens and do not spare the mother with its little brood. when we go into camp at night it is not long before the pigs are squealing in every direction. we have fine times picking black berrys which are very thick here. it is a queer sight to see a Division in a large field runing from bush to bush picking berrys. put in a sheet of paper when you write. I lost my porfolio at Gettysburgh. love to all.

Henry

85

July 29th
Camp of the 28th Regt. P.V. Catletts Station Va

Dear Sister,

After many days of dreadfull marches we have come to a halt. never has a rest been more welcome than at this time for judgeing from the appearance of our Regt. the whole army must look Consumptive. we are completely faged out, but if they allow us to remain here for a while it will not be long before we shall be recruited up and all look natural again. we are being supplied with plenty of rations such as we are not allowed to have on the march. so we think that we are now liveing like lords. The cars run every hour during the day. we receive our mails and get papers daily. I received 3 Gazzetts yesterday, but no letters of yours. I was a little disappointed but shall look for one by mail to day. I wrote to Father from Snickersville. I would like to know if you get all that I send. I am expecting more of those photos as soon as I hear from you. well there, if I did not enjoy myself looking over the list of the drafted to notice the King of Copperheads got hit.[49] it must make him feel cross. I notice that some of the old soldiers were not spared. I should like to hear from New York, to hear if Mell & Augustus or Albert are clear. I notice some of the 9 months Mass. Regts have arrived at Boston. they have come in good time to enforce the draft if necessary. the first Army Corps are encamped about 2 miles from here. if I get time I shall call to see some of the N.B. boys in the 12th. I am very certain that I saw John Burns after the Battlle of Gettysburgh. he rode by our line while we were on the march near Gettysburgh. I did not recognize him untill he had passed, then I told my Lieut that I was most certain that I knew that bugler that just rode by.[50] Lieut Devine has gone to Phil-d for Conscripts. I suppose he will be here with the poor creatures in 2 weeks at the fartherest. it will make the duties lighter for all the enlisted men except myself. I send enclosed a Photo of Sergt. Wm. H. Hiles, Co D. he was when with us the gayest boy in the Regt. he always had a story to tell or [was] ready for a song. he was wounded at Chancellorsville and died shortly afterwards in Washington. you will take good care of it as I prize it highly. it is comfortable cool to day. we can set still and not sweat much. water is very scarce here. all of the regts are diging wells but they do not make out to find much water. we use water from a sluggish stream to cook with but to get good spring water to drink we have to walk 2 miles. why they keep us in such a camp as this I cannot tell. I guess the conscripts will grumble when they come. will you write soon[?]

love to all,
Henry

86

Camp of the 28th Regt. P.V. 5 miles below Kelleys Ford Va Aug. 5th
Dear Father,

As I feel in very good humor this morning, I will write a few lines not knowing when another such favorable oppertunity may present itself. The fact is we had a very refreshing shower last evening which makes the morning air cool and braceing. we moved from Catletts Sta-n to Kelleys Ford on the Rappahannock. it is well we did not stay longer for their was much sickness oweing to the bad water and swampy nature of the ground. The Star Corps is at present guarding the fords along the river, the 3d Brigade (Gen Green) being on the extreme left at United States ford. I think we must be near Richards and Barnetts fords. we have not yet become familliar with the Country about here, but what few family there are living here are in the most wretched condition. they beg for crackers from the Yankee Soldiers and I know of one instance where they were so starving that Gen Geary orderd a box of Crackers to be sent for their releif. we have a beautifull camp, shady trees near at hand with an abundance of Cold spring water to drink and bathe. I think the prospects are good for us to remain here for some time. the chances are so favorable that all wear a smile and are begining to get fat. we console ourselves with the opinion that we can never suffer as much again from long burning, thirsty, dusty marches as we have endured of late. Men of iron constitutions who have supposed they could stand everything belonging to the duties of a Soldier have had to drop by the way side. is it not strange that I bare up under the hardships so well[?] I am astonished at it myself, but I could tell you of many a sleepless night that I have passed after a severe march. but I will not complain of my poor bones now for they have ceased to ache. the aspect of affairs looks so cheering that we forget the many trials that we have passed and cease to be troubled for those to come. I hope the people at home will not set quietly down thinking that peace is certain to follow our victorys imediately. now is the time for renewed and double efforts on the part of all. we expect the Conscripts here about the 15th. we occupy a position which will afford an excellent oppitunity to make good soldiers of them. they will have a chance of being sent to the out post on picket where they can see occasionaly a Rebel cavalry man which will nerve them in to the dangers by degrees. I can imagin their feelings for a while when they tread their lonely beat and are startled by the breaking of a dead twig from a tree by the wind (that will be a Rebel) or a stray cow may pass between him and the light of the moon (that will be a Rebel Cavalryman) and if he watches him long his imagination will make it appear to him that there are two of them. of course he must fire and alarm the post. I look for good times when they come. the boys have many serious joke prepared for them, but I tell them they must use them well for they will have enough to try their pacience without being poked at by the Old Vets. I am in hopes we shall get good steady men, for the Majority of what is left of our Company are wild vulgar boys. Lieut Devine told me that he thought he would be allowed the choice of his men. he and Capt. Flyn are great friends. I have a full supply of paper on hand. I am satisfied the way you send the Gazzette. the last letter I wrote home was to Cora. we get late papers and mail quite regular. enclosed you will find another (young) veteran Private Wm McAllister, Co D.[51] I hope Cora received the Photo of Sergt. Hiles. I expect Sergt Peppers from Phila-d. Lieut Lazarus has sent for a few. he was one of the Old original Sergts. [He] was discharged at Bolivar Heights. he is a fine man. his father was one of the first men of Phila-d —12 ock AM. Yes, I have been to dinner. this sheet has been laying around all day. it will soon be filled for the mail leaves soon and the southern sun shines hot. I must away to seek some shady spot where I can while away the time by brushing away the flies and scratching muskeeto bites untill the evening shades appear.

love to all,

Henry

87

Camp of the 28th Regt. P.V. 5 miles below Kelleys Ford, Aug. 7th

Dear Brother [Albert],

Yours of the 3d inst came to hand last night and as I am not at present engaged in company affairs I hasten to answer it. I wrote a long letter home yesterday. I generally keep them well posted concerning my movements. I have received the Gazzette with the list of the drafted. I notice that it hit a great many of my old acquaintences and did not spare the Copperheads. I now look with much interest to know who are exempt. Father writes me that he expects Melville home soon. I hope he will take his lady friend with him as it is high time that that affair had resumed a more serious aspect. we are enduring very hot weather at present, but while we remain quiet we manage to live quite comfortable. we have a camp beautifully located where there is plenty of shade and water in every direction. we have planted cedar trees all around our Company quarters which adds to our comfort, besides beautifys the camp, and with every appearence of remaining here we are very happy. we are all looking more like ourselves once more now that we are rested and are begining to gain flesh from the effects of an abundance of Uncle Samuels provender. we expect the Paymaster here to day. then there will be the usual raid on the sutlers of all the lovers of ginger cakes, cans of fruit, &c. Lieut Devine left us at Catletts Station to go to Phila for Conscripts. we look for his return about the 15th. then we shall have our hands full of buisness drilling recruits. Sergt. Chas Longsworth died of his wounds received at the Battle of Gettysburgh. I help take him from the field. he was promoted from Corporal after the battle of Chancellorsville. this makes 4 Sergts we have had wounded in the leg, 2 of whome have died. I have received a number of papers from Melville lately. I am glad to see that you are doing so well and that you are determined to give your buisness your whole attention. you must certainly succeed. if you should be drafted the money which I have in Fathers care is at your service. I do not think there is much danger of them molesting Augustus if he does not look more robust and hearty then when I last saw him. tell him to take off his whiskers. I do not know about Melvilles case. he has been a Soldier. they will nab on to him pretty quick. tell him to bend over and swallow a chew of tobacco just before he goes to get examined. it is unfortunate that both of Uncle Alberts sons should have been drafted.[52] what will they do[?] one of my messmates has fallen to sleep. he is makeing a noise simillar to a large (swine). I suppose you see A. & M. often. remember me to all and write soon.

Henry

88

Sergt Hayward
28th Penn Vols

Sir,

Some time ago, a number of opened letters, official papers, and various other articles were placed in my charge and amongst them the enclosed photograph. I have no doubt but there were also some letters, but in the course of our movements, they were either lost or destroyed. I find however from Capt. Fitzpatrick of this Regt.[53] that you are the owner of the enclosed. I forward it to you regretting that I have not the accompanying papers. but as I have the charge of all Mail Matter coming to the regiment I will take especial care of all that may be sent by accident here and send them by the first opportunity to you. reiterating my regrets for the loss of your letters.

I have the honor to be
Your obdt servt
Edward F. O'Brien[54]
Sergt Major
28th Mass Vols
Irish Brigade
1st Div 2nd Corps

You will please acknowledge the receipt of this.

89

Camp of the 28th Regt. P.V. Eliss Ford, Aug. 16th

Dear Father,

I received Melvilles letter of the 8th inst. and intended to answer it before he left N.B. but on looking over his letter I notice he intends to leave for N.Y. on the 17th. I have not yet received Coras letter with the Photos enclosed. it has been delayed somewhere on the way, prehaps lost. although it is often the case, they appear at a time when least expected. The weather continues hot but we are thouroghly Climated and do not mind it much. We have been very busy for the last week makeing bowers and planting shade trees around our quarters. although it is for our own comfort, the boys commenced the work reluctantly growling like bears. I do not blame them for marching orders are so sure to follow. as you will notice by looking over my back letters, where we have built up log villages [we are forced] to leave them half finished or [are] occupying them but a few days. we had nearly compleated ours yesterday when an order came from Gen Meade to have 3 days rations in Haversacks [and] to be ready to move at a moments notice. the steady old Soldiers received the order like men. they laid their axes [and] gatherd in Clusters under their arbors, determined to enjoy them while they remained. they talked of the Probability of going to Charleston or advancing towards Culpepper and of the many rumors going around camp. some are busy frying meat to put in their Haversacks, while all (as is generally the case) dive into the extra rations that have accumulated and eat their fill that they may not be wasted, but more particular as they do not know when they will get another chance. Well, we were let alone untill 1 ock this morning when we were arroused from our slumbers and orderd to releive the 29th Ohio who were on Picket, Companys D, E, G remaining in camp. my Lieut told me that the Ohio Regts have been orderd to their owne State to enforce the Draft. the 147 & 28 is all that is left of the invincible 1st Brig. they left us this morning at 6 ock, Gen Geary having first addressed them. Copperheads of Ohio lay low in the grass when they reach the Buck Eye State for Braver and truer men do not carry musketts than they have proved to be. who knows but we may be orderd to our 'homes' in Pen-a to kill Snakes. we consider ourselves good Soldiers and have done the State some service. it is now 12 ock A.M. 24 hours have passed since we received orders and no move yet. we may not move atall. but the chances are more in favor that we will if we can place any reliances in half of the rumors. there is no doubt but what the 5th Corps has gone to Alexandria to take Transports. rumor says more are to follow and that the remainder of the army will retire towards Washington (we will watch and see). I think it looks reasonable for North Carolina wants to be liberated. Charlestown must fall, and the Rebels will have it that we have been reinforced from the western army, so of course we can spare them.—just wait a few minutes. Diner is ready. another cup of bean soup before we move anyway.

now I hope I can write a little better. my nerves are steady. you may have roast lamb and green peas with the extras, but give to us our bean soup. why[?] What was the reason Jack wouldnt eat his supper[?] never mind. we are satisfied. it must be a healthy place where we are for the boys all complain of having such extraordinary appetites which is very uncomon for this time of the year. I sent you my Old morning report by mail yesterday. I hope it will reach you for it may be of interest to you and give some information of the causes in the decrease of our army. you will notice that it is for the months begining with Jan. up to the Middle of August. the Adjutant gave us new ones in the place of them, they being so much worn carrying them in our knapsacks while on a march. I received a letter from Albert last evening. he wrote me a very good letter. I think his change of base to New York will prove benificial to him. I notice by the manly tone of his letters that he is trying to work himself up, and at some future day we shall know him as a man of buisness. I also received one from Augustus a few days ago giving me an account of the riot. he speaks of it being very hot there. Lieut Devine writes from Phil-d that he will not be ready to join us with the Conscripts for 3 weeks. there was 200 arrived for the 147 Regt a few nights since. they were all substitutes (but 3) and they were the most depraved looking set of beings I ever saw togeather. a number of them escaped on their way here by jumping off the cars while they were at full motion. some became unmanageble on the road. the guard fired at one wounding him in the arm. there are 3 among them that served in the Rebel army in Mississipi Regts. nearly all of them are from New York. the guard that accompanyed them from Alexandria says they told them they had to leave N. York, they having been engaged in the late riot, and I beleive it by their appearance for many of them have Singed Eyes and broken noses. I hope we shall be delivered from substitutes if they are a sample. Lieut Devine is so long coming that he may wait untill the drafted men cannot get Subs—then we shall get good men. you spoke in your last letter of a Div of the 12 Corps going to the support of Kilpatrick at Kellys ford. it was Gearys Div. we laid a Pontoon. our Brigade crossed. there was not much skirmishing by Infantry. one of my mess mates says the sutler told him that Geary told him we should not remain here 24 hours. I shall keep this open untill the last moment that you may know if we do move. we were payed off yesterday 2 months dues settling our Clothing accounts. one man got no pay in our company, he having over run his allowance for Clothing. but in most cases the government owes the men, they not having taken up all the money allowed them for Cloths. I received $42.35 cts. I drawed $8.35 which I did not expend in clothing. enclosed find $20. I shall send more in my next. (I will put $20 [of] it in Coras as I am going to write a few lines to her this morning.)

Aug. 17 I will make you acquainted with Corp Henry C. Fithian one of the Old Stand bys. Honest as the day is long, [he is] always at his post. has been with us in every battle and skirmish.[55]

dont forget to write Vols. when you direct as there is a 28 Pena Militia at Harisburgh. send more stamps. I forgot to mention that that report Book was in sergt Barnes Knapsack when he was wounded and taken Prisoner at Chancellorsville.

Henry, Pen. Vols.

90

Camp of the 28th Regt Pen Vols. Aug 17th

Dear Sister,

It may be sometime since you have heard from the 28 Mass Vols. I will send you a letter from the good Sergt. Major of said Regt. which I received last night togeather with one Photo. I feel under great Obligation to him for interesting himself so much in my behalf. it will also be some satisfaction to you to know where your precious epistles have strayed to. I would have rather received the letter than the Photo for I can get more of them, but you cannot again bring your mind to bare upon the same subjects which were contained in the letter that is lost. I know it has done some poor Soldiers heart good for I always read yours with great pleasure. try it again as soon as you receive this. we have no further orders about moveing this morning. send me more of them Photos. if there is not many left, have another half dozen struck of 3 of each kinds. those which I get in exchange for mine I prize more than double the value of what mine cost. I send enclosed $20. if that gets home safe [I] will send more. we are so far in the enemys country that it is risky sending by mail. if you should let Father direct your letters I think there would be no trouble. I always receive his very quick. the Corps is the principle directory. they are given to Corps Post masters at Washington. from Corps to Div, from Div to Brig, from Brig to Regt, from Regt to Orderly Sergts.

love to all,
Henry

91

Camp of the 28th P.V. Eliss Ford Aug 20

Dear Brother [Albert],

Yours of the 13th inst has been promptly received, and not having particulars to call my attention to, I hasten to answer. there has been a considerable [amount] of a stir among the troops in the Army of the Potomac for the past week. no one knows or can even guess where they are going to. so quiet and misterious have been their movement. last night, the 2nd Corps marched. they have been encamped on our left. the 12th Corps is the only body of troops left in this section. I suppose we shall move soon as we have been under orders to be in readiness for 4 days. I beleive we shall retire towards Alexandria when we do move. I hear they are buissily at work throwing up entrenchments. I hear that a portion of the A. of the Poto- have embarked on transports for South Carolina, but I think we shall wait untill we are filled up with recruits which will not be long for we expect a squad to leave Philadelphia on the 21st. The weather continues warm with cool nights. we do not sleep any to warm with our blanketts. I was fortunate in having my blanketts haulled this sumer. when we march I take it up to Lieut Devine tent and he has it rolled up with his. all of the boys have thrown theirs away during the last campaign. we have got a Paddy regular over us commanding the Regt. he boasts of the name Capt John Flyn. he was Adjutant when we came out under Geary. he expects his commission as Colonel every day. he is disliked by all in the Regt. he is a brave enough man in battle but forgets at night what he learns during the day. one of Coras letters which I have been looking for so long with Photographs has turned up in the Mass 28. I presume it was through Capt Fitzpatrick (your former acquaintence) that I got it. the Sergt Major of that Regt wrote me a letter saying that he would look after my letters if there should be any more [that] find their way into his camp. I suppose Melville has arrived in N.Y. by this time and John Parker is looking after the Elephant. I shall have to direct this to 78 Chatham St as I have neglected to take your directions. I wrote to Augustus a few days ago. I must Close this. hopeing you will write soon.

love to all,
Henry

92

Eliss Ford, Va. /63
Camp of the 28th Regt. P.V. Aug 24th

Dear Sister,

Yours of the 20th inst came to hand last evening. I will answer imediately enclosing $20 and request you send another pair of those Sergts. tell Father this last draw—draws pretty hard on my Suttler money. but if I fall short before another pay day, I know where to call. I had a few dollars coming to me from the men in the Company the last pay day. so I guess I shall make out. there will be 2 months due us by the first of Sept. I was thinking to day that the 3 months for which I subscribed for the Inquirer must soon be out. I intend to have it Continued. I receive the Gazette regular. I notice you have a number of returned Soldiers in N.B. has Fred Goddard returned yet[?][56] I should be pleased to hear from him if he has. I do not hear what John is doing lately, wheather he is preaching or at home on the farm.[57] I suppose Johny P. is viewing the Elephant in New York. tell him I want him to write all about the sights when he returns and is well rested. this is the last day that I shall have of peace and quietness untill after the Conscripts get settled down. we expect them tonight. my Regt goes on Picket at 4 ock PM. the Orderly Sergts are exempt. There is quite a change in the weather to day, much Cooler with a good breeze stirring. I have just got in from Guard

Mounting and have concluded to lay this by untill morning. the mail does not leave untill 11 ock A.M. tomorrow. I will now prepare my supper, and as my messmates are all absent on picket, [this] of course leaves me alone. I have put some crackers to soak and [I] am going to have them fried. this is a meal very common among Soldiers. they all eat fried crackers.

Tuesday morning Aug 25th

I have just eaten my breakfast of fried Crackers & Coffee. my morning report has just gone to the Adjutants Office, and now I am at leisure, subject to calls for details or other affairs connected with the Company. the boy will be releived from picket at 4 ock this afternoon. untill then, time will wear slowly away, but I am fortunate in having yesterday Phila Inquirer full of news. its heading says full particulars of the terriffic Bombardment of Sumpter, Late Rebel news, &c. there is every appearence of a storm. we should be much benefitted by a good shower to Cleanse the Camp and fill the springs. send Photos in the first letter that leaves 48 Green Street. [Please send] A few more stamps as I am writing often now while we are in Camp. I received 4 in your last. write soon.

> I would be remembered
> to all enquiring friends,
> Henry

93

> Elis ford
> Camp of the 28th Regt. P.V. Aug 25th /63

Dear Mother,

You have heard of the famous King Cotton. I will present you with a sample of his highness in all his youth and beauty. There is a large field of it growing near our Camp. the Plant grows about 2 feet high bareing these blossoms of red and white. it looks beautifull when in full blossom early in the morning. this is the first that I have ever seen growing. the farmer that ownes it says it is very backward this Summer. I suppose it is afraid to grow when the Yankees are about. we do not bow to his Majesty or acknowledge his mighty power, but trample it under our feet the same as the Southerners do our American Flag. I think he must have hurt himself when he fell lately in England. You will please find enclosed two Shares of the afore said Cotton Loan. I hope you will be sattisfied with it. I can assure you it is just as good and is worth as much as you can purchase in England. I have wrote to Cora and shall mail this at the same time I do hers. I send $20 in Coras. the Conscripts have not come.

> Henry

94

Camp of the 28th Regt. P.V. Sept 12 63

Dear Father,

I received your last letter a few days since—still later one from mother. I supposed the next time I wrote I could inform you of the arrival of our Conscripts, but they do not come. I think they are filling up Regiments that have a longer time to serve than ours. We will soon be nine months men while there are many others that have nearly 2 years to serve. The Ohio Regiments will soon be with us again. they are now in Alexandria. we shall wellcome them back to us again for many reasons, but the first is it will make Picket duty much lighter. one of our Wounded from Chancelorsville Battle arrived yesterday. he thinks they will all be with us soon.[58] I have not heard directly from Sergt Barnes lately, but [I] beleive he is recovering slowly but will never be able for field service. a few days ago a little negro boy came into our lines (wishing to be some service to his country) and informed Gen Geary that his master had killed one of our men at the time we were on the march to Chancelorsville. Gen Geary imediately sent the Colonel of the 29th Regt P.V. with a squad of men to inquire into the matter.[59] arriving at the house he made search of the premises, finding many overcoats & Blankets. he asked him how he came by them. he said they were left there by deserters. he asked if there were any guns about his place. he said no. looking up in a corner under the caves of the house, he noticed an old stocking. he pulled it down and found it full of cartridges. the Colonel then asked him for his son. he told him he was down in the Cornfield. the Colonel started to find him when the old man insisted upon accompanying him that he might give his son the wink. the Colonel placed a guard on the house with instructions to let no one leave. when he found the son, he said to him your father told me you should show me where those guns are concealed. he droped his hoe and walked some distance into the woods and there hid in the bushes and stones were 17 Rifels. not long after, the whole family broke up house keeping and took up the line of march towards the headquarters of the White Star division where their case will be attend to by the Kansas Ruffian. serch has since been made for boddys around their premises, but none have been found. if they are proved guilty it will not be Gearys fault if they are not hung.[60] we hear great news almost daily from every department but ours. I suppose the people at home will begin to growll soon because we are inactive. if they want to know why we do not move tell them it is none of their buisness. it is not our turn yet. I should like to know how Jeff [Davis] enjoys life these times. he must certainly be troubled with the night mare or else Greek Fire.[61] Battery F is Hamptons, the one we supported at Chancelorsville.[62] enclosed you will find a Photo of Edward Pepper. he enlisted as 2d Sergt, discharged at Boliver after we recrossed the Potomac from Antietam. he was just as good as he looks. take good care of it. I received 2 Photos in mothers letter. [I] get the Gazette regular. is it printed up to the Cider mill now[?] tell Cora to write. remember me to Fanny.[63] love to all.

Henry

95

Sept 18th

Camp of the 28th Regt. Raccoon Ford on the Rapidan R

Dear Father,

I have 30 minutes to write before the mail leaves. I have no time for long words. our Conscripts came to us the day before we left Eliss Ford. Co D received 37. I am satisfied with our suces. they are mostly old Soldiers, those that are not are as dumb as sticks. we have 2 Germans that have not been over 8 days before they went as substitutes. when I want to talk to them I have to get a Interpriter. we have one man that was a Captain in the 40 Regt N.Y.V. (the Mozart Regt),[64] 2 or 3 Sergts, and a number of Corps. Lieut Devine did not come on with them. he will remain in Phila untill the draft is over. we have just come in from the place of execution where 2 men from our division were shot for desertion. they did not kill them [on] the first volley. the reserve had to come up. it was an awfull sight. after the first volley, one of them was still setting on his Coffin.[65] it has rained hard for the past 24 hours but it is now Clear. Skirmishing is continually going on down to the river. we are one mile from the Rappidan. I must make a detail. [I] will write soon again. I am well. love to all.

Henry

96

Sept 24th

Camp of the 28th Regt P.V. Raccoon Ford

Dear Sister,

Yours of the 16th has been received and was read with much interest. I cannot give as much of my time to writing as I have in former days as you are aware by this time that the Substitutes are among us in all their ignorance. you have no Idea what a wretched creature a dumb man is. we have 2 out of our squad of 37 that Bobby Williams would call Block heads. I think sometimes that they will never learn. they are both Irishman of the Pick & Spade school. the rest of the our squad are already good soldiers. Lieut Devine put [fifty-one] in their cars before they left Phil-d. yesterday. 14 of the Subs left for Washington, they having been found unfit for duty.

it is surprising to see how the government is imposed upon by the men who pass these cripples. one man that left yesterday had no heel on his left foot, it having been shot away in battle. he was discharged from his Regt and received a pension and was passed by surgons in Phila- for a Subs-.[66] yesterday a deserter from the 12 Georgia came over to our men on Picket. he was shot at 4 times. he told the boys that a great many of the troops from Lees army had gone South and that many of the N.C. troops were deserting. we can see them fortifying the hills from our picket line. both sides are very friendly. they have ceased firing at each other. they are very anxious to exchange papers. yesterday a Sergt from the V [5th] Ohio went down to the river and changed with them. Corp Porter brought one in with him.[67] our boys are in the habbit of killing pigs if any chance to come in their way and if the Rebels here them squell they shout over to our boys to drop that Pig. we can hear their drums beat very plain. we are not allowed to beat any in our Div. we expect the Pay master soon. you may have three more of those Photos taken. did you get Sergt Peppers[?] I send by this one more old Vet. I have not heard from N.Y. lately. I suppose it is because they have had so much company. I am waiting with much anxiety to hear from Burnside and Rosecrans.[68] the Rebels Cheer often of late and their Bands Play ever be Happy, but I do not take that as a sure sign that Rosecrans is defeated for these grey backs Cheerd on the night of the 3d at Gettysburgh. we are makeing up a Company Memorial. it will be here next week. it will be a very interesting affair, being a complete history of the Company. I will send it on by mail. the nights are very cold here [and] warm day times. thus far I have enjoyed good health. Substitutes dont like Pork & Crackers. the Sutlers are getting the $300. love to all,

Henry

Chapter 9

"IF A BATTLE, LET IT BEGIN WITH THE RISEING OF THE SUN"

THE CHATTANOOGA CAMPAIGN, SEPTEMBER 24, 1863–JANUARY 10, 1864

HAYWARD AND HIS FELLOW SOLDIERS TRAVELED ABOARD RAILROAD cars for ten days, arriving at Duck River Bridge, Tennessee, on October 4, after covering a distance of 1,120 miles. The journey was a harrowing one, taking them through West Virginia, Ohio, Indiana, and Kentucky. Along the route, they encountered multitudes of friendly citizens, especially in Ohio, where a heated gubernatorial campaign was in full swing. This election gained notoriety because it pitted Copperhead Clement Vallandigham against Union candidate John Brough. William Roberts of Company D remembered the election scenes vividly:

> We reached London [Ohio], about 10 o'clock A.M. Here they were having a Brough meeting, & we got a glorious reception. Little girls beautifully dressed in white with red & blue sashes waved the American flag, & a band of music struck up its enlivening strains. Everybody was for John Brough. I asked a man how many votes Vallandigham would get there. He said "about three." We regretfully bade this delightful place good-bye, & continued our journey. But at Xenia, the climax of our happiness was reached. No sooner had the train stopped at this beautiful and wealthy town, than crowds of beautiful girls, ladies, children, & gentlemen swarmed around the cars with baskets full to repletion with every luxury. We were loaded down with every delicacy, & the beaming eye, the cordial welcome, the unmistakeable "love of the soldier" were shown. We had an

hour here, but it seemed a moment. I conversed with two or three very pretty, & very intelligent young ladies, and we all enjoyed ourselves hugely, when the envious whistle called us away. Three rousing cheers for the loyal people of Xenia went up from the train, as we slowly & regretfully rolled away. Bright eyes bade us adieu, & hundreds of white handkerchiefs bade us God-speed. May God bless this noble little City; it was an oasis in the desert of our weary soldier-life, & cheered our hearts for many an hour. Next in this beautiful Ohio Valley, come we to Dayton the home of the Arch traitor. But no whisper of treason was heard. As the train rolled into the depot every man on the train cheered for John Brough & groaned for Vallandigham. The populace acquiesced, and shouted for Brough also. One fool shouted for Vallandigham. Twenty or more soldiers jumped from the train, caught him & beat him so severely that he will be unable to vote for his favorite traitor. The spirit of the troops was so universally against Vallandigham that it will be productive of the greatest good in the coming election.[1]

Several accidents marred the trek. On September 30, another train collided with the 28th Pennsylvania's train at Bellton Station. Hayward jumped from the cars in the nick of time to avoid being crushed. "I shudderd to see the wreck," Hayward wrote, expecting to find all of his company smashed to pieces. Miraculously, no one was killed. Other accidents also disturbed him. Many soldiers in the 7th Ohio became uproariously drunk and recklessly climbed on the outside of the cars. One soldier was struck in the head by a bridge, while another fell from the cars to have his legs crushed. Hayward felt the sickening thud as the car rolled over him. He could not understand why so "many of the brave Soldiers who for 2 years have withstood hardships & escaped the enemys bullets became perfectly reckless for their lives." Hayward expressed himself much relieved when this "long and fearfull journey" finally came to an end.[2]

The cause of this tortuous trek stemmed from a Union military disaster in northwest Georgia. On September 19–20 the Union Army of the Cumberland had been defeated by the Confederate Army of Tennessee. In the aftermath, the routed bluecoats withdrew to the vital supply center at Chattanooga, but quick-moving Confederates cut the two Union-controlled railroads that brought supplies into the city. Major General Braxton Bragg positioned his Confederate army on the principal heights surrounding Chattanooga: Missionary Ridge and Lookout Mountain. Now, with forty thousand Union soldiers completely cut off and starving, President Lincoln called on reinforcements from Major General Ulysses S. Grant's Union Army of the Tennessee and also more than twenty thousand men from the Army of the Potomac's 11th and 12th Corps. Major General Joseph Hooker commanded these two corps, and he now reported directly to General Grant.

After twenty-four days at Duck River, the 28th Pennsylvania boarded trains bound for the Union railhead at Bridgeport, a station west of the Tennessee River and about twenty-eight miles from Chattanooga. The regiment arrived at Bridgeport on October 29 and, once the soldiers disembarked the cars, they began a forced march to the besieged Union army. This march took the soldiers over rough, muddy roads, through treacherous mountain streams and rainy weather. The Pennsylvanians arrived at Wauhatchie Station along the Nashville and Chattanooga Railroad on October 30. Once there, the regiment joined the 2nd and 3rd Brigades of Geary's division, which had gone ahead of them. Just two days earlier, these two brigades had been involved in a desperate night battle at the station. The men of the 28th Pennsylvania found General Geary in a state of unshakeable despondence. Presently, he mourned the death of his son, Lieutenant Edward Geary, of Knap's (now Atwell's) battery, killed in the recent battle. Geary immediately put the 28th Pennsylvania to work corduroying the roads between Kelly's Ford and Brown's Ferry, two key crossing points on the Tennessee River. Once completed, this road helped to bring supplies to the besieged Army of the Cumberland in Chattanooga. All the while, Confederates on Lookout Mountain bombarded the Pennsylvanians with artillery in order to disrupt their work.

The 28th Pennsylvania encamped at Wauhatchie for the next two weeks. On November 19 Colonel Thomas J. Ahl arrived to assume command of the regiment, supplanting the widely disliked Captain John Flynn. During this period, skirmishing continued almost daily; however, Confederate desertions proved equally common. Lieutenant Colonel Ariovistus Pardee, commander of the 147th Pennsylvania, remarked, "Desertions from the enemy are very frequent. At times whole companies come into our lines." Meanwhile, Union soldiers speculated on their next move. Pardee guessed correctly that it would be an assault on Lookout Mountain. He wrote his father, "I think an attempt soon will be made to take Lookout Mtn, so that we can control the Railroad. This work

will undoubtedly be assigned to Gen. Hooker. It is an ugly looking place, some thing after the style of Mt. Pisgah [near Mauch
Chunk, Pennsylvania] in height. . . . The side of the mountain
facing us is very steep and about ²/₃ up there is a bluff, which appears to be at least 30 ft. high. This extends along the side of the
mountain from Pt. Lookout for at least one mile. Altogether it is
rather an ugly looking place to charge up."[3]

On November 24, as anticipated, General Grant directed
Hooker's men to seize Lookout Mountain and drive in the Confederate left flank. At 9:30 A.M., the 28th Pennsylvania crossed
Lookout Creek. The regiment composed part of the "left storming party," a unit of 1,010 officers and men drawn from Colonel
Charles Candy's First Brigade. Along with three other brigades arranged into two other storming parties, Candy's men assaulted the
northwest slope of the mountain, thus commencing a foggy, all-
day battle, known as the "Battle above the Clouds." Confederate
defenders put up feeble resistance, giving way at every encounter.
The gray coats held briefly at Craven's Terrace, a small plateau half-
way up the mountainside, but Candy's storming party and another
storming party led by Colonel David Ireland easily brushed these
defenders aside. Eventually, the remaining Confederate defenders
fled or surrendered, and on the morning of November 25, as the fog
evaporated and the sun shone resplendent, Geary's weary troops
could see the national colors and the flag of the White Star Division waving proudly upon the summit. The soldiers sent up a rousing cheer that echoed across the valley. After the battle, Hayward
considered this fight the most impressive display of military talent in world history. He wrote his father, "Lookout Mt is ours &
Napoleon out done. Come and see Lookout Mt or you will never
know what wonderfull deeds the American Soldiers have done."[4]

The next day, the 28th Pennsylvania and the rest of the division slowly descended the southeast slope of Lookout Mountain.
When the White Stars reached the foot of the mountain, a flooded
stream—Chattanooga Creek—delayed their passage, since all the
bridges had been destroyed by retreating Confederates. Nevertheless, Geary's division pushed across the creek and entered Ross-
ville, Georgia, a town at the southern end of Missionary Ridge.
The division turned north to ascend the steep ridge, driving Confederates from Major General A. P. Stewart's division out of their
defensive positions. Geary's men reached the top of the ridge at
6:00 P.M., after capturing dozens of prisoners and three Confederate battle flags. The successive fights at Lookout Mountain and

Missionary Ridge cost the 28th Pennsylvania ten men wounded. Company D suffered no casualties.[5]

On November 26 the 28th Pennsylvania descended Missionary Ridge and pursued the retreating Confederate army through Chickamauga Valley and Pea Vine Valley, capturing large numbers of prisoners along the way. On the morning of November 27, the 28th Pennsylvania entered the town of Ringgold, Georgia, where a Confederate division under Major General Patrick Cleburne mounted a last-ditch defense. A lofty precipice called Taylor's Ridge stood just east of the town. The Western and Atlantic Railroad passed through a gap near the ridge's southern end, but Cleburne covered this gap with artillery and a brigade of Texas infantry. Two more brigades sat firmly entrenched atop the summit. When the 28th Pennsylvania arrived at Ringgold, they saw that a Union division from the 15th Corps, led by Brigadier General Peter J. Osterhaus, had already commenced an assault on the ridge. Osterhaus had dispatched a brigade of Iowans under Colonel James A. Williamson to probe the Confederate position. The Iowans, however, advanced cautiously up the steep incline. General Geary's 1st Brigade double-quicked through Ringgold at 8:00 A.M. and arrived at the bend in the Western and Atlantic Railroad. Colonel William R. Creighton now commanded the brigade, having replaced Colonel Charles Candy, who had dislocated his hip after falling from his horse during the Battle of Lookout Mountain. Upon seeing the sluggish advance of Williamson's Iowans, Geary ordered a direct assault, assigning Creighton's men the task of pushing through the Iowans' ranks and defeating Cleburne's men beyond. In his after-action report, Geary claimed that he received verbal orders from General Hooker to attack the ridge; however, a postwar account claimed that Geary made the decision "without advice or direction from a superior."[6]

Nevertheless, Creighton appeared more than happy to carry out Geary's instructions. He formed his brigade behind the railroad embankment with the 28th Pennsylvania and 66th Ohio (left to right) in the front line and the 147th Pennsylvania and 7th Ohio (left to right) in the rear line. Standing in front of his old regiment, the 7th Ohio—known as "the roosters"—Creighton called out, "We are ordered to take those heights, and I expect to see you roosters walk right over them!" The 7th Ohio sent up a yell, crowing like roosters, and were soon joined in by the rest of the brigade. In minutes the four regiments surged over the embankment, advanced to the foot of the ridge, scaled a rail fence, and

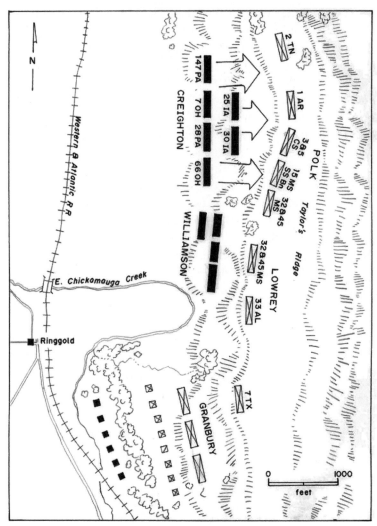

The Battle of Taylor's Ridge, November 27, 1863. Map by John Heiser.

began ascending a steep ravine in the ridge's western face. During the attack, Creighton moved his two rear regiments to the left so that the 7th Ohio and 28th Pennsylvania (left to right) now held the center of a massive battle line. Believing Cleburne's Confederates would run without much provocation, Creighton's men ascended the ridge in parade ground, shoulder-to-shoulder formation. When they came up behind two of Williamson's regiments, the 25th and 30th Iowa, Colonel George Stone, commander of the 25th Iowa, begged the easterners to alter course and maneuver around the Iowans' flanks. Stone wrote, "I spoke to one of the officers in the center column, ordering him to go up the hill to my left, but he refused to do so, and when asked by what authority he went up where he did, replied he was so ordered." Colonel Williamson also asked Creighton's men not to march over his prone soldiers, but, in Williamson's words, "They replied that they would teach 'Western troops a lesson.'"[7]

If there was a lesson to be taught, the Confederates did the instructing, for they poured a lethal fire into Creighton's brigade, tumbling men out of the ranks at every step. Once shot, the dead rolled down the steep slope until they lodged against a rock or a tree. Here Hayward lost another of his close friends, Corporal Henry C. Fithian, killed by his side. When recounting Fithian's death, Hayward exhibited signs of emotional damage. Hayward remembered, "I turned away dreading to see him roll down the mountain. I could tell you more of such tales but it is as unpleasent for me to bring them back to my memories as it is for you to read them." Hayward's post-battle letters appear to confirm the theory of independent scholar Eric T. Dean, that despite the limitations of mid-nineteenth century social science, Civil War soldiers exhibited severe psychiatric problems. Hayward's deliberate repression of painful memories may indicate that he suffered from post-traumatic stress disorder.[8]

The attack of Creighton's brigade stalled about forty yards below the crest. Corporal Joseph L. Cornet of the 28th Pennsylvania admitted, "[O]ur fire was not delivered with the accuracy and effect that we might have hoped for. It was as much as we could do to climb the rough and steep mountain-side without having to fight a larger army in front of us."[9] After a sharp conflict, Creighton's bluecoats retreated down the ridge. Colonel Williamson, whose Iowans still held a position about thirty yards behind the easterners, remembered, "when they gave way . . . [they] came down like an avalanche, carrying everything before them, and to some extent propagating the panic among my regiments." Williamson blamed the rout on the easterners' stubborn insistence on attacking in line of battle. Williamson continued, "The fault of these regiments seemed to be more the way in which they attempted to go up the hill than in anything else. While Colonel Stone preferred the method of taking it by skirmishing and cautiously advancing, the regiments above named tried to go up it as if on parade where the men could barely have gone clinging to rocks and bushes."[10]

In all, the Battle of Taylor's Ridge cost Union forces 432 casualties, most of them from Creighton's brigade, and this total included Creighton himself. Upon Creighton's death, Colonel Thomas J. Ahl of the 28th Pennsylvania assumed command of the First Brigade, and he collected the survivors behind the railroad embankment. The 28th Pennsylvania had lost thirty-five men: thirteen men killed or mortally wounded and twenty-two wounded. Of these, Company D lost five: three killed and mortally wounded and two wounded. The disastrous affair at Taylor's Ridge forced Hayward to reconsider his own mortality once again: "I saw more of my Comrades shot down at Taylors ridge than in any other battle of the War. . . . I am not unmindfull of the particular care with which I am allowed to live through such dreadfull sceans as those of last week."[11]

In the wake of this bloody fight, on November 29, the 28th Pennsylvania returned to Wauhatchie, where General Grant reviewed the White Star Division. At Wauhatchie the regiment began building winter quarters. While there, its soldiers received word that the War Department now wanted them to reenlist as veteran volunteers and serve for three more years or until the end of the war. If any of the 1861 volunteers chose to reenlist, they would receive a thirty-day furlough and a $402 veteran bounty. On December 24 the regimental officers submitted this arrangement to the men of Company D. Sixteen soldiers, including Hayward, reenlisted as veterans. Along with 215 other reenlistees from the regiment, they returned to Philadelphia on January 10, 1864, and paraded through the streets.[12] On January 14 Hayward proudly announced his decision to his father: "They tell me I am a Vetran for I have sworn to stand by the Old Flag for 3 years more which means untill the end of the War. I think I can hear you say 'well done' if so then I am satisfied."[13] Despite the recent carnage, Hayward promised to keep fighting until he was dead or the Union claimed victory.

97

Oct 10
Camp of the 28th Regt. Duck River Bridge Tenn.

Dear Father,

You are much surprised I know to hear of my change of base so sudden, but it is true I am now in Tenessee. I have no time at present to give you a description of my journey. I only write this time that you may know where I am and that I am well. the 12th Corps is stretched along the Railroad from Nashville to Tullahoma. Gen Gearys Headquarters are at Murfreesborough. Slocums are at Nashville. the 28th Regt & 147 are at present guarding the Railroad Bridge over duck river. how long we shall remain here I cannot tell. last night was the first nights sleep that we have had since we left the Rapidan. we disembarked from the Cars last Monday morning at 2 ock AM makeing 7 days of constant Railroading. we came here in a very fortunate time to save Rosecrans comunications, for Forrest & Wheeler, with all the Cavalry Bragg could give them, were determined to destroy this Road.[14] they made their first attack on a Bridge near Wartrace about 3 miles from here. they gobbled up a company of Indiana troops that were stationed there. we were orderd under arms and every preperation was made for a fight. we remained in this state of suspense for 2 days and nights, when, as I suppose, Hooker orderd an Advance to Shelbyville where they were known to be in force. we made a forced march and so did the Rebs for when we were within 2 miles of the town we heard that they had left. Shelbyville is a great Union place. it looked so strange to see the fair ladies of the place wave their hankerchiefs and throw their smiles upon us. most of the houses showed the stars & stripes. the people praised our Soldierly apperance and told us we were the finest body of troops they ever saw and wished they had Bread for us. the first train came over the road this morning. we have had our comunications cut off for 4 days and have been liveing on half rations. there was a Regiment of Colord troops passed by here to day on the cars. I suppose they are going to the front. we expect our stragglers up to day. we had 19 out of our Company. some of them will never come back. they were all subs- but 2. I received John Parkers letter to day also 2 Gazzettes. we get no news. I have not seen a paper with war news since we left Washington. let me know when peace is declared. direct as before. dont forget the 12th Corps. I will write to morrow if possible. [I] shall not be so busy when we get once settled. enclosed find a photo of Sergt Shadell wounded at Gettysburgh. he is now in Hospital in Phil.

Henry

98

Camp of the 28th Regt. Duck River Bridge Tenn Oct 12

Dear Father,

My long and fearfull journey has at last come to an end and I find myself once more at ease on the banks of the Duck River. it will form one of the principle events of my History which I have in store for you, but which is impossible for me to give to you now. A brief decription of its pleasures & Horrors will for the present suffice. We were withdrawn from the Army of the Potomac on the evening of the 24th of Sept. & marched to Bealton Sta. Va. we took the cars from there and as we rolled away we wondered where we could be going. none could tell and we cared less. we kept on singing untill we came to some familliar spot where we had in the early days of the Rebellion met the Rebels or had prehaps been one of our many old Camp Grounds. we soon neared Alexandria. then our hearts gladened with the hope that we were to leave the detested soil of Virginia, the blighted land sickening to the sight of all Soldiers where 2 years of dreadfull marches and numerous struggles we have endured and the object not yet accomplished. thus we bid a long and hope last farewell to old Virginia. we passed through Washington at night. at the first break of day there is a rush at the car door to get a view of My Maryland. it is a releif to the eye to gaze once more upon fertile land covered with vegeatibles & grain, to see cattle grazeing with (fences) around them and houses containing occupants, and what is more, to see them throw out the stars & stripes as we near them. we pass the Relay House about noon. here we were met with Cheer upon Cheer. the same loyal feeling was manifested through the state. most every house displayed the stars & stripes and every window a flag of truce. towards night we neared the Point of Rocks. now the 28 boys began to feel at home and watch closely for their old picket posts. I noticed my place at Quarter Branch where we drove the Cattle over. we crossed the bridge at Harpers Ferry to find ourselves once more in the enemys Country. at every post of importance there were stationed Iron Clad cars mounting 2 Guns. we reached Martainsburgh at 7 P.M. on the evening of the 28th. here we found smileing ladies and hot Coffee which had been prepared for us on our arrival. we chose the latter and with cups in hand we made an impetious charge, filled our cups, seized a loaf of bread and returned good naturedly to our dens ready to move at the sound of the whistle. Three cheers for the ladies of Martainsburgh and we are off. Night is now coming on but there is no thought of sleep. the weary hours are passed with much noding and dull songs. joy commeth with the morning. we make New Creek where we again get hot Coffee & Bread. we venture to run down to the stream to take a wash and once more seated in the cars we feel better prepared to pass on with our journey. the people of Western Virginia are loyal and greeted us, as we passed the many towns, with Colors flying and that certain God-speed, the wave of the white handkerchief. on the morning of the 30th we arrived in Bellton. here occurred one of the most mirraclous accidents that ever happened. the Station was arround a sharp curve and we had been stopping there for some time. most of the boys took this time to take a lunch from their haversacks and were all inside. I had finished and stepped to the door of the Car. I had been there but a moment when I noticed men rushing up the steep bank beside the rail road shouting Collision. I had just time to Clear myself of the Car as I felt the wind of it as it rushed by me. I clung to the steep bank not daring to look behind me untill the noise was all over. then I shudderd to see the wreck which I had just left expecting to find that all of my Company were smashed to peices. the first one I saw was Lieut Lazarus crawling from the ruins. I ran and shook him by the hand. I was so glad to find one alive. our car was the rear car. Co F came next. the engine struck our Car [and] drove it through the car of Co F resting upon it. now if you can tell me how it is that one car going through another containing 35 men and not killing one I should like to know. Co D had 3 men cut and bruised [and] Co F [had] 8 men. Co D & F were loaded upon a flat car and we were soon under way again thinking of nothing but smash ups. the road through Western Virginia runs continually on the side of the mountains. I saw much beautifull sceanry and as always took up my seat by the door. I had plenty to gaze upon to satify my taste for wild sceanry. we passed through a tunnel one mile long. this is called Kingwood tunnel.[15] we were some time passing through as they are obliged to run very slow. we reached the Ohio River at noon on the 30th. we crossed the River on a bridge made of boats, stacked arms, washed up and brushed up, picked a few sinders from our eyes, marched up and got crackers & Coffee, seated ourselves upon the banks of the River surrounded by Hundreds of people stareing and asking questions as if they never saw Soldiers before. we took the cars again at this place (Bellair) 40 men to a Car. it seemed to us as if they thought we were so many cattle being sent to the western market. we felt that we were true blues going to the assistance of Rosecrans. the Result was that the butts of the guns soon made the cars quite airy in spite of the remonstrance of the Rail Road Agent. We had come thus far with but few serious accidents having occured. but here, rum flowed free and the effects of it showed itself upon the men. many of the brave Soldiers who for 2 years have withstood hardships & escaped the enemys bullets became perfectly reckless for their lives. they would reel backwards & forwards on the top of the Car or climb up the sides when at full speed. I saw one man struck in the head by a bridge. another fell between the cars, the wheels passing over both thighs. at the time the later accident occured I was standing in the door. I heard the cars as the[y] jumped over him. when our car came to him it was awfull to feel the shock of the car and to see him laying upon the track, watching the wheels as they rolled towards him. he had his canteen around his neck which I suppose was full of whiskey.[16] there were a number more killed upon the train. Gen Hooker issued an order warning all citizens on the road against selling it [alcohol] to the Soldiers. Ohio out ranks all the other states that I have passed through for thriving towns and the patriotism of its people. Nearly every house showed the starry Flag and the word Brough. I never saw people take such an interest in Politics as the men, women, & Children do of Ohio. it was not hurrah for the Flag or the Union but hurrah for Brough.[17] the Soldiers soon picked it up and it was nothing but hurrah for Brough way into Indiana. at every station the people gatherd by the hundreds with their baskets well filled with eatables and would not allow us to pay them. they poured apples by the bushell into the cars. the ladies brought their arms full of papers and books. they would hand us a slip of paper and pencil for us to give them our names and Regt. and I would not be surprised if we did not have to enlarge our mail bag soon. we enquired after the Valandigham men, but could not see many. the ladies told us they kept very shady but that most of the railroad hands were of that stamp. so as we moved along when we came to a gang of them by the road side we would hurrah for Brough and if they shook their head in the Negative we knew we had one and some unruly soldier would let drive at them a peice of pork. they kept it up untill each man had thrown away his ration, then they would call them traitors and shake their fists at them. I feel certain that the election of Brough will save the Union [and] then the Country is safe.

we stop to wash & write at Columbus & Dayton. we met with great reception at both of these fine Cities. it is now late in the evening and we have already passed 4 sleepless nights upon the Cars. some are streached upon the floor, others are reclining upon the side of the man to his right who has fell to sleep thus sleeping in rows. they think not of the danger untill a sudden jerk of the Car tips one off when away they go upon the floor like bricks spilled upon their ends. there was one amusing incident occured which I noticed. a lucky fellow had a seat to himself, and while sleeping soundly, another conceives of the Idea of rolling him off upon the others who cover the floor without awakeing him. he does so, and after a while the thief gets well to sleep upon his board when another sleepy Soldier rolls him off and is soon fast to sleep upon the board. thus they sleep 3 deep. occasionally, one will ask whose leg is this[?] I wish you would haul it in. we arrive at Richmond, Indiana on the morning of the 2d of Oct. this is a large City, the headquarters of the Quakers of the West. a full Regt left this place for the War.[18] we now come to Centerville. this place without any exception gave us the warmest reception of any on the route. the Citizens turned out enmass. the ladies stood over the black kettles makeing Coffee for us, dealing it out to us as we croweded around them. there was a salute fired and the bells were rung. they told us that it was a signal for the people to turn out with eatables for the Soldiers. soon they came flocking towards the depot on foot and in carriages loaded with goodies. the Soldiers would run to meet them and the cakes and pies would soon disappear. one good farmer brought a whole hog cooked and as the boys croweded around him to lighten him of his load he would tell them to go into him he is a good hoosier hog. during the time we remained here there was a big fat Clever old lady [who] came up to the Car (and pointing to a man comeing towards the depot) told us he was a butternutt, take him along with you. I know he is a Copperhead and we dont want him around here. many a name was exchanged among the Soldiers & Ladies of this place, and while the cars move slowly by, three rousing Cheers for the ladies of Centerville are given and their good deeds are praised by the Officers and men untill we soon come in sight of Indianapolis. here we change Cars. we form line and march to the other side of the City. after stacking arms, we prepare ourselves to march to the Soldiers Retreat where Hot Coffee & Substantial food await the attack. there are many Copperheads in this place, and all they cared for the Soldier was to get his money. they would sell the boys rum for 3 or 4 dollars a bottle. it seemed as if the whole of the Regt were crazy from the effects of it. I saw a man in Co I raise his gun and knock one of his comrades dead to the ground for nothing else but that he was following him.[19] at Midnight we were all aboard of the Cars again takeing a southerly direction for the Ohio. at noon on the 3d we made Jeffersonville on the Ohio. here we took the Ferry for Louisville KY. [We] marched to the Nashville Depot. [We] took the Cars again and continued on our journey without noticeing anything worthy of notice for we are now in a Slave State and the country looks as if there was a curse upon it. we did not make a long stay in Nashville. after leaveing the city we were orderd to load and be ready for any emergency. (but he did not come) we arrived at Duck River Bridge at midnight and however anxious we were to take the cars in Virginia we were doubly glad to leave them. the distance traveled by rail sums up to 1122 miles. our Company alone had 19 Stragglers only 5 of which have yet come up.

Oct. 14th   All is quiet in the department of the Cumberland. we have recived but one mail since we arrived. I look for one to day. I must write to New York to day. it has rained for 2 days. the Climate has not effected me yet. I am in the best of health. [I am] happy as a Clam. [I] shall answer Parkers good letter soon. tell Cora if she loves her Country to write imediately. I would like for you to find out what would be the expense of sending a box by express to me. love to all.

Henry

99

Camp of the 28th Regt. Duck River Oct 14th

Dear Brother [Augustus, Melville, or Albert],

I suppose you will be surprised to hear of the sudden change which has taken place since I last wrote. we were withdrawn from the front of the Army of the Potomac on the evening of the 24th of Sept. we took the cars at Bealton Sta Va. at night on the 27th. we could not imagin where we were going. we passed through Washington at night arriving at the Relay House early in the morning. we were all in high spirits at the prospects of leaving Old Virginia and hoped that we would never tread on her soil again. leaving the Relay House we took the Balt. & Ohio R.R. the people along the route greeted us with Cheers, displaying the Stars & Stripes while the windows of the Houses were alive with the wave of the White Handkerchief. we crossed the Potomac at Harpers Ferry arriveing at Martinsburgh at 7 P.M. on the 28th. here we are soon under way again and as night is coming on the weary Soldiers fall to sleep as they set careless of all dangers. the road through West Virginia passes along the side of the Mountains. the sceanry is wild and beautifull. we passed through a Tunnel one mile long called Kingwood Tunnell. we met with a rail road accident at a Station called Bellton which liked to prove more disastrous. the Car Containing Co. D was in the rear. the train Coming up behind us did not see us as we were around a sharp curve. they came on at full speed driving our car completely through that of Com F. I was standing in the door at the time and jumped just in time to feel the rush of the Car as it passed by me. there were only 3 men injured in Co D. in Co F there were 8 [injured, but] none were killed. we crossed the Ohio at Bellair. here we were croweded 40 men to a Car like so many Cattle. the old vets would not stand this and they soon made them quite airy with the Butts of their guns in spite of the remonstrance of the Rail Road Agent. there was many a fatal accident occured on our journey and rum was the cause of all. I saw one poor fellow struck by a bridge [and] another was run over [on] both of his thighs. we passed through many fine towns in Ohio and the people cannot be excelled for their Patriotism. they flocked to every Station loaded with eatibles. we Changed Cars at Indianapolis takeing a southerly direction untill we came to the Ohio. we crossed the river in [a] steamboat, landing at Louisville Ky. we made a short stay here to get Coffee when we were soon under way again, continuing on our course untill we reached duck River bridge. our Regt with the 147 are now guarding the bridge. Gen Gearys headquarters are at Murfreesbourah, Slocums at Nashville. I have had to catch the time by minutes to write this. [I] will give you more particulars in my next. remember the 12 Corps when you direct. love to all.

Henry

100

Camp of the 28th Regt. Bridgeport Ala or Ten. Oct 29

Dear Sister,

I have just been made happy by reading your letter, and as time and circumstances will not allow me to write such a letter as I would like please except such as you have received. I am puzzeled to know where I am, and many that are writing are in the same fix. the maps say that we are in Alabama while the oldest Inhabitents say Tennessee, but we dont beleive them for they are very Ignorant. please look at the map and sattisfi yourselves. we left our Comfortable Quarters on Duck River on the morning of the 28th and took cars for this place, which is for present the terminus of the railroad. there was nothing to be seen on our journey worthy of mention. the country has the same appearences as portions of Virginia which has not been frequented by the Armies[:] poor miserable houses with Tenants to match. they wear Clothes the Color of bricks with out a change untill they are ready to drop off. we passed through another Tunnel one mile long which the Rebels in a recent raid tryed to destroy. Accidents still attend us in our Travells. last night when we were within 12 miles of this place the third car in our rear jumped from the Track and was dragged ¼ of a mile over the rough sleepers (greatly to the inconvience of its occupants) the train was stopped just as we came to a very steep bank. it was very fortunate for if they had run from the track a dreadfull accident would have been the result as it was night and the cars were filled with Soldiers. we passed the wreck of a train which had been thrown from the track by the rebels—as soon as they had accomplished this, they fired upon the Soldiers as they were crawling from the ruins, but with out effect. they fled as soon as they had done this. they are now building a large bridge over the River at this place. Hooker with the 11th Corps and most of our Div. are on the move towards Lookout Mountain. we are waiting for the 29 & 66 Ohio to come up. we have orders to march tomorrow morning at 7 ock with 3 days rations & 60 rounds of Amunition (Hooker) to a man. we were releieved by the first Div of our Corps. some of Ambitious Gearys work I suppose. It may be that Hooker, knowing our Deeds at Chancellorsville, feels that we are reliable. I hope that the substitutes will not injure our good name (for we have many in our Div) if we go into action. I am sorry to say that there are some ill feeling between the Soldiers in this Department and those from the Army of the Potomac caused by evil disposed men on both sides. we look neat and uniform, shave our faces, blacken our shoes, wear figures of the number of our Regt. [and] letter, and the bright Star, which to them appears vain and showey, while they are course looking men and not over particular in their dress. they say that we are feather bed Soldiers and can make a fine parade, that we have not seen any hard fighting compared to them. I now it is false and take no notice of them for I know many of them cannot read and are not to blame for their ignorance. the Western boys in our Div will not stand to hear them after all they have endured in Virginia and give them the lie to their teeth.[20] I received [the] Inquirer & journal. did you get the long letter I wrote with particulars of my journey[?] it is rumord that Gen Green was killed in action yesterday.[21] he was in command of 3d Brig of our Div. I am in the best of health.

love to all,
Henry

101

Camp of the 28th Regt. Wauhatche, Tenn.
near Lookout Mt. Nov 6th 1863

Dear Brother [Augustus],

I have not been as well as usual since our last march from Bridgeport or I should have wrote to you before. It rained when we started and did not cease untill 2 days after we arrived here. The roads were in a dreadfull condition and the many Mountain streams which we were obliged to cross were much swollen. I have never in all my marches passed through such a wild unsettled country. we saw no houses and only 3 huts, 2 of which were occupied. we followed along the line of Railroad and near the River. the former is in good order with the exception of 3 bridges. the one nearest Chattanooga must have been a very costly structure by the looks of the ruins. It run from Mountain to Mountain and with the rest were destroyed by Bragg in his last retreat. he saved his waggon Train by boarding the Track from rail to rail. we encamped the first night on the Mountains it raining young rivers but we were glad enough to come to a halt that we may wring out our Clothes and dry ourselves but it was no use. we could dry one side but as soon as we turned around the other would get wet and like drownded rats we crawled in. we moved of again at the rising of the sun with light heads and heavy knapsacks (every thing being wet). after Climbing many mountains high we came in sight of Lookout Mt. we noticed a number of fires upon the top and side and supposed our men held it, but we learned to the Contrary as we neared it and turned of behind a hill where we received orders to make fires where they could not be seen and to hurry up with our Supper as we would move off again in a short time. we run around in the dark and gathered up some wood and soon got up steem. Coffe down, we again followed our leader while we could turn our eyes to the lights on the Mountain and with that they were warming friends instead of foes. we soon came to the Pickets of the 11th Corps. they told us of the fight Geary had with the Rebels, which was the first we had heard of it.[22] from what I can learn by reports, the 11th Corps had passed the place where the Battle was fought. Geary came up with his white Stars and went into Camp. they had all got under their Blanketts when the Rebels got around them and then advanced on our Pickets. the out post halted them saying, who comes there, and the only reply was, forward 4th Alabama.[23] our Pickets fired and alarmed the camp. they now opened on our men from all sides and had it not been a body of men of unflinching bravery they would have fled. Knapps Battery (the pride of our Division) served their peices as they laid in Park. they had 28 killed and wounded, 38 horses killed or wounded out of 48 which they had. [They fought] with 4 peices (2 Guns being absent) Capt Atwell of the Battery has since died of the wounds received. Gen. Geary lost his noble Son who was 1st Lieut in [the] Batt- at one time the Rebels charged on the Battery.[24] any got within 15 paces. the Adjutant of the 109th P.V. with a number of his men were between the Guns and the Enemy, but they had to fire knowing when they done it they would kill them. they fired and drove the Rebels back but killed the Adjutant and 3 men.[25] we rested on the battle field. [When] we come up I saw the Graves of 14 of 137 N.Y. in a row under a large Tree.[26] they all had head boards with their names. the Tree was shaved off flat and on it were written here lies the bodys of 14 men from the Army of the Potomac. our loss in killed is 4 Officers, 30 men, 15 Off Wounded 159 men wounded—10 missing. the Rebel loss is much larger. our men buried 139. Prisoner[s taken include] 59. the Rebels did not expect to run against their old Antagonist as they owned up to afterwards. they thought they would have an easy thing of it in meeting the men who have been use to fighting Bragg. I have thought so before but I am sure of it now and that is the White Starr Division is the best in the service. I beleive Hooker thinks so. we have been hard at work throwing up breastworks since we arrived but we are nearly done now. the Rebels throw their shells from Lookout Mt. but with know effect. we are encamped opposite of Lookout on a high Mountain. we are worse off than when we were on Louden Heights. we have to bring our rations and water from streams below. we do not live as well as we did in the Old Army of the Potomac. we get nothing but Crackers & Coffee, Pork, Soap & Salt. It is very warm here. it seems so unnatural for this time of year. the boys go down to bathe as they use to in July. the birds are singing and the flowers are in blossom. you need not think of sending me a box with winter Clothing. at the foot of the Mt-. lives a man in a hovell. his family consists of [a] wife and two white headed urchins, Cow & Dog. all they get to eat is boiled corn. I think it does not agree with the young ones for they keep up a continual squalling from morn till night. for my part I like to hear it occasionally for it reminds me of my younger days, but most of the boys get outrageous and threaten to go down and take them over their knee. There was 66 Rebels came in and gave themselves up to day. they said they came over to get something to eat. when we were at Bridgeport we saw a great many that had come from Chattanooga. they all said that there were plenty more behind only waiting for the chance. Our Mailes are very irregular. we received one to day, the first since we left Bridgeport. it contained one for me from Albert which I must answer to night. I got no papers. [I] was of course disappointed. I think more of the Gazzette than I use to. the Editorials are Able and contain much information. Your account of the Engine Trial was very interesting. I wish I had them here to squirt over on to the Rebels on Lookout Mt. or to force water up the mountain for us to make Coffee. enclosed you will find a pettrified fishes head, a relic from Duck River. it was cut out of a rock by one of my company. there were many different kind of specimines to be found there on the banks and if we had remained there I would have got more of them.

Saturday Morning Nov 7th

The Mail will leave in a few minutes. [I] would rather let this go for what it is worth than to add more to it and have it delayed. it is warm and lovely this morning. I can see you all at home standing over the stove. I would rather freeze in Massachusetts than live in the Orange Groves of the Sunny South. good morning.

love to all,
Henry

PS) I have to assist the Lieut in makeing out the Pay Rolls to day. When we do get paid I think we shall get 4 months. send a sheet of paper when you write.

102

Camp of the 28th Regt Near Lookout Mt. Tenn Nov 11 /63

Dear Brother [Augustus, Melville, or Albert],

I know it is a long time since I wrote to you, but I think my excuse will pass. We have been hard at work building fortifications. now that is over. we can rest without any fear of being [driven] away by the Rebels. we never occupied a Stronger position than the one we now hold, and Longstreet can not drive us from it. he run against the White Starrs the other night when they fought them for 3 hours in the dark. the moon (11th Corps) came up in their rear when he took advantage of the bright lights and ran away but not untill he was soundly whipped. our Regt was not in the fight. we were on the march coming up. Capt Atwell & Lieut Geary of our Battery were killed. Gen Geary mournes the loss of his son. he was well liked in the Battery. the Rebels thought they were going to meet the men that have been accustomed to fighting Bragg and that they would have an easy thing of it, but they found out their mistake when our boys would not give although they were surrounded. if any one should want to know which are the best troops in the field you can make no mistake by saying Gearys Division. Deserters from Bragg come in to our lines every morning. they come over to our lines and make arrangements for our boys not to fire at them. our Picketts talk with them and exchange papers, trade coffee for tobacco. they say they are very hard up for provisions. they keep up a continual shelling from Lookout Mt. but they cannot reach us. our boys shut them up with their big 84 any time they open upon them.[27] we were encamped upon a Mountain untill yesterday when we moved down upon a level flatt on the side. the weather has been uncomfortably warm during the day untill a few days past. it seems more natural for this time of the year being clear and cool. I received the Illustrated (the roguish baby tore) yesterday. you thought your long letter went astray but I received it. when you write you can put in an extra sheet for paper cannot be had here for Gold. we expect to be payed off tomorrow [for] certain for 4 months. we are encamped in Tenn and send our Picketts into Georgia. we have had a change in the weather from hot to cold. water freezes in our canteens. we have just received orders to right Pay Rolls and I must Close.

love to all,
Henry

103

Nov 14th
Camp of the 28th Regt Wauhatche Tenn

Dear Father,

I was just thinking that it was time I had another letter on its way North, feeling certain I would be repaid by receiving one before this reaches its destination. since I last wrote, we have been favored with weather delightfull. we do not think of winter Quarters thus far, but in the middle of the day seek shelter from the sun under trees and in our tents. I cannot think but what there will be change soon. I hope there will. it will seem more natural. I like weather for this season of the year that will harden the pork so we can cut it in slices and make Sandwiches of Crackers, but I would not have our appetites increase, no not here for our rations have been very short even to ½ [rations] some times. [We even went on] ⅓ [rations] untill we went 2 days without a mouthfull. Geary heard the yells and shouts of the boys (for they make a large noise when their rations are short) mounted his horse and rode to the landing. somebody caught particular fitts for the rations came up that night and his boys went quietly to bed after supper. to day we had been soup, the first we have had since we left Duck River. I do not expect we shall live as well [as] we did in the Army of the Potomac. we have bid good bye long ago to fresh bread, dried apples, & peaches, Potatoes &c. It is most encouraging to us to see so many Deserters coming in every day. it is not in squads of 2 or 3 but by the Wholesale. our boys that were to work in the road yesterday said they counter a squad of 72. the Rebels told them that they were only the first relief. there would be another squad of 50 over to morrow. our boys were building a bridge over a small creek. the Rebels told our boys that the Bridge had a better foundation than Old Braggs Army. I look to see his Whole army come over some morning. Officers of all grades come with them. there is a Brigade of Tenneseans waiting for an oppitunity to come over, the General at their head. never were Picketts so friendly as ours and the Rebels. they talk with each other from morn till night, exchange papers, trade Canteens, give each other tobacco, and act like warm friends. only for the stream that seperates them (Lookout Creek) both lines would mingle to geather so that it would be impossible to get them to fight. it will have to be stopped or the next battle when we meet instead of the bloody charge both parties will drop musketts and run and shake hands. I told the boys that went out this morning to take plenty of crackers and when they were talking with the Johnneys to eat crackers all the time. I guess our boys tell them to come over when they get a chance. a Rebel Major offerd $30 worth of Tobacco for a pair of boots. We have moved down from the mountain near water and are very comfortably fixed. we expect to be paid to morrow. when you write send sheet of paper in [an] envelope. please send more stamps. send me a large plug of Tobacco by mail and Charge the some to me with expense of postage. it is very scarce here. [It is all of] poor quality and a big price. Lieut Barnes is on a visit to Philadelphia. he may be well enough to come on and he musters as Lieut. I can not be promoted to first Sergt untill he does so or gets discharged. I wrote to John Parker H. about a week ago. did it go through safe[?] I get the Gazzette quite regular. I received a letter from Albert a few days ago. he will have a chance to see the Great Russian Bears now on exhibition there.[28] Rebel Batteries on Lookout Mountain are silent to day. Tell Cora to eat a Wing for me [on] Thanksgiving day.

love to all,
Henry

104

Camp of the 28th Regt Wauhatche Ten Dec 2d

Dear Father,

I take the earlyest Opportunity to inform you that I am alive and well after 8 days of the hardest work I have yet experienced for the good cause against the Rebels. It is glorious to be a Soldier after the Battle is over when we have returned to our comfortable quarters to rest on our Laurells bravely won, to think and talk of dareing deeds we each and all have done, to show the narrow escape from the enemys bullets. one has had his haversack shot away, another his Clothes riddled, another his bayonett scabbard cut off. such has been our occupation for the past week. I have lost another of my messmates, Corp Fithian known through the Regt as an honest and faithfull Soldier. I saw him fall with others of my Company. I saw more of my Comrades shot down at Taylors ridge than in any other battle of the War. when I am rested and feel [like] myself again I will try to give you some Idea of my experience in all different engagements at Missionary ridge, Lookout Mt., & Taylors Ridge. Lookout Mt is ours & Napoleon out done. Come and see Lookout Mt or you will never know what wonderfull deeds the American Soldiers have done. then try to Climb Missionary ridge and you will ask how it was taken. go to Taylors ridge and you will not wonder that the White Starr Division were repulsed trying to gain the summit. but you will call them brave men for leaving their dead so near the top. I am told that it was a mistake in ordering us to storm the ridge, but it is to late. now the bravest men in our Brigade are gone. Col Creighton & Crane of the 7th Ohio were sacrificed.[29] they were Idolized by their men and familliar with all in the Brigade. I did not intend to write a letter for I must let Mell know that I am all right and I have only a few minutes to do it. I slept well last night, the first time I have slept for 7 nights. we were paid off before we marched. I will send by this $40. write as soon as you get this.

I am not unmindfull of the particular care with which I am allowed to live through such dreadfull sceans as those of last week.

love to all,
Henry

Ambrose Hayward
North Bridgewater Mass

105

Camp of the 28th Regt. Wauhatche Ten Dec 10th

Dear Brother [Augustus, Melville, Albert, or John Parker],

I received your letter a few days ago, but in consequence of the busy times in camp [I] have not been able to answer untill now. We have this minute come in from Inspection, and as the mail leaves in one hour, I must gather in my Ideas with a rush. we left our Log Huts on the mountain to cross the Valley to build again which has kept us very busy since our return from Georgia. we are now fixed as snug as a bug in a rug. We are in winter Quarters, the best ever built, and are waiting anxiously for it to rain so that it will—I am called again. send me a good silk handkerchief by mail—[I] received one peice of Tobacco by way of Nashville, none by Washington. [I] will write soon.

Henry

106

Dec 19th

Camp of the 28th Regt. P. V. Wauhatche Tenn

Dear Father,

I have laid aside the Gazette of the 8th inst. for the purpose of writing to you. It brings me near to my home when I look over its pages and read of the many events which are transpiring in your midst, And to notice the many familiar names, some of which were my former associates. I look back to my School Boy days at times and wonder at the Changes time has made. I never dreamed that I would be a Soldier In those days of Compositions. Rhoderic, Olive, & Bertram,[30] when with my school mates we appeared as such to please the Children of the Center School.[31] I mark the contrast when I think of Lookout Mt, Mission & Taylors Ridge. We left our Camp in Lookout Valley on the morning of the 24th of Nov and marched to the encampment of the 11th Corps to hold their position (as we supposed) untill they returned. Nothing unusual occured untill the next morning when heavey fireing was heard in the direction of Chattanooga, the Rebs replying from their Batteries opposite to us on Lookout Mt. we thought nothing of them as it was an everyday occurence untill towards evening when we were assured that they were in earnest from the continuous rattle of muskettry which we could hear to our left. That night we lay down to rest as we had done before to think what the morrow would bring forth. if a Battle, let it begin with the riseing of the Sun. for to know that we must fight and not be engaged, the suspense is most unbearable. we were up early the next morning so as to get breakfast before we should be called into line. (for our Generals do not ask us if we have had Coffee if they should want us to the front.) It was very foggy when Gen Geary rode along our lines. we soon followed him, moveing by the right flank along our picket line untill we came to a thick wood when we were orderd to unsling knapsacks and load at will. This looked like work. The boys gatherd in groups to express their views of the prospect before them. most all were of the opinion that we were to Storm Lookout. I could not beleive it for I thought it was not possible that it could be taken by assault. We moved forward in light marching order across Lookout Creek forming in line of Battle on the opposite side. Skirmishers were orderd to the front when we advanced with no more doubts as to the task we had before us. we moved without much opposition for nearly a mile at the base of the mountain driveing in the Rebel pickets and opening comunications with the center storming party who soon crossed the Creek. All being ready, we began to Climb. The 3d Brigade who were on the extreme right soon became engaged with the enemy, but their well known Valor was to much for the Rebels to stand and they drove them from their breastworks before we had time to get up.[32] we were often encouraged by the appearence of squads of Prisoners and were fully Convinced of the surprise when we reached their camp and found knapsacks, Uniforms, &c., guns, and their mush, left to cook itself upon the fires. we were yet but half way up, but Geary orderd us to halt to let (as we supposed) the left wing have time to get up. While we were thus resting, the Rebels opened upon us with Grape and Canister from 2 small peices. we took shelter behind rocks, the missels flying harmlessly over our heads. we soon heard the well known Cheer which follows the Charge, and in a few moments the Rebel guns were silent. we had been purposely shown to attract their attention, and, before they were aware of it, the 3d Brigade were upon them. This was a grand affair and gave us high hopes that our great attempt would yet prove a great success. we moved on passing the Captured Guns and a large squad of Prisoners. We came to a road which the Rebels had made to bring down Artillery. along this road lay the Rebel dead & wounded. we made slow progress as we neared the top, finding that it grew steeper & more impassible. we soon learned that the Rebels had made another stand. they had found their last ditch and were now defending behind natural breastworks of rocks their only road by which they could withdraw their Artillery. here they made a stubborn resistance. their artillery was of no use to them for they could not depress them low enough to get range upon us as we were nearly under the bluff where their Guns were in Position. we lay down flat upon the ground under fire of their Muskettry, there being no chance for a third of the troops to fight. Thus we passed 2 hours listening to the different tones of the Rebel bullets. a few had been wounded. I saw one man in Co F hit in the brest.[33] our Brigade was soon orderd to the rear and then to the right as a support to the 3d Brigade which had done most of the fighting during the day. We gladly welcomed the night which was fast coming on, if with it, it would put an end to that heart sickening sensation which the Whistleing bullets produce. the position we now occupied was far from being Comfortable, the Right of the Regt resting under the high Bluffs of Rocks which towerd perpendicular over our heads like a massive Fortress. From this bluff the Rebel Sharpshooters annoyed us much. They would come out of their hideing places and walk down to the edge of the Cliff and deliver a rakeing fire along our Regt.[34] but their boldness ceased when one of their number fell headlong among the rocks below near where we stood. our Sharpshooters stood ready to repeat it, but they did not dare to show their heads again. I cannot tell you how much we sufferd while here among the rocks 2000 feet above the river below. a cold drissily rain having commenced at noon still continued. the wind howled among the rocks and there was no chance of walking to and fro for one misstep might prove fatal. besides there was great dangers of killing our men below us from the rolling of loose stones down upon them. we have passed a portion of the night when the moon appeard from under the Clouds and the storm passed away but it is bitter Cold and our Overcoats never were needed so much before, but they were left with our Knapsacks at the foot of the mountain. we thought it strange that we were not relieved. has Geary forgot that his boys are on duty yet under the fearfull bluff, for we could see the fires springing up on the mountainside below. it was not long before we Cheerd up by word coming from the left that we were to be relieved. it was as slow going down as coming up, each man for himself holding on to the trees and climbing over the rocks untill we came to the Rebel path where we formed the Regt and moved a short distance untill we came to a ravine where Gen Geary had established his Head Quarters. We stacked Arms, took 40 extra rounds of Amunition, built fires, and tried to get warm. The hours passed slowly away. we talked of our days work done and the renewal of the Battle more desperate in the morning for we had heard Geary while in conversation with the Rebel Prisoners tell them that he intended to take their road from them in the morning. we knew Gearys temper and we knew that his Division must bleed freely, if by doing so he could win the day. Why should I ever forget that night we passed on Lookout Mt[?] There was no merry Faces. the moon (which was nearly eclipsed) shown cheerless upon us. we could look on the mountain side opposite and see the light of our own Camp fires and only wish we were there. At times as the Clouds would lift, Chattanooga appeared with its hundreds of Camp fires. then to make perfect this grand Panoramic view, the Tennessee with its silvery like waters moved on its winding course among the hills untill the clouds, like a curtain, closed the view for a while from our sight. Thus we pass the cold sleepless night. The sun as it rose shone first on the Rebels at Mission Ridge, then rising over the mountain Crest, put new life into the shivering Yankees. we watched anxiously the movements of Geary. High over our heads towerd the rocky bluff. we could see no signs of the enemy. The picket fireing had ceased, but we yet felt uneasy untill word came that the mountain was ours. the Rebels had fled. what we supposed was impossible had been accomplished. Lookout Mt. is ours and nothing hearafter is impossible. They could not hold Lookout which is proof enough that they cannot hold on to their Confederacy. In a few moments the Stars & Stripes with Gearys Head Quarters flag (The White Stars)[35] were flying from the bluff above. then we made old Lookout ring with Cheers, feeling that the American Flag never floated so gloriously before. Hooker soon came up and not far behind him were plenty of rations. although he loads us heavily with amunition, all give him Credit for his good attention to our rations. we were soon a lively set of Yankees and now that it was all over we were glad that we were present at the Storming of Lookout Mountain. The Sun was not more than two hours high when our guns in the works around Chattanooga opened a furious canonading upon the Rebels at Mission Ridge. soon after the Army of Gen Thomas[36] moved out in line of battle up the Valley towards the Rebel camps. a few moments would decide whether there was to be a fight or a foot race. the Rebels opened with new batteries and ours seemed to be on the increase all along the crest of mission ridge. dense Couds of smoke rolled upward and there was no mistake but what the Battle had opened in earnest. a great portion of our Infantry had moved from our sight into the woods, but we were sattisfied that they had not been Idle for soon the Rebels set fire to a portion of their Camps and fled to mission Ridge. It was a grand sight to watch the battle from the mountain where we stood, but quite unusual that we should be allowed to quietly look on. We notice a number of horsemen moveing along the road below us. Geary is on the move for we can see the White Star Flag following them in the rear. Fall in is the order, and we are soon winding our way down the steep mountain road which but yesterday could not be traveled without a pass from Bragg. Nearly the whole of the day was passed in manouvering from place to place in the valley, forming new lines of battle, Changeing position, &c. when at about 4 P.M., we moved off quickly by the flank [and] crossed Pea Vine Creek. [We] formed line of Battle at the foot of Mission Ridge. A Brigade of Osterhauses Division[37] had gained a position on the top of the ridge and heavey skirmishing soon commenced. we advanced up the side with a yell and a Charge. the Rebels seeing that they were out flanked fled in great disorder. Geary who had been waiting for this oppitunity opened on them from a battery of flying Artillery, completely demoralizing them. Thomas on the left had not been as succesfull. he had been fighting them stubbornly all day. we could hear the roar of muskettry and the thunder of his artillery, but it would not be long before we could come to his assistance, for our boys were driving all before them. we soon gained a position where we could see them fighting desperately. I saw one line charge up the side but they were repulsed. the second came up and made the top of the ridge. it was all up with the Rebels for they saw that they were surrounded, and when we gained the top we saw the Rebel prisoners enmasse surrounded by the Victorious Yankees. On the ground lay, as they had thrown them, their Rifels and Equipments. Imagin the noise we made when we saw what we had done. I should have thought the war was Over, were they not yet fighting down the Valley below us. There was such a granduur to this scean that it is yet fresh in my memories. the full moon was just peeping over the distant Mountain and the flash of the distant guns of Sherman[38] who was following up the retreating Rebels in the Dark Valley below makeing a picture none to grand to Close the day in which the Union boys had given [the] Rebellion such a mighty blow. Hooker again makes his appeerence and we open to the right and left to allow him to pass. Cheer upon Cheer are given him as he approaches. he raises his Hat and nods his head acknowledging the compliment. Uncle Sam ownes no better team than Hooker & Geary. I wish the Army of the Potomac had them untill they get to Richmond. The

Western troops took posesion of Mission Ridge While the White Star Division took possesion of the Rebels and marched them down the Mountain. A strong guard having been detailed, We take charge of them. we set about to get Coffee. we were occupieing the deserted Camp of the Rebels. there had not been as many of their shantys destroyed as we supposed, but they did not stand long for the exulting Yankees made a furious attack upon them and in a few moments they were levelled to the ground. little did the Rebels think the night before when they were so snugly fixed in their winter quarters that the yankees would so soon cook their coffee over their ruins. we all felt much in need of sleep but to attempt it with out our Blanketts, cold as it was, would be useless. I passed most of the night among the Rebel prisoners who were also without Blanketts. they expressed themselves freely on the War question, admiting the hopelessness of their cause. they were very bitter against their leaders, especially the Alabamaans.[39] they told us that the war would soon close with us, but to them there would be no peace untill their leaders were exterminated. The most wretched one among them was a little Frenchman belonging to a Louisiana Regt.[40] he shed tears while I was talking with him. he could speak English but poorly, but I could understand enough to know that he had sufferd much. he was barefooted and had been with out food for several days. he said I get 2 buiscuit when on Lookout Mt. to last me 2 days. I get no shoe, no blankett. I go with Bragg no more. he plaid out. he took out a Confederate note saying, this plaid out to. we were under marching orders before the brake of day with 3 days rations to last 5. we felt like aged Soldiers lame an tired. we took the Atlanta Pike. then we knew that "Joe" was going for "Bragg". we made a hurried march nearly all day passing waggons, Cassons, Tents, &c. which the retreating Rebs had Abandond during the night. at one time we made a short halt near a house when, as usual, many of the curious yankees called on the people to see if they had anything good. soon the Barn yard was blue with men Clubing Chickens and raceing for sheep. Madam Secesh came out, walked up to Gen Osterhause, and told him that the men were getting all of her Chickens. he said, madam, my boys like Chickens. she left. shortly after, a Soldier came to the General with his arm full of Rifels and informed him that there were many more in the house. search was made and 58 Enfield found. I think they had been thrown away by Braggs men and these people gatherd them up. we marched untill after dark leaving the road and takeing to the woods & field. we thought at first we were going into camp but we continued on. when at some distance ahead, we could see the fires of the rear guard of the Rebels. they were on the mountain and seemed to be holding the Gap through which the Road passed. Hooker is going to flank them. that is why we left the road. we pushed on untill we came to by roads when we halted. Osterhause took another road and was to get on the other side of the mountain when we were to move up and attack them while he gobbled them up. but they were not napping and quietly left while we were resting, leaving behind them 2 peices of Artillery and many willing prisoners. We made fires where we were and stood around them untill morning when we started again in the chase. we passed many squads of prisoners going to the rear. Nothing of interest occured untill we neared Taylors Ridge. Osterhause Division were in the advance and were skirmishing with the Rebels when we came up. we Crossed the Chickamauga Creek as we enterd Ringgold. each side had now become warmly engaged. the Rebels were fireing from the mountain with Artillery. we had none to reply. the first Brigade were orderd to the left to form line of Battle and to Charge the Ridge. [It is a] terrible order but we must obey. Brave Creighton of the 7th (Commanding Brigade) came along the line (which was now under fire) and said boys, remember, you are the 1st Brigade, go right up that hill, never stop. we Advance! coming to a rail fence, each man pushes against it and we are over it. a number of men have already been wounded. we reach the base of the Mt and with Rifel in one hand (and the other to assist in Climbing) we rush with a Yell up the mountain passing through the broken line of one of Osterhauses Brigade that had been repulsed.[41] on we went fearless of Death untill the men sank down exausted. we opened upon the Rebels with a fearfull Volley which seemed to cause them to waver for we could see their Officers spring up from behind their breast works and wave their swords as if rallying their men. we raise up to renew the Charge, a Cheer runing along our lines. we did advance but only to meet death more certain. many a good fellow in the first Brigade had fallen not to lay where they fell, but wounded and dead rolled togeather down the steep rocky soil of the mountain. I saw poor Fithian when he was struck. he had just spoke to me about his gun. it would not go off. the ball struck him in his side. he droped his Rifle. I saw that I could not reach him. I turned away dreading to see him roll down the mountain. I could tell you more of such tales but it is as unpleasent for me to bring them back to my memories as it is for you to read them. we fought the Rebels in this position for 2 hours. how unequal the Conflict. we could scarcely see the enemy who were concealed behind Breast Works while we stood exposed to their murderous fire. the 7th Ohio next on our left began to fall back. I knew we must go soon for we could keep up but a feeble fire against the enemy. I remember the feeling of dread when we were orderd to fall back slowly for I knew they would rise up out of their works and pour the bullets into us. down we went, half Slideing, catching the trees and holding on to the bushes, frequently passing men wounded or dead that had lodged against a rock or tree. we reformed again near the spot where we first advanced to the Charge. the Rolls were called and many who were present in the morning never would answer again. most of the wounded were dangerous as the enemy's position was over us, giving us a plunging fire. Knapps Battery came up on a double quick for 5 miles. when they opened on the Rebels, it was with their usual telling effect. they, with the assistances of a strong flanking Collum coming up on the other side, put the Rebels to flight and thus ended the Bloody strife for Taylors Ridge. we took up Quarters in the deserted buildings, makeing frequent raids on our Neighbors live stock of Pigs, Poultry, and corn meal, &c. we remained at Ringgold 4 days, destroying the Rail Road, burning Bridges, and doing many things for the good of the Service. we withdrew from the town at night, setting fire to many of the public buildings by order of Gen Hooker. we returned to our Old Camp after this severe Campaign, Completely worn out and Exausted. I experienced more fear & dread at Taylors Ridge than at either Chancellorsville, Antietam, or Gettysburgh. I saw no real Generalship displayed at either of those three Battles. Lookout Mt, Missionary Ridge (I did not like Taylors Ridge) were carried by good Generalship, beit Grant, Hooker, or Geary, but I beleive Hooker is the man. it has come out that some one blunderd in the assault at Taylors Ridge. Hooker did not intend to make the attack untill the Artillery came up.

You have now received what I promised you, my plain, simple story, telling you of my experience in my last Campaign of 9 days.

I received 2 letters from Home of the 11th & 12 inst. I have received all the papers—paper—& Tobacco. I also received one from Aunt Henrieta. I am in the best of health. the weather has been quite Cold. there is prospects of a Storm to day. Ed Cowell[42] called to see me the other day but I was absent with the Regt who were detailed to guard a train on a foraging excursion. My Regt talks of reenlisting for the War. the 29 has already gone home to recruit.[43]

I received a letter from Mell the other day.

> I must Close this for to
> days mail.
> love to all,
> Henry

Chapter 10

"The White Starr Shines in Philadelphia"

VETERAN FURLOUGH,
JANUARY 10–MAY 3, 1864

Hayward journeyed to North Bridgewater in late January. Unfortunately, little information is known about his journey. Hayward returned to Philadelphia on February 14 and he took temporary lodging with his friend William Murry Hall, a veteran from the 71st Pennsylvania. During this time, Hayward attempted to obtain an officer's commission, but in so doing he suffered disappointment. He had been serving as Company D's acting orderly sergeant for the past nine months, and he believed he had earned the right to a promotion, not merely to orderly sergeant but to second lieutenant. Orderly Sergeant Barnes had still not recovered from his leg wound, and Company D possessed only two of its three authorized officers: First Lieutenant James Devine and Second Lieutenant Aaron Lazarus. While on furlough, Devine and Lazarus applied for commissions as captain and first lieutenant, respectively. Barnes, many supposed, planned to accept a lieutenancy in the Veteran Reserve Corps. This left the second lieutenant and orderly sergeant positions vacant. Many in Company D supposed that Hayward would assume the second lieutenancy. As Private William Roberts wrote of Hayward to his sister on January 22, "I expect he'll go back as 2d Lieut."[1]

However, another soldier attempted to thwart Hayward's promotion. Third Sergeant John Oppell Foering began the war as Company D's sixth corporal. Due to friction with Company D's original captain, George Hammar, Foering had been passed over for promotion several times. Using his father's influence with three prominent Philadelphia politicians, Foering schemed to assume Company D's second lieutenancy ahead of Hayward. State

Treasurer Henry Dunning Moore sent a recommendation to the adjutant general's office at Harrisburg endorsing Foering. Captain Charles Borbridge, the officer who helped Hayward rescue Hector Tyndale at Antietam, saw this recommendation when it arrived at Harrisburg and did his best to arrest Foering's scheme. Hayward wrote to his father that "it is true that Foering has been trying to get a commission over me, but I think he has failed. . . . my case has been cared for by my owne good friends out of pure motives of Justice while I was absent."[2]

In mid-February, Hayward received a promotion to orderly sergeant, backdated to January 1, 1864. Company D's second lieutenancy remained vacant, perhaps to placate the politically connected Foering. This affair distressed Hayward, who on February 26 sent his father a *carte-de-visite* taken wearing his new orderly sergeant's chevrons. He remarked: "I send you a Photograph of the would be 2d Lieut if he could."[3]

After spending a week in Philadelphia, Hayward rendezvoused with his company at Chester Barracks. The soldiers despised their treatment at this facility; many believed that the sentinels treated them as prisoners. Although a few of his colleagues ran the guard, Hayward refused to violate orders, and he gamely stuck it out inside "this Coop of misery." After five days in the barracks, Hayward boarded railroad cars with seven other members of Company D and commenced his long return trip to the front. After seven days of railroad travel, Hayward rejoined the other members of the 28th Pennsylvania—those who had not reenlisted—at Bridgeport, Alabama, on March 8.[4]

The remaining eight veterans of Company D arrived at Bridgeport within the next week. Company D also received several new recruits—both fresh volunteers and substitutes. Hayward remarked that the quality of soldiers had steadily diminished since the war began. One man, Private Hugh Nawn, in Hayward's words, was "simple and crazy." Hayward wrote his sister that "he is the strangest man I ever saw. he will do anything the boys tell him. he is the victim of many a serious joke during the day. the boys often fill his pipe with powder and place a little tobbaco on the surface and after he smokes a few minutes it explodes." Hayward did his best to keep order in his company. He continued, "I have found quarters for him a little ways from the camp so that he may have some peace."[5]

For seven weeks, the 28th Pennsylvania drilled and prepared for the coming campaign. Once again, command of the regiment fell to newly promoted Colonel John Flynn. On March 18, after a bitter argument with Flynn over the preeminence of their commissions, Colonel Thomas Ahl chose to resign. This pleased Flynn's cabal of officers, but most members of the 28th Pennsylvania expressed displeasure at this change in command. Referring to Flynn, Lieutenant Isaiah Robison of Company A wrote his sister, "We have a miserable specimen of a man at the head of our Regt. without stability, judgment or good sense; the Regt., in regard to Regl. commanders, has about used up its material for such, and I now think it [is] almost time we look somewhere else for them; . . . there is a vast contrast in our regt. now compared to what it was when first organized. I hope there will soon be a change for the better."[6]

A few other command changes occurred at this time. On April 15 the 28th Pennsylvania joined the 20th Corps, a new organization authorized by Major General William T. Sherman that combined the Army of the Potomac's 11th and 12th Corps. The 20th Corps adopted the 12th Corps' star badge, pleasing Geary's soldiers, but many of them felt uneasy about joining forces with the 11th Corps, since it contained German-speaking troops who had acquired a poor reputation thanks to several controversial performances at recent battles. An officer in the 147th Pennsylvania complained that this consolidation created "considerable dissatisfaction among the 'Stars' who were on not very good terms with the Teutonic Crescents, from the days of Chancellorsville to that of 'Wauhatchie' where they *did not* come up in time to assist in the repulsing of Longstreets superior numbers."[7] Nevertheless, orders were orders, and they had to be respected.

Under President Lincoln's direction, General Sherman now commanded three cooperating armies: the Army of the Cumberland, the Army of the Ohio, and the Army of the Tennessee. The 20th Corps belonged to the Army of the Cumberland, commanded by Major General George Thomas. Major General Joseph Hooker commanded the 20th Corps, Brigadier General Geary still commanded the 20th Corps' 2nd Division, and Colonel Charles Candy returned to command the 2nd Division's 1st Brigade which still included the 28th Pennsylvania.

On May 1, Sherman's three armies—98,000 men strong—began moving southeast, following the axis of the Western & Atlantic Railroad. Their destination was Atlanta.

107

Philadelphia Jan 14th, 64

Dear Father,

They tell me I am a Vetran for I have sworn to stand by the Old Flag for 3 years more which means untill the end of the War. I think I can hear you say "well done." if so, then I am satisfied.[8] I have not been hasty in takeing upon myself renewed trials and privations, but have thought long and delibritely upon it untill I am convinced that, come what will, I never will be sorry for it. I am stopping with Murry Hall on Race St. I am enjoying myself greatly but am anxious to be with you. [I] Will be in a few days. We are waiting for our furlough. We had a great reception.[9] the White Starr shines in Philadelphia.

(in great haste)

love to all,

Vetran

108

Head Qus. 28th Pa. Vet. Vols.
204 Dock St. Philada. Pa.
February 11, 1864

Orders

No 4   } I. The following promotion is hereby ordered to be made in Co. "D" 28th Pa. Vet. Vols.

Sergeant Ambrose H. Hayward Co "D", 28th Pa Vet. Vols. to be "First Sergeant" vice Barnes transferred to date January 1, 1864.[10]

By Order of
Col. Thomas J. Ahl[11]

Aaron Lazarus
Lieut. & Actg. Adjutant
28th Pa. Vet. Vols.

109

Philadelphia Feb 17th /64

Dear Father,

I arrived here on Sunday night. [I] took up my Lodgeings at the States Hotel, it being so late. I did not think it best to call on Mr. Hall untill morning. I found the boys all right. they were glad to see me. it is true that

Foering[12] has been trying to get a commission over me,[13] but I think he has failed even with such powerfull influence as Thomas, the Collector of the Port,[14] Moor, congressman from his district,[15] Fox, the Politician,[16] his father,[17] and others. my case has been cared for by my owne good friends out of pure motives of Justice while I was absent.

Capt. Borbridge discovered the documents laying on the table while he was in Harisburgh.[18] he imediately Telegraphed to Lieut Lazarus, telling him to look after it. I was in company with the Lieut last night at Mr. ex Sergt Peppers. [I] enjoyed myself much. he is a great friend of mine. Lieut L. gave me my promotion yesterday as Orderly. I now wear the diamond.[19] Curtains orders read promotions must go by seniority.[20] I am now next on the list when there is a vacancy. I saw Lieut Barnes yesterday. he looks well. my promotion reads that he has been transferd. I do not understand it yet. he talked as if he intended to return with us. we expect to remain here untill after the 22d when we are to take part in the great Celebration.[21] we report to Chester when we do go instead of Harisburgh. recruits are coming in slowly. I am stopping with Murray Hall at the same place on Race St. if you write soon direct [to] 315 Race St. Phila. it is very Cold here this morning, Coldest of the Season. I had a genuine Yankee dinner at Aunt Eliza Sunday noon. [We had] Bake Beens and Indian Pudding. it was excellent. I left them all well in New York with the exception of one case of Western fever. Oh I am having such good times in Phila. I do not care if we stay here two weeks. love to all.
direct as before Sergt A. H. &c.

Henry

110

Philadelphia Feb. 19, 1864

Dear Brother [Augustus],

In much haste, I write a few lines, excuseing myself for not doing so before for reason of my having been very busy. I found the boys all right. [They] were glad to see me. that affair concerning Commissions of Foering "Vs" Hayward is all right. I learn from headquarters that he was played out, or in other words, will not succede. my Lieut gave me my promotion as Orderly the next day after I arrived to date from the first of January. we did expect to be present in the great Celebration of the 22d, but we are disappointed. we leave for Chester to day at 1 P.M. I do not know how long we shall remain there. I have been enjoying myself very much since I arrived. I want you to go to Lewis Chathoms St. and order ½ dozen Photos from the Old Negetive and send 2 of them to North Bridgewater (when you write) and the other 4 to me. let me know the expense and I will send [it] by return mail after receiving them. my time has expired.

love to all,

Henry

direct to Chester untill you hear from me again.

111

Dear Father,

We arrived here on the 23 inst. after enjoying ourselves in Phila-d for a week. we were orderd to report here on the 16 but they could not get the boys out of the City untill after the 22d. The Parad was one of the finest I ever beheld. Col Ahl and Flynn had some trouble. the consequence was we did not turn out. it caused much disatisfaction in the Regt for we all expected to join in the Celebration. some of our men have not yet reported. we are kept very Close here. no passes [are] granted unless on urgeant buisness. it is reported that we are to move monday. we expect to get our City bounty in a few days. the rolls went to the City yesterday. there is only one of my Company here this morning, the rest having run the Blockade to Phila. this morning. we have had fine weather for a few days, but there is prospects of a change. I suppose Cora will have arrived home by the time you receive this. I would like her to write, telling me of her visit. I think I shall send my bounty home by express if I get a chance. I send you a Photograph of the would be 2d Lieut if he could. is Aunt M. with you yet[?][22] remember me to her and all the rest,

I am in good health.

Henry

(PS) direct to Chester.

112

Chester Barracks Sunday Feb 28

Dear Father,

We are having dull times in this Coop of misery. we can look out of our windows through a high pickett fence on to the beautifull town of Chester and see the People promanading on the walks and only wish we were Chickens that we might gain our Liberty for a few hours. most of my boys stay in Philadelphia. they have a nack of tareing off the Slats as soon as it comes dark. The Guards dont see them when there are no Officers about. We are to be musterd for Pay monday, after which we take the cars for Phil-d, thence to Pittsburgh, Nashville, [and] Bridgeport. We received our

Wards Bounty of $25 yesterday. the City Bounty is all right. our Regt has been Credited to the quota of Phila. an Officer will be remain behind and draw it for the Regt. I shall be glad when I can have free range of the Fields once more. I walk out in the yard occasionaly to while away the hours untill the cars come up for Phila-d, then I go right strait into the house. I have not received a Gazzette since I left home. if I get them when I get out in the Field I will be satisfied. I sent you a Letter with Photos in it. we are having fine weather. it is getting late and the boys are takeing out their Blanketts which makes me feel sleepy.

love to all,
Henry

you can see by the papers if we are on the travell. if so direct by the way of Nashville.

113

Aboard the Cars, Gallatin Pa. March 2d 1864.

Dear Father,

We left the Barracks at Chester yesterday morning on our journey to Tennessee. we passed through Philadelphia makeing no stop. my Company, [at] present, Consists of 3 Sergts, 1 drummer, 2 prvts, and 2 recruits. the rest took a French leave[23] at Phila. they are old Vets and will come up in a few days. We have a Car to ourselves with a stove, benches, and everything comfortable. we got some sleep last night. [We] shall be more use to it to night. it is quite laughable to see the boys roll of the benches on to the floor when we go over a rough portion of the road. we are now on top of the Alleghaneys Mt. it is a great sight to see how the Rail Road runs among these Mt. we can look accross the Valleys from mountain to mountain and see several trains in sight. soon they come Whizeing past us. there is one place [on] the other side of the tunnel which we just passed where you can throw a stone across the Valley, but it is 5 miles around by rail. we expect to make Pittsburgh this after noon where I shall mail this. There is much more snow here than in Phila. Co. F of our Regt was recruited at or near this place. they are now scatterd through the Village. of course many will be just in time to miss the train when we start. I wish you would look and see if you can find my furlough in the house. I can get my subsistence money on it for one month amounting to $6. send it by the way of Nashville. it may be to late but I can try it. the Cars are going to start. I will finish it at the next watering place.

2d Edition) we are now within 40 miles of Pittsburgh. I expect there will be a grand raid made on the eating Saloons when we arrive. I shall go for a wash tub first. we have 2 boys in the Car with us about the age of John P.

they came aboard at Lancaster. they say they want to go to war, that they have no home, no Parents, &c. I shall not allow them to go any further than Pittsburgh. the boys have just got in a Stock of pies at this place. we are off again. Pittsburgh 7 P.M. we are all aboard again, Changed cars. I will hand this to a citizen to mail for me.

love to all,
Henry

114

Louisville Ky. March 5th /64

Dear Father,

I wrote you a Railroad letter mailing it at Pittsburgh. we have had a very pleasent journey thus far. we arrived at Indianapolis yesterday afternoon. [We] refreshed ourselves at the Soldiers Home. [We] took a tramp arround the City, leaving it at 9½ P.M. of the same day. we met our old comrades there, "Knapps Battery", who are also returning from a furlough. we arrived here at 4 this morning. [We] marched into the Soldiers Home. [But, we] found it so crowded and dirty that our Colonel would not permit us to remain there. he gave us free range of the City with orders to report there at 8 A.M. in the morning. we brought our Knapsacks and have taken up quarter in a (kind of Grocery shop) kept by a Dutchlander. here we find everything to our comfort, &c. we have engaged a corner in the dineing room to spread ourselves to night. there is only 5 of us here (Co D). the rest are in Phila-d. we expect to leave here to morrow at 8 A.M. for Nashville. it was warm and pleasent yesterday. [It] looks like rain to day. there is a great many Western Regiments passing through here who have reenlisted.

love to all,
Henry

115

Zollicoffer Barracks, Nashville Ten
March 7th /64

Dear Father,

I have just come in from a walk arround the City, having obtained a pass for the Company. we walked down to the levee, which by the appearence of the Steamboats looks much like buisness. Nashville, like Louisville, looks much neglected. the Houses and streets are dirty and worn out. the only place of note is the mansion of the deceased Prest Polk. this is a fine house with [a] beautifull garden of shrubbery in front. under the shades of the trees to the left and front of the house stands the monument under which, in the Vaults, rests the Illustrious Dead.[24] around the Arch which covers the monument are planted a hedge of Box wood. I send you a slip of it. see if you can make it grow. we expect to leave here for Bridgeport this afternoon at 3 ock. I saw Gen Grant in Louisville. he does not put on as many airs as many of our Gens but has the appearance of a man of buisness.[25] This large building we occupie was the property of the Rebel Gen Zollie.[26] it is not yet finished. there are 365 rooms in it (one for every day of the year) it is now confiscated. (US) I have a Copy of Parson Brownlows paper[27] with me which I will mail with this. some of our Straglers have got up. the Country begins to show the appearence of Spring. will this do[?] I have not the time to write more. love to all,

Henry

116

Bridgeport Ala, March 9th /64

Dear Father,

We arrived here last night after a good long shakeing up of one week aboard the Cars. we took up our quarters for the night in a large new warehouse where we are now waiting for the officers to find us a Camp ground. I took dinner with the old boys we left back. they were very glad to see us. they are in the 147 Regt P.V. which was formerly a part of the old 28th, so they feel quite at home. Gen Geary is in command of this post which is one of great importance as all the rations for the use of Thomas army are stored here. he is at work in his old style of fortifieing all the available positions around here. our Brigade is encamped here. the rest of our Division is doing picket duty along the rail road. the 2d Brigade has not returned from their furlough. we expect to build good quarters as soon as we get our camp ground. we may remain here some time if I can judge from appearences. There is a great Change in the Climate from where I was a week ago. it is fly time here with us now[;] warm, sunny june weather. the guard dutys will be quite light for the boys. besides, we get plenty of rations of all kinds. It looks like good times for us for a while. we are where we can get our mails regular, late papers, Sutlers in abundance, Sanitary Commissions, &c, &c. I got six letters this morning and one paper. the Handkerchief was among them and your last letter of the 2d inst. I wrote you from Nashville. [I] also sent a paper. [I] have not received any Gazzetts. I must go out and see the green grass and here the birds sing. they are building 2 gun boats here.

love to all,
Henry

117

Bridgeport Ala, March 29th /64

Dear Sister,

This is but a few days later from the seat of War for I suppose you have all listened to Alberts letter which I wrote on the 27th.[28] I often find it difficult to find subjects of interest to write upon, feeling that what is not interesting to me is the same with you. I look impaciently for the mail this morning for this is my day for letters from home that are wrote on Sundays. I received the Gazzette yesterday of the 22d. they often come as that did yesterday without stamp or post mark on it. do they come free[?] There is to be a Paper printed here by the Talent of the White Star Division [with] Elliot, Gearys Adjutant General, as Editor. I suppose we shall have to go on recconasances to make news for them. It will be such a grand oppitunity for Geary to put his name before the Public again. It seems like old times to have the Old Boys back again. we all assemble togeather evenings and talk of Marches we have endured, of Battles fought, and of pleasent times when we have been Stationed for a while in towns or on Railroads in the early days of the War. I should like to have been with you to hear the great Organ. I am so fond of music that I might have got enchanted. I suppose you could not hear that machine of yours within a mile of it. Lieut Lazarus has just left my tent. we have been talking over affairs of the Regt. He has asked to be releived from the acting adjutant and will take command of the company soon. he can not get along with Paddy Flynn. [He] does not like him. he was a favorite with Col Ahl. Lazarus is a very Independent man. he acts and speaks as he thinks. Capt. Devine has not arrived yet. March is going out like a Lion with us. [It] blowed hard last night. many a Soldiers house was made roofless while the rain poured down in torrents. it is clear and pleasent this morning. Lazarus has just come in with a letter from Devine. he will Start from Phil on the 22d for the Regt. there was no letter for me to day. it is just as well for I can live with brighter hopes for the morrow. the boys have Come in from fishing with many fish. there are plenty of them in the river. some times they can catch a good mess. I notice they have changed the Administration of N. B.[29] it is a wonder I do not wear choakers now or eat fried Oysters. love to all,

Henry

118

Bridgeport, Ala. April 14

Dear Brother [John Parker],

I have not heard directly from you for a long time, but I know you are engaged in a proffitable buisness, and hope it keeps you very busy. You are very fortunate in having the oppitunity to finish your Education at the Academy and I beleive you will take advantage of the time and come out No 1. I have this morning received letters from Cora And Albert. I was prompted to write this early to know if you had heard anything from my City Bounty which should have arrived there by the first of the month. some of the boys have heard from theirs in Phild. which went through all right. Gen Geary has gone on another recconsance with 4 Regts and a detail of 200 men from our Regt. 15 men from my Comp went. they embarked on board the Steamboat Chickamauga. they have 4 peices of Artillery with them. I do not know their destination, but [I] think they will be trouble for Forrest if they find him.[30] Capt Jas. Devine has been here and gone back. he only came on with a squad of Recruits. he told me Barnes was coming on and would get discharged. we have Company & Battalion Drills also, Sour Krout for Dinner once a week. I am getting tolerable Fat. [I am] Enjoying myself in a high degree while the Company is away. they only left enough men to make 2 releifs on guard every other day. I get the Gazetts quite regular. Tell Cora I wish she was down here where she could breath the warm Southern breeze and gather such beautifull wild flowers as Northerners never looked upon. I wonder why such choice plants grow in this region where the Natives cannot appreciate them. Well! I got April Fooled nicely upon opening the letter which I got from Mell. it was for Albert, and you had the one that was intended for me in N. B. it was a buisness letter I got full of Laurence Foster & Co, Idahoes &c. say to Cora I will write to her before the expedition gets back. I received a letter from Joe Freeman. I hope this will find you as well as I am. love to all,

Hen.

119

Bridgeport Ala. April 15th /64

Dear Brother [Melville],

I received a Short time ago what I supposed to be a letter for me, but upon opening it I discovered that I was April Fooled. you must have been full of buisness, much confused, &c. Albert sent me the one that was intended for me, but I did not have time to remail his before I heard he was in New York. I received one from him this morning. I suppose he is on his way to the West by this time. he was very fortunate in having the assistence of Mr. Foster. I think everything looks favorable for a success. there is nothing like makeing an advance once in a while. if he goes out there and gets settled with a fair prospect for the future, I shall have a place to go when this cruel war is over, if I cannot stay at Home. the most I fear is his health, but if he can bare up under the hardships for two weeks, he will grow stout and be healthy. Gen Geary with 4 Regts. and a detail of 200 men from our Regt. has embarked aboard the Steamboat Chickamauga on a Scout down the Tennessee River. I have enjoyed myself very much since they left. my dutys are very light. I only have to parade the guard in the morning. when they return we shall begin again with Company Drills, Battalion Drills, &c. While I am writing I can hear heavey fireing down the River. prehaps they have run into Forrest. Capt Devine of my Company was with us last week a short time. he came on from Phild. with a squad of recruits. he told me that Barnes would come on and get his discharge soon. we have been consolidated, the 11 & 12 Corps forming the 1st Army Corps under Joe Hooker.[31] Gen Slocum reviewed us the other day, takeing his last farewell of his Old Corps. he spoke with much feeling of the History of his Corps since he took Command which was 18 months ago, which is longer than any General in the army ever commanded a Corps. he was very much attached to his men and they were to him. we are having delightful weather. the boys go a fishing, Play Ball, &c. It will be so warm here soon that we shall be busy trying to keep cool. Remember me to all. how shall I direct a letter to Aunt Eliza[?][32]

I am in the best of health,

Henry

120

Bridgeport Ala. April 17th 1864

Dear Sister,

We have passed through our regular Sunday morning Inspection and we are now at Liberty untill Dress Parade at Sun Set. most of the men take pride in brushing themselves up, and by their appearences and actions show that they have been taught in their younger days to respect the Sabbath. When I wrote to John P. a few days since Geary was on an Expedition down the Tennessee R. They have since returned without serious damages. They did not reach the point for which they started but when ever oppitunity offerd, they showed their usual destructive qualitys against Rebels & their Property. the Rebels were discovered Fortified near Decatur with artillery, determined to dispute the passage of the River, but Geary knowing his Steamboat would not stand the firing of the Rebel Guns thought it best to right about, but not untill many shots were exchanged between the Rebel Riflemen and our men. the artillery from the boat kept the Rebels at safe distance and they did not annoy them after they started to return. Generals and their Staff do not like to fight aboard Steamboats. they cannot go to the rear without takeing their men with them. The boys arrived home Friday morning at 2 ock.[33] they were overjoyed to reach their quarters once more for they yelled and shouted like Indians, which is the way Soldiers express themselves when they are happy. The consequence was that I was awakened from a sound sleep. [I] thought the camp was attacked and the Rebels were upon us. I shook Shadel (my mess mate) and while pulling on my boots, hollerd for Co D to fall in. by this time I had got out of my shanty with both Eyes open, turned back quickly and asked Shadel what he was getting up for. get back to bed, says I. it is only the boys coming home from the reconnoissance. I was not heard from again that night, but after roll call the next morning I had to acknowledge that I was April fooled. I found out afterward that some of the Officers were ahead of me by having their Sword on. —After dinner P.M. we had sour krout. I suppose you do not know much about the Dish. it is as common in Phil-d as bake beans are in New England. the doctors have orderd it once a week togeather with other vegetables to prevent Scurvy. this disease has broke out to an alarming extent in our Brigade, but it is only among those who did not reenlist. there is not one case where a vetren has had [it], as yet. are you not glad that I reenlisted[?] William Atkinson[34] my old mess mate with 2 others from D company are in the Brig Hospital with the Scurvey. The former has gone home on a furlough. I have been out to day to take a walk and see the country. I do like to get away from camp once in a while, that I may free my mind of the cares and responsibilities of my position, take in a fresh supply of Ideas, &c. I walked over a mile on the banks of the Tennessee R. there are many varieties of Fish and plenty of wild game which are eagerly sought after by the Soldiers. at present the river is to high for them to be succesfull, but the boys keep at it all day without a bite, looking forward to the time when the River shall fall and there will be plenty of fish in Store for them. did I ever tell you about the Recruits we got when we were in Phil-d.[?] Co. D recruited 5 men. 3 of them deserted before leaving the city, the fourth is simple and crazy, while the last is most dead with Consumption. The fool is named Hugh Nawn.[35] he is the strangest man I ever saw. he will do anything the boys tell him. he is the victim of many a serious joke during the day. the boys often fill his pipe with powder and place a little tobbaco on the surface, and after he smokes a few minutes it explodes. I have found quarters for him a little ways from the camp so that he may have some peace. we have no trees around our camp, nothing but stumps. I will leave this space for tomorrow as I am late for to days mail.

Monday morning, April 18

We shall have a beautifull day for monthly Inspection. the mail has arrived. I got a Gazette. I notice buisness is flourishing in N.B. is aunt Eliza with you[?] you speak of her in your letter. We have Target practice twice a week. Lieut Reynolds of Co K Commands our Company.[36] Bonsall has gone back to his owne Company. I feel Gay. love to all,

Henry

121

Bridgeport Ala. April 21st /64

Dear Father,

I was about sending this Order to you when it occured to me that it would be more acceptable if this blank sheet was filled up. I received your last letter informing me of your visit to Boston, also acknowledgeing the receipt of $250 by express. did you pay the express or did they at Pittsburgh[?] The 11th & 12th Army Corps have been Consolidated and now form the 20th Army Corps under command of Joe Hooker. Geary Commands the 2d Division and we are the 1st Brig as before. direct as you have been for a while yet. all the Officers of the 28th on detached service in Phil or elsewhere have been orderd to report to their Regt. that will bring Devine back which will make the chances much better for D company to get filled up for Devine and Pat Flynn are chums. I shall look for him by the 15th of May. I have wrote to Cora and to John P. I shall want a few stamps when you write again. I have received [the] Gazette of the 12th. the weather is getting uncomfortable warm and I am in my shirt sleeves from morn till night. love to all,

Henry

122

/64
Phila- April 25th

Mr. Ambrose Haywerd,

Respected Sir, the Person adressing you is a Stranger to you at present and a word of explenation is necessary. I left Bridgeport, Alabama on the 15th of this month on a sick furlow and your Son Ambrose H kindly loaned me $30.00 to defray my expences home with instructions to send you the seam amount on my arrival here. Your Son was enjoying splendid health when I last seen him and I sincerely trust that the seam all seeing eye will watch over him still that has so mercifully speared and shielded him through so many dangers.

I have been connected with the 28th Regt P. V. since the 12th of Sept 1862 and was spared up to my present illness. in February, a kind of scurvy made its appearance and after our Regt returned, I received a furlow. I am verry much indebed to Your Son for using his influence in procuring the furlow as well as in loaning me the money to bring me home.

I arrived in Phila on the morning of the 19th. I was verry much fatigued with the long ride or I should have written to you sooner. I feel my health improoving and I hope soon to enjoy good health again. I enclose

to you the $30.00 which I borrowed from your Brave and Gennerous Son
A. H Hayward. I hope you will let me know if it arrives safe.

Yours most Respectfully
William Atkinson
Private of Co D, 28th
P. V.
Residence,
Front St Above Harrison
19th Ward Phila
Penna

123

Bridgeport, Ala. April 28th /64

Dear Father,

I have a few moments to spare which I will consume in writing a few lines Home. We are having a very warm spell at present. The springs are drying up and but for the Green appearence of the trees and the fresh flowers, I should think it was August. I received a letter from Murry Hall a few days ago. he has been in East,[37] but was in so much of a hurry, he did not stay but one Night in N. B. I notice by the papers the Governors of the different States are to call out their Militia so as to let the old Troops go to the front. That looks like buisness. I would willingly be releived to day to go to the Front to take part in the decisive blow, if strikeing the blow we can hit old Rebellion in the Head and Knock his brains out. I do not think it will do to allow this war to live through another winter. I think I can see Desperate men useing desperate means to accomplish their owne selfish desires. I hope I am mistaken, but I said at the beginning of this war that I thought this Country has seen its brightest days. we are fighting to sustain a Government That supports such Traitors as Long in Leuxury & Comfort. they allow the Rebels to be recognized in Congress. I expect to hear it in the Army soon. I hope Banks can clear himself from all blame in his late disaster. Why did they not wait for Smith to come up[?] the same reason why Geary did not wait at Taylors Ridge[: He] wanted all the Glory, never mind the sacrifice.[38] I received a letter from you this morning. That $250 which you received by Adams Express is my City Bounty. I thought I mentioned it in one or more of my letters. it is all you will receive for the Present untill we are paid off. we are to muster for pay Saturday. Geary is makeing a Bridge under the Railway Track accross the Tennessee. it will be used for waggons or troops. some of the Boys are returning to duty from the effects of the Scurvey. I noticed a death at Uncle Sumners house,[39] also one of your Neighbors, Mrs. Hovey.[40] one year ago today we were makeing a forced march to the Rapidan. many fell dead on that march. it was very hot. I remember the crossing of the Rapidan at Night. it was a grand sight. I am in the best of health.

love to all,

Henry

124

Bridgeport, Ala. April 30th 1864

Dear Father,

We are having the last of our April Showers. the rain comes down at intervals, then the Sun Shines out, bursting the buds and bringing forth such beautifull flowers as none but the natives of the Clime ever beheld. Sergt Shadel has just Come in with a boquet and presented it to me. I have just finished makeing out an Ordinance Return and while I am in the Ink, [I] will write a few lines on purpose to send you & Cora specimens. many of the plants that grow wild here are cultivated in the gardens [of the] North. we were musterd for Pay this morning. I hear that the paymaster is here. two of our boys Came back from Philadelphia yesterday. we are under marching Orders. [We] expect to leave here for Wauhatchie, Chattanooga, Cleavland, or Ringgold, or some other seaport on Monday. It may be an advance.[41] I see by the Papers Grant is getting to be quite active. the Boys are going into the work in earnest. we are disposing of Overcoat, Blanketts, and all extra Clothing. I sold my Overcoat for $2. we must go light in this Country where it is so hot—Niggers wont care. I beleive I acknowledged the receipt of your last of the 21st inst. the mail leaves in 10 minutes.

love to all,
Henry

Chapter 11

"CARRIEING THE WAR INTO AFRICA"

THE ATLANTA CAMPAIGN,
MAY 3–JUNE 19, 1864

CAMPAIGNING BEGAN IN EARNEST. ON MAY 3 GEARY'S WHITE STAR Division left Bridgeport and marched forty-four miles over the next two days. On May 8 it reached the foot of Chattoogata Mountain (also known as Rocky Face Ridge), a massive summit defended by Confederates under Major General Joseph Johnston. General Sherman hoped to dislodge Johnston's defenders and gain access to Mill Creek Gap, an aperture cut into the mountain through which the Western and Atlantic Railroad passed. Sherman's first attack, delivered by a portion of Thomas's army, bogged down when it encountered a section of Mill Creek intentionally dammed and flooded by the Confederates. After Thomas's first attack stalled, he directed Geary's division to attempt a penetration five miles farther south at Dug Gap. Under Thomas's instructions, Geary's troops had to storm an 800-foot-high gap in the mountain where a small country road passed through it. If the White Star Division forced out the six Confederate regiments protecting this opening, they could threaten the Confederate rear at Dalton. Geary formed six regiments into a line of battle at the foot of the mountain, and he put two additional regiments in close support. The 28th Pennsylvania—numbering about 350 officers and men—held a position in the front line, second from the left, with its left flank resting on the Lafayette-Dalton Road. At 2:00 P.M., preceded by a line of skirmishers, the White Stars advanced, splashing across Mill Creek and then ascending the steep slope. All the while, Johnston's soldiers—elements from two dismounted cavalry brigades—poured a destructive fire into Geary's men.

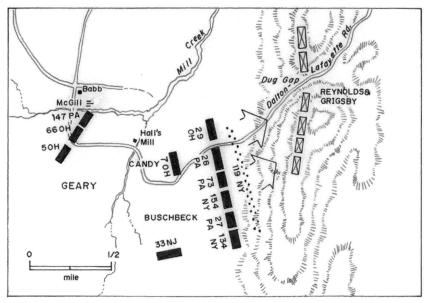

The Battle of Dug Gap, May 8, 1864. Map by John Heiser.

The Confederates had the added advantage of protective rock palisades. In fact, along the entire western face of Chattoogata Ridge, Geary's attacking line encountered nearly impassible terrain. Geary wrote that the sides of Chattoogata Mountain were "steep, covered with forest, and corrugated with ridgy spurs and formations of rock. . . . Along the top facing westward for miles on either side of the pass, rise palisades of rock impossible to scale and to be passed only through a few narrow clefts filled with loose rocks and wide enough to admit five or six men abreast." Predictably, the attack faltered just below the summit. Colonel Candy remembered that the 28th Pennsylvania made a stubborn climb: "The regiment went at the work bravely, and ascended the mountain to within thirty yards of its summit, but on arriving at that point found it so naturally defended, in addition to obstructions placed by the enemy, as to be impossible to proceed any farther. They held their ground bravely, losing heavily in both officers and men."[1]

The Battle of Dug Gap lasted until after dark, when orders from Sherman reached Geary, telling him to call off the attack. In all, the White Star Division lost 357 men. Of these, the 28th Pennsylvania lost 43, including 7 killed and mortally wounded. Hayward called it "another Taylors Ridge affair, a mountain nearly impassible."[2] However, the effort was not in vain. The men of the 28th Pennsylvania discovered later that their attack had served as a diversion, allowing Major General James McPherson's Army of the Tennessee to pass through Snake Creek Gap ten miles south.

McPherson's advance caused Johnston's army to fall back precipitously, giving up its supply base at Dalton. On May 12 the 28th Pennsylvania followed McPherson's army through Snake Creek Gap, and two days later, after a march of ten miles, the regiment arrived at Resaca, a station on the Western & Atlantic Railroad. Johnston's army now positioned itself around Resaca with its flanks protected by two deep rivers, the Conasauga to the north and the Oostanaula to the south. Sherman commenced battering Johnston's position on the fourteenth, but the 28th Pennsylvania did not engage in this fight. In the evening Sherman shifted the 20th Corps to the left wing to attack Johnston's army near the banks of the Conasauga. On May 15 the 28th Pennsylvania lightly engaged Confederate forces. While other elements of the 20th Corps attacked the Confederate breastworks, the regiment held a safe position near the Dalton-Resaca Road, where it performed provost duties, preventing skulkers from fleeing the battlefield. At 7:00 P.M. the regiment moved forward to relieve Union soldiers in their own hastily erected entrenchments. There the 28th Pennsylvania skirmished with Confederates throughout the evening, suffering no casualties. After midnight, upon learning that McPherson's army had crossed the Oostanaula River farther south, Johnston evacuated Resaca and commenced another long retreat to Allatoona Pass.[3]

After the victory at Resaca, the 28th Pennsylvania kept advancing south, covering forty-one miles in the next four days. On May 19 Geary's division reached Cassville, where it rested for two days. Hayward did not have much time to write about his experiences, since his regiment engaged continually in marching or skirmishing. Nonetheless, Hayward managed to revel in the excitement. On May 14 he wrote to his father, "Do not Concern yourself about me. I think of nothing but Victory." On May 21 he celebrated his twenty-fourth birthday and reflected upon the direction his life had taken. In a hurried note to his father, Hayward wrote, "I have never wittnessed such a sight as the sun sett of last night. everyone was out. it was grand beyond description. This is my birth Day. 3 years ago to day I booked my name for a Soldier."[4]

After the respite at Cassville, the 28th Pennsylvania, along with the rest of the division, resumed its march toward Atlanta. The weather grew increasingly hot, and all along the way scores of ex-slaves flooded into Union lines. Pleased to witness this collapse of the southern slave system, Hayward quipped, "we manage to keep in excellent spirits now that we are carrieing the War into Africa."[5] On May 25 the 28th Pennsylvania reached the banks of Pumpkin Vine Creek. Hayward lost his writing portfolio when a packhorse carrying his extra knapsack died midstream. That same day, the 28th Pennsylvania encountered skirmishers near New Hope Church. In the morning, the Pennsylvanians and the 7th Ohio drove back the Confederate skirmish line, and in the afternoon, a few miles north of the church, the regiment commenced building breastworks. The next day, under orders from Geary, it advanced southeast into the so-called Hell Hole, a thick den of brush and trees. The entire 1st Brigade had instructions to find a weak point in the Confederate line and breach it.

For the next three days Hayward and his comrades remained on the front lines skirmishing with Confederate sharpshooters. The Hell Hole's underbrush made fighting difficult. The men fought on their bellies, shooting into the thicket at anything that moved. During a Confederate counterattack, a fierce thunderstorm broke, soaking the ground until the men were caked with Georgia clay and the battlefield was enshrouded in a curtain of rain. Geary wrote, "The night was intensely dark, and a very severe thunder-storm, with cold, pelting rain, added to the gloom. It was, therefore, impossible to form a regular line with the troops, and all the dispositions we could make was by the fitful flashes of lighting."[6] On May 28 Hayward wrote to Augustus, describing the intensity of this fight: "we were under fire for 8 days. [This is] the most trying time of the war, being obliged to live among the dead bodies of our owne Soldiers, which we could not get at for the Rebel Sharpshooters kept up a continual fire from morn till night. the night attack was the most Terrific affair I ever experienced. the Rebels were repulsed at every point."[7] The fighting in New Hope Church's Hell Hole cost the 28th Pennsylvania twenty-four men, including three killed, but the battle served its purpose. Another flanking maneuver turned the Confederate left near Dallas, and on June 1 Johnston abandoned this position as well.

On June 1 the White Star Division resumed its advance, shifting east, reaching the foot of Pine Mountain on June 6. Little occurred here until June 14, when an altercation at the base of Pine Mountain forced the Confederates to retreat. The next day, the White Stars marched to a position near the center of the Confederate line. Geary's line faced southeast, confronting a steadily ascending wooded ridge called Pine Knob, a small protrusion at the foot of Pine Mountain near the Sandtown Road. There the

Confederates from Major General Patrick Cleburne's and Major General William H. T. Walker's divisions had dug impressive breastworks and hid in them to await the bluecoats' next move. Pine Knob occupied an important tactical position because it connected the Army of Tennessee's flanks between Lost Mountain and Kennesaw Mountain. The overstretched Confederate line appeared dangerously thin at this point, and Sherman hoped a celeritous attack in the center might snap it in twain. Orders passed down from Sherman's headquarters instructed four of his division commanders to commence an assault on the afternoon of June 15. Although the White Stars did not yet know it, the divisions to their right and left either refused to attack or did not receive these new orders in time. This unfortunate oversight meant that Geary's division advanced unsupported, with its flanks in the air.

At 2:00 P.M. Geary advanced three regiments as skirmishers. Behind them he arranged fourteen of his other regiments into two lines of battle, eight in the first line and six in the second. The 28th Pennsylvania held the extreme left of the first line. At 2:15 P.M. Geary sounded the attack, and his men staggered onward. Geary recalled, "The ground on which my division was now placed was entirely in the woods, and formed a series of steep ridges with narrow ravines between, their general inclination being east and west, with frequent deviations by the way of irregular spurs and small hills." Geary's men drove Confederate skirmishers over two consecutive ridges and then into heavy log works atop a third ridge. Geary added, "All of my brigades were handled very handsomely by their commanders, preserving their formation in two lines of battle while advancing, and fighting desperately over very rough and timbered ridges."[8]

At the foot of the third ridge, the White Stars broke into a run, rushing headlong into the teeth of massed Confederate artillery and infantry. The Confederate defenders blunted Geary's assault all along the line, but stubbornly the White Stars refused to give way. Rather than retreat they dug entrenchments below the Confederate breastworks and continued firing at the enemy until after dark. Of all the participating regiments, the 28th Pennsylvania came closest to the Confederate position, reaching a distance thirty yards from a lunette of four artillery pieces. A veteran from the 29th Ohio, on the immediate right of the 28th Pennsylvania, later remembered, "[T]heir artillery opened with murderous discharges of grape and canister, which produced terrible destruction in our ranks. Still the line stands firm. Another instant and our men are laying flat upon the ground and the deadly missiles go harmlessly through the air over our heads. We now open fire upon their cannoniers, so deadly in its character that the guns are soon silenced."[9] Divisional Surgeon in Chief H. Ernest Goodman, who witnessed the attack from a distance, jotted in his notes, "Character of fire: musketry and artillery; continuous; range from 100 to 25 yards; enemy strongly entrenched; one continued charge; enemy's works rendered useless, but not carried; slaughter of Federals severe."[10] During the evening, Johnston ordered his men to abandon the works, for he believed that Sherman would attack with redoubled fury the next day. Geary wrote to his wife that the final result of this battle was that "the enemy is driven three miles nearer 'Atlanta.'"[11]

During the Battle of Pine Knob, the White Star Division lost 519 men, including 82 killed. The 28th Pennsylvania lost 47, including 15 men killed or mortally wounded. Hayward commanded Company D that day, as he had done throughout the campaign. Captain James Devine still had not reported from Philadelphia, and First Lieutenant Aaron Lazarus had been acting as regimental adjutant. During the fight, Hayward received a gunshot wound to the left thigh.[12] His comrades carried him from the field and placed him in an ambulance. The ambulance trains carried the

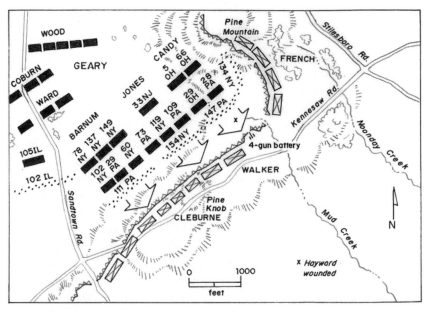

The Battle of Pine Knob, June 15, 1864. Map by John Heiser.

The Life and Letters of First Sergeant Ambrose Henry Hayward wounded over muddy roads to Acworth, and once there the ambulance operators placed them on trains to Chattanooga. Surgeon Goodman noted, "Ambulance horses and mules so worn out as to be scarcely able to remove wounded to Acworth. Have no reports of the deaths in transportation; suffering described as very great."[13] When Hayward arrived at Chattanooga, he received an assignment to the army's General Hospital Number 1. On June 17 Adjutant Lazarus wrote to Hayward's father, informing him that his son had been wounded. Lazarus assured him that the wound "is not of a serious character being only through the fleshy part of the thigh." Lazarus added, "Harry is a noble soldier and you may feel proud in the knowledge of his being your son, he commanded the company in the battle and led on his company bravely to the charge. He will write to you himself in a few days. Hoping this will relieve your anxiety."[14]

Undoubtedly, Hayward's time spent in the hospital passed in complete agony. Cooked by stifling summer heat, the twelve poorly ventilated wooden buildings that composed Hospital Number 1 overflowed with wounded from the Atlanta Campaign. Harriet A. Dada, a Union nurse, recalled, "Car-loads of the wounded were daily being brought in from the front[.] . . . [O]nly the most severely wounded were left there—such as were brought on stretchers. . . . Never was I in a hospital where there was so much suffering as at Chattanooga." During the month of June 1864, 261 patients died. Dada continued, "It would be impossible for me to write of all the heartrending scenes that were witnessed during this month of June[.] . . . It seemed as if the 'Angel of Death' was constantly hovering over the hospital." Dada made it a point to visit the 20th Corps soldiers, whom she knew well from prior nursing experience in Virginia. Often she helped sufferers write their final letters home. Mournfully, Dada remembered, "Daily I saw devoted Christian young men dying on their country's altar—costly sacrifice—men that the country could not well afford to spare. Many a heart and home were made desolate, while heaven seemed to be garnering rich treasures." Did Dada speak to Henry Hayward during his final hours? Sadly, her memoir did not mention him.[15]

First Sergeant Henry Hayward died on June 19, 1864, four days after receiving his wound. His death came as a shock to his comrades, who lamented not being at his side when he breathed his last. Private William Roberts wrote a letter to his father on June 25, explaining why Hayward's seemingly minor wound claimed his life:

I regret to state that in the fight for the possession of Pine Bluff on the 15th of the month Harry Hayward was badly wounded in the leg. The ball could not be found, though it was ascertained that it had passed upward. I learned today to my unspeakable sorrow that the poor boy is dead. He died in Genl. Hospital at Chattanooga. The ball it was discovered had penetrated his stomach & mortification ensued. He was a noble, brave, & excellent young man & enlisted with as pure & patriotic a heart as any volunteer who ever swore to defend his Country's flag. He has been in every battle with the Regiment & never shirked duty once. At the time of his death, he was Orderly Sergt of the Company, & would soon have been promoted to a Lieutenancy. He was, I have every reason to believe, a good & sincere Christian, & I know from conversations with him that he was a firm believer in the New Church Doctrine. His parents are members of the West Bridgewater Society. I hope some fitting obituary may be published in the Messenger regarding him.

> "How sleep the brave who sink to rest
> By all their country's wishes blest."

I shall ever hold his memory, & that of poor Hiles green.[16]

The soldiers of Company D had little time to mourn Hayward's death, as the duties of the hour demanded that they continue their trek to Atlanta without pause. By July 8 Sherman's armies broke the Confederate hold on Marietta and began crossing the Chattahoochee River. That day, the men of Company D gained a few moments' respite at Nickajack Creek. There they drafted resolutions lamenting the loss of their "Companion in Arms, and Brother Soldier." Adjutant Lazarus sent these resolutions to Hayward's parents along with a letter of condolence. Mourning the death of his friend, Lazarus stated, "Harry was a noble and true hearted soldier and his untimely decease is mourned by a large circle of friends in this army to whom he had endeared himself by his manly and courteous deportment. . . . The Government in your son has lost one of its most ardent supporters, one who had the interest and welfare of his country deeply at heart and whose whole aim was to render such assistance as would eradicate this unholy rebellion."[17]

Medical personnel buried Hayward's body in Chattanooga's National Cemetery, grave 231. His parents did not learn of his death and burial until receiving Lazarus's letter of July 10.

Ambrose Hayward made inquiries about receiving his son's effects, hoping to discover if Henry had left any final messages for friends or family. Surgeon Joseph P. Wright tersely replied that Henry Hayward left no effects or messages.[18]

In late July, Augustus Hayward wrote to Private William Roberts in Philadelphia, asking for any information pertaining to the final moments of Henry. Roberts had just arrived in the city, having mustered out of service on July 20. On August 17 Roberts replied that he could not provide any details, since he had been at the front when Hayward died. But he did his best to assuage Augustus Hayward's grief. In his characteristically scriptural way, Roberts wrote:

> It may perhaps soften the grief of his family & friends to Know the estimation in which he was held, & to Know moreover that he lost his life in the defense of our great & glorious heritage of freedom. With promotion awaiting him, loved & respected by all, he fell, but not forgotten, not unwept. His memory shall ever be respected & cherished by the gallant band of survivors of the 28th Regiment.
>
> *"None Knew him but to love him*
> *None named him but to praise."*[19]

These words may well have allayed the pain that the Hayward family felt, but undoubtedly, Henry's sacrifice was paid by his family in the form of innumerable tears.

125

In line of Battle to the rear of Dalton
=Ga=18m May 14th 64

Dear Father,

We have just recived word that a mail would be allowed to go at one o'k. I have no time for particulars. Everything looks bright for the Union Cause. we fought a hard Battle at Mill Springs. our Regt lost 42 killed & wounded.[20] it was another Taylors Ridge affair, a mountain nearly impassible. we were repulsed, but the Object was accomplished which was to draw their attention from Snake Gap while McPhearson & Logan passed through.[21] we have been driving the Enemy all day slowly. we hear the great News from Virginia.[22] the troops are in high spirits & very enthusiastic. I look for the Great Battle to morrow.[23] Howard[24] will then be up with his Corps. we have a powerfull army here. do not Concern yourself about me. I think of nothing but Victory. will write when ever I get the Chance.

love to all,

Henry

126

Cassville, Ga. May 21st 1864

Dear Father,

mail leaves in ½ hour. we have been resting here 2 days. [We] are preparing for a march, resting, washing, &c. [I] Saw Ed Cowell the other day. he was well. I have passed through the late Battles of Spring Mill or Dug Gap, and the last fight at Resacca with out harm.[25] I have no time for particulars. [I] received your last with Stamps. I have never wittnessed such a sight as the sun sett of last night. everyone was out. it was grand beyond description. This is my birth Day. 3 years ago to day I booked my name for a Soldier. Company buisness Calls me.

love to all,

Henry

127

Camp Near Cassville Ga. May 22d /64

Dear Father,

We have received orders that we will not move to day, so I must write as the few hurried lines I wrote yesterday were hardly possible. we are getting well rested and newly shod preparetory to another advance which will most likely begin tomorrow. we have seen very hard service since the opening of the Campaign. Hooker opened the Ball with the assault on buzzards roost with our Division. it was an awfull place for men to climb, worse than Taylors Ridge. the loss in our Regt Was 42 killed & wounded. while we were fighting here, McPhearson with his Corps was passing through Snake Gap. it seems the papers make no mention of the Battle. I suppose it is because Hooker is from the Army of the Potomac. Since the Battle of Resacca, there is no one who is not loud in Praising the Great bravery of the Star Corps. the western men that use to ask us how long we had been without our soft bread & butter or paper Collars treat us with much respect. the same day which I wrote you when in line of Battle, a part of the 4th Corps were nearby cut off while trying to join us. our first Div. was sent to their assistance and came up in time to see the Rebels driving our men away from their Battery. the Red Stars went in with a charge, drove the Rebs, retook the Battery, and the 4th Corps acknowledge [this] was the means of saveing them from a disastrous defeat. The next day was to be the decisive Battle. the Rebs were massing their forces on the left. Hooker Corps was again orderd to the critacle Point. we had hardly reached the position where our men were fighting when the Rebels fell upon our men with great fury, compelling them to fall back. again the 1st & 3d (Williams & Butterfields Div) were orderd up at a double quick with the 2d, Gearys in reserve). again, the Old vets from the Army of the Potomac showed their superior fighting qualitys by repulsing every onset made by the Rebels, and in turn chargeing the Rebels, driving the Rebels in dis order from their position. as we had been engaged a few days back at Buzzards Roost, we supposed they would be easy with us, but troops were wanted to the front which could be depended upon and we were orderd to releive the 3d [Division] just in time to receive a furious charge from the Rebels, but we repulsed every attempt, and just before dark our boys gave them a Charge driving them from their Guns in the forte and takeing a line of Breast works. continual fireing was kept up untill after dark. the 5th Ohio of our Brigade crept up and hauled off the Guns.[26] when morning Came the Rebs were gone. we got off the Cassons and togeather with the Guns, hauled them down to the Road in rear of our Div. that they might speak louder than words the Valor of the White Star Div. The Western men said to us after the Battle, does Hooker always fight with his men as he did ysterday[?] You can always find him there we replied. Dan Sickles[27] was with him throughout the fight, often exposing himself to a heavey fire. in pursuing the Rebels the next morning, our Div was in the advance. we heard great cheering far to the rear coming nearer and nearer. soon the Cause showed itself. it was Hooker passing his troops going to the front. we opened right & left and cheered him as he passed, the first time we have done so since his triumph at Missionary Ridge. we found a Rebel paper on the march which spoke of our Corps as being the flower of the Army of the Cumberland. we are in a fine Country. [It is] very productive, but we are very destructive so the Crops will not be large. the boys are living on sheep meat, Chickens, honey, &c. Peas are most ripe. Strawberrys & fruits of all kinds will soon be ripe. the sun is getting no Cooler, and we are out of ice, but we manage to keep in excellent spirits now that we are carrieing the War into Africa.[28] [I] will write as often as I can.

love to all,

Henry

128

Near Marietta Ga May 28th /64

Dear Brother [Augustus],

I am alive and well way down in Georgia. I came down with Joe Hooker. you know how he got here if you have read the Papers. I have no time for Particulars. It seems as if they intend for the 20th Corps to do all the work. Geary was in the advance at the last fight. The 7th Ohio who were in front as skirmishers came suddenly upon the advance of the Rebels (Hoods Div). we were run up at a double quick and were soon engaged. we were supported by the 1st Div. before night. our loss was Considerable. Co D has been quite fortunate this Campaign. we have had none killed as yet, but a few wounded. untill this, we always sufferd most of all the others. we were under fire for 8 days. [This is] the most trying time of the war, being obliged to live among the dead bodys of our owne Soldiers, which we could not get at for the Rebel Sharpshooters kept up a continual fire from morn till night. the night attack was the most Terrific affair I ever experienced. the Rebels were repulsed at every point. I received a letter from Mel when we were at Kingston. in much haste. love to all,

Henry

this Paper shows the Effects of war. I had my Portfolio and change of Clothes in another knapsack on a pack Horse. so if I had to throw away my knapsack in the fight I could save my shirt and writing materials. the old horse fell into the River on the last march and they all got wet, spoiled all my stamps, paper, &c. send a sheet of paper and envelope when you write for there will be no sutler up untill after we get into camp. what makes you keep Gold up so high in N.Y.[?] will you bring it down if we get Atlanta[?][29]

Vet

129

Head Quarters 28th P.V.V.
Pine Hill Georgia
June 17, 1864

Mr Ambrose Hayward
North Bridgewater Mass.

Dear Sir,

I take this method of informing you that your son 1st Sergt. A. Henry Hayward Co. "D", 28th Pa. Vet. Vols. was wounded slightly in the left thigh in the action of the 15th inst. at this place and he requested me to inform you of the fact. His wound is not of a serious character being only through the fleshy part of the thigh and he will be able to move about in a few days and he and the balance of the wounded will be sent north to one of the hospitals. Harry is a noble soldier and you may feel proud in the knowledge of his being your son, he commanded the company in the battle and led on his company bravely to the charge. He will write to you himself in a few days. Hoping this will relieve your anxiety.

I am Respectfully Yrs,
Aaron Lazarus
1st Lieut. Co. "D", 28th
Pa. Vet. Vols.
Acting Adjutant 28th
P.V.V.

130

Head Quarters 28th Pa. Vet. Vols.
Chattahoochie River near Atlanta Ga.
July 10, 1864

Mr. Ambrose Hayward
North Bridgewater Mass.

Dear Sir,

It becomes my painful duty to inform of the death of your son 1st Sergt. Ambrose H. Hayward from the effects of wounds received in the Battle of "Pine Knob" Georgia June 15, 1864. Sergt. Hayward died in the hospital at Chattanooga Tenn. June 19, 1864 and was interred in the "National Cemetery" at that place. His grave has been properly marked and can easily be designated. (Enclosed find [a] slip containing the notice of interment.)

Harry was a noble and true hearted soldier and his untimely decease is mourned by a large circle of friends in this army to whom he had endeared himself by his manly and courteous deportment. At the time he received his wound he was in command of his company and had been during the campaign, having led the company in several engagements, the Captain being on detached duty and I for the past seven months being Acting Adjutant of the regiment.

The Government in your son has lost one of its most ardent supporters, one who had the interest and welfare of his country deeply at heart and whose whole aim was to render such assistance as would eradicate this unholy rebellion.

Hoping you and your family may bear up under this heavy affliction.

I am

Very Respectfully
Yr most Obdt. Svt.,
Aaron Lazarus
1st Lieut. Co. "D", 28th
P.V.V.
Acting Adjutant

P.S. Enclosed find Preamble and Resolutions of the Non-Commissioned Officers & Privates of Co. "D", 28th P.V.V.

[*Enclosed resolutions:*]

At a meeting of the Non Commissioned Officers and Privates of Co. "D", 28th Regiment Pennsylvania Veteran Volunteers, held at Nickajack Creek, Geo. July 8th 1864 the following preamble and resolutions were unanimously adopted.

Whereas, it has pleased an all wise Providence to remove from our midst our late Companion in Arms, and Brother Soldier; 1st Sergeant Ambrose H. Hayward, who was among the first to enter the service in behalf of his country's welfare, And at a time which tried all men's souls, and who has shared with us the Privations of a Soldier and the dangers of the Battle Field, to at last fall a victim of wounds received while nobly battling for his country in the engagement at Pine Knob Georgia, June 15th 1864.

As a mark of respect and just appreciation of his worth, service and estimable qualities, a solemn sense of the just Providence, which has cut short his useful career, in his promise of manhood, induces us, therefore to adopt the following resolutions.

Resolved, That while submitting to the Decrees of Him who is all powerful, we deeply deplore the loss which has caused so great a void in the hearts of all who knew him.

Resolved, That we the Non Commissioned Officers and Privates of Co. "D" 28th Regiment Pennsylvania Veteran Volunteers, do offer our heartfelt sympathy to the bereaved family of the Deceased, and trust that they may find some consolation in the knowledge that it was caused by Him who doeth all things for a wise purpose.

(Resolved,) That a copy of these Resolutions be forwarded to the family of the Deceased and be published in the "North Bridgewater Gazette" Mass., Philadelphia Sunday Morning Times, Dispatch, and Inquirer.[30]

Committee{
Corporal John N. Moyer[31]
" Cyrus J. Shenkle
Private John Thorp[32]
" James P. Sharp[33]

Sergeant J. Oppell
Foering, Chairman

Corporal John N. Moyer
Secretary

Aaron Lazarus
1st Lieut. Co. "D", 28th
Pa. Vet. Vols
Acting Adjutant

131

North Bridgewater Mass
August 3d 1864

Superintendent of Hospital No 2

Dear Sir,

It has been reported to me from Headquarters of the Army near Atlanta Geo that my Son Ambrose Henry Hayward 1st Sergt of Co D, 28 Reg Pa Vols was wounded in the Battle of Pine Knobb Geo—June 15th last past—and that he was sent with others to the Hospital at Chattanooga—and that he died of his wounds on the 19—of the Same month—which fact if So I received a few days Since. a slip of News paper was enclosed with the mark of his grave National Cemetery Sec E Grave 23 or 231 I am not Sure which as the print is very imperfect.

I wish to be informed of the facts in the case—and what has become of his Effects and if he had any message to his friends. by so doing a grate favor will be conferred on his parents.

Very Respy
Yours,
Ambrose Hayward

132

Respectfully returned-
Your son, Ambrose
H. Hayward Sergt
Co. "D" 28th Pa. Vols
died at this Post in
Genl Hospl No. 1[34]—June
19th 1864 leaving

no effects
J. P. Wright[35]
Asst. Surg. US
Asst. Med. Dir. Dept.
Hd Qurs Dept Cumberland
Med. Directors office
Chatt. Tenn. Aug. 15th /64

[*in margin*]
No Effects
Died June
19th 1864

133

Philadelphia Pa, August 17th 1864

Augustus Hayward Esq.

Dear Sir,
Your letter of 2d inst was duly received & would ere this have received the attention it merited but that I was absent from the city at the time it arrived & did not return till yesterday.

With regard to the circumstances of your brother's death, I can unfortunately furnish you with no information derived from personal Knowledge, as I was in front with the command at the time his death occurred at Chattanooga.[36]

The Surgeon in charge of Genl Hospital No. 1 can without doubt furnish you with the desired information, as it was in that Hospital that poor Harry breathed his last. Two members of the Company were in the same Hospital at the time, Steen & Atkinson.[37] They are I believe both in this city & I shall make it my business to hunt them up & see if they cannot give some further particulars. He is buried in the National Cemetery at Chattanooga; his grave numbered & the No corresponding with the name recorded in the Hospital books so that at any time this fall you want his body sent home for interment you can have it attended to on proper application to the Military Authorities.

His commanding officer Lieut. Aaron Lazarus now Act'g Adj't of the Regiment would be the proper one to write to in relation to the matter. Genl Sherman has issued an order that no bodies shall be disinterred until after the 1st of September as infection is to be feared in that climate.

In conclusion, Mr. Hayward, let me express to you, on behalf of the company, the deep & heartfelt sorrow of the shattered band of survivors at

Harry's loss. His character was a noble one, Pure, disinterested, unassuming, patriotic, brave. His career in the service has been glorious, his record untarnished, and his name held in grateful remembrance by one and all.

Relinquishing a profitable employment, he was one of the first to respond to the call for volunteers, & after facing death & danger for nearly three years, he reenlisted not for any hope of reward, but from the purest motives of patriotism as he thereby influenced some 15 men to tender their services to the Government for a renewed term who would not otherwise have done so.

It may perhaps soften the grief of his family & friends to Know the estimation in which he was held, & to Know moreover that he lost his life in the defense of our great & glorious heritage of freedom. With promotion awaiting him, loved & respected by all, he fell, but not forgotten, not unwept. His memory shall ever be respected & cherished by the gallant band of survivors of the 28th Regiment.

> "None Knew him but to love him
> None named him but to praise."

If you think this communication worthy of notice, please send it to your parents & sister. It may afford consolation to their wounded hearts to Know the truth, and allow me in conclusion to express my own heartfelt sympathy with you all in your affliction.

He who "tempers the wind to the shorn lamb" will surely aid & comfort you, & you will eventually realize the truth of the beautiful scriptural affirmation: "He doeth all things well."

With deep respect & sympathy I remain,

> Truly Yours
> Wm Roberts Jr
> Late of Co D 28th Regt
> P.V.I.

P.S. If I should hear further, will advise you at once.

Epilogue

"At His Country's Call"

Sometime during the last week of June 1864 a detachment of Union soldiers buried First Sergeant Ambrose Henry Hayward's remains inside the newly established Soldiers' National Cemetery in Chattanooga. An Ohio soldier who likely oversaw Hayward's burial described the earnest and dedicated work of the mass interment: "Every pain and especial care is taken in the burial of the poor fallen soldier at this place. His grave is marked with his name, regiment, company, where killed, or when and where wounded or sickened, and died. And it should be a consolation to the relatives of the dead here to know that no trouble will be occasioned in finding the grave of the father, brother, son, or husband of those who have fallen and are buried on this spot." By early July, burial crews had laid to rest over 4,000 Union soldiers—casualties from the Chattanooga and Atlanta campaigns. The Ohio gravedigger reflected, "The National Soldiers' Cemetery here is from eighty to one hundred acres of beautiful[,] rolling land situated high and commanding a beautiful view of Lookout Mountain, Mission[ary] Ridge, Chattanooga Valley, and all the magnificent scenery therewith. . . . [W]hen it is finished, the friends of the poor[,] fallen soldiers may rest assured that their bodies lie in one of the most beautiful and magnificent spots to be seen in our country. . . . [N]ow buried here are soldiers from every Northern state. It is truly a national cemetery."[1]

To this day, Hayward's body remains at Chattanooga National Cemetery buried alongside 12,800 other Union soldiers who died during the war. His burial place is currently marked as Plot E, grave number 11428, and his headstone incorrectly reads "A. J. Hayward."

While gravediggers busily committed Hayward's remains to the National Cemetery, his comrades in the 28th Pennsylvania battled on. The volunteers from the regiment who did not reenlist in December 1863 mustered out in late July 1864. The remaining soldiers of the 28th Pennsylvania—a mix of veterans, recruits, draftees, and substitutes—experienced thirteen additional months of arduous service, lasting until the end of the war. These soldiers fought with Sherman's armies for the rest of the Atlanta

Campaign. On September 2, after four months of continuous combat and siege warfare, Atlanta finally fell to Union forces. The Confederate Army of Tennessee, now under Major General John Bell Hood, abandoned its entrenchments and eventually withdrew to Alabama. Briefly, Sherman's weary soldiers became an army of occupation, but the feisty Union general soon ordered all of Atlanta's citizens to evacuate the city, as he feared the strains of war could no longer allow the Gate City to sustain community life. After seventy-four days of much-needed rest, the 28th Pennsylvania struck tents again, and along with 60,000 men in two of Sherman's armies—now redesignated the Army of Georgia and the Army of the Tennessee—it participated in the renowned March to the Sea. The 28th Pennsylvania became a part of the Army of Georgia, and after a grueling campaign, described by one veteran as a "bold undertaking . . . of such stupendous magnitude, and encircled with . . . many . . . tremendous obstacles," it reached Savannah on December 10. After a ten-day siege at that place, it aided in the city's capture.[2]

The well-used veterans wintered in Savannah, and on January 19, 1865, the 28th Pennsylvania followed the rest of Sherman's command across the Savannah River, contributing to a destructive war in the Carolinas. By late April 1865 the regiment reached Raleigh, North Carolina, and went into camp there, the last state capitol to fall to Union forces. The war finally came to an end for the 28th Pennsylvania on April 26, when General Joseph Johnston surrendered his decimated army to General Sherman at nearby Durham Station. The 28th Pennsylvania then returned to Washington, where it participated in the "Grand Review," and its survivors mustered out at the national capitol on July 18. The regiment's wartime service had taken it through twelve states, and it had lost 284 men through combat or disease. One historian noted, "Their soiled, torn, and tattered flags, carried triumphantly through so many bloody battle-fields, attesting to the unfailing courage of them who bore them, have received a hallowed place in the archives of the Commonwealth, whilst the brave and noble soldiers who fought beneath and around them, have returned to peaceful pursuits of life and the enjoyment of the multiform blessings their struggles and triumphs have secured to their country and the world."[3]

Unfortunately, precious little is known about the lives of the Hayward family after the war. Many of them, it seems, continued to live on and prosper in North Bridgewater well into the twentieth century. However, the shadow of death was not long in claiming some of them. Ambrose Hayward, Henry's father, died of "paralysis of the brain," probably a stroke, on November 9, 1870. In the wake of this heartbreaking tragedy, the five surviving children and Ambrose Hayward's aggrieved wife, Hannah, divvied up his estate according to his last will and testament.[4] Death for another

Hayward came soon after. Three years after the passing of Ambrose, on January 8, 1873, the successful lawyer and veteran of the "Dandy Seventh," Melville Hayward, died at his residence, 98 Lee Street, Williamsburgh, New York. Melville had recently married a Brooklyn woman, Sarah W. Pierce, and had been an active member of the American Tract Society of the New Church. That organization remembered him this way: "A very worthy and efficient member of the executive committee of the Tract Society, Mr. Melville Hayward, passed away during the past winter. Mr. Hayward was secretary of the society for several years, and performed his duty with a faithfulness that deserves our especial notice. His character and worth are, however, so well known to the Convention, as to require only this passing tribute to his memory."[5]

However, even as the specter of death diminished their numbers, the Hayward family managed to grow and rejuvenate. During the years of Reconstruction, the surviving Hayward children all married. In August 1872, Cora, Henry's sister, married George H. Clark, a local justice of the peace. Unfortunately, this marriage did not last, and after a divorce Cora reclaimed her maiden name and lived unmarried in a two-house plot on Green Street for the remainder of her life. On December 9, 1873, Albert, Henry's younger brother, married Louise Miranda Belden. During this marriage Louise bore Albert five children: Henry, Melville, Corinne, Marden, and Carle. John Parker, the youngest Hayward sibling, also married, raising one child, Edith.[6] The four surviving Hayward children—Augustus, Cora, Albert, and John Parker—survived the depression of the 1890s and witnessed the controversies of the Spanish-American War, the exciting and tumultuous arrival of America's Imperialist Age, and the advent of Progressivism. In many ways, the course of American history had swept this family along its tortuous path since the end of the Civil War. However, the Hayward family could never escape the memory of this tragic conflict. The loss of Henry, it seemed, always lingered. Most conspicuously, Albert named his son after his older brother, who had heroically served and sacrificed his life for the maintenance of the Union and the republican government.

The decades bordering the turn of the century eventually saw the remaining Haywards pass off the world stage. Hannah Howland Hayward, the longtime mother and recent grandmother of the family, died from the effects of pneumonia in Knoxville, Tennessee, on March 14, 1885, at age seventy-eight. The remaining Hayward children passed away during the early twentieth century. Cora and John Parker both died in 1906, Augustus died in 1916, and Albert died in 1920. Albert's son, Henry P. Hayward—so named for his fallen uncle—survived his father by thirty-seven years, passing away in 1957. Nearly all of the Hayward clan had their ashes buried in Union Cemetery, on Centre Street, in North Bridgewater, present-day Brockton, Massachusetts. Over 1,024 miles away, Henry's remains sat—and still sit—alongside his brothers-in-arms, reunited with his family only in spirit.

Courage, patriotism, and sacrifice marked Henry Hayward's service during the Civil War. Although he was not unlike 360,000 other Union soldiers who also gave their "last full measure of devotion," Hayward's service was unique for its unreserved bravery. During the war, many heroic souls occasionally quailed under fire or doubted their chances of survival. But even in his country's most desperate hours, Hayward could always be found in the thick of the fray. He adhered to an extreme notion of service: "He who dares not come at his country's call is a coward," he wrote in April 1861.[7] Hayward never allowed others to do the fighting for him. It was that ethos that defined his military career. At every battle, he resolved to be the first to spring forward and the last to leave the field.

NOTES

Introduction

1. These are all the letters that are known to have survived. Hayward's correspondence proves that he wrote other letters—even others to his immediate family—but for unknown reasons, these letters were not with the collection when Gettysburg College purchased it from a rare book dealer in New York.
2. Letter 1.
3. Gerald F. Linderman, *Embattled Courage: The Experience of Combat in the American Civil War* (New York: Free Press, 1987); James M. McPherson, *What They Fought For, 1861–1865* (New York: Anchor Books, 1995); and *For Cause and Comrades: Why Men Fought the Civil War* (New York: Oxford Univ. Press, 1997).
4. Letter 76.
5. Letter 106.
6. Letter 73.

1. "Independence Still Lives"

1. Bradford Kingman, *History of North Bridgewater, Plymouth County, Massachusetts, From Its First Settlement to the Present Time with Family Registers* (Boston: Author, 1866), chap. 1 (pp. 1–11).
2. Letters 15 and 106. It is interesting to surmise how the peculiarities of the New Church may have shaped Hayward's service in the field. The New Church's inspiration, Emanuel Swedenborg, was an eighteenth-century scientist who experienced a spiritual awakening in 1742; he claimed to receive the Lord's word directly. Swedenborg viewed nature as a living scripture through which the pious could read God's message. "Swedenborgianism" might explain Hayward's uncanny fascination with the natural world. Throughout his service, Hayward admired America's diversity of landscapes, weather, and vegetation. Writing to his sister from Dumfries, Virginia, in March 1863, Hayward marveled at the serenity that surrounded him: "we are having some beautifull weather now and it will not be many days if it

continues before the army can move. I took a ramble yesterday over the hills and it was very pleasant after having been shut up in our rude huts for many days to breathe in pure air and hear the birds sing. the climate here at present is like your owne May." Swedenborg's notions of antimaterialism and heavenly salvation through earthly charity might have reinforced Hayward's longing for a peaceful restoration of the country, encapsulated by the frequent moments when he admired his picturesque surroundings. (See letter 69.)

3. William Roberts Jr. to sister, Jan. 22, 1864, William Roberts Jr. Papers, Historical Society of Pennsylvania, Philadelphia (hereafter HSP).

4. Letter 90.

5. Letters 59 and 60.

6. Letter 69.

7. Sidney George Fisher, *A Philadelphia Perspective: The Diary of Sidney George Fisher Covering the Years 1834–1871*, ed. Nicholas Wainwright (Philadelphia: Historical Society of Pennsylvania, 1967), 385 (Apr. 15, 1861); Evan Morrison Woodward, *Our Campaigns, or, The Marches, Bivouacs, Battles, Incidents of Camp Life, and History of Our Regiment during Its Three Years Term of Service: Together with a Sketch of the Army of the Potomac, under Generals McClellan, Burnside, Hooker, Meade and Grant* (Philadelphia: J. E. Potter, 1865), 13.

8. Letters 1 and 2.

9. *Philadelphia Daily Evening Bulletin,* July 29, 1861.

10. Letter 7.

11. *Philadelphia Daily Evening Bulletin,* July 29, 1861.

12. John W. Geary to wife, July 30, 1861, in *A Politician Goes to War: The Civil War Letters of John White Geary,* ed. William A. Blair (University Park: Pennsylvania State Univ. Press, 1995), 2; "D. B. H.," *Philadelphia Daily Evening Bulletin,* Aug. 3, 1861.

13. Confederate forces in South Carolina fired on the federal garrison at Fort Sumter on Friday, April 12, 1861, and forced its defenders to surrender. This outbreak of hostilities prompted war fever to spread across the North and South.

14. The U.S. Navy Yard in Philadelphia stood south of Washington Avenue along the Delaware River. Workers began outfitting ships for military service in February 1861. During the war, the Navy Yard employed 2,500 to 3,000 workers. The *Water Witch* and the *St. Lawrence* were among the first to be rearmed. The USS *Water Witch* was a 378-ton paddle sloop with side wheels and an inclined condensing engine. On June 3, 1864, it was captured by Confederate boarders in Ossabaw Sound, Georgia, and was taken into service by the Confederate navy. The USS *St. Lawrence* was a 1,726-ton Potomac-class frigate built by the Norfolk Naval Yard between 1826 and 1847. The USS *Princeton* was a 900-ton screw steamer operated by a crew of 190 officers and men and armed with a battery of four eight-inch rifles and six thirty-two-pound smoothbores. The *Princeton,* famous for its participation in the Kane Arctic Expedition, was considered by one chronicler to be "the fastest ship of her time." *Philadelphia Inquirer,* June 1, 1861; Frank H. Taylor, *Philadelphia in the Civil War, 1861–1865* (Philadelphia, 1913), 201–2;

Paul H. Silverstone, *The Sailing Navy, 1775–1854* (Annapolis, MD: Naval Institute Press, 2001), 36–67, 75–76.

15. The Hayward family lived at 48 Green Street in North Bridgewater.

16. The Columbian Number 5, one of North Bridgewater's fire engine companies, protected Centre Village. Their motto was "On the Alert." Kingman, *History of North Bridgewater*, chap. 16 (pp. 298–315).

17. On April 15, 1861, the U.S. War Department called for 75,000 volunteers to serve for three months in order to suppress the rebellion. Secretary of War Simon Cameron set Pennsylvania's quota at 14,000 soldiers, the equivalent of fourteen regiments of infantry. On April 18, acting at his own discretion, Pennsylvania's governor, Andrew Curtin, raised this quota to 25,000 soldiers, or twenty-five regiments of infantry. Curtin required Philadelphia to provide troops for eight regiments, the 17th through 24th Pennsylvania Infantry. On May 3 the War Department issued a second call for soldiers, this time for 42,000 volunteers to serve for three years. Pennsylvania raised four regiments of infantry for this call. Three of these regiments—the 26th Pennsylvania Infantry, 27th Pennsylvania Infantry, and 29th Pennsylvania Infantry—came entirely from Philadelphia. By the time Hayward wrote this letter, the Quaker City was crowded with over 11,000 soldiers waiting to leave, while private and public buildings on most city blocks became armories, temporary barracks, and recruiting stations.

18. Cora was Hayward's older sister, Hannah Corinna Hayward, age twenty-three.

19. Captain Alexander Hichborn, age thirty-nine and a physician, raised a company of soldiers from Hayward's hometown of North Bridgewater, Massachusetts. This company organized on April 20, 1861, during a mass rally held at the New Jerusalem Church, to which Hayward's family belonged. Over 1,000 people attended the rally, and 109 joined the North Bridgewater infantry company, which mustered into service on June 26, 1861, as Company F, 12th Massachusetts Infantry. Hichborn served as Company F's commander until May 1862, when he resigned to accept a position as acting assistant surgeon of the 7th U.S. Regular Infantry. He was killed in action during the Battle of Chancellorsville, May 3, 1863. Kingman, *History of North Bridgewater*, chap. 14 (pp. 298–315).

20. Hayward is referring to the *North Bridgewater Gazette*, a weekly paper started by George Phinney on May 16, 1851. Kingman, *History of North Bridgewater*, chap. 16 (pp. 298–315).

21. Henry Hayward's older brother Melville, an attorney living in Williamsburgh, New York, enlisted in Company D, 7th New York State Militia, on April 16, 1861, five days before his twenty-fifth birthday. His company mustered into service at New York City on April 17, and they arrived in Philadelphia via the Camden Ferry at 3:30 A.M. on April 20. Unfortunately, the regiment could not leave because the engineers of Philadelphia, Wilmington, and Baltimore Railroad refused to transport troops to Baltimore after secessionist mobs attacked a Union regiment the previous day. The men of the 7th New York lingered in Philadelphia until 4:20 P.M., when their colonel

chartered a steamer—the *Boston*—to ferry them to Washington via the Delaware River and the Chesapeake Bay. The 7th New York was among the first regiments to arrive at the Capitol. They quartered at "Camp Cameron" until May 31. Military Records of Melville Hayward, National Archives Records Administration, Washington DC; William J. Roehrenbeck, *The Regiment that Saved the Capitol* (New York: Thomas Yoseloff, 1961), 69–85.

22. This letter was probably written Friday, May 24, 1861.

23. Joseph W. Freeman, age twenty-two, was Hayward's childhood friend from North Bridgewater. Like Hayward, Freeman was also a needle maker. Joseph Freeman and his brother, Henry, age thirty-three, both enlisted in Company F, 12th Massachusetts Infantry, on June 25, 1861. Joseph Freeman rose to the rank of corporal, but he eventually received a discharge for disability on December 12, 1862. Henry Freeman remained in the ranks. He received a wound near Petersburg, Virginia, on June 24, 1864, and he mustered out of service two weeks later. Massachusetts Adjutant General's Office, *Massachusetts Soldiers, Sailors, and Marines in the Civil War* (Norwood, MA: Norwood Press, 1932), 2:37.

24. The Scott Legion—named for Major General Winfield Scott, a military hero of the Mexican-American War—was an independent prewar militia regiment based in Philadelphia. Like many peacetime militia units, it consisted of the city's social elite. The Scott Legion served as the organizational foundation of the 20th Pennsylvania Infantry, a three-month regiment that organized on April 30 under the command of Colonel William A. Gray, and the 68th Pennsylvania Infantry, a three-year regiment that mustered in on September 2, 1862, under the command of Colonel Andrew H. Tippen.

25. Hayward's bosses were Horace Grenville Keith, age thirty, and Joseph Battles, age twenty-seven, both former residents of North Bridgewater. Kingman, *History of North Bridgewater*, 559, 458.

26. Alice and Rebecca Shotwell ran the boardinghouse where Hayward lived. The building, known as the Quaker Hotel, stood at 402 North Front Street.

27. On May 21, 1861—his twenty-first birthday—Henry Hayward enlisted in the 2nd Company, Independent Grays, a unit raised in downtown Philadelphia. The Grays' attachment to the Chippewa Guards Regiment was unofficial. Several mobilizing companies in Philadelphia pledged to serve with this unit in May, but the regiment did not organize officially until early August, when Colonel James Miller arrived to take command. By that time, the Independent Grays had grown impatient and joined another regiment.

28. Hayward's friend William Murry Hall, age twenty-three, enlisted in Company A, 71st Pennsylvania Infantry, on May 11, 1861, and he mustered into service on May 21, 1861. Hall received a discharge from a surgeon's certificate on December 19, 1862. The 71st Pennsylvania was nicknamed the "California Regiment" because a few far westerners enlisted in its ranks. It was commanded by Colonel Edward Dickinson Baker, a Republican Party U.S. senator from Oregon. Baker's regiment also had one New York City company. Samuel P. Bates, *History of the Pennsylvania Volunteers, 1861–1865* (Harrisburg, PA: B. Singerly, 1869–71), 2:803.

29. Captain George D. Hammar, age twenty-five, commanded the 2nd Company, Independent Grays. His younger brother, Joseph W. Hammar, age twenty-two, served as the company's second lieutenant. Gilbert Lafayette Parker, age twenty-eight, served as the company's first lieutenant.

30. This passage refers to his brother, Melville. The 7th New York left Camp Cameron in Washington at 3:30 P.M. on May 31. It arrived in Baltimore at 11:00 P.M. and marched to Camden Street Station, where the soldiers took a train to Philadelphia. They arrived in Philadelphia at 10:00 A.M. on June 1, and they marched down Prime Street to Camden Ferry, spending little time in the city. From Camden, the 7th New York found passage to New York City, where it arrived at 5:00 P.M. on June 1. The regiment mustered out on June 3, after forty-six days of service. Roehrenbeck, *The Regiment that Saved the Capitol*, 173–78.

31. The identity of Colonel Seymour is unclear. According to local newspapers, the Independent Grays awaited the arrival of a "Colonel William T. Seymour" to assume command of the Chippewa Guards Regiment, but the Grays may have been under a false impression. "Colonel Seymour" might have been Truman B. Seymour, a Vermonter from Norwich University who came to Pennsylvania to seek a brigadier general's commission in Governor Andrew G. Curtin's state-funded Pennsylvania Reserve Division. If Seymour made an informal pledge to organize a volunteer regiment in Philadelphia, there is no record of it. If the men of the Independent Grays mistakenly believed that he was their colonel—hampered by the fact that they did not know his exact name—it explains why they waited so long to muster in. *Philadelphia Inquirer*, May 30, 1861.

32. Zouave infantrymen wore stylish uniforms influenced by the French-Algerian light infantry. Philadelphia had several Zouave Regiments organizing in the summer of 1861: the 23rd Pennsylvania Infantry, the 72nd Pennsylvania Infantry, the 95th Pennsylvania Infantry, and the Zouaves de'Afrique Company.

33. The brother was Albert Francis Hayward, age eighteen.

34. Due to the surplus of enlistments in May and June, the City Council incorporated a number of independent companies into the Philadelphia Home Guard. Hayward is probably commenting on the City Grays Company, a unit that organized on May 25 at the Bank Building. Since the city treasury paid these soldiers directly, they received preferential treatment in regard to uniforms and weapons, hence Hayward's low opinion of them.

35. Hayward is referring to the War Department's request to send the Hibernia Engine Company's engine, designed by Reanie and Neafie, to Washington. Taylor, *Philadelphia in the Civil War*, 238.

36. The abbreviation "F. W." could not be determined.

37. Havelocks were linen cap covers designed to protect the head and neck from the sun. Ladies' voluntary organizations often sewed them to demonstrate their support for the war.

38. Mrs. Bassett was probably Catherine Elizabeth Bassett, age thirty-two, daughter of Zibeon French of North Bridgewater. Catherine had just

married Jaazaniah Bassett on June 17. Mrs. Bassett died the next year, March 16, 1862. Kingman, *History of North Bridgewater,* 463, 507.

39. Colonel Fletcher Webster, son of the famous Whig senator Daniel Webster, commanded the 12th Massachusetts Infantry.

40. Mr. Ansilin could not be identified.

41. The Independent Grays were housed in the armory at 602 Arch Street.

42. One of Hayward's closest companions in the army was William Roberts Jr., age twenty-four, a graduate of Philadelphia's prestigious Central High School. Roberts mustered into service on July 6 as second corporal of Company D, 28th Pennsylvania Infantry. In January 1862 he became a clerk in the army adjutant's office. His company officers filled his position during his absence, and upon his return to Company D in 1863 he received a reduction to private. Roberts mustered out on July 20, 1864. On October 31, 1864, he married Mary Greble of Baltimore, a woman he proposed to while still in the service.

43. Mr. Goddard was Reverend Warren Goddard, age sixty-three, of the New Jerusalem Church in North Bridgewater. Goddard was born in Portsmouth, New Hampshire, graduated from Harvard University in 1818, studied theology in Dorchester, Massachusetts, served as a lawyer for two years in Barnstable, and was eventually installed as a preacher and pastor at the New Jerusalem Church in North Bridgewater in September 1839. Goddard was father of ten children and a noted Swedenborg. He presided over Augustus Hayward's marriage to Eveline Pratt and probably baptized Henry when he was seven years old. Kingman, *History of North Bridgewater,* 172, 516.

44. Private Samuel P. Swope, age twenty-eight, served as a member of the Independent Grays (Company D, 28th Pennsylvania). He received a discharge from the company on a surgeon's certificate, November 26, 1862. Bates, *History of the Pennsylvania Volunteers,* 1:453.

45. Reverend Henry Augustus Boardman's Tenth Presbyterian Church stood at the corner of Walnut and Twelfth streets. It was among the most prolific soldiers' aid organizations in Philadelphia. The reference to the "stomach ache belt" might be a play on words indicating Hayward's discomfort at wearing such an article.

46. John Parker Hayward, age twelve, was Hayward's youngest sibling.

47. On July 6, 1861, the Independent Grays mustered in as Company D, 28th Pennsylvania Volunteer Infantry. This company consisted of one captain, two lieutenants, five sergeants, eight corporals, two musicians, and seventy-two privates. As Hayward states, the Grays expected to attach themselves to "Colonel Seymour's" Chippewa Guards Regiment, but no officer arrived to assume command during their scheduled muster date on June 10.

48. Colonel John White Geary, age forty-one, was one of the most colorful figures of the Civil War. A native of Mount Pleasant, Pennsylvania, Geary once served as lieutenant colonel of the 2nd Pennsylvania Regiment during the Mexican-American War. He became the first mayor and postmaster of San Francisco. Between October 1856 and November 1857, he served as governor of Kansas Territory, administrating during that territory's turbu-

lent "Bleeding Kansas" period. Although Geary was a staunch Democrat, he received his commission directly from Republican President Abraham Lincoln. The War Department authorized Geary to recruit fifteen companies to form the 28th Pennsylvania Infantry, one of the first three-year regiments from the Commonwealth of Pennsylvania. Geary had a reputation as an outstanding orator, a courageous leader, and a fearsome commander. By the end of the war, he attained the rank of brevet major general. After the war, he served as governor of Pennsylvania, winning election in 1866. Geary served as governor until 1873. Only weeks after leaving office, he died of a heart attack at age fifty-three.

49. Hayward is referring to the men of Company A, 28th Pennsylvania, a unit that actually organized in Hazleton, Pennsylvania. This company, also known as the "Pardee Rifles" contained coal miners employed by Ariovistus Pardee Sr., an affluent coal baron and philanthropist. Pardee organized and equipped the company at his own expense. His son, Ariovistus Pardee Jr., served as captain.

50. Gabriel De Korponay, a Hungarian who had seen extensive military action in Europe, served as the 28th Pennsylvania's lieutenant colonel.

51. Hayward was elected eighth corporal of Company D.

52. The widely deplored army cracker, known as hardtack, was a simple mixture of flour, salt, and water. Hardtack possessed an amazing resilience, but it was difficult to chew. Many soldiers preferred to soften it by boiling.

53. Dress parade was the formal review of the regiment.

54. This was Hayward's oldest brother, Augustus, age twenty-seven. Augustus worked as a clerk in New York City. Augustus's wife was Eveline M. Pratt of West Braintree, Vermont. They married on August 20, 1858, when he was twenty-two and she was twenty-three. Eveline Hayward gave birth to a son, Arthur Augustus Hayward, on March 19, 1862.

55. On July 21, 1861, Union forces sustained a defeat near Manassas Junction, Virginia, at the First Battle of Bull Run, losing 2,900 men.

56. The 28th Pennsylvania received British-made .577-caliber Enfield rifled muskets. Unlike other Union soldiers, the 28th Pennsylvania infantrymen received heavy sword bayonets instead of the lighter triangular bayonet.

57. Major General Nathaniel Prentiss Banks, age forty-five, commanded the division to which the 28th Pennsylvania belonged. Formally, Banks commanded the "Department of the Shenandoah," directing about 35,000 men along the shores of the Potomac River. Banks, known as the "Bobbin Boy from Massachusetts," due to his boyhood occupation in a cotton mill, was a former U.S. congressman, Speaker of the House, and governor of Massachusetts. In 1861 he received an appointment as a major general of U.S. Volunteers. He commanded an army during the Shenandoah Valley Campaign of 1862, a corps during the Second Manassas Campaign, and later the federal forces occupying New Orleans. He managed to secure the surrender of Confederate forces at Port Hudson, Louisiana, in July 1863, but his forces were routed during the Red River Campaign of 1864. After the Civil War he resigned his commission and returned to politics, serving six

more terms in Congress, one term as state senator, and nine years as U.S. marshal. Ezra J. Warner, *Generals in Blue: Lives of the Union Commanders* (Louisiana State Univ. Press, 1964), 17–18.

2. "We Are Not Without Our Sport"

1. "Zoovie," *Philadelphia Inquirer*, Aug. 9, 1861.
2. "D. B. H.," *Philadelphia Daily Evening Bulletin*, Aug. 31, 1861.
3. "Enfield," *Philadelphia Inquirer*, Oct. 24, 1861. Johnston's force probably numbered about 8,000.
4. Ibid.
5. John W. Geary to wife, Sept. 29, 1861, in Blair, *A Politician Goes to War*, 15.
6. Letter 14; John Geary to wife, Sept. 5, 1861, in Blair, *A Politician Goes to War*, 13.
7. *Philadelphia Public Ledger*, Sept. 30, 1861.
8. Letter 19.
9. Letters 10 and 33.
10. Letter 22.
11. "An Eye Witness," *Philadelphia Public Ledger*, 23 Oct. 1861.
12. "Enfield," *Philadelphia Inquirer*, 24 Oct. 1861.
13. "F. O. J.," *Philadelphia Inquirer*, 22 Oct. 1861.
14. "An Eye Witness," *Philadelphia Public Ledger*, 23 Oct. 1861.
15. Letter 23.
16. Letter 24.
17. "D. B. H.," *Philadelphia Daily Evening Bulletin*, 25 Oct. 1861.
18. Letter 22.
19. "F. O. J.," *Philadelphia Inquirer*, 22 Oct. 1861; "D. B. H.," *Philadelphia Daily Evening Bulletin*, 25 Oct. 1861.
20. John W. Geary to wife, 24 Oct. 1861, in Blair, *A Politician Goes to War*, 20.
21. "Arms-a-Port," *Philadelphia Public Ledger*, Nov. 4, 1861; Richard A. Sauers, *Advance the Colors! Pennsylvania's Civil War Battle Flags* (Harrisburg, PA: Capitol Preservation Committee, 1987), 1:74–75.
22. J. M. Wolff to father, Oct. 13, 1861, Luvaas Collection, U.S. Army Military History Institute, Carlisle, PA (hereafter USAMHI). Lieutenant John Milton Wolff of Company K wrote his father that "our grey uniforms have been condemned and we are to receive a blue one shortly."
23. Letter 25.
24. "Tomliot," *Philadelphia Inquirer*, Dec. 30, 1861; "Tachey," *Philadelphia Public Ledger*, Dec. 31, 1861.
25. "Teniente," *Philadelphia Inquirer*, Dec. 17, 1861.
26. "Tasker, *Philadelphia Press*, Jan. 13, 1862.
27. "Shenandoah," *Philadelphia Daily Evening Bulletin*, Jan. 24, 1862.
28. "Teniente," *Philadelphia Inquirer*, Nov. 28, 1861; "Shenandoah," *Philadelphia Daily Evening Bulletin*, Jan. 24, 1862; "Caesai," *Philadelphia Public Ledger*, Feb. 19, 1862.

29. Letter 34.
30. The citizens of Philadelphia received the 28th Pennsylvania with great en-
    thusiasm. The march began on July 27 at 3:00 P.M. when the regiment dis-
    embarked at the Walnut Street Wharf. From there it proceeded west along
    Walnut Street, made a right turn onto Third Street, and then made a left
    turn onto Chestnut Street. The regiment traveled another fourteen blocks
    until reaching Broad Street. There it turned left and marched south for an-
    other thirteen blocks until reaching the Baltimore Depot. The men climbed
    aboard trains that took them to Baltimore and then to Sandy Hook, Mary-
    land. According to the newspaper that covered the event, Philadelphia citi-
    zens "thronged" the men of the 28th Pennsylvania with "enthusiastic cheer-
    ing." *Philadelphia Daily Evening Bulletin*, July 29, 1861.
31. Confederate Major General Joseph Eggleston Johnston's Army of the
    Shenandoah, fresh from its victory at Manassas only ten days before, prob-
    ably numbered in the vicinity of 7,600 officers and men.
32. The 12th Massachusetts Infantry, the unit that contained North Bridge-
    water's Company F, received an assignment to the same division as the 28th
    Pennsylvania. The 12th Massachusetts left Fort Warren on July 23 and it
    arrived at Sandy Hook, Maryland, on July 27, one day ahead of the Pennsyl-
    vanians. The 12th Massachusetts's band was led by Band Master William J.
    Martland, age twenty-nine, a machinist from North Bridgewater. The band
    contained twenty members, ten of whom came from North Bridgewater.
    Eleven members of the band, including six North Bridgewater natives, were
    professional musicians. This band did not survive the war. All members
    mustered out in May 1862, after the War Department discontinued pay-
    ments to regimental bands. Massachusetts Adjutant General's Office, *Mas-
    sachusetts Soldiers, Sailors, and Marines in the Civil War*, 2:1–4.
33. This incident occurred on August 5, 1861. According to another eyewit-
    ness, the alarm was caused by the 12th Massachusetts Infantry, which was
    target shooting that day. The echo of one of its volleys sounded like a return
    volley, and, believing that the enemy was upon them, neighboring regiments
    sounded the alarm. "D.B.H.," *Philadelphia Daily Evening Bulletin*, Aug. 12,
    1861.
34. The man killed was Private James McGoldrick, a twenty-three-year-old
    Philadelphian. During the confusion, Private McGoldrick received an acci-
    dental gunshot wound through the head from someone in his own company.
    Colonel Geary severely reprimanded Company I for its reckless use of fire-
    arms and eventually forced its commander, Captain Thomas McDonough,
    to resign. On August 7 Corporal William Roberts described the incident:
    "We have had some excitement too, & one very sad occurrence. Viz: the
    accidental shooting of one of Co. I's men which happened day before yes-
    terday. He was standing in front of the tent & some fool was playing with a
    loaded rifle, right in front of him, when the trigger fell on the cap, & the load
    was discharged right into his temple coming out the back of his head. He
    fell a corpse without uttering a groan. He was a young fellow only 19 [*sic*].
    His body was boxed up & sent home to his friends, who will give it a decent

burial. Gov'r Geary made a good speech to the regiment on the danger & recklessness in handling firearms." "D.B.H.," *Philadelphia Daily Evening Bulletin,* Aug.12, 1861; William Roberts to Father and Mother, Aug. 7, 1861, William Roberts Papers, Historical Society of Pennsylvania, Philadelphia; Blair, *A Politician Goes to War,* 5.

35. The man who died in Company E was Private James Brown of Mauch Chunk, Pennsylvania. He died at Sandy Hook on Aug. 6, 1861 from the effects of "typhoid fever." "D.B.H.," *Philadelphia Daily Evening Bulletin,* Aug. 12, 1861.

36. This skirmish took place on August 5. Colonel Geary's letters to his wife confirm Hayward's account: the Confederates lost five killed, fifteen captured, and twenty horses taken. Blair, *A Politician Goes to War,* 5.

37. Colonel Geary was an ardent temperance advocate, and he went to great lengths to purge alcohol from the camp of the 28th Pennsylvania. His tactics included arresting vendors who attempted to sell alcohol to his men, searching mail delivered the regiment, and destroying any secreted alcoholic containers. One soldier in the 28th Pennsylvania wrote: "Colonel Geary said he had determined to make the 'Twenty-Eighth' the 'Goldstream Regiment' of Pennsylvania. He has fulfilled his word. Liquor has been put out of reach wherever found, and kindly persuasion and strict moral example has released the inebriate from his fetters." "Teniente," *Philadelphia Inquirer,* Nov. 28,1861.

38. Sergeant James B. Sampson, age twenty-four, a merchant from North Bridgewater, enlisted in Company F, 12th Massachusetts, on April 27, 1861. He mustered into service on June 26, 1861, as sergeant. He received a commission to second lieutenant on January 16, 1863. He was captured by Confederate forces during the Battle of Gettysburg on July 1, 1863, but successfully escaped confinement at Columbia Prison, South Carolina. He mustered out on January 7, 1865. Massachusetts Adjutant General's Office, *Massachusetts Soldiers, Sailors, and Marines in the Civil War,* 2:40.

39. It is not clear if this text is a continuation of the August 8 letter or a fragment of another letter written about the same time. All pages were written on mismatching paper and provide no conclusive answer. If this is only one letter, then Hayward must have written it to his brother, Augustus. But, if this is two letters, which is more likely the case, then the first half could have been written to one of his brothers, Albert or Augustus, while the second half was addressed to Augustus.

40. The arrested soldier's name could not be determined.

41. Wilson Orr, age twenty-four, was a mechanic from North Bridgewater. He enlisted as a private in a three-month unit, Company G, 4th Massachusetts Infantry, on April 16, 1861. He mustered into service on April 22 and mustered out on July 22. He reenlisted as a private in Company I, 1st Massachusetts Cavalry, a company formerly known as the "North Bridgewater Dragoons," on October 10, 1861, and mustered into service on October 31. He reenlisted as a veteran volunteer on January 1, 1864. On February 12, 1864, he and the other veterans of Company I, 1st Massachusetts Cavalry,

received a transfer to Company I, 4th Massachusetts Cavalry, through Special Orders Number 70. Orr served with that unit until mustering out on November 14, 1865. Massachusetts Adjutant General's Office, *Massachusetts Soldiers, Sailors, and Marines in the Civil War,* 1:221, 6:196, 468.

42. At this time Geary did not have an official brigade, but he did receive authority to direct a number of units in the area, including the 28th New York Infantry, three companies of the 13th Massachusetts Infantry, the 1st Rhode Island Battery, and a company of U.S. Cavalry. As Hayward states, Colonel Geary was quite familiar with the area, having served as an officer on the Baltimore and Ohio Railroad, managing the Potomac Furnaces in 1859. Blair, *A Politician Goes to War,* 5, 9.

43. This line indicates that Hayward and his company liberated slaves when they fled to Union lines. Congress had passed a Confiscation Act on August 6, 1861, allowing Union commanders the authority to seize slaves impressed by Confederate officers for military construction projects; however, the Union army had no general policy telling its soldiers what to do when slaves asked for refuge. Hayward's letter suggests that some Union soldiers liberated slaves of their own volition, advancing the cause of emancipation. This incident concurs with the recent study by Chandra Manning, who wrote, "Between August and December 1861 a striking pattern took shape, as soldier after soldier began to insist that because slavery had caused the war, only the destruction of slavery could end the war." Although many bluecoats had enlisted to fight for the Union, some added emancipation to their cause as a pragmatic means of defeating the Confederacy. Chandra Manning, "A 'Vexed Question': White Union Soldiers on Slavery and Race," in *The View from the Ground: Experiences of Civil War Soldiers,* ed. Aaron Sheehan-Dean (Lexington: Univ. Press of Kentucky, 2006), 34.

44. This letter was probably written on Thursday, August 15, 1861.

45. Colonel Geary wrote a letter to his wife on the same date as this letter, but he did not mention any of his mistakes that resulted in the unnecessary twenty-three mile march. Geary added in his postscript: "Our march was 16 miles on foot, wet weather & bad roads." Geary to wife, Aug. 15, 1861, in Blair, *A Politician Goes to War,* 9.

46. This letter was probably written on Saturday or Sunday, August 17 or 18.

47. The retreat was ordered by Major General Nathaniel Prentiss Banks on the night of August 13.

48. Frank Leslie, age forty, published a popular illustrated journal, *Frank Leslie's Illustrated Newspaper,* or *Leslie's Weekly.*

49. Elliot was an editor of the *Philadelphia Inquirer.* His son, First Lieutenant Thomas H. Elliot of Company H, age twenty-five, was attached to Colonel Geary's staff. He was killed in action at Peach Tree Creek, Georgia, on July 20, 1864.

50. "Con-fist-to-taked" is a play on words meaning "confiscated."

51. "Ruf" was Hayward's boyhood friend from North Bridgewater, Rufus Emery Brett, age twenty-one. Brett's father, like Hayward's father, was a dry goods trader. Rufus, running his father's business, remained in North

Bridgewater throughout the war. He married Martha Jane Studley on June 15, 1864. "Fred" was Rufus Brett's brother, Frederic Lyman Brett, age eighteen. Like his brother, Frederic married on June 15, 1864. Kingman, *History of North Bridgewater,* 452–57.

52. The leader of the expedition was Second Sergeant James C. Devine, age twenty-two. Devine remained with Company D throughout the war. On December 8, 1862, he received a promotion to first sergeant. Then on March 27, 1863, he received a commission to second lieutenant. He received a promotion to first lieutenant on May 22, 1863, and then another promotion to captain on April 4, 1864. In December 1863 he and fifteen other men from Company D, including Henry Hayward, reenlisted as veteran volunteers. Devine participated in many of the 28th Pennsylvania's major engagements, including the Battles of Bolivar Heights, Antietam, Chancellorsville, and Gettysburg. He mustered out with the regiment on July 18, 1865. *Philadelphia Daily Evening Bulletin,* Sept. 10, 1861; Bates, *History of the Pennsylvania Volunteers,* 1:449.

53. "Mr. Grub" could not be identified. In a letter to his wife, Colonel Geary mentioned the cattle raid: "The Capture of the 39 cattle is regarded here as a gallant affair. It showed that some things can be done as well as others." Blair, *A Politician Goes to War,* 13.

54. Ephraim Brett, age sixty-three, was grandfather of Hayward's friend, Rufus Brett. He was a father of three and in his second marriage. Kingman, *History of North Bridgewater,* 452–57.

55. The First Maryland Infantry was a Unionist regiment recruited in Baltimore in May and June 1861. Colonel John R. Kenly, a Mexican-American War veteran, commanded it.

56. The 28th Pennsylvania received five additional companies: L, M, N, O, and P between September and October 1861. The 28th Pennsylvania's Major Hector Tyndale recruited these companies from his temporary headquarters in Philadelphia. The three companies that arrived on September 1 were companies L, N, and O, raised in Pittsburgh, Hazleton, and Huntingdon, respectively.

57. The North Bridgewater Dragoons were a prewar militia company chartered in 1857. At the outbreak of the Civil War, the Dragoons were commanded by Captain Lucius Richmond, age thirty-one. All of its members eventually mustered into service on October 31, 1861, as Company I, 1st Massachusetts Cavalry. Kingman, *History of North Bridgewater,* chap. 15 (pp. 293–97).

58. Hayward is referring to Major General Benjamin F. Butler's assault on two Confederate forts on the Outer Banks, Fort Clark and Fort Hatteras. On August 28, following an offshore bombardment by the U.S. Navy, Butler ordered his troops to land at Cape Hatteras. They successfully stormed the forts. This resulted in the capture of 670 Confederate soldiers and the completion of the war's first amphibious operation.

59. This skirmish took place on September 16. Confederate skirmishers probed the river bank at 10 A.M., causing Company D to return fire. Eventually,

Colonel Geary arrived and ordered an artillery piece to fire ten to fifteen shells into the Confederate position, causing the skirmishers to withdraw to the shelter of a brick house. Again, Geary ordered the artillery to fire a few shells, driving the Confederates from their second position. Afterwards, a squad from Company D crossed the river on a skiff and burned the house. "Rammah," *Philadelphia Public Ledger,* Oct. 1, 1861.

60. The validity of this statement is murky. A postwar historical sketch of the 28th Pennsylvania confirmed Hayward's report, explaining that the fight in question occurred at Pitcher's Mill, Virginia, and that Company A inflicted a heavy loss upon the enemy amounting to eighteen killed and seventy-three wounded. Also, the sketch stated that Company A captured two unmounted cannon, two mortars, and "several prisoners." However, a statement from Company A's commander, Captain Ariovistus Pardee Jr., tells a different story. Pardee admitted that his men did little fighting and that most reports were exaggerated. On September 26, 1861, Pardee wrote, "We did not succeed in meeting the Cavalry (rebel) or in fact any of the rebel soldiers. In both cases they heard about our being over the river, and as a matter of course were very cautious in regard to their movements. . . . I am anxious for the 28th to get an honorable name; to obtain it for an action worthy of the name, and not for being the laughing stock of the community in publishing such glowing accounts of her confounded one horse skirmishes. The 28th has not yet been engaged in an action worthy of her, but if one was to believe the reports which appear in the papers, he would be led to think she has covered herself with honors." Chickamauga-Chattanooga Battlefield Commission, *Pennsylvania at Chickamauga and Chattanooga* (Harrisburg, PA: William Ray, 1897), 88; Ario Pardee to father, Sept. 26, 1861, the Pardee-Robison Collection, USAMHI.

61. This was probably Zibeon French, age sixty-one, of North Bridgewater. Kingman, *History of North Bridgewater,* 504.

62. Although a special session of the state legislature at Frederick had voted down a bill of secession in May 1861, the Maryland Assembly reconvened on September 17 to debate the merits of the state's active neutrality. Before a meeting could be held, federal soldiers arrested the legislature's pro-Southern members. The discussion of kegs of powder being placed under the state house turned out to be mere rumor and hearsay.

63. John Richardson and E. P. Couch could not be identified.

64. The idea to form an artillery battery came from Colonel Geary and First Lieutenant Joseph M. Knap of Company L, age twenty-four, a graduate of the Rensselear Polytechnic Institute (Class of 1858). Knap's Battery began organizing as the "Fort Pitt Artillery" in July 1861. By October, Knap had recruited one hundred men. Geary materially aided Knap's recruiting by assigning squads of men to the battery from each of his infantry companies. In late October the battery was sworn into service and redesignated as Independent Battery E, 1st Pennsylvania Light Artillery. Knap resigned on May 16, 1863, to accept a position at the Fort Pitt Foundry. The cavalry company never organized.

65. Private David R. Manley of Company D, age nineteen, died of "consumption" (tuberculosis) at Point of Rocks on October 1, 1861. Manley was a resident of Philadelphia. *Philadelphia Daily Evening Bulletin*, Oct. 10, 1861; Bates, *History of the Pennsylvania Volunteers*, 1:452.

66. Chaplain Charles W. Heisley, age thirty-five, a United Methodist minister and a resident of Philadelphia, joined the 28th Pennsylvania on July 20, 1861, and he mustered into service on November 1 of that year. He served with the regiment until resigning his post on July 18, 1863. Bates, *History of the Pennsylvania Volunteers*, 1:438.

67. De Korponay would eventually receive a transfer to a parole camp at Alexandria, Virginia.

68. Colonel Edward Dickinson Baker commanded a brigade of four regiments: the 1st, 2nd, 3rd, and 5th California Regiments. Most of these soldiers came from Philadelphia. After the Battle of Ball's Bluff, the Commonwealth of Pennsylvania added them to the state quota, redesignating them the 71st, 69th, 72nd, and 106th Pennsylvania Infantry Regiments, respectively.

69. The 71st Pennsylvania wore gray uniforms. On the night of September 29–30 another Union regiment, mistaking them for the enemy, fired into them at Munson's Hill, Virginia, killing four and wounding fourteen.

70. The 28th Pennsylvania wore light gray uniforms, the standard color of the Pennsylvania State Militia. Colonel Geary and Major Tyndale privately purchased these uniforms from a firm based in Oxford Park prior to mustering in. After the Battle of Bull Run, the War Department decreed that all U.S. Volunteer regiments had to wear blue uniforms, the standard color of the United States Army, in order to prevent confusion on the battlefield.

71. Company D's clockmaker could not be identified.

72. "Plasters" refers to stamps.

73. Hayward does not recount the full extent of the pay crisis that occurred within the 28th Pennsylvania. None of the 28th Pennsylvania's original ten companies had received pay since their enlistment, the paymaster having failed to show on the scheduled July, August, and September pay dates. On October 11, two days before Hayward wrote this letter, the paymaster arrived to pay these ten companies for four months of service. Owing to the arrival of four of the additional companies—Companies L, M, N, and O—numerous errors existed in the payrolls. Fearing that some of these men would not receive all their pay, Colonel Geary suggested that the paymaster leave and pay the men in full in November. When the paymaster rode off, the soldiers of the 28th Pennsylvania almost mutinied. As one soldier recalled, "a wish to refuse to perform duty commenced to take possession of the boys." Geary delivered a hearty speech to placate them, but, according to one witness, "he did not get any applause as he usually does when he addresses us." Fearing that his men might commit a rash act, Geary recalled the paymaster on October 13, the date of this letter, paying off the original ten companies for two months' service. Thus, while Hayward expressed satisfaction at finally receiving pay, the federal government still owed him for two months' service. For examples of 28th Pennsylvania soldiers' com-

plaints regarding this pay crisis, see *Philadelphia Public Ledger,* Oct. 10, 1861, and *Philadelphia Daily Evening Bulletin,* Oct. 12, 1861.

74. This engagement became known as the Battle of Bolivar Heights. It occurred on October 16, 1861, and it involved approximately 600 Union soldiers under the command of Colonel Geary and 550 Confederate soldiers under the command of Lieutenant Colonel Turner Ashby. Geary's forces lost thirteen men: four killed, one captured, one mortally wounded and captured, and seven wounded. Ashby's forces lost fourteen men: one killed, nine wounded, and four captured.

75. Colonel Ashby brought two artillery pieces with him, a four-pound gun and a twenty-four-pound gun.

76. Ashby's force contained two companies of cavalry, totaling 180 men, and two companies of mounted infantry, totaling fifty men.

77. Captain Joseph B. Copeland, age forty-one, from Elizabeth, Pennsylvania, commanded Company F.

78. The supporting units consisted of three companies of the 13th Massachusetts Infantry—Companies C, I, and K—and three companies of the 3rd Wisconsin Infantry—Companies A, C, and H. After crossing the Potomac River, Company I, 13th Massachusetts, remained at Harpers Ferry to deal with Confederate sharpshooters posted on Loudoun Heights, but the other five companies, constituting about 180 officers and men, joined Companies D and F of the 28th Pennsylvania in the defense of Bolivar.

79. This was Rogers's Richmond Battery, a unit of four guns directed by Colonel Nathan George "Shanks" Evans. They were supported by sharpshooters from the 13th and 18th Mississippi Infantry Regiments and the 8th Virginia Infantry.

80. Two Union batteries operated on Maryland Heights, the 1st Rhode Island Light Artillery and the 9th York Light Artillery. Each battery consisted of two guns.

81. This Columbiad, as Hayward indicates, was left behind by Confederate forces. The axle broke during the fighting, and despite efforts by Confederate artillerists to drag it off the field by hand, soldiers from the 3rd Wisconsin captured it at the close of the battle. Some debate exists about the size of the gun. Although Union soldiers believed that they had captured a thirty-two-pound Columbiad, Colonel Ashby reported that his forces lost a twenty-four-pound gun.

82. Colonel Geary's after-action report confirms Hayward's letter with astonishing accuracy. Geary's force lost four men killed in action, all from the 3rd Wisconsin Infantry (two more died from wounds later). Geary also reported that the dead soldiers were found afterwards, stabbed repeatedly and stripped to "almost complete nudity." Geary blamed Ashby's cavalry for the atrocities. Another 28th Pennsylvania soldier reiterated Hayward's anger in a letter written to the *Philadelphia Daily Evening Bulletin:* "The enemy during the action committed the most barbarous atrocities, stabbing our dead and stripping them naked. When these fiends in human shape again meet the Twenty-Eighth, they shall feel our vengeance." U.S. War Department,

The *War of the Rebellion: A Compilation of the Official Records of the Union and Confederate Armies* (Washington, DC, 1889–1901), ser. 1, vol. 5, pp. 239–49 (hereafter *OR*); "D.B.H.," *Philadelphia Daily Evening Bulletin,* Oct. 25, 1861.

83. Soldiers from the 3rd Wisconsin captured Reverend Nathaniel Green North, a Confederate chaplain from Ashby's Cavalry. North's horse received a wound during the fighting and wandered back to his nearby home. The sight of the animal caused his family to seek out Ashby and ask him to make a request for North's release. Geary refused, believing that North had failed to act as a noncombatant during the fighting. *OR,* ser. 1, vol. 5, pp. 239–49.

84. Two Union soldiers were captured during the Battle of Bolivar Heights, Corporal Beniah Pratt of Company A, 28th Pennsylvania, and Private Edgar Ross of Company C, 3rd Wisconsin. Corporal Pratt was captured after he mistakenly wandered into Confederate lines, believing that Ashby's dismounted cavalry was a section of Massachusetts infantry (owing to a similarity in uniforms). Private Ross received a wound to his leg and he fell into Confederate hands. Ross died at Halltown later that night. *OR,* ser. 1, vol. 5, pp. 239–49.

85. Colonel Geary received a minor wound to his leg. Geary wrote that he was "struck with a piece of shell in the early part of the action just below the knee in the front of the leg, which cut to the bone.—I did not let it be known until after the victory was won, it is healing rapidly and will soon be well." Blair, *A Politician Goes to War,* 19–20.

86. On October 22 Colonel Geary left Point of Rocks, Maryland, with 760 soldiers of the 28th Pennsylvania, marching them twenty miles to Edward's Ferry. Geary wrote that "it rained very hard all the time and was exceedingly muddy and cold." The purpose of the expedition was to reinforce the ferry crossing after the disastrous Union defeat known as the Battle of Ball's Bluff. On October 21, 1861, a Union brigade commanded by Colonel Edward D. Baker crossed the Potomac River near Harrison's Island to advance on Leesburg, Virginia. During the poorly managed battle, Baker's 1,700 men became trapped at the top of a high precipice on the Virginia shore. Baker was killed during the engagement and his men panicked, retreating down the steep bluff and across the Potomac River, while Confederate sharpshooters picked them off as they swam for safety. Baker's brigade lost 917 men, including hundreds drowned in the Potomac River. Baker's superior, Brigadier General Charles Stone, fearing that Confederate troops might cross the river and threaten his headquarters at Edwards Ferry, called for reinforcements. Blair, *A Politician Goes to War,* 20; J. Matthew Gallman, *The Civil War Chronicle* (New York: Crown Publishers, 2000), 111.

87. Captain George F. McCabe, a twenty-seven-year-old clerk from Huntingdon, Pennsylvania, commanded Company O.

88. Corporal James A. Smith, age twenty-three, was a painter from North Bridgewater, Massachusetts. He enlisted in Company I, 13th Massachusetts Infantry, on July 16, 1861, and mustered into service that same day. On April 24, 1863, he received a discharge for disability. On February 29, 1864, he reenlisted as a private in Company H, 58th Massachusetts Infantry, and

mustered into service on April 18, 1864, as sergeant. Sometime thereafter he received a promotion to first sergeant. He was wounded at the Battle of Cold Harbor on June 3, 1864, and received a commission to second lieutenant on August 8, 1864, but he never mustered. He received another wound and was captured at the Battle of Poplar Springs Church on September 30, 1864. He was discharged on account of his wounds on June 20, 1865. Massachusetts Adjutant General's Office, *Massachusetts Soldiers, Sailors, and Marines in the Civil War,* 2:122, 5:38.

89. The 28th Pennsylvania received two battle flags on October 31, a national color and a blue regimental color with the national eagle and the Pennsylvania coat of arms. Sergeant John Page Nicholson, Samuel R. Hilt, and Lieutenant Gilbert L. Parker presented the flags to Colonel Geary during a formal ceremony at Point of Rocks. A witness recalled Geary's speech: "Colonel Geary, on behalf of the Regiment, received the gift[s], and, in reply, patriotically alluded to the standing of our beloved Keystone State and its share in the present struggle, and, amid great attention, glanced at the past, present, and future of our country, concluding by remarking that he would pledge himself to the support and protection of banners thus consigned to the care of the regiment by the city of Philadelphia, and would return them, though stained with the blood of many, to be deposited in the historical records of the state." After Geary's remarks, the 28th Pennsylvania's chaplain, Charles W. Heisley, led the regiment in a prayer and blessed the flags. Remembered the witness, "A fervent 'Amen,' I know, welled from every heart." "Arms-a-Port," *Philadelphia Public Ledger,* Nov. 4, 1861.

90. This refers to the seizure of fence rails for firewood. This practice was common among Union troops, and it exhibited the subtle beginnings of a "hard war" against southern society. Historian Mark Grimsley noted, "Back home, few men would have dismantled houses, stolen fence rails, or coerced meals from unwilling hosts. Army life, however, changed things. The usual rules did not apply, and as a result men often did things as soldiers they would never have contemplated in civilian life." Mark Grimsley, *The Hard Hand of War: Union Military Policy toward Southern Civilians, 1861–1865* (New York: Cambridge Univ. Press, 1995), 40.

91. Brigadier General Charles Pomeroy Stone, age thirty-eight, commanded three federal brigades stationed at Edwards Ferry. Stone graduated from West Point in 1845, served during the Mexican-American War, and served as inspector general of the District of Columbia before the Civil War. Warner, *Generals in Blue,* 480–81.

92. The lithographs of Geary and De Korponay that adorned the top of the 28th Pennsylvania's official letterhead derived from existing photographs. The photograph of Geary had been taken during the Mexican-American War, before Geary had grown a full beard. This thirteen-year lapse accounted for Hayward's claim that the picture did not look like him.

93. Joseph Winchester Robinson, age fifteen, lived on Main Street in North Bridgewater. After the war he became a dry goods merchant. Kingman, *History of North Bridgewater,* 636.

94. H. Ernest Goodman, age twenty-five, was a resident of Philadelphia when he received an appointment to surgeon of the 28th Pennsylvania on July 23, 1861. He remained with the regiment until he accepted a new appointment as assistant surgeon of U.S. Volunteers in February 1864. He eventually rose to the rank of brevet colonel and surgeon in chief of the Army of Georgia. Bates, *History of the Pennsylvania Volunteers*, 1:437.

95. Major General John C. Frémont, age forty-eight, former explorer, U.S. senator, and former Republican presidential candidate, assumed command of the Department of the West in July 1861. His controversial declaration of martial law in Missouri, complete with summary executions of Confederate guerrillas and seizure of slaves belonging to Confederate loyalists, prompted Abraham Lincoln to relieve him of his command in early November. Hayward's dislike of Frémont's removal may be indicative of his emerging abolitionist sentiments. Warner, *Generals in Blue*, 160–61.

96. On July 22, 1861, Congress passed an act to establish a board of examiners to screen the qualifications of Union officers. On November 25 Major General George McClellan appointed Colonel Geary to review the officers in Banks's Division. The board began its first examinations on December 18, 1861, at Frederick, Maryland. Geary performed this duty at various times during the war.

97. Knap's battery, made up of transferred infantry soldiers from each of the 28th Pennsylvania's fifteen companies, became Independent Battery E, 1st Pennsylvania Light Artillery. It served alongside the 28th Pennsylvania during most of its engagements. The Parrott guns were cast iron, rifled barrels, named for their inventor, Robert Parrott.

98. *The Yankee Peddler, or Old Times in a Virginia Farce* was written by Morris Barnett in 1853. According to a playbill, during the thespian activities held by the 28th Pennsylvania on Christmas Day Hayward played the part of "Cowpens." William Roberts Jr. Papers, Historical Society of Pennsylvania, Philadelphia.

99. Major General George Brinton McClellan, age thirty-five, replaced Lieutenant General Winfield Scott as general in chief of the Union Army on November 1, 1861. McClellan graduated second in a class of fifty-nine students at West Point in 1846, and he served as a second lieutenant of engineers during the Mexican-American War. Although McClellan had achieved some minor military successes at Rich Mountain and Corrick's Ford in July, as of December 1861 he had yet to display any grand military feats. McClellan commanded the Union Army of the Potomac during the Peninsula and Maryland Campaigns of 1862 until he was relieved by President Lincoln on November 7, 1862. In 1864 he ran as the Democratic Party's presidential candidate, losing to his former commander in chief. After the war, he served a term as governor of New Jersey. Warner, *Generals in Blue*, 290–92.

100. Augustus Hayward's troubles could not be identified.

101. Geary's men received blue frock coats, blue trousers, and blue forage caps. On December 18 Colonel Geary remarked in a letter to his wife that his

men "look exceedingly well in their new dress." Blair, *A Politician Goes to War*, 26.

102. Edward R. Geary, age sixteen, was the first son from Geary's first marriage. He mustered in as a second lieutenant in Knap's Independent Battery E, 1st Pennsylvania Light Artillery, on September 8, 1861. He received a minor wound at the Battle of Cedar Mountain on August 9, 1862, and he received a promotion to first lieutenant on July 16, 1863. He was killed in action at the Battle of Wauhatchie on October 28, 1863.

103. Brigadier General William Farquhar Barry, age forty-three, was a West Point graduate, class of 1838. Before the Civil War, he served on the Canadian border. He also served as a staff officer during the Mexican-American War and as an artillery officer during the Seminole War of 1852. During the Civil War he served during the Peninsula and Atlanta campaigns. At the time of this letter he was chief of artillery to Major General George McClellan. Warner, *Generals in Blue*, 22–23.

104. Hayward is referring to the Trent Affair. On November 8, Captain Charles Wilkes of the USS *San Jacinto* boarded a British mail packet, the *Trent*, and arrested two Confederate diplomats, James Mason and John Slidell, both en route to England. The British press argued that Wilkes had committed piracy by seizing the diplomats illegally, and the English populace responded with cries for war. Although Abraham Lincoln initially desired to keep Mason and Slidell as prisoners, shortly before Christmas 1861 he decided to release them, thus avoiding an international incident. Phillip S. Paludan, *A Peoples' Contest: The Union and Civil War, 1861–1865* (Lawrence: Univ. Press of Kansas, 1988), 41–43.

105. William L. Geary, age thirteen, the second child from Geary's first marriage, served as a drummer in the regimental band, although Colonel Geary apparently offered him a measure of freedom, letting him use a Sharps carbine to fire at Confederate pickets. As of the writing of this letter, William Geary had already participated in one skirmish. William Geary mustered out on September 9, 1862. Blair, *A Politician Goes to War*, 27.

106. According to Samuel Bates's history of the Pennsylvania Volunteers, one section of Knap's Battery fired upon four Confederate artillery pieces "with such effect as to scatter them and to cause considerable loss." Bates, *History of the Pennsylvania Volunteers*, 1:421.

107. Charles Knap, a cannon founder in Pittsburgh, presented his son's battery with four "steel guns," although these were eventually exchanged for six ten-pound Parrott Rifles provided by the War Department.

108. Aunt Henrietta, age forty-four, was a younger sister of Hayward's mother, Hannah Howland Hayward. Henrietta Howland was the twelfth of thirteen children born to Jabez Howland and Hannah Parker Howland between 1798 and 1819.

109. Patented by U.S. Army officer Henry Hopkins Sibley in 1858, the Sibley tent was circular, eighteen feet in diameter, and supported by a single twelve-foot pole. Although it was not often used during campaigns, the Sibley tent saw frequent garrison use.

110. Major General Nathaniel Banks and Vice President Hannibal Hamlin arrived at Point of Rocks on January 3. The 28th Pennsylvania formed up for review at 4:00 P.M. Hannibal Hamlin, age fifty-two, was a former schoolteacher and lawyer from Paris Hill, Maine. He served as a U.S. congressman from 1848 to 1857 and served as a U.S. senator from 1857 to 1861.

111. The "Union Repeating Gun," or "coffee mill gun," was a wheel-mounted machine gun that operated when cartridges dropped from a tray into a rotating cylinder when an operator turned the crank. J. D. Mills demonstrated its use to President Abraham Lincoln in June 1861. By December the U.S. Army had ordered sixty repeating guns. Two of these guns were assigned to Captain Lansford Chapman's Company E, 28th Pennsylvania. Chapman received orders to protect two islands in the Potomac River near a destroyed bridge. Colonel Geary was not impressed with the guns' usefulness, and consequently they fell out of favor with the War Department. "Shenandoah," *Philadelphia Daily Evening Bulletin*, Jan. 10, 1862.

112. George Acorns was a character in R. J. Raymond's play *The Farmer's Daughter of Severn Side, or Mr. and Mrs. Toodles: A Domestic Drama.*

113. Geary wrote to his wife on January 10 that "Willie has a bad cold but nothing serious." Geary did not admit his own sickness. On January 3, while in Frederick, Geary wrote, "My health is very good," and on January 10, "I am well." Blair, *A Politician Goes to War*, 30–31.

114. Most Pennsylvania newspapers referred to the 28th Pennsylvania as the "Gallant 28th." See "Arms-a-Port," *Philadelphia Public Ledger*, Nov. 4, 1861.

115. First Sergeant H. E. Smith of Company E presented a privately purchased sword to Colonel Geary. Smith dedicated the sword as follows: "Most gallantly, for six months of arduous service have you led us, and we stand today living witnesses to your bravery and courage. Success has always followed you and supported and sustained those who esteem you so highly and have such unbounded confidence in your ability. I shall not be thought extravagant in saying, victory shall ever crown you." Geary received the sword and delivered one of his typical speeches: "May this sword, as it now glitters in the sun, be a pillar of cloud by day and of fire by night to lead you on to victory, and may the blessing of God rest upon it, that no act of mine may ever cause a stain to mar its spotless surface, but that it may be the beacon light to cheer you on until the glorious ensign, so proudly waving over us, shall be planted, if need be, upon the shores of the Gulf of Mexico." "D," *Philadelphia Daily Evening Bulletin*, Feb. 10, 1862.

116. "Get up his Geary" was probably a slang phrase created by members of the 28th Pennsylvania.

117. This action occurred at the end of December and lasted about two hours. According to Samuel Bates, "a large portion of the town was burned." Bates, *History of the Pennsylvania Volunteers*, 1:421.

118. Hayward is referring to Brigadier General Ambrose E. Burnside's impending effort to seize Roanoke Island. Since the capture of the forts guarding Hatteras Inlet, federal forces were preparing for another amphibious assault farther north. On January 13, 1862, Burnside assumed command of the

Department of North Carolina, and on February 8 his forces successfully took Roanoke Island. The Mississippi River flotilla, under Commander Andrew H. Foote, consisted of shallow-draft, iron-clad gunboats. On February 6, and on February 14–16, while working in conjunction with U.S. Army forces under Brigadier General Ulysses S. Grant, this flotilla helped capture two Confederate-held bastions, Fort Henry and Fort Donelson. Their capture opened passage into the Deep South along the Tennessee and Cumberland Rivers. Gallman, *Civil War Chronicle*, 138–40.

119. "Destruction of Harpers Ferry" is another reference to Geary's order to burn the town in late December.

120. A full battery consisted of six guns divided into three sections of two guns each. Under regulations, a lieutenant commanded each section.

121. This incident occurred on February 14. Geary described it in a letter to his wife: "Yesterday I was drilling my Regt. in firing blank cartridges. A Company of rebel cavalry appeared as spectators on the other side of the river. I immediately turned the cannon upon them [and] put shells into them. The discharge scattered the enemy in all directions, to the great merriment of the whole regiment." Blair, *A Politician Goes to War*, 32.

3. "We All Supposed the Time for Chewing Cartridges Had Come"

1. "H.," *Philadelphia Daily Evening Bulletin*, Mar. 3, 1862.

2. In Fort Johnston Geary's men found the following note: "Capt. Fitzgerald, of Mississippi, presents his compliments to the infernal Yankees who will soon visit this fort. He will take pleasure in paying them a similar visit in Washington, autumn next." Geary ordered the 28th Pennsylvania to unfurl its colors over the fort and declared, "For the first time the rightful flag of our country floats over these battlements." "Tomliot," *Philadelphia Inquirer*, Mar. 22, 28, 1862.

3. "Tomliot," *Philadelphia Inquirer*, Mar. 22, 28, 1862.

4. Ibid., Mar. 28, Apr. 7, 1862.

5. Letter 39.

6. "D. B. H.," *Philadelphia Daily Evening Bulletin*, Apr. 5, 1862.

7. "Tomliot," *Philadelphia Inquirer*, Apr. 25, 1862.

8. "D. B. H.," *Philadelphia Daily Evening Bulletin*, Apr. 5, 1862; unknown correspondent, *Philadelphia Inquirer*, Apr. 29, 1862.

9. Letter 42.

10. John W. Geary to wife, Dec. 24, 1861, in Blair, *A Politician Goes to War*, 29.

11. Bates, *History of the Pennsylvania Volunteers*, 1:424.

12. Ariovistus Pardee to father, June 6 and 10, 1862, Pardee-Robison Collection, USAMHI.

13. Letter 43.

14. Robert E. Erwin letter, July 14, 1862, Luvaas Collection, USAMHI.

15. Hector Tyndale, *A Memoir of Hector Tyndale* (Philadelphia: Collins, 1882), 63–66.
16. The lead elements of the 28th Pennsylvania crossed the Potomac River on February 24.
17. This letter was probably written between March 3 and March 6, 1862.
18. Leesburg fell to Union forces on March 8, 1862. The four forts—Johnston, Beauregard, Evans, and Hill—were named after Confederate generals. Leesburg's shockingly easy capture resulted from Major General Joseph E. Johnston's hasty withdrawal. Geary's crossing of the Potomac River near Harpers Ferry on February 24–26 alerted Johnston that his left flank might be turned. He pulled his forces out of Leesburg on March 5.
19. Brigadier General Nathan George Evans, age thirty-eight, of Marion County, South Carolina, was a graduate from the West Point class of 1848. He served as a dragoon officer in Texas and New Mexico Territory, fighting campaigns against the Comanche. He joined the Confederate military in February 1861 and served at the bombardment of Fort Sumter and at the Battles of Blackburn's Ford, First Manassas, Bolivar Heights, Ball's Bluff, Second Manassas, Antietam, Kinston, Goldsboro, and the Siege of Vicksburg. He survived the war, but he died in 1868 from the effects of a head injury received during a buggy accident.
20. Hayward is referring to the Battle of Bolivar Heights. During the opening phase of the battle, he and his comrades were forced to abandon their knapsacks and blankets. The Confederates summarily seized them.
21. Brigadier General John Joseph Abercrombie's brigade consisted of the 12th Massachusetts Infantry, the 13th Massachusetts Infantry, the 83rd New York Infantry, the 11th Pennsylvania Infantry, the 12th Indiana Infantry, and the 16th Indiana Infantry. Abercrombie, age sixty-four, graduated from West Point in 1822 and served during the Mexican-American and Seminole Wars. Warner, *Generals in Blue*, 3.
22. Hayward is not referring to any of the three battles commonly called the Battle of Winchester. The three "battles" around Winchester occurred on May 25, 1862; June 14–15, 1863; and September 19, 1864. What Hayward calls a battle was really a skirmish that resulted in Union occupation of the town.
23. These were three regiments in Abercrombie's brigade. The 9th New York State Militia (also known as the 83rd New York) was a three-year regiment raised in New York City in May 1861. It mustered into service with only eight companies at Washington on June 8, 1861. Three new companies (I, K, and L) joined the regiment in July, August, and September. The 9th New York State Militia mustered out in New York City on June 23, 1864. During the war, the regiment lost 164 officers and enlisted men killed or mortally wounded in action, while ninety-one officers and enlisted men succumbed from disease. The 16th Indiana Infantry was a one-year regiment raised in Richmond, Indiana, in May 1861. It served in the Department of the Shenandoah until May 1862, losing one enlisted man killed in action, while fifteen enlisted men succumbed from disease. The 13th Massachusetts was a three-year regiment raised in Boston, Roxbury, Marlboro, Stoneham,

Natick, and Westboro. In mustered into service at Fort Independence on July 16, 1861, and mustered out at Petersburg, Virginia, on July 14, 1864.

24. The Manassas Gap railroad line transported General Joseph Johnston's 12,000-man army to Manassas Junction in late July 1861 to join General P. G. T. Beauregard's 22,000-man army. This crucial movement helped unify Confederate forces, achieving victory at the Battle of Bull Run.

25. On March 12, 1862, at Leesburg, Virginia, the officers of the 28th Pennsylvania published a small newspaper, entitled the *Advance Guard*. It is not clear if the officers ever continued this publication. *Advance Guard*, Mar. 12, 1862, Historical Society of Pennsylvania, Philadelphia.

26. Brigadier General Louis Blenker, age forty-nine, commanded a division composed of German American soldiers. Blenker was born in Worms, Germany, and he was a veteran of the Revolution of 1848. Warner, *Generals in Blue*, 37.

27. Collis's Zouaves—also known as the Zouaves' de'Afrique—was a company of Philadelphia soldiers assigned to Banks's division. Their commander was Irish-born Captain Charles Henry Tuckey Collis. They wore a distinctive uniform inspired by the French-Algerian light infantry, complete with fezzes and red pantaloons.

28. Mary Good could not be identified.

29. This is likely a postscript added by Ambrose Hayward before he forwarded the letter to his wife, Hannah, who was visiting relatives in Barnstable.

30. The Battle of Pittsburg Landing, or Shiloh, occurred on April 5–6, 1862, after Major General Albert Sidney Johnston's Confederate Army of the Mississippi surprised Major General Ulysses S. Grant's Army of the Tennessee near Shiloh Church in southwest Tennessee. Although Union forces drove Confederates from the field on the second day of the battle, the victory cost Grant 13,000 casualties out of a force of 62,000 men.

31. "Uncle Corporal" is in reference to the birth of Arthur Augustus Hayward, born March 19, 1862, the first child of Henry Hayward's older brother, Augustus.

32. This letter was probably written during the first week of May 1862.

33. Turner Ashby, age thirty-three, of Farquier County, Virginia, was a privately educated planter who served as chief of cavalry under "Stonewall" Jackson. Although he had no professional military training, Ashby served in a prewar militia company called the Mountain Rangers. In June 1861 he received a commission as captain and volunteered his ranger unit for Confederate service. On March 12, 1862, he received a promotion to colonel and took command of the 7th Virginia Cavalry. He received another promotion to brigadier general on May 23, 1862, taking command of the "Laurel Brigade," a larger unit of Virginia cavalry. He was killed in action at the Battle of Harrisonburg, June 6, 1862. In 1853 Ashby bought Wolf's Crag, a square brick-and-stucco house outside of Markham.

34. Aunt Beldens was Henrietta Howland, the twelfth child of Hayward's maternal grandparents, referred to earlier as "Aunt Henrietta." She married Dr. Rufus Hibbert Belden of Amherst, Massachusetts, on February 18, 1835.

35. A Philadelphia reporter described Wolf's Crag as "a plain stone build-
    ing, and looks like a mere stopping place of a sporting old bachelor." The
    soldiers found many scattered decks of cards and empty bottles in the
    parlor, and one servant informed them that Ashby frequently entertained
    gentlemen visitors who played cards and drank all night. The reporter com-
    mented, Ashby "is represented, also, as being liberal and kind to the poor—
    one or two virtues appearing among a multitude of vices." Naturally, such
    conclusions made it easier for the Pennsylvanians to loot Ashby's house.
    Philadelphia Inquirer, June 2, 1862.
36. On April 25, 1862, Geary received a promotion to brigadier general.
37. The men of the 28th Pennsylvania felt a special attachment to Geary. Since
    the beginning of the war, Geary had spent ample amounts of energy disci-
    plining the regiment and building it into a fighting unit. "We will never look
    upon his like again," sighed one Philadelphia soldier at this time. Similarly,
    a Pittsburgher wrote, "I have been in the service with the 28th Penna. Reg't
    nearly ten months, and have had many long and wearisome marches, but
    led and stimulated by so gallant a commander as Col. John W. Geary, I am
    willing to undergo many more." "Enfield," *Philadelphia Inquirer,* May 21,
    1862; "S. M.," *Pittsburgh Gazette,* May 19, 1862.
38. On April 24, 1862, Union naval forces under Flag Officer David Glasgow
    Farragut opened passage into New Orleans after fighting a fierce night battle
    with Confederate naval forces and the defenders at Fort St. Philip and Fort
    Jackson. The next day, 15,000 Union soldiers under Major General Benjamin
    Butler took the city. New Orleans remained in Union hands throughout the
    war. Meanwhile, in Virginia, Major General George McClellan's Army of
    the Potomac moved at a snail's pace up the Yorktown Peninsula. McClellan's
    troops began their campaign on March 17, leaving Alexandria on naval
    troop carriers, but by late April they had only advanced as far as Williams-
    burg. By the time Hayward wrote this letter, the Army of the Potomac had
    just won victories at Lee's Mill, Williamsburg, and Burnt Chimneys, but it
    still had over thirty miles to advance before reaching Richmond.
39. On May 31 and June 1, 1862, the Army of the Potomac collided with the
    Army of Northern Virginia along the Chickahominy River, fighting two
    back-to-back battles, Seven Pines and Fair Oaks.
40. Kentucky-born Major General John Pope, age forty, graduated from West
    Point in 1842. He served during the Mexican-American War and later as a
    topographer for the U.S. Army Engineers in the 1850s. On June 14, 1861,
    he received a commission as brigadier general, and in March and April
    1862 he won distinction for his capture of Island Number 10 on the Mis-
    sissippi River. In June, President Lincoln appointed him to command the
    Army of Virginia, a 70,000-man force that operated in the Eastern Theater.
    He became widely unpopular among his own troops for his bombast and
    arrogance. He managed to bring his army to one major engagement, the
    Second Battle of Manassas, fought on August 28–30, 1862. He suffered a
    disastrous defeat at this battle, and Lincoln transferred him to command
    the Department of the Northwest. Warner, *Generals in Blue,* 376–77.

41. Hayward is referring to rumors that Confederate General Thomas J. "Stonewall" Jackson had been killed in action. These rumors were untrue.

42. This letter was sent by another soldier in Company D while Hayward was still at Fort DeKalb.

43. First Sergeant Edwin F. Paul, age twenty-two, was a salesman from Philadelphia. He stood five foot five and one-half inches tall. He had light hair, light complexion, and hazel eyes.

44. Private Powell Thorne, age twenty, was from Philadelphia. He received a discharge from a surgeon's certificate on April 3, 1863.

45. The retreat from Thoroughfare Gap occurred on May 26, 1862. According to Captain Ariovistus Pardee Jr. of Company A, 28th Pennsylvania, the retreat began when "a negro came breathless into camp and informed the gen'l [Geary] that a force of 20,000 was within a few miles. This fellow was believed, the officers of the cavalry were not believed." Geary promptly ordered his troops to fall back to Manassas. Apparently, Geary believed that the situation was so urgent that all unnecessary camp equipment had to be burned. Although Hayward believed that Geary never told the men of the 104th New York to burn their tents, Pardee maintained otherwise: "The camp equipage of the 104th N.Y. and the officers' baggage, commissary stores, etc., etc. were ordered to be burned although a train was at hand on which everything could have been placed and removed, but time would not permit—to burn was the quickest way of getting rid of these articles." Ario Pardee to father, June 10, 1862, Pardee-Robison Collection, USAMHI.

46. On July 10, 18, and 23, 1862, Major General Pope issued General Orders Numbers 5, 7, and 11. These orders authorized Union officers to seize Confederate property without compensation, execute captured guerrillas who fired on Union troops, and expel disloyal citizens from occupied territory.

47. Martin Van Buren, the eighth president of the United States, died on July 24, 1862, at age seventy-three.

48. Brigadier General Alpheus Starkey Williams, age fifty-one, was a Yale-trained lawyer from Saybrook, Connecticut. He served as a volunteer officer during the Mexican-American War and as postmaster of Detroit in the 1850s. He received a brigadier general's commission on August 9, 1861, and commanded a division in Banks's corps in the Shenandoah Valley. He remained with his unit after it was redesignated the 1st Division, 12th Corps, in September 1862 and also after it was redesignated the 1st Division, 20th Corps, in April 1864. After the war, he served as minister to the Republic of Salvador and as a U.S. congressman from 1876 to 1878. Warner, *Generals in Blue*, 559–60.

49. This incident is explained more fully in Melville Hayward's letter to his father, dated July 23, 1862 (Letter 54).

50. This letter could not be found.

51. The French phrase *hors de combat* means "out of the fight." Generals often used it to refer to units that could no longer function in combat situations.

52. As Hayward indicates, the 28th Pennsylvania was only lightly engaged at the Battle of Cedar Mountain. Sometime between 10:00 A.M. and 11:00 A.M. on

August 9, after Union forces passed Culpeper Court House, ten miles north
of Cedar Mountain, Lieutenant Colonel Hector Tyndale, commanding the
28th Pennsylvania, received verbal instructions from Major General Banks
and Brigadier General Geary to detach his regiment and seize Thoroughfare Mountain, an acclivity that had once been occupied by the U.S. Signal
Corps. Aided by a squadron of the 1st (West) Virginia Cavalry, the 28th
Pennsylvania carried the heights, while the rest of Banks's forces engaged
"Stonewall" Jackson's Confederates on the plain north of Cedar Mountain.
Although the men of the 28th Pennsylvania could hear the fighting below,
Tyndale decided not to join the battle. He conferred with his company officers and deemed it best to remain on Thoroughfare Mountain until he
received further instructions. As a consequence, the 28th Pennsylvania was
spared the grim fate that befell Geary's brigade, which suffered 465 casualties. Although decimated, Geary's brigade performed admirably during
the fight. Geary was wounded by a musket ball that broke his left arm and
disabled him from field command until October. Tyndale's inaction sparked
controversy after the war when a Union staff officer accused Tyndale of de-
liberately avoiding combat while his regiment "passively witnessed the carnage." Banks's corps was soundly defeated and sent in retreat to Culpeper.
Tyndale, *A Memoir of Hector Tyndale*, 63–66.

53. This letter was probably written between August 17 and August 24, 1862.

54. The four Ohio Regiments in Geary's Brigade were the 5th Ohio Infantry,
the 7th Ohio Infantry, the 29th Ohio Infantry, and the 66th Ohio Infantry.

55. This was probably Captain Alpheus K. Harmon, age thirty-five, a painter
from North Bridgewater and the new commander of Company F, 12th
Massachusetts Infantry. Harmon received a wound at the Second Battle of
Manassas, and he received a discharge on July 8, 1864, for the expiration
of his term of service. Kingman, *History of North Bridgewater*, chap. 14 (pp.
249–92).

56. This was Susanna Fish Hayward, the second wife of Ira Hayward, Ambrose
Henry Hayward's paternal grandfather. Susanna Fish was born about 1799
at Kingston, Massachusetts. After her first husband died, she married Ira
Hayward on February 19, 1820. She died on June 9, 1862.

57. These margin notes were probably written by Augustus Hayward.

58. Augustus Hayward is referring to New York's militia draft. On August 4
President Lincoln called upon the states to provide 300,000 nine-month
militiamen. If the states failed to raise this number through volunteering,
he required them to hold a draft. In preparation for this, state draft boards
began recording the names of all fencible males onto local militia rolls.

59. Colonel Michael Corcoran, age thirty-four, was an Irish immigrant trained
in the British army. After his immigration to the United States in 1849,
he settled in New York City, found employment as a clerk, and joined the
69th New York State Militia as a private, rising to the rank of colonel by the
outbreak of the Civil War. On July 21, 1861, during the Battle of Bull Run,
he was captured by Confederate forces. The War Department eventually
negotiated his parole and exchange. After one year in a Confederate prison,

Corcoran returned to New York City on August 22, 1862, amid great fanfare and celebration. A portion of his old regiment, the 69th New York State Militia, having been called up by Governor Edwin Morgan back in May, escorted Corcoran to New York City. Warner, *Generals in Blue*, 93–94.

4. "Baltimore Is a Slumbering Volcano"

1. Letters 52 and 53.
2. The 7th New York Militia received a second call to service and left New York City on May 25, 1862. It mustered into three-month service on May 29, 1862, at Camp Hamilton, Virginia. It served most of its time in Baltimore, Maryland, and returned to New York City, mustering out on September 5, 1862.
3. Mary Howland was a maternal cousin of Melville and Henry Hayward.
4. This was Eliza Howland, wife of Paul J. Fish. Eliza was also the younger sister of Hannah Hayward, the mother of Henry and Melville. Eliza Howland married Paul Fish on July 6, 1837. Their wedding was conducted by Reverend Edward Andrews.
5. This is a mistake. Major General Irvin McDowell commanded the 1st Corps, Army of the Potomac. Henry Hayward never served with this corps. At the time, he was still serving in Banks's Army of the Shenandoah.
6. P. J. Fish was Melville Hayward's law partner at Williamsburgh, New York. Melville studied law under Fish from May 1851 to 1857 until he passed the New York bar.
7. Fanny was another maternal cousin of the Hayward brothers, probably Frances E. Howland, daughter of Freeman Howland and Adeline Parker.
8. The seminary was Greenback Female Seminary, a converted mansion once owned by a deceased widow. Founded by Eliza Romeyn in 1837, it was described by one visitor as "a spacious and beautiful mansion, on an eminence, looking down upon the pleasant little village, . . . [w]ith competent instructors in every branch of female education; a fine climate, delightful scenery, and easy access to the town; above all with grounds laid out in gardens, walks, and orchards, for purposes of recreation." *Knickerbocker* 15 (1840): 360.
9. This was probably Reverend William Hull Hinkley, pastor of Baltimore's New Jerusalem Church.
10. Formed on June 28, 1861, the Union Relief Association provided meals, comfort, and aid to Union soldiers stationed in or in transit through Baltimore. Dozens of women volunteers ran the Union Relief Association's facilities, two rented warehouses with kitchens, several dining halls, and a fifty-bed hospital. By April 1864 the Union Relief Association had distributed aid to over one million Union soldiers, Confederate prisoners of war, and southern refugees.
11. The Eutaw House was a hotel built in 1836 at the northwest corner of Eutaw and West Baltimore streets. During the Civil War, it served as a recruiting station and a headquarters for prominent Union officers. Scott Sumpter

Sheads and Daniel Carroll Toomey, *Baltimore during the Civil War* (Linthicum, MD: Toomey Press, 1997), 178.

12. The 47th New York State Militia organized nine companies in May 1862. The 47th New York left Brooklyn on May 30, 1862, and mustered into three-month service at Fort McHenry, Maryland, backdated to May 27, 1862. It returned to Brooklyn on September 1, 1862, and once there it mustered out.

13. Uncle F. was Freeman Howland, age fifty, the ninth child of Hayward's maternal grandparents.

14. Aunt Howland was Dorcas Jenkins, who in 1832 married Jabez Howland, the older brother of Hannah Howland.

15. Colonel Joseph V. Meserole commanded the 47th New York State Militia. His field officers were Lieutenant Colonel George Sangster and Major George W. Young. E. R. Johnson had been the previous major. Sangster, Young, and Johnson all held membership in the 7th New York State Militia, thus explaining their close association with Melville Hayward. Mrs. Culbert could not be identified.

16. Arthur Cleveland Coxe, age forty-four, a graduate of the University of the City of New York and the General Theological Seminary of the Protestant Episcopal Church, served as rector of Baltimore's Grace Church from 1854 to 1863.

17. The Baltimore Basilica of the National Shrine of the Assumption of the Blessed Virgin Mary, America's oldest Catholic cathedral, stood at the corner of Cathedral and Mulberry streets. It was built between 1806 and 1821. Monument Park was in central Baltimore. A 178-foot column and statue of George Washington designed by Robert Mills was erected in the park between 1815 and 1829. The Mercantile Library Association headquartered at the Athenaeum Building at the corner of Saratoga and St. Paul streets.

18. Jabez Howland, age fifty-nine, was the fourth son of Hayward's maternal grandparents.

19. America's first New Church temple stood at the southwest corner of Exeter and Baltimore streets in Baltimore. The temple was dedicated on January 2, 1800.

20. Major General Ambrose Everett Burnside, age thirty-eight, graduated from West Point in 1847, served during the Mexican-American War, and worked for the Illinois Central Railroad. After his successful campaigns in the Carolinas in 1861, Burnside and a portion of his troops were transferred to the Army of the Potomac. They arrived in July 1862 and became the 9th Corps. Warner, *Generals in Blue*, 57–58.

5. "I Have Seen Death in Every Shape"

1. Letter 55.

2. Ariovistus Pardee Jr. to father, Sept. 8, 1862, Pardee-Robison Collection, USAMHI.

3. Bates, *History of the Pennsylvania Volunteers*, 1:427–28.

4. As it advanced along the Smoketown Road, the 28th Pennsylvania moved at the double-quick in "close column by division"—that is, two companies front. Tyndale gave the command: "Deploy from the left and right!" Each division, as it arrived, broke by companies to the left and right until the regiment fully deployed.

5. Joseph A. Moore, "Rough Sketch of the War as Seen by Joseph Addison Moore," in *George Washington Irwin: The Civil War Diary of a Pennsylvania Volunteer,* ed. Jane B. Steiner (Lafayette, CA: Hunsaker, 1991), 162; "J.," *Pottsville Miner's Journal,* Oct. 4, 1862; J. O. Foering, MS, Sept. 17, 1862, John O. Foering Collection, HSP.

6. At this point, Private Patrick McShay of Company A picked up the abandoned colors of a Georgia regiment inscribed with the battle honor "Seven Pines." Another soldier from Company A spoke with a wounded Georgian who wailed that the "flower" of his brigade had been annihilated.

7. Joseph A. Moore, "Rough Sketch of the War as Seen by Joseph Addison Moore," in Steiner, *George Washington Irwin,* 162; "J.," *Pottsville Miner's Journal,* Oct. 4, 1862; Foering MS, Sept. 17, 1862, HSP; Letter 58.

8. Letter 57.

9. Letter 56.

10. Letter 63; 28th Pennsylvania Infantry Papers, HSP.

11. Tyndale, *Memoir,* 58, 105.

12. Letter 73.

13. Letter 64.

14. Thirteen picked men from the 28th Pennsylvania, including Henry Hayward, made a valiant expedition during the first week of September. Hayward describes this expedition more fully in letter 58, dated September 28, 1862.

15. The 28th Pennsylvania faced elements from five Confederate brigades: Colonel Duncan K. McRae's brigade, Colonel Alfred H. Colquitt's brigade, Brigadier General Joseph B. Kershaw's brigade, Colonel Vannoy H. Manning's brigade, and Brigadier General Robert Ransom Jr.'s brigade. The battery they supported was Captain John A. Tompkins's Battery A, 1st Rhode Island Light Artillery, and the two artillery pieces they captured came from Captain George M. Patterson's Battery B, Sumter Artillery. Sources boast that Tyndale's brigade captured seven battle flags. Evidence verifies four of these captures. Private John P. Murphy (Company K, 5th Ohio) captured the colors of the 13th Alabama, Corporal Jacob G. Orth (Company D, 28th Pennsylvania) captured the colors of the 7th South Carolina, Private Patrick McShay (Company A, 28th Pennsylvania) seized the colors of an unnamed Georgia regiment, and First Lieutenant Charles W. Borbridge (Company I, 28th Pennsylvania) most likely took the colors of the 8th South Carolina. Hayward's estimate of the fight's duration is fairly accurate. Most accounts claim that Tyndale's brigade fought for six to nine hours. Eight hours, from 7:00 A.M. to 3:00 P.M., seems to be the most reasonable estimate.

16. Tyndale was wounded at approximately 3:00 P.M., shortly after his horse was shot from under him. As he turned to rally his retreating troops, a

Confederate musket ball slammed into the back of his head, glanced off the lower occipital bone of his skull, and lodged in his neck between his jugular vein and his carotid artery. The impact caused a compound fracture of his skull and knocked him unconscious. Hayward and an officer from Company I, First Lieutenant Charles W. Borbridge, carried Tyndale off the field. Tyndale never received an opportunity to thank Hayward for saving his life. In 1864 Tyndale replied to an army circular, providing a brief overview of his military service. Not having written an after-action report for the Battle of Antietam, he took the opportunity to explain his role in the battle in great detail. When describing his rescue by Hayward and Borbridge, he wrote: "I wish to record here a disinterested, noble, and courageous action. First Lieutenant, now Captain Charles W. Borbridge, of my own regiment, who was one of the last to retreat, seeing me fall, at once turned back, in the face of a heavy fire from the advancing enemy, who were within a hundred yards. He had a rebel battle flag (of which my brigade that day captured, I think, seven) in his hands, but with the aid of a sergeant, whose name I could never learn, dragged my apparently dead body, seemingly shot through the head, behind a haystack at least fifty yards distant." It is certain that the unnamed sergeant was Corporal Hayward. Tyndale regained consciousness that evening after the ball was extracted from his neck by the 28th Pennsylvania's surgeon, Henry Ernest Goodman. Although Tyndale's wound was of serious nature, he recuperated and resumed active service as a brigade commander in June 1863. Tyndale served with distinction at the Battle of Wauhatchie on October 29, 1863, but the pain caused by his wound forced him to resign in August 1864. The compound fracture did not heal properly, placing intense pressure on his brain. Although he continued to lead an active lifestyle during the postwar years—even running for mayor of Philadelphia in 1868—his wound induced a severe attack of *angina pectoris,* which claimed his life on March 19, 1880. Tyndale, *Memoir,* 13–21, 58.

17. The New York regiment was probably one of Colonel William H. Irwin's 3rd Brigade, 2nd Division, 6th Army Corps. This brigade included the 20th, 33rd, 49th, and 77th New York Infantry Regiments. Irwin's brigade arrived behind Tyndale's position just as his brigade began its retreat.

18. Major General Alpheus Williams commanded the 12th Corps' 1st Division and, later, the 12th Corps itself. The corps commander, Major General Joseph Mansfield, was mortally wounded during the fighting.

19. "General White" was probably Major William Capers White of the 7th South Carolina Volunteer Infantry, a native of Georgetown, South Carolina. White was killed in action during the 28th Pennsylvania's attack. Hayward probably mistook White as a general because a Confederate major's insignia—a single star on each collar—resembled the insignia for a U.S. Army brigadier general, a single star on each shoulder. White's horse was captured as Hayward mentioned. It was grabbed by a private in Company A, 28th Pennsylvania, and was then purchased on the battlefield by Major William Raphael of the same regiment.

20. Hayward's estimate of the 28th Pennsylvania's casualties is remarkably accurate. The official records place the regiment's loss at 44 killed, 217 wounded, and 2 missing.

21. Major General Edwin Vose Sumner commanded the 2nd Army Corps.

22. Geary received command of the 2nd Division, 12th Army Corps, upon his arrival at Loudoun Heights. In a letter to his wife written two days later, Geary recalled the greeting: "My Old Veteran Brigade received me with great enthusiasm, and I find myself in command of a Division. God grant that I may guide them to victory and success, under the direction of the God of Battles." As Hayward indicates, Geary had not recovered from the arm wound he received at Cedar Mountain. In the same letter, Geary remarked that his arm was still "very painful & sore." Blair, *A Politician Goes to War*, 57–58.

23. The reconnaissance consisted of one volunteer drawn from each company. Every company supplied one volunteer with the exception of Companies A and P—not for want of volunteers—but because the mission parameters limited the party to thirteen men. The party consisted of Sergeant Frank B. M. Bonsall (Company H), Sergeant George H. Grady (Company G), Sergeant Hiram F. Ely (Company L), Sergeant Samuel S. Diffelbaugh (Company O), Corporal Ambrose Henry Hayward (Company D), Corporal Douglas McLean (Company E), Corporal Luke Behe (Company F), Corporal Arnold B. Spink (Company I), Corporal Almon Smith (Company K), Corporal Henry Carse (Company M), Corporal John O'Connor (Company N), Private Lentillus L. Frazier (Company B), and Private Charles Hickey (Company C). Sergeant Grady, age twenty-five, was a resident of Sewickleyville, Pennsylvania. He received a wound at the Battle of Antietam on September 17, 1862, while carrying the regimental colors. This wound led to his discharge on December 27, 1862. Corporal O'Connor, age twenty-five, was a resident of Hazleton, Pennsylvania. He also received a wound at the Battle of Antietam and was discharged on December 28, 1862, at the U.S. General Hospital in Philadelphia. Sergeant Diffelbaugh, age twenty-four, was a resident of Coalmont, Pennsylvania. He died of chronic diarrhea at Harpers Ferry, Virginia, on December 13, 1862. Corporal Smith, age twenty-five, was a resident of Philadelphia. He died of disease at Frankford, Pennsylvania, on February 5, 1863. Private Hickey, age twenty-four, also resided in Philadelphia. He received a discharge on July 20, 1864, due to the expiration of his term of service. Corporal Carse, age twenty-six, was a gardener from Philadelphia. He received a promotion to sergeant on March 1, 1863, and later a discharge due to expiration of service on August 29, 1864. Corporal Behe, age twenty-four, resided in Elizabeth, Pennsylvania. At his own request, he received a reduction to private on March 9, 1863. He received a discharge on July 20, 1864, due to expiration of his term of service. Sergeant Ely, from Pittsburgh, also received a discharge from expiration of service in July 1864. Corporal Spink, age nineteen, resided in New Cumberland, Pennsylvania. He received a promotion to sergeant on March 14,

1863, a promotion to first sergeant on September 1, 1864, and finally a promotion to first lieutenant on April 3, 1865. He reenlisted as a veteran volunteer on December 24, 1863. He was wounded during the Battle of Resaca, May 15, 1864, and he commanded Company D from July 3, 1864, until the end of the war. Corporal McLean, age twenty-two, resided in Mauch Chunk, Pennsylvania. He received a promotion to sergeant on September 18, 1862. He was wounded at the Battle of Gettysburg on July 3, 1863. He reenlisted as a veteran volunteer on December 24, 1863, and he mustered out with the regiment on July 18, 1865.

24. Colonel John S. Clark, age thirty-eight, the former colonel of the 19th New York Infantry, served as an additional aide-de-camp on the staff of Major General Nathaniel Banks. Clark had been a civil engineer in his hometown of Throopsville, New York. Roger D. Hunt and Jack R. Brown, *Brevet Brigadier Generals in Blue* (Gaithersburg, MD: Olde Soldier Books, 1990), 113.

25. Major Generals Phillip J. Kearney and Isaac I. Stevens were both killed at the Battle of Chantilly on September 1, 1862.

26. It is unknown which soldier returned to Union lines.

27. Sergeant Frank B. M. Bonsall, a twenty-five-year-old Pittsburgh resident, commanded the reconnaissance. Bonsall received a promotion to second lieutenant on March 9, 1863, and another to first lieutenant seven days later. He received another promotion to captain on June 9, 1864, and received a wound at the Battle of Peach Tree Creek on July 20, 1864. He mustered out with the rest of the 28th Pennsylvania on July 18, 1865.

28. Hayward inserted this line at the bottom of the letter next to the asterisk: "*we had received orders from Col. Clark before we started to avoid if possible any Engagement with the Rebels as that was not the object of which we came."

29. Private Lentillus L. Frazier, age twenty-six, from Mount Pleasant, Pennsylvania, was the soldier captured. Private Frazier was later exchanged and returned to the regiment. He reenlisted as a veteran volunteer on December 15, 1863, and mustered out with his company on July 18, 1865.

30. Hayward is mistaken, since Lieutenant General James Longstreet's wing did not contain the 34th Virginia Infantry. This soldier could have been from either the 14th or 24th Virginia Infantry Regiments.

31. This was probably Selden Island, located in the Potomac, northwest of Dranesville.

32. The general order came from Major General Alpheus Williams, who temporarily commanded the 12th Corps, following Banks's transfer to the defenses of Washington. Williams's order read: "The General commanding takes great pleasure in commending the conduct of Sergeant Bonsall and twelve men of the Twenty-Eighth Pennsylvania Volunteers, who being detailed on important special duty beyond the lines of the army, discharged that duty promptly and faithfully, and on their return, captured nineteen armed Confederates, sixteen of whom they brought safely to camp. This act is deemed worthy of special commendation as an example to their comrades."

33. Second Corporal Jacob George Orth, age twenty-four, captured the colors of the 7th South Carolina Infantry during the 28th Pennsylvania's advance at Antietam. According to Orth's testimony after the war, he killed the 7th South Carolina's color bearer during a fierce hand-to-hand combat. Orth received a slight gunshot wound to his right shoulder during the encounter, but the wound healed rapidly and left no scarring. Orth received a promotion to color sergeant on December 8, 1862, and in 1867 received the Congressional Medal of Honor, the only member of the 28th Pennsylvania to receive such a distinction. W. F. Beyer and O. F. Keydel, eds., *Deeds of Valor: How America's Civil War Heroes Won the Congressional Medal of Honor* (Stamford, CT: Longmeadow Press, 1994), 86.

34. President Abraham Lincoln, along with two corps commanders, Major General Edwin Sumner and Major General William Franklin, reviewed Geary's division at 8:00 A.M. on October 2. The salute was a twenty-one-gun salute. Judging from the above evidence, this undated letter was probably written during the second week of October, probably on October 10 or 11, 1862. Blair, *A Politician Goes to War*, 58.

35. The *Philadelphia Press* article is reprinted here as follows:

> Honor to the Brave
> Headquarters 1st Brigade 2d Div. Banks' Corps.
> Near Frederick, Md., Sept. 13, 1862.
> I take pleasure in calling your attention to the accompanying General Order, a deserved tribute to some of the uncommissioned brave of this army, men whom I am very proud to command. Their names I send herewith.
> Respectfully, your obd't serv't,
> HECTOR TYNDALE,
> Lieut. Col. 28th Reg't P.V., Commd'g Brigade.
> Headquarters Banks' Army Corps,
> Camp near Damascus, MD, September 10, 1862.
> GENERAL ORDER.
> The General commanding takes pleasure in commending the conduct of Sergeant Bonsall, and twelve men, of the 28th Pennsylvania Volunteers, who, being detailed on important special duty beyond the lines of the army, discharged that duty promptly and faithfully; and, on their return, captured nineteen (19) armed Confederates, sixteen (16) of whom they brought safely to camp. This act is deemed worthy of special commendation, and is recommended as an example to their comrades.
> By command of Brigadier General A. S. Williams:
> S. E. Pittman,
> First Lieutenant and A. A. A. General.
> Names of the squad detailed from the 28th Regiment Pennsylvania Volunteers, on the 1st of September, 1862, for—duty,

commanded by general order from Gen. Williams, commanding corps:

Sergeant F. B. M. Bonsall, Company H.
Sergeant G. H. Grady, Company G.
Sergeant Hiram F. Ely, Company L.
Sergeant Samuel Diffe[l]baugh, Company O.
Corporal A. H. Hayward, Company D.
Corporal Douglas McLean, Company E.
Corporal Luke Behe, Company F.
Corporal A. B. Spink, Company I.
Corporal Olman Smith, Company K.
Corporal H. Carse, Company M.
Corporal John O'Connor, Company N.
Private L. L. Frazier, Company B.
Private Charles Hickey, Company C.

Note—It is but justice to say that the above was the number designated by General Banks himself, and that the two
companies (A and P) of the regiment, which were not represented were so by decision of lot, the men selected were from
those companies being eager to go with their comrades upon
their most dangerous and important duty. Private Frazier has
not yet returned, and is supposed to have been taken by the enemy's cavalry, who, in large numbers, surrounded and attacked
them—these men of ours extricating themselves only by their
courage and address from a seemingly hopeless position.

H. TYNDALE, Lieut. Col., &c.

36. President Lincoln relieved McClellan of command of the Army of the Potomac on November 7, 1862.
37. "F.F.V.," meaning "First Family of Virginia," is a slang term referring to the
affluent planter-class of Virginia.
38. Hayward is referring to the Battle of Harpers Ferry, September 14–15,
1862. After two engagements on Maryland Heights and Bolivar Heights,
Colonel Dixon S. Miles, the Union garrison commander at Harpers Ferry,
surrendered to Lieutenant General Thomas J. Jackson's Confederates.
Miles took little precaution to fortify the ferry, and his quick surrender resulted in the capture of 12,700 Union soldiers.
39. Hayward received a promotion to fourth sergeant on December 1, 1862,
following the discharge of Third Sergeant Edward Pepper on a surgeon's
certificate on November 21, 1862. Bates, *History of the Pennsylvania Volunteers*, 1:449.
40. First Sergeant Edwin F. Paul was captured at Charlestown on December 5.
He was paroled on December 16 near Strasburg, Virginia, sent to Camp
Parole, Maryland, and then sent to the provost marshal's office on January 8, 1863. There he was subsequently reduced to ranks. He was officially
relieved of his duty as first sergeant on April 13, 1863, but he continued to

serve faithfully with the 28th Pennsylvania as a hospital steward until he was discharged on October 5, 1863. Bates, *History of the Pennsylvania Volunteers,* 1:452.

41. Major General Franz Sigel, age thirty-eight, was born at Sinsheim, Duchy of Baden, Germany. He participated in the Revolution of 1848 and immigrated to New York City in 1852. Prior to the war, he directed schools in St. Louis, Missouri. Although he possessed questionable military abilities, his popularity among the German American population proved essential in recruiting soldiers. He participated in the Missouri Campaign of 1861–62 and the Shenandoah Valley Campaign of 1864. Warner, *Generals in Blue,* 447–48.

42. Vinegar Swamp rested at the southwest edge of North Bridgewater.

43. The Battle of Fredericksburg took place on December 13, 1862. Major General Ambrose Burnside launched a series of assaults against heavily entrenched Confederate forces costing his army 12,600 casualties.

44. General Banks had recently assumed command of Union troops in New Orleans. The Mississippi Expedition referred to General Ulysses Grant's effort to seize Vicksburg, Mississippi. On December 20 he left Memphis with 40,000 troops separated into two columns. Both columns stalled after running into Confederate resistance. One column halted near Holly Springs, the other at Chickasaw Bayou. Together they suffered 3,800 casualties, and they commenced retreating on December 29. Gallman, *Civil War Chronicle,* 261–62.

6. "These Are America's Dark Days"

1. Letter 66.

2. *Congressional Globe,* 37th Cong., 3rd sess., appendix (Washington, DC: Government Printing Office, 1863), 55.

3. Letter 69.

4. Unknown correspondent, *Philadelphia Inquirer,* Mar. 23, 1863.

5. Letter 69.

6. Undated newspaper clipping, Ambrose Henry Hayward Papers, Gettysburg College Special Collections Archive. For a fuller discussion of Pennsylvania soldier resolutions, see Timothy J. Orr, "'A Viler Enemy in Our Rear': Pennsylvania Soldiers Confront the North's Antiwar Movement," in *The View from the Ground: The Experiences of Civil War Soldiers,* ed. Aaron Sheehan-Dean (Lexington: University Press of Kentucky, 2006), 171–98.

7. Unknown correspondent, *Philadelphia Inquirer,* Mar. 23, 1863.

8. Ariovistus Pardee to father, Jan. 7, 1863, Pardee-Robison Collection, USAMHI.

9. Unknown correspondent, *Philadelphia Inquirer,* Feb. 11, 1863.

10. George W. Irwin diary, Apr. 28, 1863, in Steiner, *George Washington Irwin,* 99.

11. Major General Henry Warner Slocum, age thirty-five, a West Point graduate from the class of 1852, commanded the 12th Army Corps. Warner, *Generals in Blue,* 451–53.

12. Brigadier General George Sears Greene's 3rd Brigade, 2nd Division, 12th Army Corps consisted of five regiments: the 3rd Delaware Infantry, the 60th New York Infantry, the 78th New York Infantry, the 1st District of Columbia Infantry, and the Purnell Legion (Maryland) Infantry.

13. Brigadier General James E. B. Stuart led a 1,800-man raiding force against Dumfries and Fairfax Station on December 27–29. Geary's division forced Stuart's withdrawal following a smart action that nearly captured a portion of Brigadier General Wade Hampton's cavalry brigade. Blair, *A Politician Goes to War*, 77.

14. The town of Dumfries, Virginia, was established at the head of the Quantico River on May 11, 1749, but settlements existed as early as 1690. It was the oldest continuously chartered town in Virginia.

15. President Lincoln's Emancipation Proclamation took effect on January 1, 1863.

16. De Korponay took command of a parole camp at Alexandria, Virginia. He was discharged on a surgeon's certificate on March 26, 1863.

17. Tyndale received his promotion to brigadier general on November 29, 1862. However, he did not take field command for several months. His head wound left him enfeebled, partially paralyzed, and deaf in one ear. After a slow convalescence, he took command of a brigade at Fort Monroe in June 1863. Tyndale, *Memoir*, 14.

18. Second Lieutenant Joseph W. Hammar received a promotion to Captain of Company D on April 1, 1863. He resigned on May 14, 1863. Bates, *History of the Pennsylvania Volunteers*, 1:449.

19. Captain George D. Hammar resigned on March 22, 1863. Bates, *History of the Pennsylvania Volunteers*, 1:449.

20. Northern antiwar Democrats were known as Copperheads, so-called because they wore copper badges on their lapels to signify their association with secret fraternal societies. Republicans used the name to suggest that Peace Democrats treasonously supported the Confederacy. Like the copperhead snake, Peace Democrats gave no warning before striking their prey. The most notorious Copperhead was Clement Laird Vallandigham, age forty-two, a "lame duck" congressman from Dayton, Ohio. In 1861 Vallandigham proposed several controversial measures designed to placate the South, including a plan to divide the United States into four sections, each administrated by its own president. In November 1862 Vallandigham lost reelection after Republicans gerrymandered his district. Following this, he delivered a series of anti-administration speeches on the floor of Congress, and then he commenced a tour of several northern states to drum up support for the peace movement. He denounced President Lincoln as a tyrant and called the military "an army of public plunderers." On May 5, 1863, the commander of the Department of the Ohio, Major General Ambrose Burnside, arrested Vallandigham in Dayton, charging him with treason. Despite protests from other northern Democrats who demanded his release, Lincoln ordered Vallandigham banished to the South.

Vallandigham eventually secured passage to Canada, and during the autumn of 1863 he unsuccessfully ran for governor of Ohio. Vallandigham secretly made his way back into the United States in 1864. Gallman, *The Civil War Chronicle*, 275, 306.

21. For the past eight months, Union forces had attempted to capture these two important cities. Major General Ulysses S. Grant's Army of the Tennessee had been moving down the Mississippi River toward Vicksburg since late December, but his men did not reach the city until May. By that time Confederate forces under Major General John C. Pemberton had fortified the city in preparation for a siege. Union forces had also moved by land toward Charleston in June 1862, but they were forced back after a fight near Secessionville. Afterward, U.S. Naval forces prepared for a seaborne assault to begin in April 1863.

22. General Orders Number 3 of the Army of the Potomac granted ten-day furloughs to selected men in any company that did not have outstanding unauthorized absences.

23. Many Union regiments sent "unanimously adopted" resolutions to local newspapers to indicate their support for the war. Officers often circulated these resolutions during dress parade. The officer in command of the 29th Ohio Infantry was Lieutenant Colonel Thomas Clark, a temperance advocate from Cleveland.

24. On January 26, 1863, Major General Joseph Hooker, age forty-eight, a West Point graduate from the Class of 1837 and a veteran of the Mexican-American War, assumed command of the Army of the Potomac. His nickname—"Fighting Joe"—derived from a press wire sent during the Battle of Williamsburg that read "Fighting—Joe Hooker." Newspaper editors mistakenly left out the dash. Warner, *Generals in Blue*, 233–34.

25. The 147th Pennsylvania Infantry was a new regiment added to the 1st Brigade, 2nd Division, 12th Army Corps. Five of its companies (Companies A, D, C, B, and E) had once been companies L, M, N, O, and P of the 28th Pennsylvania. Colonel Ariovistus J. Pardee, Jr., the former major of 28th Pennsylvania, commanded this unit.

26. One of Hayward's close friends in Company D was Second Lieutenant Aaron Lazarus, age twenty-three, a clerk from Philadelphia. Lazarus began the war as Company D's fourth sergeant. His promotion to second lieutenant became official on May 22, 1863. He received a promotion to first lieutenant on April 9, 1864, and he served as the 28th Pennsylvania's acting adjutant for several weeks. He mustered out at the expiration of his term of enlistment on July 20, 1864. First Sergeant George T. Barnes, age twenty-seven, began the war as a private. On December 28, 1861, he received a promotion to fifth sergeant by special order from Colonel Geary. His promotion to first sergeant became official on May 24, 1863. Bates, *History of the Pennsylvania Volunteers*, 1:449.

27. This incident could not be identified.

7. "Last to Leave the Field"

1. *OR*, ser. 1, vol. 25, no. 1, pp. 727–33; *Philadelphia Inquirer*, May 12, 1863.
2. *Philadelphia Inquirer*, May 12, 1863.
3. *OR*, ser. 1, vol. 25, no. 1, pp. 727–33.
4. Letter 73.
5. *OR*, ser. 1, vol. 25, no. 1, pp. 727–33.
6. Letter 73; Twenty-eighth Pennsylvania Infantry Papers, HSP.
7. Letter 72.
8. Samuel Goodman to Andrew Curtin, Aug. 31, 1863, RG 19, Pennsylvania State Archives (hereafter PSA).
9. Letter 74.
10. Letter 73.
11. Letter 82.
12. Lieutenant Colonel Hiram Cale Rodgers, age twenty-nine, a bank teller from Sauquoit, New York, served as the assistant adjutant general for the 12th Corps commander, Major General Henry Slocum. In 1861 Rodgers helped organize Company D, 27th New York Infantry, and he served as its first captain. On March 13, 1865, Rodgers was brevetted to brigadier general for gallant and meritorious service. Hunt and Brown, *Brevet Brigadier Generals in Blue*, 515.
13. As Hayward indicates, the 28th Pennsylvania's commanding officer, Major Lansford Foster Chapman, age twenty-nine, from Mauch Chunk, Pennsylvania, was killed in action on May 3, 1863, while leading the regiment's final charge. According to most accounts, Chapman's panicked horse dragged his body into enemy lines, preventing its recovery until May 1865. Hayward states incorrectly that First Sergeant George T. Barnes was also killed in action. Barnes survived his severe leg wound. In January 1864 he received both a promotion to second lieutenant and a transfer to the Veteran Reserve Corps, the U.S. Army's invalid unit. Barnes remained on duty until discharged one year later. Color Sergeant Jacob George Orth, seriously wounded in the right leg, also survived. Orth, likewise, never saw combat again. He received a discharge in July 1864, but he never fully recovered from his wound. Forty-four years after the battle, his wound completed its intended work. A 3.5-inch by 4.5-inch gangrenous scar formed on his right leg, causing immense blood clots to form in his leg veins. On September 11, 1907, one of these clots broke free, inducing a severe heart attack that resulted in Orth's death. Only Third Sergeant William H. Hiles, age twenty-eight, died shortly after receiving his leg wound at Chancellorsville. Hiles died in a field hospital on May 7, two days before Hayward wrote this letter. Bates, *History of the Pennsylvania Volunteers*, 1:449; Jacob George Orth, military pension files, National Archives Records Administration, Washington, DC.
14. Company D's casualties for the Battle of Chancellorsville included twelve men: One killed, Private John Donnelly; two mortally wounded, Sergeant William Hiles (died May 7) and Private Richard Bingley (died May 4); five

wounded, Sergeant George Barnes, Sergeant Jacob Orth, Corporal Philip F. Worsely, Private James Morrison, and Private Henry Till; one captured, Private Charles T. Murphy; and one wounded and captured, Private Godfrey Goldsmith. Two other privates, John N. Moyer and John H. Eagan, were also listed as missing in action immediately after the battle but turned up unscathed shortly thereafter. Bates, *History of the Pennsylvania Volunteers*,1:449–53; *Philadelphia Public Ledger*, May 22, 1863.

15. Official estimates placed the 28th Pennsylvania's casualties at 17 killed, 60 wounded, and 24 missing, a total of 101 men. William F. Fox, *Regimental Losses in the American Civil War, 1861–1865* (Albany, NY: Albany Publishing Co., 1889), 264.

16. Captain Conrad U. Meyer, age twenty-eight, from Allegheny, Pennsylvania, commanded the 28th Pennsylvania after Major Lansford Chapman's death.

17. The document kept in the Special Collections Archive at Gettysburg College is only a portion of the actual document written by Lieutenant James Devine. A preceding paragraph existed describing the bravery of First Sergeant George T. Barnes. That paragraph is reproduced as follows: "In compliance with Genl. Orders No. 53 dated Hd. Qrs. Army of the Potomac, May 12th 63, I have the honor to submit the names of 1st Sergt. George T. Barnes and Sergt. Ambrose H. Hayward for gallant and meritorious conduct at the Battles of Chancellorsville Va, May 1st, 2nd, & 3rd. The conduct of 1st Sergeant George T. Barnes during the entire engagement is worthy of mention, by his calm and cool behavior when under a galling fire and during the confusion incidental to a breaking of a portion of the Army, he restored confidence among the troops and by his example encouraged the men to renewed efforts. On the morning of the 3rd inst. after being driven from our position, Sergt. Barnes used voice and example to cheer and encourage, and partly through his instrumentality the Regt. formed and made a decisive charge driving the enemy handsomely. In this charge he was found in the front and while nobly fighting was struck in the knee and seriously wounded; although the wound was of a dangerous character he utterly refused to allow any person engaged in the fight to convey him from the field: saying their presence was required there. Sergt. Barnes was engaged in the Battle of Antietam and did his part nobly for which he received the commendation of his officers. I would respectfully request that he receive honorable mention in Orders." 28th Pennsylvania Infantry Records, Historical Society of Pennsylvania, Philadelphia.

18. In summarizing Hayward's actions during the Battle of Chancellorsville, Devine refers to the confusing action that occurred on May 2 when a large body of Confederate soldiers—nearly 28,000 men under the command of Lieutenant General Thomas J. Jackson—undertook a fourteen-mile flank march through dense undergrowth, surprising Union soldiers holding the right flank of the Army of the Potomac. This attack occurred at 5:00 P.M. and swept the bulk of the Union army's 11th Corps from the field. It was these men—many of whom were German Americans—that Sergeant Hayward managed to rally, and for whom he furnished rifles. On May 3,

the 28th Pennsylvania held a position in the center of the Union line near the Chancellor House. There they met a series of Confederate attacks, one of which temporarily drove them from their entrenchments. During the close of the fight, Major Lansford Chapman led the 28th Pennsylvania in a countercharge to retake the breastworks. The charge succeeded, but Chapman was killed in the process. It was most likely during this attack when Hayward was "conspicuous in the advance." According to an undated, unsigned extract kept at the Historical Society of Pennsylvania, Major Chapman was the officer who complimented Hayward during the attack: "Sergeant Hayward was highly complimented by the major commanding the Regiment May 2nd [3rd] for the coolness and courage he manifested when charging the enemy. His coolness is proverbial." 28th Pennsylvania Infantry Records, Historical Society of Pennsylvania, Philadelphia.

19. This refers to Captain Charles Borbridge, who at the time of this extract was in command of Company C.
20. These were the actions described in Hayward's letters of September 18, 21, and 28, 1862. "Sergeant B." referred to Sergeant Frank Bonsall.
21. Alice and Rebecca, his former landladies.
22. Augustus, Melville, and Albert.
23. Mr. Glover was probably Amasa Glover from North Bridgewater. Glover moved to North Bridgewater from Dorchester, Massachusetts, in 1834. He was the father of four children, one of whom, Walter Scott Glover, age twelve, served as a musician in Company F, 12th Massachusetts Infantry. Amasa Glover himself served in the regimental band of the 12th Massachusetts until its disbanding. Kingman, *History of North Bridgewater*, 517.
24. Captain Hammar resigned on May 14, 1863. Bates, *History of the Pennsylvania Volunteers*, 1:449.
25. "Kingdom Coming," a song written by Henry Clay Work in 1862, was popular among soldiers in the Union Army.
26. This was probably First Lieutenant Edward D. Muhlenburg, commander of Battery F, 4th U.S. Light Artillery.

8. "I Have Done My Duty in the Last Great Contest"

1. Letter 76.
2. Letter 77.
3. Letters 78 and 79.
4. Letter 79.
5. Foering MS, July 2, 1863, HSP.
6. Henry E. Brown, "The 28th and 147th Regiments Penna. Vols. at Gettysburg," 28th Pennsylvania, Vertical File, Gettysburg National Military Park Library, p. 6.
7. Letter 83.
8. Brown, "The 28th and 147th Regiments," 7.
9. Letter 83.

10. Letter 81.
11. Letter 84.
12. Ibid.
13. Letters 95 and 96.
14. Letter 98.
15. Colonel Charles Candy of the 66th Ohio Infantry, a regular army officer who served in New Mexico territory during the 1850s, commanded the 1st Brigade, 2nd Division, 12th Army Corps. David T. Thackery, *A Light and Uncertain Hold: A History of the 66th Ohio Volunteer Infantry* (Kent, OH: Kent State Univ. Press, 1999), 31–32.
16. Frank Nash was Francis Howard Nash of North Bridgewater. Nash moved to North Bridgewater from Braintree, Massachusetts, in 1836. He was a father of six children. Although Nash was not drafted as Hayward desired, one of his sons, George Morton Nash, was called to service by the first federal draft in July 1863. George Nash, who was Hayward's age, began service with Company K, 32nd Massachusetts Infantry, on September 18, 1863. He received a mortal wound during the Battle of Spotsylvania on May 10, 1864, and died five days later. The $300 to which Hayward refers was a commutation fee established by the new federal draft law. Mr. Webster could not be identified. Kingman, *History of North Bridgewater*, 584.
17. Vicksburg, Mississippi, remained under siege from Major General Ulysses S. Grant's Army of the Tennessee. After several disastrous assaults against Confederate fortifications in late May, Grant decided to outlast Vicksburg's garrison. The Confederate defenders surrendered on July 4.
18. The 28th Pennsylvania exchanged its .577-caliber Enfield rifled muskets for .58-caliber Springfield rifled muskets.
19. George Gordon, the Sixth Lord Byron (1788–1824), was a popular English poet and satirist from the Romantic period best known for his brooding characters and melancholic poetry. He authored such works as "Lara" and "Childe Harold's Pilgrimage." John Godfrey Saxe (1816–1857), an American Romantic poet from Vermont, authored such poetry and prose as *The Proud Miss MacBride*, "The Money-King," and "Rhyme of the Rail."
20. Private George F. Zellar, age twenty-five, was present at the forthcoming Battle of Gettysburg. On August 1, 1863, he received a transfer to the Veteran Reserve Corps.
21. Captain Meyer, who assumed command of the 28th Pennsylvania following Major Lansford Chapman's death, resigned in early June 1863 after charges of cowardice were filed against him for his performance at the Battle of Chancellorsville.
22. Captain John Hornbuckle Flynn, age forty-four, was a native of Waterford, Ireland. Flynn had served as a noncommissioned officer with the U.S. Army during the Mexican-American War, earning distinction at the Battle of Molino del Ray. By the outbreak of the Civil War, Flynn worked as a lawyer in Pittsburgh. Flynn served as the 28th Pennsylvania's first adjutant, and later he received a promotion to colonel of the regiment. Flynn received two gunshot wounds during the Civil War, one at the Battle of Gettysburg

and another at North Edisto, Georgia, during the Atlanta Campaign. The latter wound resulted in partial amputation of his foot. After the war, he served as superintendent of Little Rock National Cemetery in Little Rock, Arkansas. He died on December 25, 1875. Bates, *Martial Deeds of Pennsylvania*, 915–16.

23. Corporal John Thomas Ashton, age twenty-eight, received a slight wound during the Battle of Gettysburg, July 3, 1863, and a second wound during the Battle of Kennesaw Mountain, June 27, 1864. The latter wound resulted in his discharge in August 1864. Bates, *History of the Pennsylvania Volunteers*, 1:450.

24. Third Sergeant Edward Pepper, age thirty-four, was discharged on a surgeon's certificate, November 21, 1862. He kept in touch with the soldiers in the 28th Pennsylvania after his discharge. Bates, *History of the Pennsylvania Volunteers*, 1:449.

25. On June 15, 1863, President Lincoln called up 120,000 six-month emergency troops to help repel the Confederate invasion of the Shenandoah Valley. New York State mobilized twenty-six regiments, including the 7th New York State Militia, which left New York City on June 17 and returned for provost duty on July 20. The 6th Massachusetts was a nine-month militia regiment from Boston called to service in August 1862. It served at Fort Monroe and in the defense of Suffolk. It returned to Boston on May 29, 1863, and it mustered out of service on June 3. Massachusetts Adjutant General's Office, *Massachusetts Soldiers, Sailors, and Marines in the Civil War*, 1:398.

26. Philip F. Worsley, age twenty-three, was a corporal in Company D. He had been promoted from private on April 1, 1863. He received a wound during the Battle of Bolivar Heights on October 16, 1861, and he received another wound during the Battle of Chancellorsville on May 3, 1863. He received a discharge in July 1864. Bates, *History of the Pennsylvania Volunteers*, 1:456.

27. The execution took place on June 19, 1863. The three deserters were Privates William Grover (or Gruver), age unknown, and William McKee, age nineteen, Company A, 46th Pennsylvania Infantry; and Private Christopher Krubart, age thirty-six, Company B, 13th New Jersey Infantry. The chaplain was T. Romeyn Beck of the 13th New Jersey. Most accounts agree that the executions proceeded flawlessly. One eyewitness remembered, "The day was a perfect one. The sky was cloudless; the sun shone resplendent." All three men died instantly on the first volley. Samuel Toombs, *Reminiscences of the War, Comprising a Detailed Account of the Experiences of the Thirteenth New Jersey Volunteers in Camp, on the March, and in Battle* (1878; repr., Hightstown, NJ: Longstreet House, 1994), 68–69.

28. Sumner Augustus Hayward, a fifty-year-old blacksmith, was Ambrose Hayward's younger brother. His "little girl" was Julia Bradford Hayward, age twelve. Otis Hayward, a fifty-six-year-old deputy sheriff of Plymouth County, was Ambrose Hayward's older brother. Kingman, *History of North Bridgewater*, 517–21.

29. The Battle of Hanover occurred on June 30, 1863. Brigadier General Hugh Judson Kilpatrick's Union cavalry division engaged three brigades of Major General J. E. B. Stuart's Confederate cavalry. Tactically, this fight was inconclusive, but operationally it prevented Stuart from reaching the main body of the Army of Northern Virginia before a major battle was joined. The Battle of Hanover produced 215 Union casualties and 117 Confederate casualties. George Rummel, *Cavalry on the Roads to Gettysburg: Kilpatrick at Hanover and Hunterstown* (Shippensburg, PA: White Mane, 2000).

30. Prior to the Battle of Gettysburg, rumors circulated that Major General George McClellan had returned to command the Army of the Potomac. These rumors were untrue; on June 28 Major General George Gordon Meade, age forty-eight, a graduate of the West Point class of 1835, a military engineer, and a veteran of the Mexican-American War, assumed command.

31. The United States' first national draft law planned to go into effect during the second week of July. In places where money was scarce and eligible draftees could not purchase substitutes or pay commutation, some citizens reacted with violence. On June 11, citizens in the Ohio River Valley murdered two federal agents charged with registering those eligible for the draft. Gallman, *The Civil War Chronicle*, 313.

32. Regulations required infantrymen to carry forty rounds in their cartridge boxes at all times. If they expected a battle, officers sometimes ordered their men to stuff their pockets and knapsacks with extra ammunition.

33. This line is unclear. Hayward left no evidence explaining why he believed this man was a deserter.

34. Corporal James D. Butcher, age twenty-four, was from Philadelphia. He received a leg wound on July 3 and died that night at the Henry Spangler farm before an amputation could be performed. According to William T. Simpson, a drummer from Company A, Butcher refused to have his leg cut off. Simpson recollected, "One especially I will always remember. He was a corporal and had been badly wounded. They wanted to amputate his leg. He said to me: 'Will, they won't do it, for I will shoot the first man who touches me. I am married and won't go home to be a burden on my wife.' He was certainly earnest in every word he said. When the surgeons went over to him the second time, intending to cut off his leg, he was dead." Butcher was buried on the north side of the Henry Spangler house and later moved to the Soldier's National Cemetery in Gettysburg, plot D-53. William T. Simpson account, 28th Pennsylvania vertical file, Gettysburg National Military Park Library; John W. Busey, *These Honored Dead: The Union Casualties at Gettysburg* (Hightstown, NJ: Longstreet House, 1996), 239.

35. On July 11 the federal draft took effect in New York City. The next day, the names of draftees appeared in local papers alongside lists of casualties from the recent Battle of Gettysburg. On July 13 a mob led by a volunteer fire company stormed the city's draft office and looted the building. Following this, a series of mobs rampaged the city for three days, resulting in the

nation's most destructive urban riot. Although various strata of New York City society participated in this mayhem, laboring-class individuals who lacked the means to procure a substitute or pay the commutation fee led the most violent actions, including attacks on police and lynching of African Americans. In the end, over one hundred people were killed.

36. In May, with an army of 24,000 men, Major General Nathaniel Banks laid siege to the Confederate bastion at Port Hudson, Louisiana, on the Mississippi River. Although Banks's force suffered 4,000 casualties in two assaults against enemy entrenchments on May 27 and June 14, the Confederates eventually surrendered their fortifications on July 9.

37. Captain James Devine wrote the extract. It is included as letter 73. There is no indication that this extract was ever acted upon following the Battle of Chancellorsville.

38. Between 1:00 P.M. and 4:00 P.M. on July 2 the men of Brigadier General George Sears Greene's New York Brigade constructed elaborate fieldworks on the slopes of Culp's Hill. Most historians agree that these crude but effective breastworks turned the tide in favor of Union forces during the engagement on the Union Army's right flank.

39. Brigadier General Thomas Leiper Kane's 2nd Brigade, 2nd Division, 12th Army Corps contained the 29th, 109th, and 111th Pennsylvania Infantry Regiments. Kane's Brigade was the first to return to the entrenchments on Culp's Hill following a confusing march led by Brigadier General Geary. By morning, after their ammunition gave out, Kane's men were gradually relieved by regiments from Colonel Candy's Brigade, to which the 28th Pennsylvania belonged.

40. Private Lewis K. Boyce, age thirty-four, was shot through the head and killed instantly. His body was returned to Philadelphia. Busey, *These Honored Dead*, 239.

41. Hayward is slightly mistaken. The unit he witnessed firing over his head was the 1st Maryland Eastern Shore Regiment, a unit in the same brigade as the 1st Maryland Potomac Home Brigade and equally new to combat. According to sources, several companies of the 1st Maryland Eastern Shore became lost trying to relieve units already in the trenches. Its commander admitted to accidentally firing over the heads of men in a Pennsylvania regiment. The identity of this unit has long been a mystery, but Hayward's account clearly proves that it was the 28th Pennsylvania. Colonel James Wallace of the 1st Maryland Eastern Shore wrote: "Upon reaching the brow of the hill, the five companies halted for an instant upon the discovery of the enemy attempting to rush upon our works, and then delivered a very effective volley over the heads of the men occupying the position we were ordered to relieve. The officer in command of the men in the breastworks, supposing we were firing into his command, requested that the fire should cease. That volley, however, with the fire from the regiment in the works, effectually checked all farther advance from the enemy." *OR*, ser. 1, vol. 27, pt. 1, pp. 808–9.

42. The cannonade to which Hayward refers was an artillery barrage begun by the Confederates at 1:00 P.M. on July 3, made by about 140 cannon in all,

just prior to the infantry attack known as Pickett's Charge. This barrage lasted approximately two hours and was intended to soften the Union center before a Confederate infantry assault. It is unclear where the 28th Pennsylvania was positioned in order to witness this cannonade. Hayward's letter suggests that his unit was in reserve, probably in an area between the Baltimore Pike and Taneytown Road where a number of artillery projectiles may have landed after overshooting their intended targets on Cemetery Ridge.

43. Brigadier General John M. Jones commanded a brigade in Major General Edward Johnson's "Stonewall Division." The brigade consisted of the 21st, 25th, 42nd, 44th, 48th, and 50th Virginia Infantry Regiments.

44. Third Sergeant Charles Longworth, age twenty-six, was shot through the calf and knee joint on July 3. He died of his wounds at the 12th Corps field hospital, the George Bushman farm, on July 14. He was temporarily buried in the Bushman orchard until his body was recovered by his family. Busey, *These Honored Dead*, 239.

45. Corporal Henry Shadel, age twenty-nine, had been wounded previously at Middleburg, Virginia, in March 1862. At Gettysburg, he received a wound to his shoulder. He survived this wound and eventually returned to duty. On July 15, 1864, he received a promotion to sergeant. He received a discharge five days later.

46. Private Cyrus J. Shenkle, age twenty, received a wound to the head. Shenkle recovered from his wound and eventually returned to duty. In December, Shenkle reenlisted as a veteran volunteer. He received a promotion to corporal on May 1, 1864, and another to sergeant October 1, 1864. He eventually mustered out with Company D on July 18, 1865. According to Drummer William T. Simpson of Company A, Shenkle and Corporal Shadel had a brief exchange as they were being carried to the rear on stretchers. Shadel called out to Shenkle, "Shake [Shenkle's nickname], we're good for Philadelphia!" Simpson claimed that surgeons removed the bullet from Shenkle's skull after the war, and supposedly he kept the relic in his pocket wherever he went. Bates, *History of the Pennsylvania Volunteers*, 1:449; William T. Simpson account, 28th Pennsylvania vertical file, Gettysburg National Military Park Library.

47. Private George W. Williams, age twenty-nine, survived his wound at Gettysburg. He was discharged on July 20, 1864. Bates, *History of the Pennsylvania Volunteers*, 1:453.

48. Private William S. Murphy, age twenty-one, survived his wound at Gettysburg. He was discharged on July 20, 1864. Bates, *History of the Pennsylvania Volunteers*, 1:452.

49. This is probably a reference to the drafting of George M. Nash, son of Francis H. Nash, as mentioned in letter 75, note 16.

50. This reference is not entirely clear. Hayward could be referring to the famous John Burns, age seventy, an ex-constable from Gettysburg and a veteran of the War of 1812, who during the first day of the Battle of Gettysburg shouldered a flintlock musket and briefly joined the ranks of a Pennsylvania regiment and a Wisconsin regiment. After fighting for several hours, he received

four bullet wounds. Burns's service earned him considerable fame after the battle. However, Hayward might also be referring to Private John W. Burns, age thirty-six, a shoemaker from North Bridgewater who served in Company H, 12th Massachusetts. The reference to the bugler is not completely understood. Timothy Smith, *John Burns: "The Hero of Gettysburg"* (Gettysburg: Thomas Publications, 2000); Massachusetts Adjutant General's Office, *Massachusetts Soldiers, Sailors, and Marines in the Civil War,* 2:49.

51. Private William McCallister, age twenty, reenlisted as a veteran volunteer in 1863, received a promotion to corporal on February 1, 1865, and mustered out with the company on July 18, 1865. Bates, *History of the Pennsylvania Volunteers,* 1:450.

52. Albert Howland, age sixty-four, was the eldest son of Hayward's maternal grandparents. Howland's two eldest sons—those that were drafted—were Nathaniel Perkins Howland, age thirty-two, and George Briggs Howland, age thirty. Neither son saw service.

53. Captain James Fitzpatrick, age thirty-one, came from Luzerne, Pennsylvania. He commanded Company A, 28th Pennsylvania. Fitzpatrick received a promotion to major on March 27, 1864, and another to lieutenant colonel on August 9, 1864. He received a wound to the head during the Battle of Antietam and another to the leg during the Battle of Dug Gap, Georgia, May 8, 1864.

54. Sergeant Major O'Brien, age thirty, was a civil engineer from Burlington, Vermont. He enlisted in Company G, 28th Massachusetts Infantry, in October 1861 and mustered in as his company's first sergeant in December. In March 1863 O'Brien received a promotion to sergeant major, and in October he received another promotion to first lieutenant of Company A. He received two wounds in the service, one on August 30, 1862, during the Second Battle of Bull Run, and another on June 3, 1864, during the Battle of Cold Harbor. The second wound resulted in amputation and warranted his discharge in October 1864. It is unclear how O'Brien knew Captain Fitzpatrick of the 28th Pennsylvania, but the acquaintance proved beneficial because Hayward would have certainly lost his photograph otherwise. Massachusetts Adjutant General's Office, *Massachusetts Soldiers, Sailors, and Marines,* 3:243.

55. First Corporal Henry C. Fithian, age twenty-five, was one of the original corporals of Company D. Fithian was killed in action at the Battle of Taylor's Ridge, Georgia, on November 27, 1863. He is buried in Chattanooga National Cemetery, grave 329. Bates, *History of the Pennsylvania Volunteers,* 1:450.

56. James Frederic Goddard, age twenty-one, was son of Warren Goddard, pastor of the New Jerusalem Church in North Bridgewater. Kingman, *History of North Bridgewater,* 516.

57. John was probably John Goddard, age twenty-three, another one of Reverend Goddard's sons. Kingman, *History of North Bridgewater,* 516.

58. The wounded soldier was Corporal Philip F. Worsely.

59. Colonel William D. Rickards Jr., age forty-three, commanded the 29th Pennsylvania Infantry.

60. General Geary admitted that he arrested "many" Virginians for stealing federal arms and accoutrements, but he left his account very brief. He did not mention a search for bodies but commented, "The meanest, lowest, vilest people on earth, purporting to be civilized, is to be found here, and if it were not for a principle it would be no great loss socially to lose the whole of them. The more the condition of the local affairs of Virginia are examined into, the more desperate and rotten we find its society." Blair, *A Politician Goes to War,* 112.

61. This is a reference to any type of hand-tossed, fuel-burning incendiary weapon. These weapons—essentially the Civil War equivalent of napalm—were rarely, if ever, used. Nevertheless, citizens in both the North and the South widely feared their deployment. In this letter, Hayward speculated that disenchanted Confederates might attempt to torch Jefferson Davis's residence in Richmond.

62. Pennsylvania's Battery F, Independent Light Artillery, organized for three-years' service in October and November 1861 in Pittsburgh under the command of Captain Robert F. Hampton. During the Battle of Chancellorsville, Battery F held a position near the Chancellor House, where it withstood repeated Confederate attacks. During the fighting, Captain Hampton was killed. Bates, *History of the Pennsylvania Volunteers,* 5:893–94.

63. This was one of Hayward's cousins, Frances E. Howland, the daughter of Freeman Howland and Adeline Parker.

64. The 40th New York Infantry, also known as the "Mozart Regiment," organized in New York City in June 1861 with the support from the politicians of Mozart Hall, one of the city's well-known Democratic political machines. The substitute referred to by Hayward was ex-Captain Marriott N. Crofts, age forty, who mustered in as captain of Company A, 40th New York, on June 21, 1861, and who later received a discharge on November 28, 1861. Crofts went as a substitute on July 17, 1863, but on January 1, 1865, he transferred to accept a commission in the 82nd New York. Bates, *History of the Pennsylvania Volunteers,* 1:450.

65. These two deserters were Privates William Smith, age thirty-five, and Cornelius Treece, age twenty-three, from Companies E and K, 78th New York Infantry. General Geary's account of the event was more antipathetic than Hayward's. Geary wrote to his wife, "Such is military life and discipline. . . . Thus you see the crime of desertion will no longer go unpunished." Robert Alotta, *Civil War Justice: Union Army Executions under Lincoln* (Shippensburg, PA: White Mane, 1989), 82–83; Blair, *A Politician Goes to War,* 115.

66. It was not uncommon for medically unsound individuals to pass as substitutes. To meet quotas, recruiters accepted them without question, and slapdash medical inspections by surgeons failed to uncover physical deficiencies.

67. Corporal Edwin T. Porter, age twenty-four, was discharged from service on July 21, 1864.

68. Hayward is referring to operations led by Major General Ambrose E. Burnside and Major General William S. Rosecrans to seize Knoxville and Chattanooga. Burnside's campaign met resounding success. His 24,000

soldiers entered Knoxville on September 3, Confederate defenders having retreated without firing a shot. Rosecrans's endeavor proved less fortunate. Although his Army of the Cumberland occupied Chattanooga on September 9, on September 19–20, it engaged in a two-day battle with Major General Braxton Bragg's Confederate Army of Tennessee near Chickamauga Creek, Georgia. Rosecrans's army was defeated, suffering 16,000 casualties.

9. "If a Battle, Let it Begin with the Riseing of the Sun"

1. William Roberts to father, Oct. 7, 1863, William Roberts Jr. Papers, HSP.
2. Letter 98.
3. Ariovistus Pardee to father, n.d., Pardee-Robison Collection, USAMHI.
4. Letter 106.
5. Ibid.
6. *OR*, ser. 1, vol. 31, pt. 2, p. 43; Keith Bohannon, "Preservation Plan for Ringgold Gap Georgia Battlefield," report (Washington, DC: American Battlefield Protection Program, 1997), 27.
7. *OR*, ser. 1, vol. 31, pt. 2, pp. 616–17, 623; Lawrence Wilson, *Itinerary of the 7th Ohio Infantry* (New York: Neale, 1907), 367.
8. Letter 106. For further explanation of post-traumatic stress disorder in the Civil War, see Eric T. Dean, *Shook Over Hell: Post-Traumatic Stress, Vietnam, and the Civil War* (Cambridge, MA: Harvard Univ. Press, 1997), 4–6.
9. Joseph L. Cornet, "Dedication of the Monument: Twenty-eighth Regiment Infantry, Near Craven's House, Lookout Mountain, Tennessee, November 15th, 1897," in *Pennsylvania at Chickamauga and Chattanooga,* ed. William Stanley Ray (Harrisburg, PA: State Printer, 1897), 84.
10. *OR*, ser. 1, vol. 31, no. 2, pp. 616–17.
11. Letter 104.
12. *Philadelphia Inquirer,* Jan. 11, 1864.
13. Letter 107.
14. Major General William Starke Rosecrans, age forty-four, a graduate of the West Point Class of 1842, commanded the Union Army of the Cumberland, recently defeated at the Battle of Chickamauga. Brigadier General Nathan Bedford Forrest, age forty-two, commanded a corps of cavalry in the Confederate Army of Tennessee. A veteran of the Fort Donelson, Shiloh, Stones River, Vicksburg, and Chickamauga Campaigns, Forrest became well known for helping to organize the first klavern of the Ku Klux Klan in Tennessee in 1866. Major General Joseph Wheeler, age twenty-seven, a graduate of the West Point Class of 1859, commanded the other cavalry corps in the Confederate Army of Tennessee. A veteran of many of the same campaigns as Forrest, Wheeler survived the war and later rose to the rank of major general in the U.S. Army and served during the Spanish American War. Major General Braxton Bragg, age forty-six, a graduate of the West Point Class of 1837, commanded the Confederate Army of Tennessee, recently

victorious at Chickamauga. A veteran of the Mexican-American War and
the Shiloh, Perryville, and Stones River campaigns of the Civil War, Bragg
commanded this army until his removal in December 1863. After the federal defeat at Chickamauga, Rosecrans withdrew his men to Chattanooga,
Tennessee. Bragg ordered his energetic cavalry commanders, Wheeler and
Forrest, to sever all the railroad connections to the city. They succeeded in
cutting all the rail lines but one. They failed to sever the railroad that connected Chattanooga to Nashville. The timely arrival of Union reinforcement
prevented this. Warner, *Generals in Blue*, 410–11; Ezra J. Warner, *Generals
in Gray: The Lives of the Confederate Commanders* (Baton Rouge: Louisiana
State Univ. Press, 1959), 30–31, 92–93, 332–33.

15. Between 1849 and 1852, the Baltimore and Ohio Railroad Company constructed the West End Line to connect Cumberland, Maryland, to Wheel-
ing, West Virginia. During this time, the railroad company constructed
Kingwood Tunnel, a 4,100-foot tunnel that burrowed through Laurel
Mountain.

16. The drunken soldier run over by the train was Private Mitchell St. Onge of
Company B, 7th Ohio Infantry, who was known by his nickname, "Santa."
According to the 7th Ohio's unit history, the accident occurred near Graf-
ton, West Virginia, on September 29, 1863. Apparently, Private St. Onge attempted to leap from one car to another but lost his balance. The next day,
St. Onge's leg was amputated at the middle third. St. Onge—who had been
wounded in the arm at the Battle of Chancellorsville—received a discharge
on January 23, 1864. Wilson, *Itinerary of the Seventh Ohio Volunteer Infantry,
1861–1864*, 547, 650.

17. "Hurrah for Brough" was an endorsement of John Brough, the Republican
candidate for the Ohio gubernatorial election.

18. Situated in Wayne County, the city of Richmond was founded in 1806 by
North Carolina Quakers. The 16th Indiana Infantry organized there in
May 1861.

19. This soldier might have been Private Michael McVoy, age twenty-one.
He died in Tullahoma on October 17, 1863, of a "gen[eral] disability" and
was buried at Stones River, Tennessee. Bates, *History of the Pennsylvania
Volunteers*, 1:470.

20. A mutual animosity existed between the eastern soldiers in the Army of
the Potomac and western soldiers in both the Army of the Cumberland and
the Army of the Tennessee. Colonel Ario Pardee Jr., who commanded the
147th Pennsylvania—a unit in the 28th Pennsylvania's brigade—remarked
similarly: "We 'A. of P.' [Army of the Potomac] do not think much of the
troops we have seen. They are mighty loose and negligent in all their military duty." Ario Pardee to father, Oct. 11, 1863, Pardee-Robison Collection,
USAMHI.

21. Hayward is incorrect. Brigadier General George Greene received a wound
to the face at the Battle of Wauhatchie, October 28–29, 1863. This wound
crushed his jaw and carried away several teeth, but Greene returned to service after six weeks of medical leave.

22. The Battle of Wauhatchie, Tennessee, took place on the night of October 28–29, 1863.
23. The 4th Alabama Infantry, recently removed from the Virginia theater, attacked Colonel Orland Smith's 11th Corps brigade on the northernmost hill of Wauhatchie Battlefield, adjacent to Lookout Creek.
24. As Hayward indicates, the night battle of Wauhatchie, which began at approximately 10:00 P.M., swirled around four guns from Knap's Battery, parked in rear of the Union line. Amid the confusion, the artillerymen unlimbered their pieces and fired them, repelling the Confederate attack. The battery lost twenty-two officers and men killed or wounded, including the battery's commander, Captain Charles Atwell, who died of his wounds on November 1, and Lieutenant Edward Geary, General Geary's son, who was killed instantly while sighting one of the cannon. According to Geary, the battery lost thirty-three out of forty-eight horses. Blair, *A Politician Goes to War*, 131.
25. Hayward is slightly mistaken. The 109th Pennsylvania did lose its adjutant, First Lieutenant James Glendening, but the officer killed by friendly fire from Knap's Battery was Second Lieutenant Marvin D. Pettit of the 111th Pennsylvania. Pettit was decapitated by an undershot artillery round. Bates, *History of the Pennsylvania Volunteers*, 3:691, 1027; *OR*, ser. 2, vol. 31, pp. 120–22.
26. Hayward's casualty figure is remarkably accurate. The 137th New York reported fifteen men killed or mortally wounded. Richard Baumgartner, *Echoes of Battle: The Struggle for Chattanooga* (Huntington, WV: Blue Acorn Press, 1996), 132.
27. This is a reference to an eighty-four-pound siege gun, a "James Rifle," named for its designer, Charles T. James. These guns were actually modified seven-inch, Model 1841 smoothbores, which James had adapted for siege use.
28. This is a reference to the arrival of the Russian fleet at New York harbor. To spur strong diplomatic relations with the United States, Czar Alexander II sent his fleet to New York City in the autumn of 1863. The Russian flagship *Alexander Nevskii* arrived there on September 24, and the fleet remained docked until April 1864. During the intervening period, the Russian dignitaries became minor celebrities in the city, and politicians loyal to the Lincoln administration held frequent balls and banquets in their honor. Although this meeting failed to promote a long-lasting alliance, the Russians and the North found much in common, as Czar Alexander II then dealt with the suppression of a rebellion on the Polish frontier.
29. Colonel William R. Creighton, age twenty-six, an employee of the *Cleveland Herald*, commanded the 1st Brigade, 2nd Division, 12th Army Corps. In 1861 he raised Company A, 7th Ohio Infantry, and he mustered in as its captain. He received a promotion to lieutenant colonel on May 7, 1861, and another to colonel on May 20, 1862. He received a wound during the Battle of Cedar Mountain on August 9, 1862, but he returned to command only a few weeks later. After Colonel Charles Candy received injuries by falling

from his horse during the Battle of Lookout Mountain, Creighton received command of the 1st Brigade. On November 27, 1863, Creighton received a mortal wound to his chest at the Battle of Taylor's Ridge and died within minutes. Lieutenant Colonel Orrin J. Crane, age thirty-five, a ship carpenter from Cleveland, mustered in as first lieutenant, Company A, 7th Ohio Infantry, on April 19, 1861, and he received an appointment to captain one month later. He received a promotion to major on May 25, 1862, and another to lieutenant colonel on October 6, 1862. Crane commanded the 7th Ohio during the Battle of Taylor's Ridge and was killed in action just below the summit by a bullet to the forehead.

30. These three childhood friends could not be identified.

31. North Bridgewater was divided into fourteen school districts. Hayward attended Public School District Number 1, or Centre District. Centre School consisted of a single building erected in 1847 described as a "neat, roomy building, two stories in height, with a cupola and bell, and is painted white, with green blinds, and enclosed with a substantial fence." Kingman, *History of North Bridgewater*, chap. 6 (pp. 110–33).

32. The 3rd Brigade, 2nd Division, 12th Army Corps was commanded by Colonel David Ireland. Ireland's brigade bore the brunt of the Lookout Mountain assault.

33. The identity of this soldier could not be determined. Whoever he was, his wound was not of sufficient character to receive a mention in Bates's roster of Company F. Bates, *History of the Pennsylvania Volunteers*, 1:456–59.

34. Located near the Robert Craven house, this bluff stood over 100 feet high.

35. This was the popular nickname for Geary's Division. In March 1863 Major General Joseph Hooker assigned corps badges to all units in the Army of the Potomac to facilitate rapid identification. The shape of the badge indicated the corps designation and the color indicated the division (red for 1st Division, white for 2nd Division, and blue for 3rd Division). The 12th Army Corps' badge was a five-pointed star, and since Geary's division was 2nd Division, its badge was a white star.

36. Major General George Henry Thomas, age forty-seven, a graduate from the West Point class of 1840, commanded the Army of the Cumberland.

37. Prussian-born Brigadier General Peter Joseph Osterhaus, age forty, a veteran of the Revolution of 1848, commanded the 1st Division, 15th Army Corps, Union Army of the Tennessee.

38. Major General William Tecumseh Sherman, age forty-three, a graduate from the West Point class of 1840, commanded the Union Army of the Tennessee.

39. The Alabamians that Hayward encountered were likely men from Colonel J. T. Holtzclaw's brigade, which lost hundreds of men as prisoners during the Chattanooga campaign. Holtzclaw's brigade consisted of the 18th, 32nd/58th (consolidated), 36th, and 38th Alabama Infantry Regiments.

40. This Louisianan probably came from Colonel Randall Lee Gibson's brigade, which also lost numerous men as prisoners. Gibson's brigade consisted of the 13th/20th (consolidated), 16th/25th (consolidated), and 19th

Louisiana Infantry Regiments, the 4th Louisiana Battalion, and the 14th Louisiana Battalion Sharpshooters.

41. Creighton's brigade collided with men from the 25th and 30th Iowa Infantry Regiments, under the direction of Colonel J. A. Williamson, commander of the 2nd Brigade, 1st Division, 15th Army Corps. Apparently, Williamson's Iowans and Creighton's men exchanged harsh words as the easterners passed over. According to most accounts, the Ohioans and Pennsylvanians boasted that they would teach the westerners a "lesson in fighting."

42. Corporal Edwin Tucker Cowell, age twenty-two, was a baggage master from North Bridgewater. He enlisted in Company F, 12th Massachusetts, in June 1861. Sometime in 1863 he received a transfer to a contingent of the U.S. Signal Corps assigned to the 4th Army Corps, Army of the Tennessee. In February 1864 he reenlisted as a sergeant in the Signal Corps, and he received a discharge on August 25, 1865. Kingman, *History of North Bridgewater,* 479; Massachusetts Adjutant General's Office, *Massachusetts Soldiers, Sailors, and Marines,* 2:36, 7:68.

43. The 29th Pennsylvania Volunteer Infantry returned to Philadelphia on December 23 to enlist more recruits.

10. "The White Starr Shines in Philadelphia"

1. William Roberts Jr. to sister, Jan. 22, 1864, William Roberts Jr. Papers, HSP.
2. Letter 109.
3. Letter 111.
4. Letter 112.
5. Letter 120.
6. Isaiah Robison to sister, Apr. 17, 1864, Pardee-Robison Collection, USAMHI.
7. Joseph A. Moore to "dear old home," Apr. 14, 1864, Pennsylvania Save the Flags-Moore Family Collection, USAMHI.
8. The men of the 28th Pennsylvania received an opportunity to reenlist as veteran volunteers and acquire a thirty-day furlough on December 24, 1863. Approximately 230 of the regiment's 350 soldiers chose to reenlist. This included sixteen men from Company D: First Lieutenant James C. Devine, Second Sergeant Ambrose Henry Hayward, Third Sergeant John Oppell Foering, Corporal James Morrison, Private John H. Eagan, Private John Cardiff, Private Joseph Foll, Private William McCallister, Private John N. Moyer, Private John Ribble Jr., Private John Thorp, Private Cyrus J. Shenkle, Private Charles R. Goodman, Private Edward D. Foulke, Private John A. Ferguson, and Musician Henry Stanwood.
9. The veterans of the 28th Pennsylvania arrived in Philadelphia on Sunday, January 10, 1864. A reporter for the *Philadelphia Inquirer* described the scene: "The men, generally, wore a rugged, weather-beaten appearance and gave the outward sign of having seen hard service. Everywhere along the line of march the quiet Sabbath day was broken by the cheers of those assembled

along the sidewalks; and at numerous points the ladies waved the brave veterans a welcome home with handkerchiefs from windows and doorsteps. . . . The Twenty-Eighth is one of the most popular regiments that ever left the city, and has probably seen more active service and performed more active duty than any other in the field." *Philadelphia Inquirer,* Jan. 11, 1864.

10. First Sergeant George Barnes, whose convalescence had been holding up promotion within Company D for some time, received a transfer to the Veteran Reserve Corps, the U.S. Army's invalid unit. Barnes mustered out the next year, January 4, 1865. Bates, *History of the Pennsylvania Volunteers,* 1:449.

11. Colonel Thomas Jefferson Ahl, age thirty-four, was a native of York County, Pennsylvania. At the outbreak of the war, Ahl worked as a lumber dealer in Arkansas. He rejected an offer to serve in a Confederate regiment, returning to Pennsylvania where he helped recruit the Pittsburgh Zouave Cadets, a company that became Company H, 28th Pennsylvania. Ahl served as Company H's original captain. Following Captain Flynn's wounding at Gettysburg, Ahl took command of the 28th Pennsylvania and received a promotion to colonel on November 15, 1863. Ahl temporarily assumed command of the brigade following Colonel Creighton's death at the Battle of Taylor's Ridge. He lost both brigade and regimental command upon the return of Colonel Charles Candy (the old brigade commander) and newly promoted Colonel Flynn. Being supernumerary, Ahl accepted an honorable discharge on March 18, 1864. Bates, *Martial Deeds of Pennsylvania,* 924–25.

12. Third Sergeant John Oppell Foering, age twenty-two, was a veteran volunteer in Company D. He received a promotion to second sergeant following Hayward's promotion to first sergeant. Foering began the war as Company's D sixth corporal. He received a promotion to fourth sergeant on May 24, 1863, following Sergeant Jacob Orth's wounding and Sergeant William Hiles's mortal wounding at the Battle of Chancellorsville. After Hayward's mortal wounding at the Battle of Pine Knob, Foering became first sergeant. Following this, he rose rapidly in rank, becoming first lieutenant in October 1864 and captain in March 1865. After the war, he served as chancellor of the Military Order of the Loyal Legion. He died in 1933, one of the last survivors—if not the last—of the 28th Pennsylvania.

13. This kind of political interference was not uncommon. No doubt Hayward's rapid promotion in December 1862 did not sit well with Foering, who used his political connections to acquire the second lieutenancy ahead of Hayward. It is worthy to note that the individual who uncovered Foering's plot was none other than Captain Charles Borbridge, the officer who aided Hayward in carrying Lieutenant Colonel Hector Tyndale off the battlefield at Antietam.

14. This was William B. Thomas, a Republican delegate to the national convention of 1860 who unsuccessfully ran for mayor of Philadelphia in 1855. In 1861, upon the request of Secretary of War Simon Cameron, Thomas received an appointment to the post of collector of the Port of Philadelphia, perhaps the most lucrative position in the Commonwealth.

15. This was Henry Dunning Moore, age forty-three. As a member of the Whig Party, Moore had served as a U.S. representative from 1849 to 1853. In 1855 he campaigned for the Philadelphia mayoral election as a member of the American Party, but he was defeated by Democrat Richard Vaux. Later, as a Republican, Moore served as Pennsylvania State Treasurer from 1861 to 1865 and he became collector of the port in 1869.

16. This was Daniel Fox, Democratic candidate for the Philadelphia mayoral elections of 1862, 1865, and 1868. Fox was defeated during these first two elections but prevailed in 1868, defeating the Republican candidate, Hector Tyndale, former commander of the 28th Pennsylvania.

17. This was Frederick Foering, former brigade inspector and deputy quarter-master general of Philadelphia's city militia.

18. These documents still exist, and they are kept at the Pennsylvania State Archives in Harrisburg, in Record Group 19. They include a letter from Sergeant Foering to Henry Dunning Moore, the Pennsylvania state treasurer; a letter from Moore to Eli Slifer, secretary of the Commonwealth; and a letter from Captain James C. Devine, presumably written to Adjutant General Andrew L. Russell. They are reproduced here:

> [undated]
> [To Hon. Henry D. Moore,]
> I left Philadelphia on the 27th day of July 1861 as a Corporal in Company "D" 28th Regt. Pa Vols. Capt. Geo. D. Hammar was commanding the company at that time. While we were quartered at Point of Rocks, Md. In the winter of 1861, Private Geo. T. Barnes was appointed Corporal by Capt. Geo. D. Hammar. In a short time afterwards, he was appointed 5th Sergeant over all the old Corpls by Capt. Geo. D. Hammar. He was wounded at the Battle of Chancellorsville, and while he was at Douglas Hospital, Washington D.C., he received a commission as 2nd Lieut. of Co. "D" 28th Regt. Pa. Vols. He has not been mustered yet. He still remains on the Company Roll, as 1st Sergt. In the month of Dec. 1862 while we were quartered at Bolivar Heights, Va., Corporal Ambrose H. Hayward was appointed 5th Sergeant to fill a vacancy in the Company by Capt. Geo. D. Hammar. Ambrose H. Hayward left the City as 7th Corporal. He is now 2nd Sergeant in the Comp. Private J. Geo. Orth was appointed corporal in the month of Sept. 1861 by Capt. Geo. D. Hammar. In the month of Dec. 1862 [he] was appointed 5th Sergt. to fill a vacancy by Capt. Geo. D. Hammar. I was appointed 5th Sergeant by Capt. Jas. C. Devine on the 24th of May 1863. So there has been 3 men promoted over me, and what is the reason I do not know. I have been with the Regt. ever since I left the City, In all the Battles with the Regiment, And always done my duty to the best of my ability. I am home now on furlough of 30 days, having reenlisted for 3 years more.

I remain Your Obedient
Servt.
Sergt. John O. Foering

[undated]
Hon. Eli Slifer,
My dear Sir,
The enclosed case of Foering is one of much merit. —He
is a brave soldier, has been in the service near three years, in all
the battles, and really deserves promotion. —
If you can have it done you will very much oblige me. It is
a shame that men have been promoted over him.—
Yours truly,
Henry D. Moore

Jan 16/64
I take much pleasure in recommending to your favorable con-
sideration the case of Jno. O. Foering of my Company. his
character as a soldier, scholar, and gent is good. his promotion
has been retarded by the fact of the former Capt. having pro-
moted men over him. Unfortunately, there is no vacancy in my
company. There is a number in the regt. Hoping to hear of the
Sergt. being commissioned in some other Co.
I am sir,
Yours,
Jas. C. Devine
Capt. Co, "D," 28th P.V.

19. Hayward is referring to his promotion to first sergeant. A first sergeant's in-
    signia included three chevrons on each sleeve and a diamond insignia above
    the top-most chevron.
20. Andrew Gregg Curtin, the Republican governor of the Commonwealth of
    Pennsylvania, directed all requests for officer's commissions to State Adju-
    tant General Andrew L. Russell. Although a few individuals undoubtedly
    received spoils late in the war, in order to prevent squabbling, commission
    requests went by order of seniority.
21. The celebration was a parade held in honor of George Washington's
    birthday.
22. Aunt M. was Mercy Howland, age sixty-two, the third child of Hayward's
    maternal grandparents.
23. "French leave" is a slang term meaning "absent without leave."
24. James Knox Polk, the eleventh president of the United States, lived in a
    mansion in downtown Nashville called "Polk Place." Polk died on June 15,
    1849, three months after leaving office. After his death, he was buried tem-
    porarily in the Old City Cemetery until his widow moved him to the court-
    yard of the mansion. After her death in 1891 his body was again moved, this
    time to the Tennessee capitol grounds.

25. Lieutenant General Ulysses Simpson Grant, age forty-one, graduated from West Point in 1839, fought in the Mexican-American War, and commanded the Army of the Tennessee at the battles of Fort Henry, Fort Donelson, and Shiloh. Grant's army captured Vicksburg, Mississippi, in July 1863, and he commanded the Union armies that captured Chattanooga, Tennessee, in November 1863. Grant received the rank of lieutenant general on March 2, 1864, and he reported to Washington to assume command of all Union armies on March 12, 1864. Grant served as general in chief until the end of the war. After the war he became the eighteenth president of the United States, winning election in 1868 and 1872. Warner, *Generals in Blue,* 184–86.

26. Brigadier General Felix Kirk Zollicoffer was a Whig newspaper editor, a veteran of the Seminole War, and a former U.S. congressman. In July 1861 he received a general's commission in the Confederate army. He was killed in action at the Battle of Mills Springs, Kentucky, January 19, 1862.

27. William Gannaway Brownlow, age fifty-nine, was a former Methodist circuit preacher and editor of the *Knoxville Whig,* a Unionist newspaper. After the war, he became governor of Tennessee and a U.S. senator.

28. This letter could not be found.

29. This in reference to North Bridgewater's town "selectmen," the primary administrators of town affairs. According to Bradford Kingman, North Bridgewater's historian, "To be a Selectman or 'Townsman,' as they were sometimes called, was considered as being one of the 'fathers of the town.' The Selectmen have nearly the control of the affairs of a town. . . . Anything and everything, not otherwise provided by law, in regard to town affairs, falls by custom to the care of the Selectmen." In 1864 Nelson J. Foss, Jonas R. Perkins, and Rufus L. Thatcher replaced Josiah W. Kingman, Nathan Packard, and Franklin Ames as selectmen. Kingman, *History of North Bridgewater,* chap. 9 (pp. 197–208).

30. In what he dryly called his "first naval expedition," General Geary embarked on the steamboat *Chickamauga* with 800 infantrymen and four pieces of artillery. Geary's instructions simply ordered him to reconnoiter the river by traveling as far as he could. Blair, *A Politician Goes to War,* 164.

31. Major General William T. Sherman ordered the consolidation of these two undersized corps on April 2, and the new organization, dubbed the 20th Army Corps—not the 1st Corps, as Hayward indicates—took effect on April 15. Major General Henry W. Slocum, the 12th Corps' former commander, received assignment to the Department of the Mississippi.

32. This was Eliza Howland, age fifty-four, the eighth child of Hayward's maternal grandparents.

33. Geary's expedition traveled 110 miles along the Tennessee River. They captured Guntersville, where they burned houses, letters, and bonds. The engagement with Confederate forces occurred beyond Whitesburg, where a mixed force of Confederate artillery and sharpshooters ambushed the steamboat. Geary's loss included three men wounded. The Confederate loss

is unknown. Although Confederate forces continued to harass the steamboat with more ambushes during its return trip, the *Chickamauga* safely returned to Bridgeport. Geary declared the reconnaissance "a perfect success," although he admitted that he came close to being shot, lending some currency to Hayward's comment that generals "do not like to fight aboard Steamboats. they cannot go to the rear without takeing their men with them." Blair, *A Politician Goes to War,* 165–66.

34. Private William Atkinson, age thirty-two, enlisted in Company D on September 12, 1862. He was wounded at the Battle of Pine Knob, Georgia, on June 15, 1864, and he received a promotion to corporal on April 1, 1865. He received a discharge on June 1, 1865. Bates, *History of the Pennsylvania Volunteers,* 1:450.

35. Private Hugh Nawn, a thirty-eight-year-old-substitute, survived the war, but he was reported absent, sick at muster out, on March 12, 1865. Bates, *History of the Pennsylvania Volunteers,* 1:452.

36. First Lieutenant William Reynolds was a thirty-year-old Philadelphian. He enlisted as a private in Company K, 28th Pennsylvania, on September 7, 1861. He reenlisted as a veteran volunteer at Wauhatchie, Tennessee, on December 24, 1863, and received a commission to first lieutenant on April 1, 1864. He received a discharge on May 12, 1865. Bates, *History of the Pennsylvania Volunteers,* 1:471.

37. This refers to East Bridgewater.

38. This is in reference to Major General Nathaniel Banks's Red River Campaign. In March, Banks advanced up the Red River with 35,000 men covered by Union gunboats. Near Natchitoches, Banks made a costly decision to abandon the river, and he marched his troops northwest with slow-moving supply wagons. On April 8, 1864, Lieutenant General Richard Taylor's Confederates attacked his army near Sabine Crossroads. Lacking support from the gunboats, Banks's line of advance became clogged by the wagon train. Banks's soldiers proved easy targets for the Confederates and they routed quickly. Although Banks's men repulsed the Confederates near Pleasant Hill the following day, Banks ordered a retreat, summarily ending his campaign. Gallman, *Civil War Chronicle,* 399–400.

39. This reference is probably to Sarah Washburn, age forty-seven, the sister-in-law of Hayward's Uncle Sumner. She died on April 17, 1864.

40. The death at Mrs. Hovey's could not be identified.

41. Union forces in the eastern and western theaters prepared for simultaneous advances during the first week in May. On May 3 Lieutenant General Ulysses S. Grant led 118,000 soldiers in the Union Army of the Potomac across the Rapidan River to engage General Robert E. Lee's Army of Northern Virginia. On May 1 the three armies under Major General William T. Sherman's command—numbering 98,000 men—left their encampments at the outskirts of Chattanooga and followed the Western and Atlantic Railroad line toward their ultimate objective, Atlanta.

11. "Carrieing the War into Africa"

1. *OR*, ser. 1, vol. 38, pt. 2, pp. 114–16, 154.
2. Letter 125.
3. *OR*, ser. 1, vol. 38, pt. 2, pp. 190–91.
4. Letters 125 and 126.
5. Letter 127.
6. *OR*, ser. 1, vol. 38, pt. 2, p. 124.
7. Letter 128.
8. *OR*, ser. 1, vol. 38, pt. 2, pp. 127–28.
9. J. Hamp SeCheverell, *Journal History of the Twenty-Ninth Ohio Volunteers, 1861–1865: Its Victories and Its Reverses* (Cleveland: n.p., 1883), 106.
10. *OR*, ser. 1, vol. 38, pt. 2, p. 150.
11. Blair, *A Politician Goes to War*, 181.
12. The bullet that mortally wounded Hayward probably came from Brigadier General Clement H. Stevens's brigade of Walker's division. This brigade consisted of the 1st, 25th, 29th, 30th, and 66th Georgia Infantry Regiments and the 1st Georgia Sharpshooter Battalion.
13. *OR*, ser. 1, vol. 38, pt. 2, p. 151.
14. Letter 129.
15. Edmund J. Raus Jr., ed., *Ministering Angel: The Reminiscences of Harriet A. Dada, a Union Army Nurse in the Civil War* (Gettysburg: Thomas Publications, 2004), 43–47.
16. William Roberts Jr. to father, June 25, 1864, William Roberts Jr. Papers, HSP.
17. Letter 130.
18. Letters 131 and 132.
19. Letter 133.
20. On May 8 Major General William T. Sherman launched a diversionary attack against a Confederate position at Rocky Face Ridge—a steep, craggy crest that was penetrated only by a few small gaps, Mill Creek Gap among them. This diversionary attack encompassed elements from Major General John Schofield's Army of the Ohio and Major General George Thomas's Army of the Cumberland, to which the 28th Pennsylvania belonged. Although Union soldiers commonly called the battle of May 8 the Battle of Mill Creek Gap (or Buzzard's Roost), the 28th Pennsylvania actually engaged Confederates at Dug Gap, an opening five miles to the south.
21. The federal feints at Mill Creek Gap and Dug Gap fixed Confederate forces under General Joseph E. Johnston in their positions, allowing 24,000 Union troops under Major General James McPherson to swing south of Johnston's army and pour through an unprotected position at Snake Creek Gap.
22. On May 5–6 the Army of the Potomac and the Army of Northern Virginia fought the Battle of the Wilderness, and on May 8–18 they fought again at the Battle of Spotsylvania Court House. Although Union forces could claim a tactical victory at the latter battle because they forced Confederates to relinquish a section of their entrenchments, the results were not as encourag-

ing as Hayward claimed. Union forces sustained 34,000 losses in less than a week.

23. As of the writing of this letter, Sherman's armies stood poised to attack Confederate positions at Resaca.

24. Major General Oliver Otis Howard, age thirty-three, West Point class of 1850, commanded the 4th Army Corps, Army of the Cumberland. Warner, *Generals in Blue*, 237–39.

25. General Joseph Johnston's Army of Tennessee made a stand against the Union advance at a crossroads called Resaca on May 14–15, 1864. Union attacks battered Confederate entrenchments for two days, but a flanking maneuver slipped around the Confederate left, forcing Johnston to give up his defenses and retreat to Allatoona. The 28th Pennsylvania was only lightly engaged on the second day of battle, losing no men killed or mortally wounded.

26. On May 15, shortly before midnight, a mixed unit commanded by Captain Austin T. Shirer—consisting of five companies from the 5th Ohio and a detachment of fifty men from the 33rd New Jersey—dug their way into an abandoned Confederate redoubt. This earthen fortification contained four twelve-pound artillery pieces belonging to Captain Maximilian Van Der Corput's Cherokee (Georgia) Battery. The Confederate artillerymen left these guns behind when they retreated from the redoubt on the second day of the Battle of Resaca. Shirer's men dragged the artillery pieces out by hand at 3:00 A.M. on May 16, and they turned them over to Battery E, 1st Pennsylvania Light Artillery. Larry M. Strayer and Richard A. Baumgartner, eds., *Echoes of Battle: The Atlanta Campaign* (Huntington, WV: Blue Acorn Press, 1991), 89–95.

27. Major General Daniel Edgar Sickles, age forty-four, was a former U.S. congressman and a member of New York City's Tammany Hall political machine. He commanded the Army of the Potomac's 3rd Corps until wounded at Gettysburg. In May 1864, at the request of President Lincoln, he briefly joined Sherman's advance to observe the progress of wartime reconstruction in Union-occupied territory. Warner, *Generals in Blue*, 446–67.

28. This is a clever reference to the classic military campaign waged by Roman General Scipio Africanus. In 204 BCE, Scipio Africanus petitioned the Roman Senate for permission to invade North Africa in order to draw Hannibal's Carthaginian army out of Sicily. "Carrying the War into Africa"—the substance of Scipio's plan—became a popular phrase among antebellum abolitionists during the 1850s.

29. This is probably in reference to New York City's "gold hoax" of 1864. On May 18 the editor of the *Brooklyn Eagle*, Joseph Howard Jr., forged an associated press release announcing a wave of Union defeats and a new call for troops. Without confirming the press release's validity, two New York City papers, the *World* and the *Journal of Commerce*, ran this proclamation in their own columns, which in turn caused an economic panic and a dramatic increase in the value of gold. This benefited Howard, who had invested in gold the day before. When Lincoln learned of Howard's scheme, he ordered

him arrested but released him after Lincoln issued a real call for troops in July. Hayward, of course, knew that a Union victory—the fall of Atlanta—would lessen the economic strain on the North and decrease the value of gold, hoax or no hoax. Jeffery Wert, "The Great Civil War Gold Hoax," *American History Illustrated* 15, no. 1 (1980): 20–24; Mark E. Neely Jr., *The Union Divided: Party Conflict in the Civil War North* (Cambridge, MA: Harvard University Press, 2002), 11–17.

30. The *Philadelphia Inquirer* ran these resolutions in their July 25, 1864, issue.

31. John N. Moyer, age thirty-one, was a veteran volunteer. Twelve days after he drafted these resolutions, he received a mortal wound at the Battle of Peach Tree Creek. He died in a general hospital at Nashville, Tennessee, on September 19, 1864. Bates, *History of the Pennsylvania Volunteers*, 1:450.

32. Thorp, a twenty-six-year-old veteran volunteer, received a promotion to corporal on November 1, 1864. He mustered out with the remainder of Company D on July 18, 1865. Bates, *History of the Pennsylvania Volunteers*, 1:450.

33. Sharp, a thirty-seven-year-old substitute, received a promotion to corporal on February 1, 1865, another to sergeant on April 1, 1865, and a reduction to private two months later. He mustered out with the remainder of Company D on July 18, 1865. Bates, *History of the Pennsylvania Volunteers*, 1:452.

34. Chattanooga's General Hospital Number 1 consisted of eight one-story and four two-story wooden buildings and a number of tents, over 700 beds altogether. These buildings, originally constructed by the Confederates in 1863, stood on a hill adjoining the city's academy grounds. Dr. Francis Salter was in charge of the hospital during the Atlanta Campaign. Raus, *Ministering Angel*, 43.

35. This was probably Surgeon (Lieutenant Colonel) Joseph Payson Wright, U.S. Army.

36. Private Roberts served with Company D until July 20, 1864, when he received a discharge.

37. These were Privates William Steen and William Atkinson. Steen, age twenty-two, was a three-year volunteer who enlisted in 1861 and received a discharge on July 20, 1864. Atkinson received a wound at the Battle of Pine Knob, but he eventually recovered, returned to the regiment, and rose to the rank of corporal. He mustered out in June 1865. Bates, *History of the Pennsylvania Volunteers*, 1:450, 453.

Epilogue

1. *Boston Daily Evening Transcript*, July 7, 1864. This letter was copied from the *Cincinnati Commercial*.

2. Chickamauga-Chattanooga Commission, *Pennsylvania at Chickamauga and Chattanooga*, 105.

3. Bates, *History of the Pennsylvania Volunteers*, 1:436–47.

4. The value of Ambrose Hayward's personal property bequeathed to his heirs amounted to $4,340. All of this went to his wife, Hannah, with the excep-

tion of his silver watch and Bible (given to Augustus), his gold watch chain (given to Cora), and fifteen dollars (five dollars each given to Melville, Albert, and John Parker). Last Will and Testament of Ambrose Hayward, Sept. 19, 1867, Massachusetts Probate Court Records, Massachusetts State Archives, Boston.

5. *New York Herald,* Jan. 10, 1873; *New Church Magazine* 1 (1873): 491–92.

6. Edith Howland Hayward's name surfaced in the Massachusetts Supreme Court case *Hayward v. Hayward.* In 1908 her trustee, Henry W. Flagg, attempted to sue her cousin, Corinne, over an awkwardly worded will and testament devised by Edith's and Corinne's recently deceased aunt, Cora. Cora's will and testament bequeathed to the nieces her two adjacent houses but made no specific reference regarding the mortgage. The probate court ruled that the will and testament did not exonerate Corinne from the mortgage, as the awkwardly worded passage implied. On appeal, the case went to the state supreme court, and the justices overturned the probate ruling, requiring only Edith and her trustee to assume the mortgage. No evidence indicates how this civil case altered the relationship between Albert's family and John Parker's family, although by that point John Parker Hayward had also died. Henry Walton Swift, *Massachusetts Reports, Number 199: Cases Argued and Determined in the Supreme Judicial Court of Massachusetts, May 1908–October 1908* (Boston: Little, Brown, and Co., 1909), 340–43.

7. Letter 1.

BIBLIOGRAPHY

Archives

Gettysburg College, Special Collections, Musselman Library, Gettysburg, PA

Hayward, Ambrose Henry. Papers. MS-009.

Gettysburg National Military Park Library, Gettysburg, PA

Brown, Henry E. "The 28th and 147th Regiments Penna. Vols. at Gettysburg." 28th Pennsylvania vertical file.

Simpson, William T. "William T. Simpson Account," in 28th Pennsylvania vertical file.

Historical Society of Pennsylvania, Philadelphia, PA

The Advance Guard.

Foering, John Oppell. Papers.

Roberts, William, Jr. Papers.

28th Pennsylvania Infantry papers.

Massachusetts State Archives, Boston

Probate Records of Ambrose Hayward.

Pennsylvania State Archives, Harrisburg

Adjutant General Papers. 28th Pennsylvania Infantry, RG 19.

U.S. Army Military History Institute, Carlisle, PA

Erwin, Robert E. Papers. Luvaas Collection.

Moore, Joseph A. Papers. Pennsylvania Save the Flags—Moore Family Collection.

Pardee, Ario, Jr. Papers. Pardee-Robison Collection.

Robison, Isaiah Papers. Pardee-Robison Collection.

Wolff, J. Milton. Papers. Luvaas Collection.

U.S. National Archives of Records Administration, Washington, DC

Hayward, Ambrose Henry. Military records.

Hayward, Melville. Military records.

Orth, Jacob George. Military records, pension files.

Newspapers

Boston Evening Transcript

New York Herald

Philadelphia Daily Evening Bulletin

Philadelphia Inquirer

Philadelphia Press

Philadelphia Public Ledger

Pittsburgh Gazette

Pottsville Miner's Journal

Published Primary Sources

Chickamauga-Chattanooga Battlefield Commission. *Pennsylvania at Chickamauga and Chattanooga*. Harrisburg, PA: William Ray, 1897.

Dada, Harriet A. *Ministering Angel: The Reminiscences of Harriet A. Dada, a Union Army Nurse in the Civil War*. Ed. Edmund J. Raus Jr. Gettysburg, PA: Thomas Publications, 2004.

Fisher, Sidney George. *A Philadelphia Perspective: The Diary of Sidney George Fisher Covering the Years 1834–1871*. Ed. Nicholas Wainwright. Philadelphia: Historical Society of Pennsylvania, 1967.

Geary, John W. *A Politician Goes to War: The Civil War Letters of John White Geary*. Ed. William A. Blair. University Park: Pennsylvania State University Press, 1995.

Moore, Joseph A. "Rough Sketch of the War as Seen by Joseph Addison Moore." In *George Washington Irwin: The Civil War Diary of a Pennsylvania Volunteer*, ed. Jane B. Steiner, 160–66. Lafayette, CA: Hunsaker, 1991.

SeCheverell, J. Hamp. *Journal History of the Twenty-Ninth Ohio Volunteers, 1861–1865: Its Victories and Its Reverses*. Cleveland, 1883.

Toombs, Samuel. *Reminiscences of the War, Comprising a Detailed Account of the Experiences of the Thirteenth New Jersey Volunteers in Camp, on the March, and in Battle*. 1878. Reprint, Hightstown, NJ: Longstreet House, 1994.

Tyndale, Hector. *A Memoir of Hector Tyndale*. Philadelphia: Collins, 1882.

U.S. Congress. *Congressional Globe*. 46 vols. Washington, DC, 1834–73.

U.S. War Department. *The War of the Rebellion: A Compilation of the Official Records of the Union and Confederate Armies, Series 1*. Washington, DC: Government Printing Office, 1889–1901.

Wilson, Lawrence. *Itinerary of the 7th Ohio Infantry, 1861–1864*. New York: Neale, 1907.

Woodward, Evan Morrison. *Our Campaigns, or, The Marches, Bivouacs, Battles, Incidents of Camp Life, and History of Our Regiment During Its Three Years Term of Service: Together with a Sketch of the Army of the Potomac, under Gener-*

als McClellan, Burnside, Hooker, Meade and Grant. Philadelphia: J. E. Potter, 1865.

Secondary Sources

Alotta, Robert. *Civil War Justice: Union Army Executions under Lincoln.* Shippensburg, PA: White Mane, 1989.

Bates, Samuel P. *History of the Pennsylvania Volunteers, 1861–1865.* Vols. 1–2. Harrisburg, PA: B. Singerly, 1869–71.

———. *Martial Deeds of Pennsylvania.* Vols. 1–2. Philadelphia: T. H. Davis and Co., 1876.

Baumgartner, Richard. *Echoes of Battle: The Struggle for Chattanooga.* Huntington, WV: Blue Acorn Press, 1996.

Beyer, W. F., and O. F. Keydel, eds. *Deeds of Valor: How America's Civil War Heroes Won the Congressional Medal of Honor.* Stamford, CT: Longmeadow Press, 1994.

Bohannon, Keith. "Preservation Plan for Ringgold Gap Georgia Battlefield." Report. Washington, DC: American Battlefield Protection Program, 1997.

Busey, John W. *These Honored Dead: The Union Casualties at Gettysburg.* Hightstown, NJ: Longstreet House, 1996.

Dean, Eric T. *Shook Over Hell: Post-Traumatic Stress, Vietnam, and the Civil War.* Cambridge, MA: Harvard University Press, 1997.

Fox, William F. *Regimental Losses in the American Civil War, 1861–1865.* Albany, NY: Albany Publishing Co., 1889.

Gallman, J. Matthew. *The Civil War Chronicle.* New York: Crown Publishers, 2000.

Grimsley, Mark. *The Hard Hand of War: Union Military Policy toward Southern Civilians, 1861–1865.* New York: Cambridge University Press, 1995.

Hunt, Roger D., and Jack R. Brown. *Brevet Brigadier Generals in Blue.* Gaithersburg, MD: Olde Soldier Books, 1990.

Kingman, Bradford. *History of North Bridgewater, Plymouth County, Massachusetts: From Its First Settlement to the Present Time with Family Registers.* Boston: Author, 1866.

Knickerbocker Magazine. Vol. 15. New York, 1840.

Linderman, Gerald F. *Embattled Courage: The Experience of Combat in the American Civil War.* New York: Free Press, 1987.

Manning, Chandra. "A 'Vexed Question': White Union Soldiers on Slavery and Race." In *The View from the Ground: Experiences of Civil War Soldiers,* ed. Aaron Sheehan-Dean, 31–66. Lexington: University Press of Kentucky, 2006.

Massachusetts Adjutant General's Office. *Massachusetts Soldiers, Sailors, and Marines in the Civil War, Volumes 1–6.* Norwood, MA: Norwood Press, 1932.

McPherson, James M. *For Cause and Comrades: Why Men Fought the Civil War.* New York: Oxford University Press, 1997.

————. *What They Fought For, 1861–1865*. New York: Anchor Books, 1995.

Neely, Mark E., Jr. *The Union Divided: Party Conflict in the Civil War North*. Cambridge, MA: Harvard University Press, 2002.

New Church Magazine. Vol. 1. Boston: Massachusetts New Church Union, 1873.

Orr, Timothy J. "'A Viler Enemy in Our Rear': Pennsylvania Soldiers Confront the North's Antiwar Movement." In *The View from the Ground: The Experiences of Civil War Soldiers*, ed. Aaron Sheehan-Dean, 171–98. Lexington: University Press of Kentucky, 2006.

Paludan, Phillip S. *A Peoples' Contest: The Union and Civil War, 1861–1865*. Lawrence: University Press of Kansas, 1988.

Roehrenbeck, William J. *The Regiment that Saved the Capitol*. New York: Thomas Yoseloff, 1961.

Rummel, George III. *Cavalry on the Roads to Gettysburg: Kilpatrick at Hanover and Hunterstown*. Shippensburg, PA: White Mane, 2000.

Sauers, Richard A. *Advance the Colors! Pennsylvania's Civil War Battle Flags*. Vol. 1–2. Harrisburg, PA: Capitol Preservation Committee, 1987.

Sheads, Scott Sumpter, and Daniel Carroll Toomey. *Baltimore during the Civil War*. Linthicum, MD: Toomey Press, 1997.

Silverstone, Paul H. *The Sailing Navy, 1775–1854*. Annapolis, MD: Naval Institute Press, 2001.

Smith, Timothy. *John Burns: "The Hero of Gettysburg."* Gettysburg, PA: Thomas Publications, 2000.

Strayer, Larry M., and Richard A. Baumgartner, eds. *Echoes of Battle: The Atlanta Campaign*. Huntington, WV: Blue Acorn Press, 1991.

Swift, Henry Walton. *Massachusetts Reports, Number 199: Cases Argued and Determined in the Supreme Judicial Court of Massachusetts, May 1908–October 1908*. Boston: Little, Brown, and Co., 1909.

Taylor, Frank H. *Philadelphia in the Civil War, 1861–1865*. Philadelphia, 1913.

Thackery, David T. *A Light and Uncertain Hold: A History of the 66th Ohio Volunteer Infantry*. Kent, OH: Kent State University Press, 1999.

Warner, Ezra J. *Generals in Blue: Lives of the Union Commanders*. Baton Rouge: Louisiana State University Press, 1964.

————. *Generals in Gray: The Lives of the Confederate Commanders*. Baton Rouge: Louisiana State University Press, 1959.

Wert, Jeffery. "The Great Civil War Gold Hoax." *American History Illustrated* 15, no. 1 (1980): 20–24.

INDEX

Page numbers in **boldface** refer to illustrations.